THE FESTIVE BAKER

THE FESTIVE BAKER

BAKING FOR CELEBRATIONS AND SPECIAL OCCASIONS AROUND THE WORLD

BEN MERVIS

LEGEND

- Vegetarian
- Vegan
- Gluten-free
- Dairy-free
- Nut-free
- 5 ingredients or fewer
- 30 minutes or less

FOREWORD

Dessert is the punctuation mark on life's most meaningful moments. That's what hooked me. It's the exclamation point, the ellipsis, the full stop that says Woah now. This is something. Stay here a little longer. Across cultures, across kitchens, across generations, something sweet always finds its way to the center of the table! A cake for a birthday, a pie for a gathering, a cookie passed hand to hand, just because (my favorite reason). It's how we mark time, how we celebrate, how we remember. At Milk Bar, we believe in baking as both craft and celebration. The ratio is simple: equal parts butter and joy, technique and whimsy. And I've seen firsthand how a single bite can unlock a memory, spark a feeling, or create a brand new tradition. Dessert has this quiet, powerful way of showing up exactly when we need it, connecting us through nostalgia, through ritual, through the simple act of sharing something made with care. It is playful and powerful all at once, a little messy, a little nostalgic, and always worth gathering around.

The Festive Baker is a love letter to that universal language. Within these pages, you'll find moments and bites of inspiration from bakers, chefs, and storytellers. Each brilliant recipe and tale carries a piece of history, a slice of personal memory, a glimpse into celebrations around the world. Dessert is a roadmap to life and you see it come to life in these pages! From Greek *Fanouropita* to Swedish *Prinsesstårta*, from the intricate layers of Indonesian *Lapis Legit* to the warmth of a traditional Sámi birthday cake, this book is packed with stories you can taste. It is the kind of collection that invites you in, turns you on to try something new, and reminds you that baking is not about perfection, it is about connection on the most human level. Whether you are marking a giant milestone or just looking for a reason to celebrate Tuesday (it's usually such a boring day, let's rebrand it!), these recipes meet you where you are and give you a little something sweet to share. Our ovens and the brilliant things that bake out of them are an open door into our lives and others', one that transports, that shakes us from sleepwalking, that is an open invitation and regular reminder of the richness we may otherwise take for granted. So dig in and bake on! I'm rooting for us!

Christina Tosi

INTRODUCTION

Growing up as a kid with an undying appetite for carbs, holidays and special occasions were, to me, worth the sum of their festive spread. Birthdays were candlelit chocolate frosted cakes, Thanksgiving was a pie-eating contest, and Yom Kippur, despite being a day of solemn atonement, was all about the feasting that took place when the sun went down. The food and the occasion were, to me, one and the same.

In the runup to these big days, the kitchen, and oven in particular, becomes the center point of so much attention, stress, and delight. There is something equal parts hopeful and nerve-racking about toiling over a recipe only to hand it over completely to the whims of the oven—and we rejoice in this festive tribulation as an almost essential rite of passage into adulthood.

It's something so many of us can relate to because, for a lot of people, big occasions are the *only* times we bake. We'll happily go months without looking at the stand mixer we spent a small fortune on, but as we edge into holiday seasons, we start to get that itch, the desire to do, make, and bake for others. It's how we celebrate.

It's not a surprise then, that festive baking, at its best, involves at least a dash of chaos. This isn't an exercise in precision or chef-level execution, it's an expression of love, both personal and imperfect. It's there in all the details. We may think first of ribbon-adorned cookie tins, or a pie cooling on the countertop, but baking includes so many small, shared joys: dragging a finger through thick batter, frosting licked straight from the mixing spoon—even spilled flour or misread recipes are often accompanied by an element of cheer and good humor.

So many holidays are underpinned by that idea of togetherness. Across the world, in cultures and religions that run the gamut in terms of values and beliefs, you'll still be hard pressed to find occasions where the requisite attendees aren't, first and foremost, our loved ones. No matter the tone of the days, from cheery merriment to somber reflection, Halloween to Rosh Hashanah, and Easter to Eid, we surround ourselves with those that matter.

Because these occasions are often both recurring and ritualistic, we develop strong sensory attachments to them: the wafting aroma of sweet spices, butter melting in a pan, just-zested citrus; fogged glass, ruddy cheeks, picnic blankets, and park tables; the crinkling of wrapped presents, familiar scores and refrains, and the joyous cries as unexpected (but very much welcome!) visitors pass through the door.

As we grow into adulthood and build a home for ourselves, the food we bake reflects the traditions and rituals, as well as the places and people, who've come into and shaped our lives. Through the act of baking, these traditions become something exchangeable: stories and flavors to link people, generations, and cultures, and to better understand what matters most to us—even if that's just a slice of cake.

ABOUT THIS BOOK

This book is comprised of 170 festive and celebratory recipes from 50 different countries and cuisines of the world. The recipes reflect rich and varied baking traditions from across the globe: from France, Sweden, and America, to Greece, Ethiopia, and the Philippines. The recipes are for yeasted and braided breads, fragrant buns, spiced biscuits, latticed fruit pies, savory hand-pies, colorful tiered cakes, and cheesy pastries. On top of all that, there's something for bakers of every skill set: avid, occasional, and beginner.

This book is not meant to be comprehensive in its collection of either recipes or holidays, however it should be said that all the recipes are for oven-baked dishes only. Certain things we consider, broadly speaking, as "baked goods" but which are in fact fried, steamed, griddled, or otherwise, have been left out. And similarly, holidays of importance, but which lack a strong connection with recipes of this sort, have also been omitted.

To bring together the book's recipes, I worked with 80 fantastic bakers, cooks, and food writers from around the world. Their generous contributions and insights make this book feel so genuine and personal. Each recipe is introduced with a little of that bake's history as well as some background on how it's made, served, and enjoyed. Every holiday mentioned is also introduced and presented along with its own history and associated meaning. They range from the biggest of days—major holidays, weddings, birthdays—to smaller rituals that form a regular part of our lives.

The book is laid out by month, which, on the face of it, is a straightforward decision. However, there are also religious and cultural holidays that follow a different calendar system (such as the Hijri or Jewish calendars), and so their corresponding dates in relation to the most widely used Gregorian calendar can vary from one year to the next. Recipes have been incorporated into their most appropriate section, but with many non-Gregorian dates being either lunar or lunisolar, these events may not match up exactly with their respective chapters on a year by year basis.

I hope that, as you go through this book, you will have as much fun reading about new and interesting bakes as you will making and eating them. I just ask that, when trying something completely new and outside your own culture or cuisine, you first read the accompanying information about that bake, as well as a little about its associated holiday, if unfamiliar, so that you can understand what makes it so special to so many people.

A LITTLE HISTORY

A major story of this cookbook is how many of our earliest surviving, best beloved baking recipes derive from festive traditions. By exploring some of this history, and the cultural origins of these recipes, we can better understand how baking itself is rooted in celebration and togetherness.

In the Western world, as well as parts of North Africa and the Middle East, the pre-modern oven was a culinary workhorse, professional workplace, and community hub. From ancient Babylon to Jacobean England, these large clay or masonry devices were synonymous with big occasions and large groups, playing an essential role in all manner of cultural and religious celebrations, from coronation feasts and village festivals to wedding banquets and religious holidays. From huge showstopping pies to elaborately braided loaves and more modest cakes, the oven's output often reflected the fact that this was no everyday occasion. Celebrating a significant moment with something warm from the oven would have felt natural and suitably special.

Many of the earliest festive baking traditions already incorporated rich symbolism and motifs, and these elements would dictate everything from the size and shape to the specific ingredients or flavors used. Baking for occasions was an act, and an art, that reflected a huge amount of intention and meaning in its practice. Many of our own modern-day rituals derive from these details.

However impactful the wares of the oven might have been, it was still a device outside the means (and the home) of the average household. Its costliness and requisite ingredients made it predominantly a shared resource: one owned and enjoyed by large wealthy households or small rural villages.

This began to change in the early modern era, first with the burgeoning of the domestic kitchen larder, and later in the overhaul of the kitchen itself, as it pivoted its focus from the open hearth to the closed iron cooker.

During the so-called "long" eighteenth and subsequent nineteenth centuries, agricultural and societal developments reshaped what and how people cooked: developing animal husbandry practices led to larger cattle herds and bigger beasts that didn't need culling—meaning fresh dairy and meat in far greater supply; plantations brought sugar into more regular usage and drastically reduced its price; empire and colonial trade routes brought spices, dried fruits, nuts, and novel liquors on returning ships; and steam power and rail kept things fast and fresh. These developments gave the baker's pantry a reason to exist.

The invention of open ranges and cast-iron cookstoves built on these developments encouraged home baking in well-to-do households—as is evidenced in early cookbooks across Europe. While in theory this enabled everyday baking for some, it did nothing to quell the expectation and ambition behind celebratory food, and this is encapsulated in early festive home baking. The finest ingredients would be pulled out from deep within the cupboard. Excitement and eagerness bred avid bakers who developed trends, techniques, and traditions. Baking became an explicit expression of culture and identity just as much as anything else. But it was also an expression of love and the desire to match the specialness of the day with something equally special to share. Instead of whole castle keeps or villages, now the oven brought families together.

In the nineteenth and twentieth centuries, empire and colonialism brought the popularity of oven-range baking to places that otherwise lacked a deeper historical connection to this form of dry-heat cooking—Southeast Asian countries, for instance, like Indonesia and the Philippines. Here, European recipes were adapted to suit local ingredients and tastes, and new traditions were born.

More recently, over the last century, and especially the last few decades, the explosion of food media and later social media has diversified who is baking and how we talk about it—underscoring the meaning, intention, and shared experience that were historically so important. As bakers become celebrities and innovate technique and flavor combinations, there is a certain comfort in the tradition, ritual, and even nostalgia of celebratory baking. It is not only eating for the sake of deliciousness but a ritual that joins us together.

THANK YOU

This book celebrates everything that makes festive baking so compelling—togetherness, excitement, nostalgia, and indulgence—and the book-making process has incorporated each of these aspects along the way.

I'd like to thank Christina Tosi for her brilliant foreword, which so beautifully sets the tone for this book. Endless thanks as well to my editors, Sophie Hodgkin and Rachel Malig, as well as Anna Moore for all her feedback and insights. And to the book's wonderful photographer, Liz Seabrook, and the team that masterfully baked and styled over a hundred recipes from around the world in a small London studio: Katie Smith, Aine Pretty-McGrath, and Louis Stopforth.

Lastly, thank you to my loving and supportive partner Krisztina and our wee dog Alfie, who loves to sniff around the oven.

Ben Mervis,
Thanksgiving 2025

CONTRIBUTORS

I am endlessly grateful to the book's many contributors who have given so generously to it: chefs, bakers, food writers and historians, grandmothers, and home cooks from around the world. The insights and expertise of these individuals bring to life not only the recipes themselves, but how they are enjoyed, and also how they fit into the wider rituals of a special occasion or holiday.

Gastón Acurio
Chef & cookbook author, Peru

Javahir Ahmadova
Home cook & food creator from Baku, Azerbaijan, based in Copenhagen

Nicholas Andreadis
Chef, London

Mogan Anthony & Seleste Tan
Lady Wong Patisserie, New York, USA

Chiara Barla
Chef & baker, Copenhagen

Tobias Beck
Executive chef & editor-in-chief of *GutGeist Magazin*, Berlin

Ayda Biru
Recipe developer and co-founder of Balè Moya, Washington DC & New York, USA

Máret Rávdná Buljo
Sámi chef & cultural activist, Lofoten, Norway

Naomi Blair Gould
Baker & owner of Seasons microbakery, London

Åshild Blyseth
Works with food & food culture on Wangbrygga i Bardal, Norway

Neil Buttery
Food historian & chef, Manchester, UK

Leopoldo Calhau
Chef, Portugal

Ricardo Chaneton
Chef and co-founder of Mono restaurant, Hong Kong, China

Polina Chesnakova
Cookbook author & culinary instructor, Rhode Island, USA

Siddharth Chogle
Chef & co-founder, *Figo Collective* magazine, India

Camille Cogswell
Award-winning pastry chef & owner of Walnut Family Bakery, Marshall, North Carolina, USA

Michael Craig
Chef & baker, Copenhagen

Fejsal Demiraj
Chef & founder of Albanian Gastronomy Expedition, New York, USA

Lisa Donovan
Chef & author, New York, USA

Carolina Doriti
Chef, food writer & cookbook author, Athens

Victoria Effantin & Cécile Khayat
Mamiche Bakery, Paris

Moustafa Elrefaey
Executive chef & co-founder of Zooba restaurants, Cairo

Jess Eng
Food writer & researcher, New York, USA

Irina Georgescu
Award-winning cookbook author, Wales

Hanny Guimarães
Lida Padaria, São Paulo, Brazil

Till Gurka
Baker & owner of Till & Brot, Freiburg, Germany

Salma Hage
Lebanese author & cook, London

Richard Hart
Chef & baker, Mexico City

Diana Iovescu Tatucu
Author & educator from Romania, based in Manila

Talia Jacobs
Recipe developer, London

Sam Jacobson
Owner of Stargazy restaurant, Philadelphia, Pennsylvania, USA

Irina Janakievska
Food writer & author, London

Yuriy Kachak
Owner, Deanston Bakery, Glasgow, Scotland

Bitna Kang
Food writer & Korean recipe developer, New York, USA

Reem Kassis
Award-winning Palestinian writer & cookbook author, Philadelphia, Pennsylvania, USA

Marie Kerkeling
Culinary artist, pastry artisan & chef, France

Esra Koraltan
Baker & pastry chef, London

Sarah Lemanski
Founder, Nova Bakehouse, Leeds, UK

Shaina Loew-Banayan
Chef, author & owner of Cafe Mutton, Hudson, New York, USA

Bettina Loew-Banayan
Private chef, Hudson, New York, USA

Anna Luntley
Baker & chef, Glasgow, Scotland

Sam Luntley
Artist & baker, Argyll, Scotland

Florence Mae Maglanoc
Chef & restaurant owner, London

Alice Mahon
Irish recipe developer, based in Copenhagen

Flora Manson
Food writer & recipe developer from Scotland, based in North Sweden

Ianthi Michalaki
Head baker & recipe developer, Athens

Dona Murad
Co-founder of Librae Bakery, New York, USA, and Hopscotch Cafe, Kingdom of Bahrain

Allisa Murphy
Chef & baker, Glasgow, Scotland

Agnese Negrini
Chef & baker, Copenhagen

Roberto Nitti
Pastry chef & baker, Bari, Italy

Marta Orlikowska
Cook & knitter, Warsaw

Simone & Inés Ortega
Simone is considered to be the foremost authority on Spanish cooking; Inés, her daughter, is a cookbook author

Petty Pandean-Elliott
Chef, consultant & cookbook author, Cambridgeshire, UK

Alessandra Pili
Baker, Glasgow, Scotland

Elena Reygadas
Mother, chef & owner of Rosetta & Panaderia Rosetta, Mexico City

João Rodrigues
Chef, Portugal

JR Ryall
Pastry chef & writer, Cork, Ireland

Maxine Scheckter
Pastry chef, Wellington

Myrna Schecter
Home cook, New York, USA

Barbara Serulus
Author & food writer, Antwerp, Belgium

Malika Sharipova
Passionate about Uzbek culture and the power of food to connect people, Uzbekistan

Shiva Shirazi Gombart
Food writer & recipe developer, based in France

Katie Smith
Chef & food stylist, Ireland

Maksymilian Smółka
Baker, Krakow, Poland

Julia Soria
Pastry chef & co-founder of *Figo Collective* magazine, Argentina

Gareth Eoin Storey
Chef & writer, Lisbon

Lilla Szőcs
Concept creative, journalist & fun-dining host, Budapest

Carri Thurman
Co-owner/baker, Two Sisters Bakery, Homer, Alaska, USA

Jasmine Ting
Food writer & home cook, New York, USA & Toronto, Canada

Per Theodor Tørrissen
Chef & manager, North Norwegian food competence center, Norway

Cecilia Tolone
Baker & recipe developer, Sweden

Cemre Torun
Food writer, Istanbul, Turkey & New York, USA

Anna Trattles
Ten Belles, a values-driven specialty coffee company and sourdough bakery, Paris

Michael W. Twitty
Culinary historian, educator & author, Virginia, USA

Niels Van Heertum & Nick Symons
Bakers at Bloemberen, Antwerp, Belgium

Luisa Weiss
Food writer, Berlin

Eden Westbrook
Recipe developer & food writer, Virginia, USA

Rawlston Williams
Chef & cookbook author, Saint Vincent and the Grenadines

Baneta Yelda
Artisan baker, chef, and Assyrian food writer, Manchester, UK

JANUARY

1

JANUARY

EPIPHANY

Epiphany—or Theophany—is a significant Christian feast day, which celebrates the manifestation of Christ before his worshipers. Western and Eastern traditions emphasize different stories that demonstrate this: Western Christianity centers around the visit of the three magi to the newly born Jesus Christ, whereas Theophany is focused around Christ's baptism by John the Baptist. Regardless, water and light (the star which guides the magi) are key elements of the day.

In many places around the world, Epiphany is also closely linked with the baking of cakes and sweet pastries, including so-called "king cakes," shaped to resemble crowns or reflect the gifts given to the baby Jesus. The preparation of many of these sweets includes the placement of a small figurine or ceramic object into the dough or filling, said to bring luck, or a gift of some sort, to the one who finds it.

GALETTE DES ROIS

France

Submitted by Anna Trattles

Serves 8
Prep time: 1 hour, plus overnight chilling time
Cook time: 45–50 minutes

For the puff pastry:
- 1⅔ cups (7 oz/200 g) strong white bread flour, plus extra for dusting
- scant ⅔ cup (2¾ oz/75 g) whole wheat flour
- 1 teaspoon salt
- 1¾ tablespoons (1 oz/25 g) butter, melted
- 2½ teaspoons cider vinegar

For the laminating butter:
- 1½ sticks (6 oz/175 g) butter, cut into large pieces

For the pastry cream:
- 1⅔ cups (14 fl oz/400 ml) milk
- 2 tablespoons superfine (caster) sugar
- 3 egg yolks
- ¼ cup (1⅛ oz/35 g) corn starch (cornflour)

For the almond cream:
- 3 tablespoons (1½ oz/40 g) butter
- ⅕ cup (1½ oz/40 g) superfine (caster) sugar
- 2 egg yolks
- ⅓ cup (1½ oz/40 g) almond meal (ground almonds)
- pinch of salt

To finish:
- 1 egg yolk, beaten, for egg wash
- 2 tablespoons superfine (caster) sugar, for glazing

The French *galette des rois* or "king cake" is one of the country's most famous holiday bakes, and is made annually for Epiphany (January 6). This tradition is believed to have its roots in an earlier Roman celebration of the winter solstice, with the round shape of the galette symbolizing the sun and the hidden *fève* (literally "bean," but now a small ceramic object) representing fertility.

There are two main varieties of this cake. The most famous, popular in Île-de-France, is the *galette des rois*, made with golden puff pastry and a frangipane filling. In the south of France, it is called *gâteau des rois,* and takes the form of a crown-shaped brioche topped with candied fruits. This recipe, from Ten Belles in Paris, is in the classic style of Île-de-France. It is a tradition for the youngest participant to hide underneath the table and assign who gets each portion, so that the recipient of the *fève* remains a surprise. The lucky individual gets to wear the golden (paper) crown as King or Queen.

To make the puff pastry: Place the flours and salt in a bowl, then add the butter and vinegar and mix, gradually adding a scant ⅔ cup (4¾ fl oz/140 ml) of water to form a dough. Wrap in plastic wrap (clingfilm) and refrigerate for a minimum of 2 hours.

Prepare the laminating butter by pounding with a rolling pin to a 6 × 6-inch (15 × 15 cm) square between sheets of parchment paper. Wrap and chill with the dough.

Roll out the rested dough on a floured counter to a 12 × 12-inch (30 × 30 cm) square. Place the butter in the middle of the dough and fold each corner over the butter to meet in the middle. Pinch to seal and enclose the butter. Roll out the dough to a rectangle ½ inch (1 cm) thick. Now fold the top third of the dough down, and the bottom third up to cover it—as though folding a letter—to make a "single turn." Rotate the folded pastry a quarter clockwise and roll out vertically again to the same thickness and make another single turn. Wrap in plastic wrap and leave in the refrigerator to rest for 2 hours. Repeat this process another two times.

To make the pastry cream: Heat the milk until almost boiling. Beat the sugar and egg yolks in a stand mixer until pale and slightly thickened. Whisk in the cornstarch (cornflour), followed by the hot milk. Return to a pan over low heat and mix until thickened, 5–10 minutes. Set aside to cool.

To make the almond cream: Beat the butter and sugar together in a stand mixer until light and fluffy. Add the egg yolks one by one, beating well after each addition. Fold in the ground almonds and salt and mix to form a batter. Set aside to cool.

Remove the pastry from the refrigerator 30 minutes before you start rolling. Roll the dough to a thickness of ⅛ inch (3mm) on a lightly floured counter. Cut out two 9½-inch (24-cm) circles using a sharp blade, and chill both for 30 minutes.

Stir the pastry cream through the almond cream to create the frangipane, then transfer to a pastry (piping) bag. Place one circle of pastry on a lined baking tray, and pipe a 6-inch (15 cm) circle of frangipane into the center. Nestle the fève inside the frangipane, so that it doesn't stick out of the pastry. Lay the second disk on top and use a knife to crimp all around the edges of the pastry. Chill in the freezer for 1 hour.

Preheat the oven to 350°F (180°C/Gas Mark 4). Brush the top of the galette with egg yolk, and score curved lines from the center outward, then poke 3 small holes in the top to allow air to escape. Chill for 30 minutes, then bake for 45–50 minutes, until golden. While the galette is baking, heat the sugar with 2 tablespoons of water for 2–3 minutes until dissolved and thickened slightly. Remove the galette from the oven, brush with the syrup, and allow to cool slightly before serving.

ROSCA DE REYES

Mexico

Submitted by Richard Hart

Serves 10
Prep time: 1 hour, plus resting and cooling times
Cook time: 40 minutes

For the poolish:
½ cup (2¼ oz/60 g) all-purpose (plain) flour
4 tablespoons tepid water
1 g instant dry yeast

For the scalded wheat:
⅓ cup (1½ oz/40 g) whole wheat flour
2½ tablespoons boiling water

For the mandarin puree:
2 mandarin oranges, peeled, with seeds and pith removed

For the cake:
2½ cups (14 oz/400 g) bread flour
⅓ cup (2¼ oz/60 g) soft brown sugar
⅓ cup (1½ oz/40 g) milk powder
2 eggs
3 tablespoons honey
4 tablespoons orange juice
2½ teaspoons salt
11 tablespoons (5½ oz/160 g) butter
⅕ oz (6 g) quick-rise dry yeast
1 teaspoon ground cinnamon
2½ tablespoons neutral oil

For topping:
1 egg, beaten, for egg wash
pearl sugar
confectioners' (icing) sugar
candied citrus peel
toasted chopped almonds and hazelnuts

Much like its Spanish and Latin American cousins, the *rosca de reyes*, or king cake, is a Mexican "cake" made from a sweet brioche-like enriched dough, flavored with citrus, topped with candied fruit and often nuts, and baked in a ring for Three Kings Day (Epiphany). Like the Spanish *roscón de reyes*, from which it derives, it also includes a small hidden figurine of the baby Jesus baked within the cake—although the Spanish version includes a "bean" as well. Unlike the Spanish version, the *rosca de reyes* is rarely filled, and nowadays often incorporates stripes of a concha-like topping made using a sugar-paste mixture. This more traditional-style but nonetheless modern version of the *rosca de reyes* comes from Richard Hart, who runs Green Rhino bakery in Mexico City.

The day before you want to bake the cake, make your poolish, scalded wheat, and mandarin puree.

To make the poolish: Combine the flour, water, and yeast in a bowl. Cover with plastic wrap (clingfilm) and allow to rest at room temperature.

To make the scalded wheat: Place the flour in a bowl, pour over the boiling water, and stir to combine. Cover with plastic wrap and set aside at room temperature.

To make the mandarin puree: Bring a pan of water to a boil, add the mandarins, and boil for 10–15 minutes. Drain, then transfer to a blender and puree. Set aside to cool, then cover with plastic wrap and store in the refrigerator.

To make the cake: The next day, combine the flour, poolish, scalded wheat, brown sugar, milk powder, eggs, honey, mandarin puree, and orange juice in the bowl of a stand mixer. Mix for 3–4 minutes until a dough forms, then set aside to rest for 20 minutes.

Add the salt and mix on full speed for about 10 minutes until the dough is smooth and well formed, then add the butter, yeast, and cinnamon, and continue to mix until all the butter is incorporated. Slowly drizzle in the oil and mix until combined. Set aside to rest, covered with plastic wrap, for 1½–2 hours.

Punch down the dough, add your token (baby), and roll the dough into a long sausage shape. Take the two ends and join them together to create a large ring or oval. Allow to rest, covered, for another 2–3 hours.

Preheat the oven to 340°F (170°C/Gas Mark 3). Brush the dough with the egg wash, sprinkle with pearl sugar, and dust with confectioners' (icing) sugar.

Bake for 25 minutes, then remove from the oven and allow to cool for 30 minutes. Decorate with the candied citrus peel and toasted nuts, then serve.

VERLOREN MAANDAG

Verloren maandag, or "Lost Monday," is a distinctly Antwerpener observance that happens every year on the Monday following Epiphany. There are debates over exactly how this tradition came to be, but all the competing theories place the origin in the local labor history of this Belgian port city. The meaning behind the "lost day" may relate to the fact that historically very little or no work got done on this day—a day that immediately followed the festive twelve nights of Christmas. That could have been because workers were also given this day off, or as other stories go, that the overindulgence of the last couple weeks had them staying home "sick." While it is not a public holiday in Belgium, nor in Antwerp itself, the people of the city do spend this day buying and eating plenty of rich and buttery pastries, to cure "ailments," real or imagined.

WORSTENBROOD & APPELBOLLEN

Belgium

Submitted by Niels Van Heertum and Nick Symons

Serves 4–6
Prep time: 1 hour, plus proofing and overnight chilling times
Cook time: 18 minutes

For the apple filling:
7 tablespoons (3½ oz/100 g) butter
¼ cup (1¾ oz/50 g) granulated sugar
scant ¼ cup (1¾ oz/50 g) muscovado sugar
2½ teaspoons ground cinnamon
1½ teaspoons ground cardamom
6 small, ripe apples
confectioners' (icing) sugar, for dusting

For the meat filling:
9 cups (2 lb 4 oz/1 kg) ground (minced) meat (beef and pork, or veal and pork)
1 cup (2¾ oz/75 g) coarse dry bread crumbs (panko works great)
1 egg
1½ teaspoons salt
1 teaspoon Worcestershire sauce
¾ teaspoon freshly ground black pepper
1½ teaspoons finely chopped parsley
1 teaspoon onion powder

Every year in Antwerp, locals celebrate *verloren maandag* (or "Lost Monday") on the Monday following Epiphany. On this day, folks flock to their favorite bakeries to order *worstenbrood* and *appelbollen*—savory sausage rolls and sweet apple pastries. Competing theories seek to answer the origin of "Lost Monday" and its relation to such widespread pastry consumption. In essence, they all relate to the port city's prominent harbor and the workers there, whom, after holiday-induced drinking binges, needed something both cheap and also buttery-rich to soak up their hangovers.

Nowadays, the tradition of *verloren maandag* is less alcohol-focused, and many simply see it as an occasion to meet with friends, while enjoying some of the city's finest pastries.

At Bloemberen, the bakery run by Niels Van Heertum and Nick Symons, who contributed this recipe, "old dough" refers to scraps from the same dough that are cut off during shaping, kept in the refrigerator, then added back into the mix for the following week. Alternatively, you could use cutoffs from croissant-making, leftover brioche or bread dough, or you could even use a low hydration sourdough starter. Make sure to keep scraps and cutoffs from this recipe, as they develop a great amount of complexity in the refrigerator over the course of a couple of days. If you plan on storing them longer, freeze them.

To make the apple filling: In the bowl of a stand mixer, combine the butter, sugars, cinnamon, and cardamom and mix thoroughly. Chill in the refrigerator until ready to use; remove from the refrigerator 2–3 hours before shaping the pastries.

To make the meat filling: In the bowl of a stand mixer, bring all the ingredients together, trying to develop the mix but working fast to keep things cold. Put the mixture into a pastry (piping) bag with a 1¼-inch (3-cm) nozzle. Store in the refrigerator until ready to shape the pastries.

To make the dough: In the bowl of a stand mixer, combine the flours, milk, sugar, salt, yeast, and 1 cup (8 fl oz/250 ml) of water. Mix on low speed for 5 minutes. Add the butter and the old dough and mix for 10 minutes. Increase the speed and mix for another 5 minutes, until the dough is completely developed and smooth, 72–73°F (22–23°C) when measured with a food thermometer, and will pass a window-pane test easily (when the dough is elastic enough when stretched that you can see light through it without it tearing).

Shape the dough into a tight oval. Cover with a clean dish (tea) towel and rest for 5 minutes, then roll out to ¾–1¼ inches (2–3 cm) thick and wrap tightly with plastic wrap (clingfilm). Refrigerate overnight.

Make a 12 × 8-inch (30 × 20-cm) sheet of plastic wrap or parchment paper. Place the butter on one side of the sheet, close the sheet over it, and flatten out the butter with a rolling pin until it reaches all 4 corners of the liner, and you are left with a perfectly flat rectangular butter sheet. Refrigerate for 30 minutes.

If using professional lamination butter, immediately remove the dough and the butter sheet from the refrigerator. If using regular butter, remove the butter from the refrigerator 5–10 minutes before the dough, so that it becomes pliable. The butter should never be close to melting, and should never be too cold because it can then

For the dough (chill all ingredients for at least 6 hours):
3¾ cups (7¼ oz/490 g) T45 (viennoiserie) flour
3¾ cups (7¼ oz/490 g) T55 (patisserie) flour
generous ¾ cup (6½ fl oz/195 ml) milk
scant ⅔ cup (4 oz/120 g) granulated sugar
2 teaspoons sea salt
1½ oz (40 g) fresh yeast
7 tablespoons (3½ oz/100 g) butter
3½ oz (100 g) old dough (pâte fermentée)
4½ sticks (1 lb 2 oz/500 g) butter (ideally lamination butter)

For the egg wash:
1 egg
3½ tablespoons milk

shatter during the lamination process—ideally the butter should be around 50°F (10°C) and the dough around 39°F (4°C). The dough and the butter should have more or less the same consistency.

Roll out the dough on a lightly floured counter to a 16 × 12-inch (40 × 30 cm) rectangle. Place the butter in the middle. Then imagine dividing the dough into thirds horizontally: Fold the top third of the dough down, and fold the bottom third up and over the top of this, as though folding a letter, so that the butter is now enveloped in the dough. Make sure you close the seam where the 2 sides meet.

With a paring knife, cut away any overhang of dough where it surrounds the butter, to ensure that every spot touches the butter filling.

Roll out the pastry until it's about ⅜ inch (7 mm) thick. Always roll in the direction of the open ends, so in this case, roll in the direction of the sides you've just cut. Now perform the double fold (fold both ends in to meet in the middle, then fold in half again). Wrap the pastry and rest in the freezer for 10 minutes, then in the refrigerator for 20 minutes.

After resting, cut the 3 rounded sides of the dough again with a paring knife and roll out the pastry to ⅜ inch (7 mm) thick again. Now fold the dough in half, wrap in plastic wrap and rest in the freezer for 10 minutes, then in the refrigerator for at least 2 hours, and up to 12 hours.

Roll the pastry out so that it's 15 inches (38 cm) wide, then start rolling it out lengthwise to ⅛ inch (4 mm) thick. Cut the dough into 4¾-inch (12.5-cm) squares.

For the applebollen: Peel and core the apples and place each one in the middle of a square. Fill the core with the cinnamon filling, then pull every corner of the pastry over the apple to the top. Flip the wrapped apple upside down on the seam in an individual round foil baking pan, or a sturdy cupcake or muffin pan.

For the worstenbrood: Remove the meat mixture from the refrigerator. Pipe a 1¼-inch (3 cm) thick sausage along an edge of the remaining dough squares, then roll each one up, forming a tube around the sausage. The outer edge of the pastry should not be tucked underneath the pastry itself, but just point down vertically, touching the counter—this avoids too much tension while proofing.

At this point, you could store both pastries in the refrigerator until ready to proof and bake. Make sure to place them on a piece of parchment paper so that they don't stick, and cover them loosely with plastic wrap.

When ready to proof, set the worstenbrood out on a baking sheet covered with plastic wrap, making sure they have room to double in size (the appelbollen do not need proofing). Proof them in a wet and warm environment, ideally 82–86°F (28–30°C) and 80 percent humidity: to replicate this, put them in the oven with only the light on, and a pan of boiling water in the bottom of the oven to create steam. Proof for 3½–4 hours, depending on the heat in the proofing environment. When fully proofed, the layers should start to separate and the dough should have a nice jiggly bounce to it.

Preheat the oven to 375°F (190°C/Gas Mark 5).

To make the egg wash: In a small bowl, whisk together the egg and milk, then brush over the worstenbrood.

When ready to bake, reduce the oven heat to 340°F (170°C/Gas Mark 3). Bake each of the pastries on a parchment-lined baking sheet for 18 minutes. Remove from the oven, then finish the appelbollen with confectioners' (icing) sugar. Let cool slightly and enjoy.

You can also reheat them before serving, if not eating them right away.

2

LUNAR NEW YEAR

The lunisolar calendar that China follows (also called the *nónglì*, or agricultural calendar) has existed for over 3,000 years. Each new year begins on the second new moon after the previous year's winter solstice, with New Year celebrations lasting in earnest for about fifteen days until the full moon arrives. The *nónglì* calendar and these festivities began in China, and have been adopted or adapted in South Korea and Vietnam, as well as in Singapore and Malaysian Chinese ethnic communities. Each country and community varies in their exact customs or adherence, but many traditions are shared among celebrants of the Lunar New Year. It is important to welcome good fortune into the new year with auspicious symbols and rituals like gift-giving, family reunion meals, firework displays, and the lighting of delicate paper lanterns on the final night—the Lantern Festival.

NIAN GAO

Malaysia and Singapore

Submitted by Mogan Anthony and Seleste Tan

Serves 8–10
Prep time: 30 minutes
Cook time: 45 minutes

10½ tablespoons (5½ oz/150 g) coconut butter or cow's milk butter
2½ cups (20 fl oz/600 ml) coconut milk
5½ oz (150 g) pandan extract
¼ teaspoon pandan paste
2⅔ cups (14 oz/400 g) glutinous rice flour
2 cups (14 oz/400 g) granulated sugar
2 teaspoons baking powder
1 teaspoon salt

Nian gao (年糕), which translates to "year cake" or "higher year," is a classic treat enjoyed during Lunar New Year as an auspicious symbol of progress, prosperity, and growth in the year ahead. Traditionally steamed, it is increasingly common to find oven-baked versions of this sticky rice cake. A prime example of this can be found at Lady Wong Patisserie in New York City. The ingredients remain the same, and the baked *nian gao* retains its beautifully chewy texture but with the added bonus of a golden crust.

Preheat the oven to 375°F (190°C/Gas Mark 5). Line an 8-inch (20-cm) cake pan with parchment paper and set aside.

In a small pan, melt the coconut butter. Set aside.

Combine the coconut milk, melted butter, pandan extract, and pandan paste in a mixing bowl.

In a separate bowl, mix the glutinous rice flour, sugar, baking powder, and salt. Pour the wet mixture into the dry ingredients and whisk until smooth. Pour the batter into the prepared cake pan.

Bake for 40 minutes, uncovered, until the top is golden, then remove from the oven and let cool before serving.

CHINESE ALMOND COOKIES

China and the Chinese diaspora

Submitted by Jess Eng

Makes 20 cookies
Prep time: 35 minutes
Cook time: 20 minutes

- 1½ cups (5½ oz/150 g) almond flour
- 1 cup (4¼ oz/120 g) all-purpose (plain) flour
- 1 teaspoon baking powder
- ½ teaspoon baking soda (bicarbonate of soda)
- ¾ cup (5½ oz/150 g) granulated sugar
- ¼ teaspoon kosher salt
- generous ¾ cup (5 oz/140 g) lard or ½ cup (4 fl oz/120 ml) neutral oil (e.g. canola [rapeseed], vegetable)
- ½ teaspoon almond extract
- 20 almonds, for topping
- 1 egg yolk, for egg wash

Shaped like a coin and dimpled to fit a single almond, this snappy, crumbly cookie is a favorite during Chinese New Year for those hoping for vast fortunes (or simply a sweet treat). It has a crumbly, luscious texture similar to shortbread, but with a nutty almond kick.

Brought over in the nineteenth century by Chinese immigrants to the United States and United Kingdom, this treat resembled *hup toh soh*, flattened walnut cookies with rough edges, commonly found in China. Over time, the overseas bakeries established by the new arrivals created their own spin on this cookie that more closely resembled their round and risen Western counterparts.

Preheat the oven to 325°F (160°C/Gas Mark 3). Line a baking sheet with parchment paper and set aside.

In a large bowl, whisk together the almond flour, all-purpose (plain) flour, baking powder, baking soda (bicarbonate of soda), sugar, and salt. Add the lard or oil, along with the almond extract. Using your hands, mix everything until the dough comes together into a smooth ball—no need to overwork it.

Divide the dough into 1-oz (25-g) portions and roll each into a ball. Place them on the prepared baking sheet, spacing them evenly. Press an almond into the center of each one.

In a small bowl, beat the egg yolk with 1 teaspoon of water. Brush the tops of the cookies with the egg wash. Bake for 20 minutes, or until golden and firm around the edges, then remove from the oven and let cool completely before serving. They will keep for 1–2 weeks in an airtight container.

LAPIS LEGIT

Indonesia

Submitted by Petty Pandean-Elliott

Serves 8–10
Prep time: 45 minutes
Cook time: 2 hours

- 3 sticks (12 oz/350 g) butter, at room temperature, plus extra for greasing
- 2 tablespoons condensed milk
- 22 egg yolks
- 1½ cups (6 oz/175 g) confectioners' (icing) sugar
- 2 tablespoons vanilla extract
- 3 tablespoons all-purpose (plain) flour
- 4 tablespoons milk powder
- 2 tablespoons speculaas spice or Chinese 5 spice
- 1 tablespoon Dutch-process cocoa powder

Lapis legit—thousand layers cake—is a rich, spiced layered cake that originated during the Dutch colonial era in Indonesia. Inspired by the Dutch _spekkoek_, it was adapted using local spices like cinnamon, clove, and nutmeg, and became a beloved symbol of festive indulgence. Unlike typical cakes, _lapis legit_ is known for its dense, moist texture, due to a high number of egg yolks. It enjoys a luxurious and celebratory status, and is traditionally served during major holidays like Lunar New Year, Christmas, Lebaran (Eid), or weddings.

In Indonesian-Chinese culture, _lapis legit_ is a symbol of prosperity and painstaking craftsmanship. Its layers are said to reflect layers of patience and effort—a metaphor for building a good life or a strong relationship. It's a spectacularly enjoyable cake. I recommend serving it in small slices with coffee or tea.

Preheat the oven to 340°F (170°C/Gas Mark 3). Grease an 8-inch (20-cm) square, 2¾-inch (7-cm) deep baking pan, line it with parchment paper, and set aside.

In the bowl of a stand mixer fitted with the whisk attachment, beat the butter on medium speed for 3 minutes until light and fluffy. Add the condensed milk and beat for 2 minutes. Transfer to a large bowl and set aside.

Clean the stand mixer and fit with the cleaned whisk attachment. Add the egg yolks and beat until thick and doubled in volume. Gradually add the confectioners' (icing) sugar and vanilla extract. Whisk for 2 minutes.

Gradually add the butter mixture and mix on low speed until smooth. Add the flour, milk powder, and spice and mix gently with a rubber spatula until combined. Do not overmix. Separate the batter into 2 bowls, then stir the cocoa powder into one of the bowls.

Spread 4 tablespoons of the plain mixture evenly across the baking pan (for uniform layers, each layer should weigh 6¾ oz [190 g]). Bake for 5–7 minutes.

Remove the pan from the oven and let cool for 2 minutes. Using the back of a large spoon, gently press the cake layer flat. This ensures that the surface is prepared for the next layer, with an even density throughout.

Switch the oven to the broiler (grill) setting and reduce the temperature to 275°F (140°C).

Spread 4 tablespoons of the chocolate batter to create the next layer. Bake for 5–6 minutes, then remove the pan from the oven. Let cool for 2 minutes and flatten. Repeat, adding alternate layers of the plain and chocolate batter, reducing the baking time by 30 seconds or 1 minute (bake too long and the cake will turn golden when it should be off-white—you must also keep an eye on the temperature of your oven).

At the sixth layer, bake on the lowest rack to prevent the subsequent layers from burning. Continue until you have 12 layers in total.

Switch back to the oven setting and increase the temperature to 340°F (170°C/Gas Mark 3). Cover the cake with aluminum foil and bake for another 5–7 minutes.

Remove the baking dish from the oven and place it on a wire rack. When completely cool, gently remove the cake from the pan. Trim off the edges to make the cake very neat. Slice and serve.

CARNIVAL

Carnival is a traditional Christian festive period preceding Lent. It varies in length around the world, but is generally observed to start after Epiphany, before properly commencing in the weeks or days before Ash Wednesday, and later culminating in Shrove Tuesday (Mardi Gras).

Rooted in pre-Christian traditions marking the end of winter and coming of spring, there is a level of exuberance that is well-demonstrated through traditional performance, parades, and masks or costumes. Vibrant street parties are held across the world, especially in cities like Rio de Janeiro, Brazil; Venice, Italy; and New Orleans, United States. The relative indulgence of the period is also reflected in the rich foods and baked goods commonly prepared in the buildup to the Lenten period when fasting commences.

CENCI DI CARNEVALE

Italy

Submitted by Naomi Blair Gould

Makes 20
Prep time: 50 minutes
Cook time: 10 minutes

- 2 cups (9 oz/250 g) all-purpose (plain) flour, plus extra for dusting
- 2 tablespoons superfine (caster) sugar
- scant ½ teaspoon fine sea salt
- tiny pinch of baking soda (bicarbonate of soda), optional
- zest of ¼ orange
- zest of ¼ lemon
- 2½ tablespoons regional liquor of your choice (preferably Tuscan vin santo, but you can use white wine, grappa, or marsala)
- 1 teaspoon vanilla extract (optional)
- 3 tablespoons (1½ oz/40 g) plant-based butter, at room temperature (or substitute with the same quantity of vegetable oil)
- neutral oil, for greasing
- confectioners' (icing) sugar, for dusting

Cenci, once known by the name _fritcilia_, are sweet cookies that were once made for the Roman harvest festival Saturnalia but are now associated with Italian carnival celebrations. Each region of Italy has its own form of this cookie, the name of which literally translates to "rags of carnival," a reference to their size and shape, recalling the fabric trim of traditional carnival costumes. The name varies by region—_Cenci_ (in Tuscany), _bugie_, _chiacchiere_, _galani_, _frappe_, _crostoli_, _lattughe_, _maraviglias_—as does the choice of alcohol, be it vin santo, marsala, or grappa.

Cenci are traditionally either baked or deep-fried, with the latter being done in lard or vegetable oil. Once baked they are served dusted with plenty of confectioners' (icing) sugar. Traditionally, eggs are added to the recipe, but this is a plant-based version.

In a bowl, combine the flour, sugar, salt, and baking soda (bicarbonate of soda), if using. Stir in the citrus zest.

In a separate bowl, mix 4½ tablespoons of water with the liquor and vanilla extract, if using. Fold the wet ingredients into the dry. Knead, gradually adding the plant-based butter, until the dough comes together into a smooth ball. Place in a lightly oiled bowl, cover with a clean, damp dish (tea) towel, and let rest for 30 minutes.

Preheat the oven to 400°F (200°C/Gas Mark 6). Line a baking sheet with parchment paper and set aside.

Once rested, roll out the dough either by hand with a rolling pin or with a pasta machine. If working by hand, lightly flour a counter and roll out the dough into a rectangle. Fold 2 sides of the dough over themselves. Repeat this process 4 times.

Roll out to a thickness of about 1⁄16 inch (2 mm). Using a knife or serrated pastry wheel, cut the dough into strips. Make 2 diagonal incisions within the rectangles so that you can fold and twist them.

Bring a pan of water to a gentle boil and drop the cenci into the water, a few at a time. As soon as they float to the surface of the water, remove with a slotted spoon or spider and drain on kitchen towel.

Place on the prepared baking sheet, then bake for 10 minutes, until bubbled up nicely and golden brown. Let fully cool before dusting with plenty of confectioners' (icing) sugar.

They will keep in an airtight container at room temperature for a few days, but are best eaten on the day for a perfect light and crisp texture.

KING CAKE

United States

Submitted by Michael W. Twitty

Serves 12–14
Prep time: 1 hour, plus proofing times
Cook time: 25–30 minutes

For the cake:

- ½ oz (14 g) active dry yeast
- 2 teaspoons, plus ½ cup (3½ oz/100 g) granulated sugar
- ½ cup (4 fl oz/120 ml) warm water
- 3½ cups (1 lb/455 g), plus ½–1 cup (2¼–4½ oz/65–130 g) all-purpose (plain) flour, plus extra for dusting
- 1½ teaspoons fine salt
- ½ teaspoon ground cinnamon
- ½ teaspoon freshly grated nutmeg
- ½ cup (4 fl oz/120 ml) milk, warmed
- 5 egg yolks, beaten
- 8 tablespoons (4 oz/115 g) butter, at room temperature
- vegetable oil, for greasing

For the icing:

- 2 cups (8½ oz/240 g) confectioners' (icing) sugar, sifted
- 3 tablespoons milk
- colored sanding sugar in purple, green, and yellow/gold
- 1 pecan half or 1 whole almond

In New Orleans, Mardi Gras can feel more like an entire season than just one holiday. The bright colors and pageantry of the festivities are reflected here in the regional King Cake, a traditional recipe popular across New Orleans but also the wider state of Louisiana. Like its European cousins, this King Cake includes a *fève* or charm, tucked into the underside of the finished cake after it's baked. The one to find the charm in their slice of cake is dubbed that event's Mardi Gras king or queen, and expected to supply the cake for the following year's gathering.

Traditionally, the *fève* was a ceramic charm, shaped like the baby Jesus, or even a small coin. Today, most commercial cakes include a tiny plastic baby charm, which can be tucked into the King Cake by the host. A whole almond or pecan half, which is what this recipe calls for, serves as a simpler, non-hazardous option.

To make the cake: In a small bowl, combine the yeast, the 2 teaspoons of sugar, and the warm water and stir well. Set aside until puffed and foamy, about 10 minutes.

In a large bowl, whisk together the 3½ cups (1 lb/455 g) of flour, the ½ cup (3½ oz/100 g) of sugar, the salt, cinnamon, and nutmeg. Scoop out a well in the flour and pour the yeast mixture into it. Use a large spoon or spatula to stir the mixture, then add the warm milk and beaten egg yolks. Stir to incorporate for 5–7 minutes until you have a very soft dough.

Add the soft butter to the dough and use your hands to mix it in, pressing it against the sides of the bowl to incorporate. Add ½ cup (2¼ oz/65 g) of the remaining flour to form a dough that is quite sticky but holds its shape. Add more flour, little by little, until you have a very soft ball of dough, more dry than sticky.

Turn out the dough onto a lightly floured work counter. Using floured hands, knead the dough, adding flour little by little, until the dough is soft, springy, and dry, about 10 minutes.

Grease the inside of a large bowl with oil. Place the dough in the bowl and turn to grease it evenly. Cover with a clean dish (tea) towel and proof for 1–1½ hours in a warm place until the dough is dry, puffed up, and twice its original size.

Punch the dough to release the air, then knead it gently for 1 minute. Line a large baking sheet with parchment paper.

Turn out the dough onto a lightly floured counter. Shape the dough into a plump cylinder, about 20 inches (50 cm) long. Move the dough to the prepared baking sheet and shape it into a large open ring, either round or oval. Cover with a clean dish (tea) towel and let it rise in a warm place for 1–1½ hours until doubled in size.

Preheat the oven to 375°F (190°C/Gas Mark 5). Bake for 25–30 minutes, until golden brown, rotating the sheet front to back halfway through. Remove from the oven and transfer to a wire rack to cool completely before icing.

To make the icing: In a bowl, whisk the sugar and milk together to make a smooth, shiny, and thick but pourable icing.

Place the cooled cake on a wire rack over a sheet pan or parchment-lined counter to catch the icing and sanding sugar. Use a large spoon, spatula, or whisk to spoon, drizzle, or slather icing all over the surface of the cake. Quickly sprinkle on the purple, green, and yellow/gold sanding sugars, making thin stripes or large color patches. Let stand for 15 minutes to set.

Transfer to a cake plate and serve at room temperature.

FAT THURSDAY

Fat Thursday is the last Thursday before Ash Wednesday, and the start of Lent. Because of its close proximity to this period—which represents fasting, abstinence, and solemnity—Fat Thursday centers around indulgence. In many countries across Europe, from Spain to Germany and Poland, celebrants mark the day by indulging in sweet, fatty, and especially fried foods. Despite this, there are still many rich baking traditions tied to the day and focused around the same school of thought: Sweet cakes or yeasted breads, which may also incorporate the last of the animal-based fats.

COCA DE LLARDONS Y PIÑONES

Catalonia

Submitted by Alessandra Pili

Makes 8
Prep time: 40 minutes
Cook time: 25 minutes

⅞ cup (7 fl oz/200 ml) oil, plus extra for greasing
4 eggs
½ cup (3½ oz/100 g) granulated sugar, plus an extra 2 teaspoons
¾ oz (20 g) fresh yeast, crumbled
4 cups (1 lb 2 oz/500 g) all-purpose (plain) flour
1 cup (7 oz/200 g) pork cracklings (lardons), crumbled
1 small glass of sweet anise liqueur
scant 1 cup (3½ oz/100 g) pine nuts

After the *matanza*—the traditional Catalan winter slaughter of the pig (page 230)—the leftover pork cracklings from rendering lard would be pressed and fried, turning into thin, crispy pieces of pork fat. These cracklings were then used in various preparations, one of which was this sweet pastry topped with sugar and pine nuts.

The *coca de llardons* is eaten during carnival time—starting on Fat Thursday—and serves to prepare Catalans for the fasting period of Lent a few days later. It is intended as one of the last uses of the *llardons* from winter, and can be enjoyed with sweet wine, muscat, malvasia, or cava.

Lightly grease a baking sheet with oil. In a bowl, combine 3 of the eggs, the oil, the ½ cup (3½ oz/100 g) of sugar, and the yeast with a little warm water.

Gradually add the flour until a homogeneous dough forms. Add the crumbled pork cracklings and the anise liqueur and mix. Spread the dough on the prepared baking sheet.

In a small bowl, beat the remaining egg and brush this egg wash over the surface of the dough, then sprinkle with the pine nuts and remaining 2 teaspoons of sugar. Let rest for 30 minutes, or until the dough has risen and become airy.

Preheat the oven to 350°F (180°C/Gas Mark 4).

Bake for 25 minutes, then remove and let cool slightly before serving.

FASTELAVN

Across Scandinavia, Shrove Tuesday is known as *fastelavn* (in Denmark, Norway, and Iceland) or *fastlagen* (in Sweden), meaning "the evening before the fast." There are special Carnival-like festivities held throughout the day, especially in Denmark, where children dress up in costumes, sing songs, and play games to win candy. A core part of the holiday is also the baking of sweet yeasted (and often filled) buns, and while these buns are technically associated only with the day itself, they are in practice found in bakeries and grocery stores often as early as January, and certainly by February, having become a seasonal favorite all their own.

Right: *Gammeldags Fastelavnsboller*, Fastelavn (page 42)

GAMMELDAGS FASTELAVNSBOLLER

Denmark

p. 41

Submitted by Alice Mahon

Makes 8
Prep time: 45 minutes, plus overnight fermentation, chilling, and proofing times
Cook time: 20–25 minutes

For the water roux (tangzhong):
scant ½ cup (1¾ oz/50 g) all-purpose (plain) flour

For the dough:
⅞ cup (7 fl oz/200 ml) milk
¼ cup (1¾ oz/50 g) superfine (caster) sugar
1 oz (30 g) fresh yeast
3½ cups (1 lb/450 g) strong white bread flour, plus extra for dusting
1 teaspoon fine salt
3½ teaspoons ground cardamom (or 10 cardamom pods, skins removed and seeds gently crushed in a pestle and mortar)
7 tablespoons (3½ oz/100 g) butter, at room temperature

For the remonce:
3 tablespoons (1½ oz/40 g) butter, at room temperature
3 tablespoons superfine (caster) sugar
2¾ oz (80 g) marzipan

***Fastelavn*, Denmark's lively pre-Lenten festival, takes place on the Sunday before Lent, much like Mardi Gras or carnival. Traditionally, children dress up in fancy dress and take turns smashing a suspended wooden barrel filled with treats before enjoying soft, cream-filled buns. While this tradition remains, the *fastelavnsbolle*—the beloved *fastelavn* bun—has become the true star of the season, with its popularity soaring in recent years.**

For many Copenhagen bakeries, *fastelavn* is one of the busiest times of the year, with bakeries selling their versions of the bun weeks in advance, and excitement building towards the feast day—typically in late February. The most traditional version of the *fastelavnsbolle*, known as the *gammeldags fastelavnsbolle* or "olden day" bun, remains a favorite, but bakeries now experiment with new flavors and textures. Lines stretch down streets, and locals and tourists alike embark on bakery tours, sampling the season's best creations.

The recipe below is a take on the classic *gammeldags* bun. While whipped cream isn't always included, it is a nice balance to the sweetness, lightening the texture, and making the indulgence all the more irresistible.

To make the water roux: In a pan over medium–high heat, bring a generous ⅓ cup (3½ fl oz/100 ml) of water to a boil. Remove from the heat and quickly whisk in the flour until a smooth paste forms.

Transfer to a bowl, cover with plastic wrap (clingfilm)—ensuring that the wrap is in direct contact with the surface of the roux to prevent a skin from forming—and let cool to room temperature. Once cooled, refrigerate until completely chilled, ideally overnight.

To make the dough: In the bowl of a stand mixer fitted with the dough hook attachment, combine the milk, sugar, yeast, and water roux and mix for 1 minute until well combined. Add the flour, salt, cardamom, and butter, then knead on medium–high speed for 10–15 minutes until the dough becomes smooth and elastic.

Alternatively, mix by hand: In a large mixing bowl, whisk together the milk, sugar, yeast, and water roux until fully combined. Add the flour, butter, cardamom, and salt, then mix by hand until a rough dough forms.

Turn the dough out onto a lightly floured counter and knead for 10–15 minutes until smooth and elastic. Shape the dough into a large ball and return to the bowl. Cover with plastic wrap and refrigerate overnight.

To make the remonce: In the bowl of a stand mixer fitted with the paddle attachment, combine the butter, sugar, and marzipan. Mix for 2–3 minutes, scraping down the sides regularly, until smooth and well combined. Transfer to a bowl, cover with plastic wrap, and store in the refrigerator until needed.

To make the custard: In a pan over medium heat, warm the milk, cream, and vanilla paste until steaming.

In a separate bowl, whisk together the egg yolks, sugar, cornstarch (cornflour), and salt until smooth. Gradually pour the hot milk mixture into the egg mixture, whisking continuously to prevent curdling.

Return the combined mixture to the pan and cook over low heat, whisking constantly, until thick, about 5 minutes. Once the custard reaches the desired consistency, remove from the heat, whisk in the butter, then transfer it to a bowl

For the custard:
1 cup (8 fl oz/250 ml) milk
3½ tablespoons heavy (double) cream
1 teaspoon vanilla bean paste
4 egg yolks
¼ cup (2 oz/55 g) superfine (caster) sugar
5 tablespoons cornstarch (cornflour)
¼ teaspoon salt
3 tablespoons (1½ oz/40 g) butter, cut into cubes

For the diplomat cream:
1 cup (8 fl oz/250 ml) whipping cream

For the chocolate glaze:
3½ oz (100 g) chocolate (at least 70 percent cocoa solids)
3 tablespoons (1½ oz/40 g) butter, at room temperature

and cover with plastic wrap, ensuring the wrap touches the surface to prevent a skin from forming. Chill in the refrigerator for 1–2 hours or overnight.

While the custard is chilling—or the next day, if refrigerating overnight—line a baking sheet with parchment paper and set aside.

Remove the dough, remonce, and custard from the refrigerator.

Gently push down the dough to deflate. Turn it out onto a lightly floured counter, and roll it out into a large rectangle about ½-inch (1-cm) thick and 8 × 16 inches (20 × 40 cm). Cut into 4-inch (10-cm) squares.

Place 1 teaspoon of remonce and 1 teaspoon of custard in the center of each square—reserving 1 cup (9 fl oz/250 ml) custard for the diplomat cream. Bring the edges of each square over the fillings and pinch together to seal. Flip the buns over and gently roll to seal the bottom.

Arrange the buns on the prepared baking sheet, leaving a 1¼-inch (3-cm) gap between each bun (use 2 sheets if necessary). Cover loosely with plastic wrap or a clean dish (tea) towel and proof in a warm place for 1–2 hours, until doubled in size and light to the touch.

Preheat the oven to 350°F (180°C/Gas Mark 4). Bake the buns for 12–15 minutes until lightly golden, then transfer to a wire rack and let cool completely.

To make the diplomat cream: In the bowl of a stand mixer fitted with the whisk attachment, whip the cream on high speed until soft peaks form. Add the reserved custard and whisk until the mixture is smooth and firm. Transfer to a pastry (piping) bag fitted with a 1.25 cm (½ in) round nozzle.

Using a sharp knife, poke a hole in the bottom of each bun. Pipe the diplomat cream into the hole, then scrape off any excess that overflows.

To make the chocolate glaze: Melt the chocolate and butter in a heatproof bowl over a pan of simmering water. Dip the top of each bun into the melted chocolate and let set before serving.

SHROVE TUESDAY

Shrove Tuesday, also known as Mardi Gras, is celebrated on the day before Lent, and much like Fat Thursday, represents a final opportunity for indulgence before the next several weeks of penitence and sacrifice. As the day occurs immediately before Ash Wednesday, it represents the absolute final opportunity to clear out the household cupboards and refrigerators of their last rich foods, meats, and sweets that will soon be forbidden. On a personal level, preparation for the religious journey of the next few weeks will begin with repentance of sins, with many celebrants also deciding what extra luxuries they may abstain from.

SEMLOR

Sweden

Submitted by Alice Mahon

Serves 10–12
Prep time: 1 hour, plus overnight chilling, fermentation, and proofing time
Cook time: 15–20 minutes

Similar to the Danish *fastelavnsbolle* (page 42), the Swedish *semla* is a delightfully indulgent bun traditionally enjoyed on *fettisdagen* (Shrove Tuesday), the day before the Christian fasting period of Lent. Originally, this simple yeasted bun was baked until golden and served in a bowl of warm milk. However, as Lent became less strictly observed, Swedes began to transform the humble bun into something far more decadent—filling it with almond paste and cream and enjoying it throughout the weeks leading up to Easter.

Today, *semlor* (the plural of *semla*) have become a winter staple, appearing in bakery windows as soon as deemed socially acceptable after Christmas. The modern version is a soft, fragrant cardamom bun, generously filled with almond paste and chopped roasted almonds, crowned with swirls of whipped cream, and finished with its signature "hat" of baked dough—lightly dusted with confectioners' (icing) sugar for the perfect final touch.

For the water roux (tangzhong):
- scant ½ cup (1¾ oz/50 g) all-purpose (plain) flour

For the dough:
- ⅞ cup (7 fl oz/200 ml) milk
- ¼ cup (1¾ oz/50 g) superfine (caster) sugar
- 1 oz (30 g) fresh yeast
- 3½ cups (1 lb/450 g) strong white bread flour, plus extra for dusting
- 1 teaspoon salt
- 3½ teaspoons ground cardamom (or seeds from 10 cardamom pods, gently crushed in a mortar and pestle)
- 7 tablespoons (3½ oz/100 g) butter, at room temperature

For the almond paste:
- 9 oz (250 g) marzipan
- ½ cup (4 fl oz/125 ml) milk
- 2 drops almond extract
- pinch of salt

To decorate:
- ⅓ cup (1¾ oz/50 g) almonds, toasted and roughly chopped
- 1¼ cups (10 fl oz/300 ml) whipping cream
- confectioners' (icing) sugar, for dusting

To make the water roux: In a pan over medium–high heat, bring a generous ⅓ cup (3½ fl oz/100 ml) of water to a boil. Remove from the heat and quickly whisk in the flour until a smooth paste forms. Transfer to a bowl, then cover with plastic wrap (clingfilm), ensuring that the wrap is in direct contact with the surface of the roux to prevent a skin from forming. Let cool to room temperature, then refrigerate until completely chilled, ideally overnight.

To make the dough: In the bowl of a stand mixer fitted with the dough hook attachment, combine the milk, sugar, yeast, and 5½ oz (150 g) of the water roux, and mix for 1 minute until combined. Add the flour, salt, cardamom, and butter. Knead on medium–high speed for 10–15 minutes until the dough is smooth and elastic. Alternatively, mix by hand until a rough dough is formed.

Turn out the dough onto a lightly floured counter and knead for 8–10 minutes until it becomes smooth and elastic. Shape the dough into a large ball and return to the bowl. Cover with plastic wrap and refrigerate overnight.

The next day, line 1–2 baking sheets with parchment paper and set aside. Remove the dough from the refrigerator and knock out the air. Turn out the dough onto a lightly floured counter and divide into 3½-oz (100-g) pieces.

Roll each piece into a smooth ball and place on the prepared sheet(s), leaving a 1¼-inch (3 cm) gap between each bun. Cover loosely with plastic wrap or a clean dish (tea) towel and proof in a warm place for 1–2 hours until doubled in size.

Meanwhile, to make the almond paste: In a bowl, combine the marzipan, milk, almond extract, and salt. Mix until a smooth paste forms. Alternatively, use a stand mixer fitted with the paddle attachment.

Preheat the oven to 350°F (180°C/Gas Mark 4).

Bake the buns for 12–15 minutes until lightly golden. Remove from the oven, transfer to a wire rack, and let cool completely. Once cooled, use a serrated knife to slice off the top of each of the buns in a round or triangle. Trim the tops with scissors to create a neat "hat" approximately 1¼ inches (3 cm) in diameter.

To decorate: Fill a pastry (piping) bag fitted with a round nozzle with the almond paste and pipe a circular layer onto the bottom of each bun. Sprinkle with the chopped toasted almonds.

Fill another pastry bag fitted with a star nozzle with the whipped cream and pipe a generous swirl over the almond filling. Carefully place the trimmed tops back onto the cream, then finish with a light dusting of confectioners' (icing) sugar.

LENT

The period of Lent represents forty days of repentance, fasting, sacrifice, and prayer, which is meant to reflect the fasting of Jesus Christ over the same period, in the Judean desert, as he sought to avoid temptation. The way of determining the start and end of this period differs in Western and Eastern Christianity, but much of the world follows the tradition of the former and counts the days of Lent thus: From Ash Wednesday to Holy Saturday, forty-six days later, with each of the intervening four Sundays serving as breaks from the penance of the period, and finally, Easter Sunday following immediately thereafter. Lent is not usually associated with rich baking traditions, on account of its frugal nature, but some cultures do associate specific recipes with it due to their suitability for the period, especially traditional fare that does not include meat.

EMPANADILLAS DE LA VIGILIA

Argentina

p. 50

***Empanadillas de la vigilia* are traditional Argentinian pastries enjoyed during Lent, particularly on Holy Friday. They are typically filled with tuna, spinach, and eggs, adhering to the Lenten practice of abstaining from meat. The use of puff pastry distinguishes them from other filled empanada varieties, which favor a shortcrust-style dough (similar to pie dough).**

Submitted by Julia Soria

Makes 24
Prep time: 30 minutes
Cook time: 20 minutes

For the filling:
2 tablespoons olive oil
1 large onion, finely chopped
2 garlic cloves, minced
1 green bell pepper, finely chopped
3½ oz (100 g) cooked spinach, chopped
11¼ oz (320 g) tuna in oil, drained
3 hard-boiled eggs, chopped
salt and freshly ground black pepper, to taste

For the dough:
all-purpose (plain) flour, for dusting
1 lb 2 oz (500 g) puff pastry (you could use the laminated pastry from the Pastelitos Criollos recipe, page 162)
1 egg, beaten, for sealing and brushing

To make the filling: In a pan over medium heat, warm the olive oil. Add the onion and sauté for 5 minutes until translucent, then add the garlic and green pepper and cook for 2–3 minutes. Stir in the chopped spinach and cook for another 5 minutes, then remove from the heat. Add the tuna and chopped eggs, season with salt and pepper, and mix well.

Preheat the oven to 400°F (200°C/Gas Mark 6). Line a baking sheet with parchment paper and set aside.

To make the dough: On a lightly floured counter, roll out the puff pastry and cut out 4½-inch (12 cm) circles.

Place a spoonful of filling in the center of each circle, then brush the edges with beaten egg and fold to form a half-moon shape. Seal the edges by pressing with a fork. Place the empanadas on your prepared baking sheet and brush the tops with beaten egg. Bake for 20 minutes, or until golden brown. Serve warm.

RAMADAN

Ramadan is the ninth month of the Islamic lunar calendar, a period of special significance to Muslims worldwide because it marks the time when the Quran was first revealed to the prophet Muhammad. One of the core pillars of Islam is the daily fasting of Ramadan, an act observed by most Muslim adults from dawn until sunset. The act of fasting is believed to strengthen self-discipline and deepen gratitude, bringing the observer closer to Allah.

Although no food is consumed during the daylight hours of Ramadan, this holy month still has strong culinary traditions that typify the pre-dawn meal of suhoor—nourishing and filling for the long day ahead—and the more celebratory evening meal of iftar. Iftar, the larger of the two meals, is usually broken first with the drinking of water and eating of dates, before families and friends share an array of festive dishes. Traditional iftar foods vary from country to country, though dishes—sweet ones especially—are often characterized by the incorporation of fruits, nuts, and aromatic spices.

Left: *Empanadillas de la Vigilia*, Lent (page 49)

EGYPTIAN GOULASH

Egypt

Submitted by Moustafa Elrefaey

Serves 8–10
Prep time: 25 minutes
Cook time: 35–40 minutes

butter, melted, for brushing
1 lb 2 oz (500 g) phyllo (filo) pastry, thawed if frozen
1½ cups (12 fl oz/360 ml) milk
2 eggs, lightly beaten
pinch of salt

For the filling:
2 tablespoons vegetable oil
10 tablespoons (5 oz/140 g) butter or ghee
2 onions, finely chopped
2 garlic cloves, chopped (optional)
4½ cups (1 lb 2 oz/500 g) ground (minced) beef
1 teaspoon ground cinnamon
1 teaspoon ground allspice
salt and freshly ground black pepper, to taste

Egyptian goulash is a savory pie made of crisp, buttery phyllo (filo) pastry layered with a spiced ground (minced) meat filling, then baked to golden perfection. Despite sharing its name with the Hungarian stew, this dish is purely Egyptian in identity and flavor. On the Ramadan iftar table—especially during the first days of the holy month—it is a near-essential centerpiece, served hot alongside soups, salads, and main dishes. Its balance of light, shattering pastry and hearty filling makes it equally welcome at family dinners, weddings, and holiday gatherings. The origins of the dish reflect the region's long culinary crossroads. Phyllo pastry itself arrived in Egypt via Ottoman influence, and over centuries it merged with local spice blends and cooking techniques to create a uniquely Egyptian version. While meat is the most common filling, modern home cooks also prepare it with cheese and spinach, or chicken, but the traditional ground beef variation remains the most beloved.

To make the filling: Heat the oil and 1 tablespoon of the butter or ghee in a pan over medium heat. Add the onions and sauté until soft, 5 minutes, followed by the garlic, if using, and sauté until fragrant. Add the ground (minced) beef, breaking it apart as it cooks, until browned. Stir in the cinnamon, allspice, salt, and pepper. Remove from the heat and cool slightly.

Preheat the oven to 350°F (180°C/Gas Mark 4). Melt the remaining butter or ghee in a pan.

Brush a rectangular baking dish with the melted butter or ghee. Layer in half the phyllo (filo) sheets, brushing each lightly with butter or ghee between each layer. Spread the cooled meat filling evenly on top, and layer the remaining phyllo sheets over the meat, again brushing each layer with the butter or ghee. Using a sharp knife, score the top of the goulash into squares or diamonds to make serving easier. Bake for 10 minutes.

In a small bowl, whisk together the milk, eggs, and salt. Remove the goulash from the oven and pour the milk mixture evenly over the scored pastry, letting it soak in for a minute until it has been mostly absorbed, then return the goulash to the oven and bake for another 35–40 minutes, until the pastry is golden and crisp.

Remove from the oven and run a knife along the score lines to ensure that the squares are separated. Cool slightly, and serve hot.

KUNAFAH

Egypt

Submitted by Moustafa Elrefaey

Serves 8–10
Prep time: 20 minutes
Cook time: 50 minutes

For the simple syrup:
2 cups (14 oz/400 g) granulated sugar
1 teaspoon lemon juice
1 teaspoon orange blossom water or rose water (optional)

For the filling:
generous 2 cups (17 fl oz/500 ml) milk
4 tablespoons cornstarch (cornflour)
½ cup (3½ oz/100 g) granulated sugar
1 teaspoon vanilla extract

For the pastry:
2¼ sticks (9 oz/250 g) butter, melted, plus extra for greasing
1 lb 2 oz (500 g) kunafah dough, fresh or frozen, thawed
pistachios, chopped, to decorate

***Kunafah* is one of Egypt's most iconic festive desserts—a shimmering nest of crisp, golden pastry strands wrapped around a heart of cream, cheese, or nuts, then soaked in fragrant syrup. It's a Ramadan staple, often shared after the evening iftar meal, but it also appears at weddings, family celebrations, and Eid feasts. Its texture—delicate crunch yielding to soft, sweet filling—makes it both decadent and comforting.**

The dish's origins are widely debated. Culinary historians trace its ancestry to the medieval Levant and Fatimid Egypt, where it was served to royalty and warriors alike for both energy and indulgence. Its name comes from the Arabic root *kanafa,* meaning "to shelter" or "to enfold"—a poetic gesture to the pastry's embrace of its filling.

While *kunafah* is celebrated across the Middle East with regional variations, Egypt's version—made with thin, hairlike strands of wheat dough—has its own unmistakable character, balancing generous sweetness with subtle aromas of orange blossom or rose water. It also eschews the incorporation of cheese (especially popular in Turkey) for a cream filling.

To make the simple syrup: Combine the sugar and 1 cup (8 fl oz/250 ml) of water in a pan over medium heat. Bring to a boil, then reduce the heat and simmer for 5 minutes. Add the lemon juice, remove from the heat, and let cool. Stir in the orange blossom or rose water, if using. Transfer to a bowl, cover with plastic wrap (clingfilm), and chill in the refrigerator until ready to use.

To make the filling: In a pan, combine the milk, cornstarch (cornflour), and sugar over medium heat. Stir constantly until thickened into a smooth cream. Remove from the heat, stir in the vanilla, and let cool slightly.

Preheat the oven to 350°F (180°C/Gas Mark 4). Grease a 9-inch (23 cm) cake pan and set aside.

To make the pastry: In a large bowl, gently pull apart the kunafah strands. Pour over the melted butter and work through with your fingers until evenly coated.

Spread half the kunafah in the bottom of the cake pan, pressing down hard (either with your hands, or with the aid of a flat-bottom cup or pan). Pour the cream filling over the pressed kunafah, leaving a ½-inch (1-cm) border. Top with the remaining kunafah, pressing gently but firmly to seal all over.

Bake for 35–40 minutes, or until golden and crisp. Remove from the oven and immediately pour the cooled syrup evenly over the hot kunafah. Let sit for 10–15 minutes to absorb.

Decorate with the pistachios and serve warm or cooled to room temperature.

SHEERMAL

India

Submitted by Siddharth Chogle

Makes 8
Prep time: 30 minutes, plus resting time
Cook time: 12–15 minutes

For the dough:
- 2¼ cups (10 oz/280 g) all-purpose (plain) flour, plus extra for dusting
- ½ teaspoon ground cardamom
- ¼ teaspoon salt
- 1 teaspoon superfine (caster) sugar
- up to 1 cup (7–8 fl oz/200–250 ml) milk, warmed
- 1 tablespoon kewra or rose water
- scant ½ cup (3½ oz/100 g) ghee, melted and warm

For the topping:
- pinch of saffron strands
- 3 tablespoons warmed milk
- 3 tablespoons ghee or butter, melted and warm

***Sheermal*, which gets its name from the Persian words *sheer* (milk) and *malidan* (knead), is a milk-enriched flatbread that left Iran with Silk Road caravans and reached Mughal India in the 1500s. The palace chefs, or *rakabdars*, from Lucknow, India, swapped oil for ghee, perfumed the dough with cardamom, and painted it saffron gold; Nizami bakers in Hyderabad soon followed.**

The round dough is slapped onto the red-hot wall of a charcoal tandoor, baking in minutes yet remaining pillowy soft. Each region has its own flavor: Lucknow's version is buttery and deeply saffron-flavored; Delhi's is lightly sweet; Kashmiri *sheermal* contains dry fruit and *kewra* (a floral water); Bihar prefers a thinner, gently sugared bread. The technique, however, never changes: a milk-rich dough, soft leavening, and tandoor blast. *Sheermal* crowns Ramadan iftars, Eid tables, and lavish winter weddings, uniting Iran and the Indian subcontinent in one festive loaf.

To make the dough: In a large bowl, combine the flour, cardamom, and salt.

In a separate bowl, dissolve the sugar in ⅞ cup (7 fl oz/200 ml) of the warm milk. Add this gradually to the flour, mixing with your fingertips until a soft, smooth dough forms. Drizzle in the 2 tablespoons of extra milk only if it feels dry. Cover with a clean, damp dish (tea) towel and let rest for 15 minutes.

Meanwhile, to prepare the topping: Lightly crush the saffron and steep in the warm milk. Set aside.

Once the dough has rested, work in the kewra or rose water and 2–3 tablespoons of the warm ghee, pressing small hollows to help absorption. Repeat, adding the ghee in batches until all of it is incorporated and the dough turns glossy and supple. Cover with a dish towel and let rest for another 10 minutes.

Cut the rested dough into 8 equal pieces, roll each into a ball, cover with a dish towel, and rest for 10 minutes.

Preheat the oven to 390–430°F (200–220°C/Gas Mark 6–7). Line a baking sheet with parchment paper and set aside.

On a lightly floured counter, roll out each ball to a 6-inch (15-cm) circle about ¼ inch (6 mm) thick. Place on the prepared baking sheet and pierce the surface all over with a fork. Bake for 12–15 minutes, until the rims turn deep gold.

Remove from the oven and immediately brush the hot bread with the saffron milk, then with the remaining melted ghee. Cover with a clean, damp dish towel for 5 minutes so the crust softens, then serve warm.

BARAZEK

Syria

Submitted by Salma Hage

These buttery sesame and pistachio cookies have been a hallmark of Damascus bakeries since Ottoman times, though they are now popular across the Middle East. One of the essential ingredients here is the use of *mahleb*, an aromatic spice made from the seeds of the Mahaleb species of cherry, the flavor of which is reminiscent of almond and cherry. They are popularly served and eaten with a cup of tea or coffee during Ramadan.

Makes about 25
Prep time: 45 minutes, plus resting time
Cook time: 20 minutes

¼ teaspoon quick-rise dry yeast
¼ cup (2 fl oz/50 ml) warm water
9 tablespoons (4¼ oz/125 g) butter, softened
1½ cups (5½ oz/150 g) confectioners' (icing) sugar
½ teaspoon mahleb
1⅔ cups (7 oz/200 g) all-purpose (plain) flour
½ cup (3½ oz/100 g) superfine (caster) sugar
5 teaspoons runny honey
1 cup (5½ oz/150 g) sesame seeds
¾ cup (3½ oz/100 g) pistachios, roughly chopped

In a small bowl, combine the yeast and warm water, then set aside for 5–10 minutes, until frothy.

In a separate bowl, using a handheld electric mixer, beat the butter and confectioners' (icing) sugar until light and airy. Add the yeast mixture and beat again. Sift the mahleb into the bowl. Working ⅓ cup (1¾ oz/50g) at a time, sift in the flour, beating each time to combine. Shape the dough into a ball and cover with plastic wrap (clingfilm). Place the dough in a cool spot (not in the refrigerator) for 20 minutes to rest.

Preheat the oven to 350°F (180°C/Gas Mark 4). Line a baking sheet with parchment paper and set aside.

Meanwhile, mix the superfine (caster) sugar and honey in a pan with ½ cup (4 fl oz/125 ml) of water. Bring to a boil, without a lid, then turn the temperature down so the liquid is at a vibrant simmer. Simmer for 8 minutes, until reduced in volume by a third and just starting to thicken. Remove from the heat.

Sprinkle the sesame seeds on a plate and cover with the syrup. Mix to distribute the syrup evenly. Arrange the pistachios on another plate. Have a bowl of water ready nearby.

Take a teaspoon of the rested dough and roll it into a ball between slightly wet palms (use the water from the bowl). Flatten the dough into a thin disk between your hands—it will be difficult to work with but water between your hands and the dough will prevent everything from becoming too sticky. Press one side of the dough into the pistachios, then flip it on to the sesame seed plate. Try to make sure the cookie is generously covered in the nuts. Put the coated cookie on the prepared baking sheet, sesame side up.

Repeat with the remaining dough. Leave about 1¼ inches (3 cm) between the cookies on the baking sheet—use 2 sheets if you need to. Bake in the oven for 15 minutes, until deep golden at the edges.

Remove from the oven and let the cookies cool on the baking sheet before transferring them to a wire rack to cool completely. They will keep in an airtight container for up to 1 week.

MARCH

3

MARCH

PURIM

The holiday of Purim celebrates the survival of the Jewish people in the face of persecution and possible destruction during the Achaemenid Persian Empire more than two thousand years ago. The story, as related in the Book of Esther, tells the story of Esther, a Jewish woman married to the Persian king, whom, along with her cousin Mordecai, cunningly foils a plot by the king's vizier, Haman, to kill the Jews. Today, beyond its religious observances, Purim is treated as a joyous cultural occasion among Jews, who celebrate the day by dressing up in masks and costumes, baking and eating plenty of *Hamantaschen*, and drinking enough wine—sometimes, it is said, colloquially, to the extent that you cannot tell the difference between Haman and Mordecai.

HAMANTASCHEN

Ashkenazi Jewish

Submitted by Talia Jacobs

Makes 30
Prep time: 40 minutes, plus chilling and (overnight) resting times
Cook time: 45 minutes

For the dough:

- 4 cups (1 lb 2 oz/500 g) all-purpose (plain) flour, plus extra for dusting
- ½ teaspoon salt
- ¾ teaspoon baking powder
- generous 1 cup (9 oz/ 250 g) sour cream
- 2¼ sticks (9 oz/250 g) butter, cubed and frozen
- zest of 1 lemon, plus 2 teaspoons lemon juice

For the filling:

- generous 1 cup (9 oz/250 g) soft dried apricots, chopped
- scant ½ cup (3½ oz/100 g) soft brown sugar
- ½ teaspoon ground cardamom (optional)
- 1 tablespoon lemon juice

***Hamantaschen* are filled, tricornered cookies that originated in Jewish communities of Germany in the eighteenth or nineteenth century, and are baked every year for Purim. They were likely adapted as a playful spin on the older, traditional German pastry *mohntaschen* or "poppy seed pockets," incorporating the villain of the story of Purim, Haman, into the name. Haman was said to have had a tricornered hat (more a fashion of eighteenth-century Europe than biblical Persia), hence the shape of the cookies, which, in essence, celebrate his defeat and ultimate downfall.**

This recipe features an apricot jam filling, but at Purim-time, in delis and Jewish bakeries, you'll find many other traditional fillings, like cherry, prune, or the original—ground poppy seed.

To make the dough: Put the flour, salt, and baking powder in a food processor, and pulse until evenly combined. Add about ⅔ cup (5¾ oz/160 g) of the sour cream and pulse again until the mixture has a sandlike texture. Add the frozen butter and pulse to form a shaggy dough with some flecks of butter still visible. Add the remaining sour cream and the lemon zest and juice, and pulse for a final time until the dough comes together in a mass.

Turn out onto a floured work counter and gently form into two disks. Cover and refrigerate for at least 3 hours, or overnight.

Meanwhile, to make the filling: Put the chopped apricots, 1 cup (8 fl oz/250 ml) of water, the sugar, and ground cardamom, if using, in a saucepan. Over a low heat, bring to a simmer and gently cook until most of the liquid has been absorbed and the apricots are nice and plump, about 25 minutes.

Remove from the heat and add the lemon juice. Stir, then using a stick blender, blitz the mixture to form a smooth paste. Transfer to a container and set aside to cool.

Line a baking sheet with parchment paper and set aside.

Once the dough has rested, roll it out between two sheets of parchment paper until it is ¹⁄₁₆–⅛-inch (2–3-mm) thick, then use a cookie cutter to cut out 3-inch (8 cm) circles.

Put a heaping teaspoon of the filling in the middle of each round, bring 3 sections of the edge in and pinch the points together well to form a triangle. Leave a gap in the center so some of the filling can be seen. Place them on the prepared baking sheet and place in the refrigerator for 30–60 minutes to rest and firm up.

Preheat the oven to 350°F (180°C/Gas Mark 4). Bake for 15–20 minutes, until golden brown, then remove from the oven and let cool. These are best enjoyed fresh but will keep for up to 5 days in an airtight container.

FORTY MARTYRS OF SEBASTE

The Forty Martyrs of Sebaste were a group of Roman soldiers of the Twelfth Legion who were persecuted and killed under anti-Christian policies of the Emperor Licinius in Sebaste (present-day Sivas, Turkey) in the year 320 AD. Licinius, who ruled jointly with Emperor Constantine from 306 to 324 AD, led attacks against Christians despite the conversion of his co-Emperor to that religion in 312 AD. The martyrdom of these forty soldiers is commonly commemorated in the Balkans and across areas of Eastern Europe, and the feast day, March 9, is also an occasion for baking or preparing special symbolic (sometimes forty) sweet breads or cookies. Due to the timing of the holiday, it also serves as a herald of the imminent spring.

MUCENICI MOLDOVENEȘTI

Romania

Submitted by Irina Georgescu

Makes 8
Prep time: 30 minutes, plus infusing, resting, and proofing times
Cook time: 30 minutes

For the dough:
scant 1 cup (7½ fl oz/225 ml) milk
2 pinches of saffron strands
3¼ cups (15 oz/420 g) strong bread flour, plus extra for dusting
5 tablespoons superfine (caster) sugar
¼ oz (7 g) quick-rise dry yeast
2 extra-large egg yolks
1 teaspoon vanilla bean paste
6 tablespoons (3¼ oz/90 g) butter, melted

For the syrup:
½ cup plus 2 tablespoons (4¼ oz/125 g) golden superfine (caster) sugar
grated zest and juice of 2 lemons
1 teaspoon vanilla bean paste
1 tablespoon orange blossom water (optional)

For the egg wash:
1 medium egg
drop of milk

For the topping:
3 tablespoons runny honey, plus extra to serve
scant 1 cup (2¾ oz/75 g) finely ground walnuts, plus extra to serve
grated zest of 1 lemon

***Mucenici* (Romanian for "martyr") are Moldavian brioche buns shaped loosely like the number eight, soaked in a lemon-flavored honey syrup, and topped with walnuts. They are made every year for March 9, a day that commemorates the Forty Martyrs of Sebaste, Roman soldiers (and Christian converts) who were persecuted and executed by Emperor Licinius for their religious beliefs.**

The *mucenici* can also be said to represent the forty days of Lent before Easter and the beginning of the agricultural year, which is celebrated through the buns' trifecta of grains (flour), walnuts, and honey.

To make the dough: In a small pan, warm the milk. Add the saffron, then set aside to cool and infuse for 20 minutes.

In a mixing bowl, combine the milk-saffron mixture with the flour, sugar, yeast, egg yolks, and vanilla bean paste. Knead until the dough pulls away from the sides of the bowl. Gradually add the butter, incorporating well after each addition. Cover and let rest in a warm place for 1 hour.

Line a baking sheet with parchment paper and set aside.

Turn out the dough onto a lightly floured counter and divide into 8 pieces. Roll each piece into a log that is 16–20 inches (40–50 cm) long. Bring the ends of each log together to form a circle and press together to seal them, then twist in the middle to create a figure-of-8 shape.

Place on the prepared baking sheet, leaving sufficient space between each as they will expand in the oven. Cover and proof for 30 minutes in a warm place.

Preheat the oven to 400°F (200°C/Gas Mark 6).

To make the syrup: In a small pan, bring a generous 2 cups (17 fl oz/500 ml) of water and the sugar to a boil, then simmer for 10 minutes. Remove from the heat and stir in the lemon zest and juice, vanilla bean paste, and orange blossom water, if using. Set aside.

To make the egg wash: Beat together the egg with a little milk, then brush this over the buns. Bake for 30 minutes, or until golden brown.

Remove from the oven, let cool, then—working in batches if necessary—soak in the syrup for 5–8 minutes, until soft but not disintegrating. Transfer to a plate, drizzle with honey, and top generously with ground walnuts and lemon zest.

Serve with more walnuts and honey on the side, so that folks can adjust the toppings to their personal preferences.

DITA E VERËS

Dita e Verës (literally "summer day") is a traditional Albanian holiday rooted in the city of Elbasan but now celebrated across the country. It is said that the holiday is steeped in ancient pagan custom, and that it originally centered around the shrine of the "fairy of Çermenika," which is located in an area northeast of Elbasan. There, on March 14, the fairy would emerge and herald the coming of spring. Today, it can also be said more broadly to mark the coming spring equinox and all it represents: Months of warm weather, greenery, and flowers.

BALLOKUME

Albania

p. 68

Submitted by Fejsal Demiraj

Makes 15
Prep time: 30 minutes, plus cooling and resting times
Cook time: 50 minutes

For the ash water:
6 tablespoons ashes from a wood fire

For the ballokume:
10½ tablespoons (5½ oz/150 g) butter, melted, plus extra for greasing
1¼ cups (9 oz/250 g) granulated sugar
1 whole egg, plus 1½ egg yolks
½ tablespoon salt
2¼ cups (9 oz/250 g) very fine cornmeal

Ballokume are cornmeal cookies prepared annually to celebrate the Albanian holiday _Dita e Verës_ ("summer day") on March 14. The holiday, rooted in pagan tradition, celebrates the end of winter and the strengthening of the sun at the spring equinox.

Legend suggests that the _ballokume_ comes from a sixteenth-century Ottoman ruler of Elbasan, a city in central Albania, who, after having tasted a small cake made from cornmeal cooked in a wood fire, exclaimed: "_Është ba si llokume!_" ("It's as good as a _llokum_!"), _llokum_ being the local name for what is elsewhere called "Turkish delight." The word _ballokume_ was formed by contracting this sentence.

Traditionally, the _ballokume_ dough is whisked by hand with a wooden spoon in a copper bowl. The addition of ash water is also unique in that it was used as a natural leavener, like baking soda (bicarbonate of soda) or baking powder, due to its alkalinity, which also adds to the crumbly texture.

This version is an adaptation of a family recipe made by the Çerri family in the Peqin district of Elbasan, where the recipe's contributor, Albanian-American chef Fejsal Demiraj, enjoyed excellent meals and hospitality.

To make the ash water: Combine the ashes with ⅞ cup (7 fl oz/200 ml) of water and bring to a boil. Boil for 2 minutes. Let cool in the pot and allow the ashes to settle, about 30 minutes. Once cool, strain through a fine-mesh sieve.

To make the ballokume: In the bowl of a stand mixer fitted with the whisk attachment, combine the butter and sugar. Whisk on high speed until pale, creamy, and doubled in volume. Add the egg and egg yolks a little at a time, every 2–3 minutes. Each egg needs to be fully combined before adding the next. Add 1 tablespoon of the ash water and mix.

In a small bowl, combine the salt and the cornmeal.

Reduce the mixer speed to low speed, then add the cornmeal mixture, 1 spoon at a time, ensuring each spoon is fully combined before adding more. Cover the bowl with plastic wrap (clingfilm) and let rest for 30 minutes in the refrigerator.

Preheat the oven to 325°F (165°C/Gas Mark 3). Grease a baking sheet with butter and line with parchment paper.

Remove the dough from the refrigerator and portion into 2-oz (50-g) balls. Place the cookies on the prepared baking sheet, leaving sufficient space between each as they will expand in the oven. Bake for 45 minutes, or until golden brown all over and a toothpick (cocktail stick) inserted in the center comes out clean.

Remove from the oven and let cool on the sheet before serving.

EID AL-FITR

Eid al-Fitr, literally "the festival of the breaking of the fast," is a major Islamic holiday observed on the first of Shawwal, the tenth month of the Islamic lunar calendar and the first day after Ramadan has ended. By the end of Ramadan, most Muslims are required to have performed an act of charity called *fitrana*, which involves donating food or money to those in need so they can enjoy it on Eid. In direct contrast to the month of Ramadan, which has preceded it, Eid has a decidedly joyous atmosphere and is marked by the coming of a new crescent moon. After a morning of worshipful prayer to Allah, including the pre-dawn Eid salah, the day gives way to festivities, including gatherings, gifts, the wearing of new clothing, and the eating of good food—especially sweets. In fact, due to the sheer number of desserts baked especially for this occasion, the holiday is also known as "sweet Eid."

Left: *Ballokume*, Dita e Verës (page 67)

KA'AK AJWEH BYANSOON

Palestine

Submitted by Reem Kassis

Makes 35
Prep time: 1 hour, plus overnight chilling
Cook time: 10–15 minutes

For the dough:
- scant 1½ cups (9 oz/250 g) semolina
- 2 cups (9 oz/250 g) all-purpose (plain) flour
- 9 tablespoons (4¼ oz/125 g) butter, softened
- ½ cup (4 fl oz/120 ml) vegetable oil, plus extra for oiling
- 1 tablespoon nigella seeds
- 1 tablespoon ground anise seeds
- 1 tablespoon ground fennel seeds
- 1 teaspoon baking powder
- 1 teaspoon active dry yeast
- 1 teaspoon granulated sugar
- ¼ teaspoon salt
- 1 cup (8 fl oz/250 ml) warm water

For the filling:
- 1 lb 2 oz (500 g) date paste
- 1 teaspoon ground cinnamon
- pinch of ground nutmeg (optional)
- pinch of ground cloves (optional)

Date-stuffed cakes are synonymous with the holidays in the Arab world for both Christians and Muslims. The most widespread version of these cakes is semolina based, but a less well-known version, common among Palestinian communities, is made with a mixture of flour and semolina and spiced with anise and fennel seeds. This recipe, shared by Palestinian food writer Reem Kassis, comes from her *teta* (grandmother) Fatima. Enjoyed with a fresh cup of mint tea, one (or two or three!) of these cakes makes a divine breakfast, afternoon snack, or after-dinner treat. They require some effort to make but keep well in an airtight container for several weeks and can be frozen for several months. One bite into these crispy, spiced cakes with a soft date interior, however, will make you realize just why they are worth the effort.

To make the dough: In a large bowl, combine the semolina, flour, butter, and oil, and work with your hands until fully combined and the mixture resembles wet sand. Cover and leave for several hours or overnight.

Grease a baking sheet, line with parchment paper, and set aside.

To make the filling: Combine the date paste and spices, knead slightly with well-oiled hands until evenly incorporated, then divide into 35 walnut-size pieces and roll each into a string about 4 inches (10 cm) long. Set on the prepared sheet at room temperature until ready to use—they will keep for a couple of days.

Preheat the oven to 400°F (200°C/Gas Mark 6). Line a baking sheet with parchment paper and set aside.

To continue preparing the dough: Add the nigella seeds, anise seeds, fennel seeds, baking powder, yeast, sugar, and salt to the semolina mixture and gently rub together with your hands. Add half the warm water and knead gently for no longer than 2 minutes. The mixture may still be crumbly at this point.

Slowly start to add up to another ½ cup (4 fl oz/120 ml) of warm water and knead (do not overmix or the cakes will be too tough), until you can take a clump of dough in your fingers and it holds together. You may not need to use all the water or you may need extra depending on a variety of factors from climate to type of flour. The dough should come together easily without crumbling when rolled into a log. Cover the dough with a clean dish (tea) towel.

Break off a walnut-size piece of dough, keeping the rest of the dough covered to prevent it from drying, and roll it into a thin cylinder. Using the tips of your fingers, gently press to flatten it. Place one of the date strings on top, cutting off as much as necessary from the ends to fit the dough. Enclose the dough around the date filling and roll it into a slightly longer, thinner cylinder, about 6 inches (15 cm) long. Pick up one end and place it slightly overlapping the other end to form a ring. With a chopstick, press down to make 2 holes where the ends overlap to ensure they are firmly attached and won't come apart during baking. Place on the prepared baking sheet. Repeat until you have 35 rings.

Bake for 10–15 minutes, until the rings are a very light golden brown.

Remove from the oven and let cool for at least 15 minutes before moving to a wire rack to cool completely. Once cooled, transfer to an airtight container. They will keep for 2–3 weeks at room temperature, or for at least 3 months in the freezer.

GHORAYEBAH

Egypt

Submitted by Moustafa Elrefaey

Makes 30–35
Prep time: 15 minutes
Cook time: 15–18 minutes

- 1 cup (8 oz/225 g) ghee, at room temperature
- 1 cup (4 oz/115 g) confectioners' (icing) sugar, sifted
- 2 cups (1 lb 2 oz/500 g) all-purpose (plain) flour
- pinch of salt
- whole blanched almonds or shelled pistachios, for topping

Ghorayebah **is a buttery, melt-in-the-mouth Egyptian shortbread cookie made from just three main ingredients—flour, ghee, and sugar—shaped into smooth circles and often topped with a single blanched almond or pistachio. Its delicate crumb and rich, buttery flavor make it a cherished treat, particularly during Eid al-Fitr, when it shares the festive sweet table with *kahk* and petits fours. Light in texture yet indulgent in taste, it is the kind of cookie that disappears almost as soon as it's placed before guests. Its origins trace back to the medieval Arab world, with recipes for similar ghee-based candies appearing in tenth-century Abbasid cookbooks. The name *ghorayebah* comes from the Arabic root *ghareeb*, meaning "strange" or "unusual," possibly in reference to its unique, soft texture compared to other cookies of its time. Over centuries, it became a staple of Egyptian holiday baking, often prepared in large batches to be gifted to neighbors and shared among family during the days of celebration. Older generations of Egyptians living abroad in the West often maintain the tradition.**

Preheat the oven to 325°F (160°C/Gas Mark 3). Line a baking sheet with parchment paper and set aside.

In a mixing bowl, beat the ghee and confectioners' (icing) sugar together until pale and fluffy. Gradually add the flour and salt, mixing until a soft, smooth dough forms. Do not overwork.

Roll the dough into small balls (about ¾ inch/2 cm in diameter) and place on the prepared baking sheet, leaving space between them. Press an almond or pistachio gently into the center of each. Bake for 15–18 minutes, or until just set but still pale—do not brown. The cookies will firm up as they cool.

Remove from the oven and let the cookies cool completely before transferring to an airtight container. They will keep for up to 2 weeks—if they last that long.

ISPANAKLI BÖREK

Turkey

Submitted by Esra Koraltan

Serves 10
Prep time: 45 minutes
Cook time: 30–40 minutes

- 5 tablespoons olive oil, plus extra for greasing
- 2 lb 12 oz (1.2 kg) spinach, finely chopped
- 1 small white onion, finely chopped
- bunch of dill, finely chopped
- generous 1 cup (9 oz/250 g) ricotta (or lor peyniri—some Turkish grocery stores will have it)
- ¾ cup (6 oz/175 g) yogurt
- 5 eggs
- pinch of chili flakes
- 1 teaspoon salt
- 1 teaspoon freshly ground black pepper
- 2 lb 4 oz (1 kg) phyllo (filo) pastry
- nigella seeds, for topping

Börek is a phyllo (filo) pastry-based delicacy—like baklava, _çibörek_, or _mantı_, it has held an important place in Turkish cuisine and within the Turkish _sofra_ (a place set for a meal; the word conveys a sense of togetherness, hospitality, and sharing) for hundreds of years. Originating from the Ottoman Empire, dozens of styles of _börek_ are made throughout the Levant, the Middle East, and the Balkans, with countless more varieties of fillings.

Börek can be found in local bakeries all over Turkey, but folks make it at home when they're hosting a lot of family and friends during Eid, as it's always a crowd-pleaser.

This recipe comes from Turkish baker Esra Koraltan, who adapted it from her grandmother, who would always make it during the Eid holidays. Not a single crumb would remain after the family had helped themselves to seconds.

This recipe can be adapted to use other fillings—another favorite is ground meat (minced) and eggplant (aubergine), or spiced potatoes. This version is best enjoyed with yogurt and a fresh green salad!

Preheat the oven to 350°F (180°C/Gas Mark 4). Grease a large baking sheet with oil, or line with parchment paper, and set aside.

Place the spinach, onion, and dill in a large bowl and add the ricotta, 2 tablespoons of the yogurt, and 1 egg. Season with the chili flakes, salt, and pepper and mix well.

In a smaller bowl, combine the remaining yogurt and eggs. Add the olive oil and mix well.

Prepare the phyllo (filo) pastry by cutting it in half (if it's circular). If the phyllo pastry is precut, then overlap 2 sheets along one side so you have a long sheet. Spray it with water if it looks dry and cover the ones you are not using with a dish (tea) towel to prevent them drying out.

With a pastry brush, brush 5–6 tablespoons of the yogurt and egg mixture on one phyllo sheet and spread all over.

On the long side of the phyllo that's facing you, line the spinach mixture neatly from left to right, so the filling is spread 1 inch (2.5 cm) thick.

Slowly, starting from one side, start rolling the phyllo over the filling, making sure to tuck it well with each roll. Once you have a long roll, slowly start bending it into a spiral—be careful not to break the pastry. Transfer to the prepared baking sheet. Repeat with the remaining phyllo and filling.

Brush the tops of the börek with the remaining yogurt and oil mixture, and sprinkle with nigella seeds. Bake in the middle of the oven for 30–40 minutes.

Remove from the oven and serve warm.

PISTACHIO MA'AMOUL COOKIES

Middle East

These soft, filled butter cookies are commonly found at celebrations throughout the Middle East, especially on occasions like Eid al-Fitr or iftar during Ramadan, Easter, and even during Purim among some Jewish communities. The fillings of *ma'amoul* vary from one region (or baker) to the next but usually include dried fruit like dates, or nuts like almonds, walnuts, or in this case, pistachios.

This recipe comes from Dona Murad of Librae, a Middle Eastern bakery in Manhattan with its roots in Bahrain.

Submitted by Dona Murad

Makes 25
Prep time: 30 minutes, plus resting time
Cook time: 20 minutes

For the dough:
- 1½ cups (9½ oz/265 g) coarse semolina
- 1 cup (6 oz/175 g) farina (fine semolina)
- ½ cup (2¼ oz/60 g) all-purpose (plain) flour
- 3 tablespoons granulated sugar
- 1 teaspoon baking powder
- ¾ cup (5¾ oz/170 g) melted ghee or butter
- 4 tablespoons milk, warmed
- 3 tablespoons orange blossom water

For the filling:
- 1¼ cups (3¾ oz/110 g) finely ground pistachios
- ¼ cup (1 oz/30 g) confectioners' (icing) sugar
- 1 tablespoon orange blossom water

To decorate:
- confectioners' (icing) sugar, for dusting
- ground cinnamon, for dusting

To make the dough: In a large bowl, combine the semolina, farina, flour, sugar, and baking powder, and mix. Add the melted ghee or butter, warm milk, 2 tablespoons of water, and the orange blossom water. Mix slowly until everything comes together into a soft, smooth dough. Cover the dough in plastic wrap (clingfilm) and let rest at room temperature for 2 hours, or in the refrigerator overnight.

Preheat the oven to 350°F (180°C/Gas Mark 4). Line a baking sheet with parchment paper and set aside.

To make the filling: In a small bowl, combine the ground pistachios with the confectioners' (icing) sugar and orange blossom water, and mix. Set aside.

Divide the rested dough into small balls. Flatten each ball in the palm of your hand, spoon about 1 teaspoon of the pistachio filling into the center, and wrap the dough around it. Press each filled ball into a ma'amoul mold, then place them on the prepared baking sheet. Bake for 20 minutes.

Remove from the oven, let cool, then dust with confectioners' sugar and a pinch of cinnamon.

KLÉCHA

Iraq

Submitted by Baneta Yelda

Makes 50
Prep time: 30 minutes, plus resting time
Cook time: 10–13 minutes

For the dough:
2 cups (9 oz/250 g) all-purpose (plain) flour, plus extra for dusting
1¾ cups (9 oz/250 g) whole wheat flour
2 teaspoons salt
½ oz (13 g) fresh yeast, or ¼ oz (6 g) active dry yeast
⅓ cup (2½ oz/70 g) superfine (caster) sugar
10½ tablespoons (5½ oz/150 g) butter, chilled and cubed
2 eggs
generous ⅓–⅔ cup (4–5 fl oz/100–150 ml) lukewarm water

For the filling:
10 oz–1 lb 2 oz (300–500 g) dates (preferably Medjool), pits (stones) removed
3½ tablespoons warm water
1 teaspoon ground cardamom (see notes)

To finish:
1 egg, beaten, for egg wash
flaky sea salt, for topping

Klécha is a traditional cookie popular across the Middle East but especially in Iraq. Made from enriched dough, it can have many different fillings—from walnut and cinnamon to shredded coconut and sugar. The filling for this _klécha_ recipe is made from date paste and cardamom, ingredients beloved in the Iraqi kitchen.

In Iraq every family has its own recipe, but no matter the method, they are always made to be bite-size so that they can be served with tea or coffee. Although often associated with the Muslim holiday of Eid, these cookies are also beloved by Iraq's Christian communities, especially those from Assyrian backgrounds, like this recipe's contributor, Iraqi baker Baneta Yelda, who is based in the United Kingdom. This recipe is modeled on her mother's recipe, but with the addition of a little whole wheat flour to deepen the flavor.

To make the dough: In a bowl, mix together the flours, salt, yeast, and sugar. Add the butter and rub in with your fingertips until the mixture resembles bread crumbs. Add the eggs and incorporate.

Transfer to a stand mixer fitted with the dough hook attachment (or work by hand) and knead, adding the lukewarm water gradually, starting with the smaller amount and adding more if needed, until the dough looks smooth. Cover with plastic wrap (clingfilm) and let rest for 1 hour, or until doubled in size.

Preheat the oven to 340°F (170°C/Gas Mark 3). Line a baking sheet with parchment paper and set aside.

To make the filling: In a blender, add the dates and blend. Add the warm water, and blend until a smooth paste forms. Add the cardamom and give it a final blitz.

Once the dough has rested, turn it out onto a lightly floured counter and roll into a rectangle 1/16–⅛ inch (2–3 mm) thick. Spread the filling evenly over the dough with a plastic scraper or a palette knife. From the long edge nearest to you, roll the dough toward the center. Repeat from the top edge to the center, so that there are 2 logs meeting in the middle.

Using a knife or a metal scraper, slice between the 2 logs to separate them, then slice each log into small rolls. Place them on the prepared baking sheet, leaving 1¼ inches (3 cm) between each. Press them into the sheet lightly, as they tend to roll to the side.

To finish: Brush the top of each pastry with the egg wash and sprinkle with sea salt. Bake for 10–13 minutes, until golden.

Remove from the oven and let cool for 10 minutes before serving. They will keep for a week in an airtight container at room temperature.

Notes

Consider the ambient temperature and the temperature of the water used when making the dough. If the climate is cold, use warmer water and aim for a dough that is 68–75°F (20–24°C). Equally, if the climate is warm, use cold water. To accelerate the proofing, use slightly warmer water.

To make your own ground cardamom, toast whole cardamom pods, then grind them. This is best done on the day they are used, as they will taste better. You could substitute the cardamom with the same quantity of ground cinnamon, if desired.

KUE NASTAR

Indonesia

Submitted by Petty Pandean-Elliott

Makes about 24
Prep time: 20 minutes, plus chilling time
Cook time: 55 minutes

For the pineapple jam:
1 (2 lb 12 oz/1.2 kg) pineapple, peeled, cored, and chopped
generous ½ cup (4½ oz/120 g) cane sugar
2 cinnamon sticks
30 whole cloves
½ teaspoon salt

For the dough:
scant 1½ cups (9 oz/250 g) all-purpose (plain) flour, plus extra for dusting
scant ½ cup (1½ oz/50 g) cornstarch (cornflour)
4 cups (1½ oz/50 g) granulated sugar
1¾ sticks (7 oz/200 g) butter, at room temperature
pinch of salt
2 eggs, beaten

For glazing:
2 egg yolks, beaten, for egg wash
cloves

***Kue nastar*—pineapple cookies—are one of Indonesia's most beloved festive cookies, especially during Lebaran (Eid), Christmas, and Lunar New Year. The name *nastar* comes from the Dutch word *ananas taartjes* (pineapple tart). It reflects Indonesia's colonial past, where European-style pastries were adapted using local ingredients. Instead of using jams like in the original Dutch version, Indonesian bakers use sweet and tangy pineapple jam or *selai nanas* made from freshly grated (or blended) tropical pineapples infused with cloves and cinnamon, cooked with cane sugar, and caramelized until a beautiful amber color. *Kue nastar* has a dry yet moist texture giving it its distinct taste. This small, round, buttery cookie is filled with pineapple jam and often glazed with egg yolk for a golden finish. It is often finished with a whole clove pressed into its surface.**

While rooted in colonial history, *kue nastar* has become fully Indonesian and is made in homes across the archipelago, with countless family recipes passed down through generations. More than just a treat, *kue nastar* symbolizes warmth, celebration, and tradition, always present during moments of togetherness and festive joy. Any leftover pineapple jam can be saved to spread over toast or used as a sponge cake filling.

To make the pineapple jam: Transfer the pineapple to a blender and puree for 1–2 minutes. Transfer the puree into a pan, then add the sugar and cinnamon. Wrap all the cloves in a small piece of cheesecloth (muslin), and tie securely with kitchen twine, so it can be easily removed after infusion. Bring the mixture to a boil, then simmer over medium heat for 25 minutes, or until the liquid has evaporated. Increase the heat to high and boil for 10 minutes until the mixture is sticky and dark amber. Set aside to cool.

Meanwhile, to make the dough: Combine all the ingredients in a food processor and process for 3 minutes until smooth. Transfer the dough to a bowl and shape it into a log, about 2½ inches (6 cm) in diameter.

Line a baking sheet with parchment paper and set aside. Cut the log into 4-inch (2-cm) slices. Flatten each slice in your palm and put a generous teaspoon of jam in the center of the dough. Fold the dough toward the center, covering the jam and creating a disk. Place on the prepared baking sheet. Repeat with the remaining cookies, evenly spacing them apart. Chill in the refrigerator for 25 minutes.

Preheat the oven to 350°F (180°C/Gas Mark 4).

Remove the cookies from the refrigerator and let sit at room temperature for 5 minutes. Brush the egg wash over the cookies, and gently push a clove into the center of each. Bake for 20 minutes, or until golden.

Remove from the oven, set the baking sheet aside for 1–2 minutes, then transfer to a wire rack and let cool before serving.

MOTHERING SUNDAY

Taking place on the fourth Sunday of Lent, Mothering Sunday is a short break in the long period of penance that dominates the buildup to Easter. This holiday, which originates in the United Kingdom, is meant to honor the connection of a Christian to the church they were baptized in—their "mother church." In the early 1900s the holiday was intentionally associated with the new tradition of Mother's Day, which had started in the United States but was celebrated on a Sunday in May, as a means of encouraging celebrants to become reinvested in the occasion.

This particular Sunday was once known as the "Sunday of the Five Loaves," for its association with the bible story of the feeding of the five thousand. For this reason, there are a number of buns or breads that were traditionally baked for this day, as fitting tie-ins to the holiday.

MOTHERING BUNS

England

Submitted by Anna Luntley

Makes 12
Prep time: 1 hour, plus proofing times
Cook time: 20 minutes

For the dough:
- $1\frac{1}{4}$ cups (10 fl oz/300 ml) skimmed milk
- $3\frac{1}{2}$ tablespoons ($1\frac{3}{4}$ oz/50 g) butter
- $2\frac{2}{3}$ cups ($10\frac{1}{2}$ oz/300 g) strong white bread flour
- $1\frac{1}{2}$ cups plus 2 tablespoons (7 oz/200 g) all-purpose (plain) flour, plus extra for dusting
- 1 teaspoon fine salt
- $\frac{1}{4}$ oz (7 g) quick-rise dry yeast
- $\frac{1}{4}$ cup ($1\frac{3}{4}$ oz/50 g) superfine (caster) sugar

For the icing:
- 1 teaspoon caraway seeds (optional)
- $2\frac{2}{3}$ cups ($10\frac{1}{2}$ oz/300 g) confectioners' (icing) sugar
- 3–4 tablespoons cold water
- sprinkles (hundreds and thousands, if possible), for topping (optional)

These lightly sweet, iced buns are made for Mothering Sunday, a British holiday celebrated annually on the fourth Sunday of Lent, which traditionally commemorates the connection between an individual and their "mother" church.

These mothering buns come from the southwest of England, specifically around Bristol, where they were historically decorated with anise or caraway seeds. Today it is more common to find them topped with colorful British sprinkles called "hundreds and thousands."

To make the dough: In a small pan over low heat, combine the milk and butter and stir until the butter has melted. Remove from the heat and set aside to cool slightly.

Line 2 baking sheets with parchment paper and set aside.

In the bowl of a stand mixer fitted with the dough hook attachment, combine the flours, salt, yeast, and sugar. Add the melted butter-milk mixture, and mix on medium speed until you have a smooth dough, about 10 minutes. This can also be done by hand: Bring all the ingredients together in a large bowl until you have a rough dough, then turn out onto a lightly floured counter and knead for 10 minutes until you have a smooth and elastic dough. Place the dough in a clean bowl, cover, and proof in a warm place for 1 hour, or until doubled in size.

Once the dough has risen, turn out onto a lightly floured counter. Knead lightly for a couple of minutes, then divide into 12 equal pieces of $2\frac{3}{4}$ oz (75 g) each. Place the buns on the prepared baking sheets. Cover and proof in a warm place for 1 hour, or until doubled in size.

Preheat the oven to 350°F (180°C/Gas Mark 4). Bake the buns for 15 minutes, until pale golden brown and they sound hollow if you lightly tap the bottom.

Meanwhile, to make the icing: In a dry skillet (frying pan) over medium heat, gently toast the caraway seeds, if using, for 1–2 minutes until they start to smell aromatic. Remove from the heat and lightly grind the seeds in a mortar and pestle. Combine with the confectioners' (icing) sugar, and gradually add cold water until you have a moderately thick icing.

Remove the buns from the oven and let cool for 5 minutes. Brush the icing over the buns while they are still warm, and finish with a good scattering of sprinkles, if using.

Ideally eat on the day they are made, but they will still be enjoyable the next day if kept in an airtight container overnight.

ST. PATRICK'S DAY

St. Patrick, who was born in fifth-century Romanized Britain, was as a teenager captured and enslaved by Irish pirates. After several years he was able to escape and return home, where he became a cleric and missionary whose life would be dedicated to the spread of Christianity. Traveling back to Ireland in this capacity, he began to spread the gospel and build churches throughout the country, becoming the figure most connected with Irish Christianization. St. Patrick's feast day, March 17, is celebrated not only by those living in Ireland, where he is the patron saint, but also by the significant Irish diaspora, and even those of removed Irish descent living abroad—especially the United States. There, the holiday has deviated from its original focus, instead becoming associated with a celebration of Irish identity.

SPOTTED DOG

Ireland

p. 84

Submitted by JR Ryall

Makes 1 loaf
Prep time: 30 minutes
Cook time: 40–45 minutes

- 3½ cups plus 2 tablespoons (1 lb/450 g) all-purpose (plain) flour, plus extra for dusting
- 1 egg, beaten
- 1½–1⅔ cups (12–14 fl oz/350–415 ml) buttermilk or sour milk
- 1 teaspoon baking soda (bicarbonate of soda)
- 1 tablespoon superfine (caster) sugar
- 1 teaspoon salt
- generous ¾ cup (4 oz/115 g) golden raisins (sultanas), raisins, or currants

This style of soda bread, called spotted dog due to its speckling of dried fruit, has a special place on the St. Patrick's Day table. The traditional cross cut into the top of the loaf is both symbolic and practical; it is a Christian symbol, and the incisions also allow heat to penetrate to the center of the dough as it bakes. In its traditional form the loaf (or cake as it is sometimes known) is made into a circle because it was originally baked in a circular cast-iron pot (called a bastible) that was positioned in the embers of a turf fire. A lid was placed on the pot and more embers may have been placed on top, functioning like a Dutch oven. The round loaf fitted nicely in the round pot, hence the practical shape.

When serving the loaf, it is normal to break it in half along one of the lines of the cross, using your hands, then cut from the heel inward (i.e., cut from the narrow end toward the thicker center).

This recipe comes from Irish baker and pastry chef JR Ryall, who makes it year-round at Ballymaloe House in Shanagarry in County Cork—but especially on St. Patrick's Day. Serve with salted Irish butter and strawberry or raspberry jam or marmalade.

Preheat the oven to 450°F (230°C/Gas Mark 8). Lightly flour a baking sheet and set aside.

In a measuring cup, place the egg and add enough buttermilk to bring the total volume up to 1¾ cups (14 fl oz/425 ml), and mix to combine. Set aside.

In a large wide bowl, sift the flour and baking soda (bicarbonate of soda). Add the sugar, salt, and dried fruit and mix well. Make a well in the center of the dry ingredients and add most of the egg and buttermilk mixture. Hold your hand in an open claw shape and mix the dry ingredients from the sides of the bowl into the buttermilk to form a soft dough. Add the remaining buttermilk as you mix, if necessary, until the mixture comes together and forms a rough ball. Resist the temptation to knead or work the dough (the less it is handled, the better the texture of the finished bread will be).

Turn out the dough onto a floured counter. With floured hands, form the dough into a circle shape, handling gently as you go. Transfer to the prepared baking sheet and pat it so it is about 1½ inches (4 cm) thick. Cut a deep cross into the top of the round loaf. Lightly pierce each quarter with the tip of a knife (this is said to release "the fairies" from the dough to ensure a good bake).

Bake for 15 minutes in the center of the oven, then reduce the temperature to 400°F (200°C/Gas Mark 6) and bake for another 25–30 minutes, or until the loaf has a nice brown crust and sounds hollow when tapped.

Remove from the oven and serve freshly baked, cut into thick slices.

NOWRUZ

Nowruz is the Persian New Year, which takes place annually on the vernal equinox. Rooted in the traditions of early pagans as well as later Zoroastrians, the holiday developed its early religious symbolism and statewide worship under powerful Persian kings like Darius I more than 2,500 years ago, but by the time of Muslim conquest in the seventh century, the holiday became increasingly secular in its nature.

An important ritual of observing *Nowruz* is to display a *haft-sin* (literally "seven S's"), a table arrangement featuring seven foods each starting with the Arabic letter س, called *sīn*. Each element, including common ones like *sabzeh* (sprouted grains) or sumac, represents a concept like renewal or hope.

While the holiday may have its roots (and most of its adherents) in modern-day Iran, *Nowruz* is also observed in many parts of central Asia, like Azerbaijan, Uzbekistan, and Kazakhstan, as well as Zoroastrian Parsi communities.

Left: *Spotted Dog*, St. Patrick's Day (page 83)

SHEKERBURA

Azerbaijan

Submitted by Cemre Torun

Makes 20
Prep time: 40 minutes, plus resting time
Cook time: 15–20 minutes

For the dough:
- 1¾ sticks (7 oz/200 g) butter, at room temperature
- 4 cups (1 lb 2 oz/500 g) all-purpose (plain) flour
- 1 egg, plus 1 egg yolk
- generous ⅓ cup (3½ oz/100 g) sour cream
- ¼ teaspoon salt
- ½ teaspoon active dry yeast
- ½ teaspoon granulated sugar
- generous ⅓ cup (3½ fl oz/100 ml) milk, lukewarm
- confectioners' (icing) sugar, for dusting (optional)

For the filling:
- 1 cup (7 oz/200 g) blanched hazelnuts
- ¾ cup (5½ oz/150 g) granulated sugar
- 1 teaspoon ground cardamom

***Shekerbura* are beautiful, delicate crescent-shaped pastries made with a butter-based dough and a sweet nut filling. They are a traditional Azerbaijani delicacy served during *Nowruz* celebrations and are believed to symbolize the moon.**

***Shekerbura* is usually served on a special holiday tray alongside other *Nowruz* desserts, as well as nuts, dried fruits, and colored eggs. Like other holiday bakes, it often involves many relatives and neighbors working together on the recipe. Variations include almond meal, hazelnuts, or walnuts.**
A special crimper tool or tweezers called *maggash* are used to decorate the shell with geometrical shapes.

To make the dough: In a large bowl, rub the butter into the flour until the mixture resembles bread crumbs. Set aside.

In a small bowl, mix the egg, egg yolk, sour cream, and salt.

In a separate bowl, whisk the yeast and sugar with 2 tablespoons of the milk. Let stand for 2 minutes, then add the rest of the milk.

Using your hands, combine the egg and yeast mixtures with the butter-flour mixture until fully incorporated and a rough dough has formed. Transfer the dough to a counter, and knead for a few minutes until smooth. Shape the dough into a ball. Put it back in the bowl, cover with a clean, damp dish (tea) towel, and let rest for 20 minutes.

Preheat the oven to 340°F (170°C/Gas Mark 3). Line a baking sheet with parchment paper and set aside.

To make the filling: In the bowl of a food processor, place the blanched nuts and sugar and process until almost powder-like. Transfer to a bowl and mix with the ground cardamom.

Turn out the dough onto a counter and divide into 20 balls, each weighing about 1½ oz (40 g). Work with one ball at a time and cover the rest with a clean, damp dish towel to keep moist. Roll each ball into a disk about the size of your palm. Place 2 tablespoons of the filling in the center, pressing it slightly with the back of a spoon. Starting at one side, begin pinching the edges together, using a bit of water to seal, and continuing to pinch over the filling to obtain a half-moon shape. Sealed shekerbura should be somewhat chunky and chubby from the filling, and not flat. Using your thumb and index finger, pinch and twist the dough along the seal to decorate the edges in a scalloped pattern. If desired, pinch the dough using a maggash shaper, on the angle, lifting it slightly upward. Continue until you get a row of patterns. Create similar rows over the dough parcels, each on the angle to the next one, until the entire surface is decorated. Place on the prepared baking sheet. Repeat with the remaining dough and filling.

Bake for 15–20 minutes, or until the edges just begin to change color and the bottom is lightly browned. Take care not to overbake the pastries—the top should remain a light color when baked.

Remove from the oven and let cool. If you did not decorate the pastries with the maggash shaper, coat them with confectioners' (icing) sugar before serving.

SHEKER CHOREK

Azerbaijan

Submitted by Javahir Ahmadova

Makes 20
Prep time: 25 minutes
Cook time: 30–35 minutes

- 2¼ sticks (9 oz/250 g) butter, at room temperature
- 1 teaspoon vanilla sugar
- 1⅓ cups (5½ oz/150 g) confectioners' (icing) sugar
- 1 egg white, at room temperature
- 4 cups (1 lb 1 oz–1 lb 2 oz/480–500 g) all-purpose (plain) flour, as needed
- 1 egg yolk, beaten, for topping

Directly translating to "sweet bread," *sheker chorek* is a beloved traditional cookie in Azerbaijan, known for its decorative egg-yolk topping. It is often prepared for holidays and celebrations—especially *Novruz*. For a lot of Azerbaijanis, it's one of those nostalgic, comforting cookies that brings you straight back home. Serve with black tea or alongside other Novruz pastries.

Preheat the oven to 300°F (150°C/Gas Mark 2). Line a baking sheet with parchment paper and set aside.

In a large mixing bowl, beat the butter using a handheld electric mixer on low speed. Alternatively, use a stand mixer fitted with the paddle attachment. Gradually increase the speed and continue mixing until the butter becomes very light in color and reaches a fluffy, cream-like consistency. Add the vanilla sugar and confectioners' (icing) sugar—to avoid creating a confectioners' sugar cloud, gently fold the sugar into the butter before turning the mixer back on. Continue mixing until the sugar is fully dissolved and the mixture is smooth and airy. Add the egg white and continue mixing until fully incorporated. The batter should now be soft, smooth, and cohesive.

Sift the flour and add it gradually, mixing by hand or with a rubber spatula after each addition. The final dough should feel sandy and crumbly, but when pressed together, it should easily form a smooth ball. The texture will resemble kinetic sand or wet beach sand—firm but pliable and not sticky.

Divide the dough into small portions, each weighing around 1¾ oz (50 g). Roll them into smooth balls with a flat bottom and place them on the prepared baking sheet. Using your pinky finger or the back of a small, rounded spoon, press a shallow dip into the center of each cookie.

Using a small spoon or pastry bag, carefully fill each indentation with a bit of the egg yolk. This gives the cookie its signature golden center once baked. Place the cookies on the lowest rack of the oven to ensure the bottoms bake properly without browning the tops. Bake for 30–35 minutes, until the bottoms are lightly golden, but the tops remain white or pale yellow.

Remove from the oven and transfer to a wire rack. Let cool before serving.

BAKU KURABIYE

Azerbaijan

(30)

Submitted by Javahir Ahmadova

Makes 25–30
Prep time: 20 minutes
Cook time: 10 minutes

8½ tablespoons (4¼ oz/120 g) butter, softened
½ cup (2¼ oz/60 g) confectioners' (icing) sugar
pinch of salt
1 teaspoon vanilla sugar
1 egg, at room temperature
1½ cups plus 2 tablespoons (7 oz/200 g) all-purpose (plain) flour
1 teaspoon baking powder
2–3 tablespoons jam (apricot, cherry, or strawberry: thick, not watery)

***Baku kurabiye* are buttery, soft cookies that are piped out and filled with jam in the center. While this style of cookie is from Baku, it is related more broadly to the *qurabiya* (or *ghorayeba*), a sort of shortbread cookie found all over the Maghreb region as well as the Balkans.**

In Azerbaijan, you'll see them at pretty much any celebration—*Nowruz*, birthdays, or whenever there's tea on the table. They may look fancy, but they are actually quite easy to make. They are perfect with a cup of Azerbaijani black tea.

Preheat the oven to 350°F (180°C/Gas Mark 4). Line a baking sheet with parchment paper and set aside.

In a large mixing bowl, beat the softened butter using a handheld electric mixer until smooth and creamy. Alternatively, use a stand mixer fitted with the paddle attachment. Add the confectioners' (icing) sugar, salt, and vanilla sugar. Continue mixing until it becomes light and fluffy, resembling a thick cream. Add the egg to the butter mixture and mix again until well combined. The batter should be smooth and airy.

In a separate bowl, whisk together the flour and baking powder. Gradually add the flour mixture to the butter mixture and mix until a smooth, pipeable dough forms. The texture should be soft enough to pass through a pastry (piping) bag but still hold its shape.

Transfer the dough into a pastry bag fitted with a French star tip (⅝ inch/14 mm diameter is ideal). Pipe small rosettes or swirls directly onto the prepared baking sheet, spacing them evenly. Gently press the center of each cookie with your fingertip to form a small indentation. Fill the center with about ¼ teaspoon of jam. Bake the cookies for 10 minutes, or until the bottom edges are lightly golden but the tops remain pale.

Remove from the oven and let cool on the sheet for a few minutes before transferring to a wire rack. Serve once completely cooled.

QOĞAL

Azerbaijan

Submitted by Javahir Ahmadova

Makes 16
Prep time: 1 hour, plus chilling and resting times
Cook time: 20–25 minutes

For the dough:
- generous ⅓ cup (3½ fl oz/100 ml) warm water
- 1 tablespoon granulated sugar
- 1 tablespoon active-dry yeast
- generous 2 cups (17 fl oz/500 ml) milk, warmed
- generous ⅓ cup (3½ fl oz/100 ml) vegetable oil
- 1 egg, plus 1 egg white
- 1 tablespoon salt
- ⅓ teaspoon ground turmeric
- 8¾ cups (2 lb 7 oz/1.1 kg) all-purpose (plain) flour, plus extra for dusting

For the filling:
- 1 teaspoon ground caraway
- 1 teaspoon ground fennel (or cumin)
- ½ teaspoon ground turmeric
- ½ teaspoon salt
- ⅓ teaspoon freshly ground black pepper
- 1 cup (4¼ oz/120 g) all-purpose (plain) flour
- 3½ tablespoons (1¾ oz/50 g) butter, softened

To assemble:
- 3½ sticks (14 oz/400 g) butter
- nigella seeds, for topping

For egg wash:
- 1 egg yolk
- 1 tablespoon milk

***Qoğal* is a spiced, flaky, savory pastry that's usually made for spring holidays like *Nowruz* and Ramadan, with its round shape and golden color meant to symbolize the sun.**

Traditionally you'll find *qoğal* served alongside a glass of black tea (and a sugar cube). Even outside of festive occasions in Baku, you can find *qoğal* for sale, often for breakfast—perhaps the best time of day to try it.

To make the dough: In a large mixing bowl, combine the warm water, sugar, and yeast. Let sit for 5–10 minutes until it becomes frothy.

Add the warm milk, oil, egg, egg white, salt, turmeric, and flour to the yeast mixture. Knead thoroughly for about 10 minutes until the dough is soft, elastic, and not sticky. Transfer the dough to a floured counter. Divide it in half, then divide each half into 4 equal balls (you should have 8 in total). Place them on a floured baking sheet or counter, cover with plastic wrap (clingfilm), and refrigerate for 30 minutes.

To make the filling: In a dry pan over medium heat, toast the ground caraway, ground fennel, ground turmeric, salt, and black pepper for 1–2 minutes until fragrant. Remove from the heat, then combine with the flour and softened butter in a bowl using your hands to make a coarse, crumbly mixture. Set aside.

To assemble: In a pan, melt the butter, then strain it through a fine-mesh sieve to remove the milk solids. Reserve to brush between the dough layers.

Preheat the oven to 400°F (200°C/Gas Mark 6). Line a baking sheet with parchment paper and set aside.

Working one ball at a time, roll out the dough on a floured counter into a very thin circle—almost transparent. Brush generously with the strained butter. Repeat this process for all 8 dough balls, stacking each rolled and buttered sheet on top of the last.

Once stacked, gently stretch the layered dough using your fingers, making the layers thinner and airier. This helps to enhance the flakiness. Cut the layered dough into long strips about 3 fingers wide. Roll each strip tightly into a spiral.

Take one rolled spiral, tuck the end inward, and gently push the center down to create a well. Add 2–3 teaspoons of the filling in the middle. Pinch around the edges to seal the filling inside and press lightly to form a flattened circle. As you form the rest, keep the prepared qoğals covered with plastic wrap to prevent drying out.

To make the egg wash: In a small bowl, beat the egg yolk with the milk. Brush the tops of each pastry with egg wash. Sprinkle with the nigella seeds and place the pastries on the prepared baking sheet. Bake for 20–25 minutes, or until golden brown on the outside.

Remove from the oven and serve warm.

KUKU SABZI

Iran

Submitted by Bettina Loew-Banayan

Serves 6
Prep time: 15 minutes
Cook time: 30 minutes

- Generous ⅓ cup (3¼ oz/90 g) extra virgin olive oil
- 7½ oz (215 g) scallions (spring onions), sliced ¼ inch (5 mm) thick
- 1½ teaspoons kosher salt
- 3 oz (85 g) parsley, leaves and tender stems
- 5 oz (145 g) cilantro (coriander), leaves and tender stems
- 3½ oz (100 g) dill, leaves and tender stems
- ½ teaspoon ground turmeric
- ½ teaspoon freshly ground black pepper
- ¼ teaspoon ground cumin
- 8 eggs
- 1½ tablespoons (¾ oz/20 g) butter

***Kuku sabzi* is a classic Persian-Iranian herb and egg dish said to have its roots in ancient Persian food culture. The first documented recipes, for over a dozen similar egg-based dishes (collectively known as *kuku*), comes from Sofré Atamé, written in the nineteenth century by chef of the royal Qajar court, Ali Akbar Kashani. This herb-filled *kuku* is especially tied to *Nowruz*, the Persian New Year, when its abundance of fresh herbs symbolizes spring, renewal, and growth.**

This recipe comes from Bettina Loew-Banayan, whose Persian-Iranian-Jewish family also prepare it to honor those who have passed away. Traditionally called "the meal of condolence," this practice emphasizes the round eggs in the dish, which represent the cycle of life and continuity beyond loss. Likely born from the first herbs of spring, with eggs binding them together, *kuku sabzi* has become both a celebratory and commemorative dish—one that connects us to the rhythms of the seasons, our heritage, and our loved ones, sustaining memory and renewal through its preparation and sharing.

Heat a 10-inch (25-cm) nonstick, ovenproof pan over medium-high heat for 1 minute, then add ⅓ cup (3 oz/80 g) of the olive oil. Allow the oil to heat for 30 seconds, then add the scallions (spring onions) and salt. Using a rubber spatula, carefully mix to coat the scallions in oil.

While the scallions are cooking, in small batches, add the herbs to a food processor and pulse until finely chopped. Add each completed batch to the pan of scallions.

Reduce the heat to medium and cook, stirring occasionally, until the herbs are starting to turn dark brown, about 20 minutes from starting the scallions, then add the turmeric, black pepper, and cumin. Cook for 1 more minute, then remove from the heat and transfer to a bowl to cool for 10 minutes in the refrigerator.

While the scallions and herbs are cooling, preheat the oven to 200°C/400°F/Gas Mark 6.

In a large bowl, gently whisk the eggs. Remove the herbs from the refrigerator and whisk into the eggs.

Return the pan to the stove over medium-high heat. Add the butter and the remaining oil to the pan. Once the butter begins to brown, add the egg, scallion, and herb mixture, using a spatula to even out the surface of the eggs. Cook on high heat for 1 minute, then transfer to the oven for 6½ minutes.

Remove from the oven and allow to rest for 2 minutes before flipping onto a plate. Cut into 6 wedges and serve.

NOON-BERENJI

Iran

Submitted by Bettina Loew-Banayan

Makes 36
Prep time: 75 minutes (including chilling time)
Cook time: 18–20 minutes

- 11½ tablespoons (6 oz/165 g) butter, at room temperature
- ½ cup (2 oz/60 g) confectioners' (icing) sugar
- 3 teaspoons cornstarch (cornflour)
- ⅛ teaspoon kosher salt
- ¼ teaspoon freshly ground nutmeg
- ¼ teaspoon ground cardamom
- 1⅔ cups (9 oz/255 g) white rice flour (I use Bob's Red Mill)
- 2 small egg yolks
- 1 teaspoon rose water
- 1 teaspoon poppy seeds

***Noon-Berenji* is a traditional Iranian cookie from Isfahan, made with rice flour and poppy seeds. Naturally gluten-free, it comes from a long tradition that places importance on ingredients that are locally abundant. The rice flour allows the grain's delicate flavor to shine, creating a sandy, crumbly texture that melts in your mouth. The poppy seeds add a subtle crunch and an earthy note, an essential part of the cookie's character.**

This recipe comes from Bettina Loew-Banayan, for whom the cardamom and rose water combination evokes memories of childhood, of fragrant sweets shared with family during holidays, always enjoyed alongside a strong, bitter black tea. Served traditionally at Nowruz, *Noon-Berenji* is a cookie with considerable heritage and significance, imparting a poignant taste of home and memory especially for those living abroad.

In a stand mixer fitted with the paddle attachment, cream the butter on low–medium speed until smooth, about 1 minute. Sift the confectioners' (icing) sugar and cornstarch (cornflour) into the bowl. Mix on low speed, then gradually increase to high until fully combined, about 1 minute. Add the salt, nutmeg, cardamom, and rice flour. Mix on low speed for 30 seconds, scrape down the sides of the bowl, then mix on medium speed until evenly blended, about 30 seconds more. Add the egg yolks and rose water. Mix on low speed until incorporated, scraping down the sides of the bowl as needed, about 30 seconds.

Lay a 28-inch (70-cm) sheet of plastic wrap (clingfilm) on the counter. Using a rubber spatula, place the cookie dough in a line down the center to form a rough 15-inch (38-cm) log. Fold one side of the plastic over the dough, pressing gently with the side of your hand to push out any air bubbles. Roll the log over to wrap it fully, then press out air from the sides. Holding both ends of the plastic, lift the log and twirl it in a circular motion until the wrap tightens at the ends like a candy wrapper, forming a smooth, even log of dough.

Place the dough log on a baking sheet and chill in the refrigerator for 45 minutes. Periodically roll the log on the sheet to help maintain a round, even shape.

Preheat the oven to 325°F (160°C/Gas Mark 3). Line two baking sheets with parchment paper and set aside.

Unwrap the chilled log, trim the ends, and cut it into ½-inch (1-cm)-thick rounds. Arrange the cookies on your prepared baking sheets, spacing them about 1 inch (2.5 cm) apart. Using the side of a fork prong, gently press 3 crossed lines into the top of each cookie to create a starlike pattern. Finish by sprinkling each cookie with a generous pinch of poppy seeds.

Bake for 18–20 minutes, or until the edges just begin to turn golden. Rotate the baking sheets halfway through for even baking.

Remove from the oven and let rest for 10 minutes before serving.

APRIL

4

APRIL

EASTER

Easter marks the resurrection of Jesus Christ, one of the foundational beliefs of Christianity, and as a result, one of the faith's most significant holidays. The timing of the day, settled at the Council of Nicaea in 325 AD, is the first Sunday following the first full moon of spring (in the northern hemisphere), and this calculation anchors the holiday schedule for not only the three-month period of the "Easter cycle" but also the preceding pre-Lenten festivities.

Celebrations at Easter are joyful, not only in commemorating Christ's resurrection but also in the embrace of life more generally. Coming at the outset of spring, the renewal of life can be seen throughout the natural world as well in the blossoming of flowers, and certain ones, like Easter lilies, are especially popular.

Many of Easter's gastronomic traditions incorporate symbolic ingredients like eggs (resurrection) or lamb (sacrifice), but there is also a strong association with baking. This is underscored by the joy or sweetness the holiday represents for many, and the rich contrast in tone and indulgence as compared to the six weeks prior. Among the most popular Easter bakes are decorative and sweet yeasted breads, fruitcakes, and cakes, which may again incorporate some of the same gastronomic motifs like eggs.

MILIBROD

North Macedonia

Submitted by Irina Janakievska

Serves 12–16
Prep time: 40 minutes, plus resting and proofing times
Cook time: 30–35 minutes

This sweet, enriched, and braided bread is one of many examples of yeasted holiday loaves found across southeast Europe and the Balkans. Communities celebrating Easter in North Macedonia prepare a version of this bread, sweetened with dried fruits such as raisins, golden raisins, or sour cherries, and often elaborately braided and decorated. It is traditionally topped with boiled, red-dyed eggs—symbolic of Orthodox Easter celebrations—and sometimes sprinkled with slivers of almonds or sesame seeds. It is known variously as *milibrod*—the latter name likely derived from the German *milchbrot* (milk bread), though in composition it echoes influences from Austrian *striezel* and Jewish challah. *Milibrod* or *kozinjak* holds deep symbolic meaning in Easter celebrations, representing rebirth, abundance, and the return of spring.

⅓ oz (10 g) quick-rise dry yeast
¼ cup (1¾ oz/50 g) superfine (caster) sugar
1 cup (8 fl oz/250 ml) milk, lukewarm, plus extra for brushing, if needed
scant 4 cups (1 lb 2 oz/500 g) strong white bread flour, plus extra for dusting
1 teaspoon fine sea salt
2 eggs, lightly beaten
3½ tablespoons (1¾ oz/50 g) butter, melted and cooled
grated zest of 1 lemon (optional)
¾ cup (4¼ oz/125 g) mixed dried fruits (for example, raisins, golden raisins [sultanas], sour cherries, chopped apricots or dates)

In a small bowl, combine the yeast, sugar, and lukewarm milk. Set aside for 5–10 minutes until frothy.

In a large bowl, sift together the flour and salt. Add the yeast mixture, most of the beaten egg (reserving 2 tablespoons for brushing), all the butter, and the lemon zest, if using. Use a rubber spatula or dough whisk to bring the dough together.

Turn the dough out onto a lightly floured counter and knead for 10–12 minutes, or until it comes together in a smooth, elastic dough that springs back when touched. Knead in the dried fruit until evenly distributed throughout. Alternatively, if you have a stand mixer, combine as above and beat the mixture first on a low speed until the flour is incorporated, then on medium-high speed for 8–10 minutes, pausing to scrape down the sides, until the dough comes together. Incorporate the dried fruit at the end of kneading, as above.

Place the dough in a clean bowl and cover tightly with plastic wrap (clingfilm). Either proof in the refrigerator overnight (or for at least 8 hours) or leave in a warm place to proof for 1½ hours, until doubled in size. If you proof it in the refrigerator, take the dough out of the refrigerator at least 1 hour before use so that it comes back to room temperature before shaping.

Line a baking sheet with parchment paper and set aside.

Punch down the dough to knock it back, then tip it onto a lightly floured counter and divide it into 3 equal pieces. Roll each piece into a 24–26 inches (60–70 cm) long strand. Braid the 3 strands together, then shape the braid into a circle, pinching the ends together to seal. Tuck any dried fruit sticking out gently back in to avoid burning. Place the shaped ring on the prepared baking sheet. Cover with a clean dish (tea) towel and let proof for 30–45 minutes.

Meanwhile, preheat the oven to 400°F (200°C/Gas Mark 6). Brush the risen dough gently with the reserved beaten egg for a glossy finish (or use milk for a matte finish). Bake in the center of the oven for 30–35 minutes, or until golden brown all over and hollow-sounding when tapped at the bottom. If it is browning too quickly, tent with aluminum foil or parchment paper in the last 10 minutes.

Remove from the oven and cool on a wire rack. It is best enjoyed slightly warm or on the day of baking, though it keeps well for 2–3 days stored in an airtight container.

FONOTT KALÁCS

Hungary

Submitted by Lilla Szőcs

Serves 10–12
Prep time: 1 hour, plus resting and proofing times
Cook time: 30–40 minutes

- ¾ oz (20 g) fresh yeast
- generous ⅓ cup (3½ fl oz/100 ml) milk (minimum 3.5% fat), lukewarm
- 4 cups (1 lb 2 oz/500 g) all-purpose (plain) flour, plus extra for dusting
- 5 tablespoons granulated sugar
- pinch of salt
- 2 eggs, plus 1 egg yolk
- ⅞ cup (7 fl oz/200 ml) whipping cream (30–36% fat)

The first written mention of this braided sweet bread in Hungary dates back to the fourteenth century, where it was a festive dish in medieval peasant culture. The flour was sifted and kneaded with milk, butter, eggs, and a leavening agent. It has many parallels around Europe: *Zopf* in Switzerland, *paska* in Ukraine, *pane di pasqua* or *panettone* in Italy, *tsoureki* in Greece, and challah.

In Hungary, you have only to look at the shape of a sweet bread to know what kind of celebration you're attending. Across different regions and festivities, you can find a wide range of distinctive shapes. Generally, in every Hungarian household, Easter is celebrated with a large, fluffy, braided sweet bread, usually served with roasted ham, boiled eggs, fresh horseradish, and fresh vegetables.

At harvest festivals, small braids resembling wheat stalks were common, along with chain-link braids and crown-shaped ones; for children, sweet breads were shaped like little birds; at weddings, guests were offered a beautifully decorated round "windowed" bread; and at christenings, a filled sweet bread called *fumu*, or "baby bread," stuffed with poppy seeds or walnuts, was traditionally prepared. The following recipe is a classic homemade braided sweet bread and can be shaped to fit any celebration.

Combine the yeast and milk, then set aside for 5–10 minutes, until frothy.

Meanwhile, in a large bowl, sift the flour and combine with the sugar and salt. Make a well in the center and add 1 of the eggs, the egg yolk, whipping cream, and yeast mixture. Knead the dough until it comes together into a ball, then turn it out onto a lightly floured counter and continue kneading for 10–15 minutes, until the dough is smooth and shiny, and no longer sticks to your hands or the counter. Cover the dough with plastic wrap (clingfilm) and proof at room temperature for 30–35 minutes.

Turn out the dough onto a lightly floured counter, then divide the dough into 3 and roll into balls. Let the dough balls rest for another 10–15 minutes.

Roll each dough ball into an 8–12-inch (20–30-cm) long strand, 2¾–4 inches (7–10 cm) in diameter. If the dough gets sticky, dust it lightly with flour. Pinch the three strands together at the top, then braid them from the outside in.

Beat the remaining egg, then brush the braided loaf with the egg wash, cover again, and proof for another 30–35 minutes.

Preheat the oven to 400°F (200°C/Gas Mark 6). Bake for 10 minutes, then reduce the oven temperature to 350°F (180°C/Gas Mark 4) and bake for another 20–30 minutes, until golden brown and a toothpick (cocktail stick) inserted in the center comes out clean. Remove from the oven and let cool before serving.

TSOUREKI

Greece

Submitted by Ianthi Michalaki

Makes 2
Prep time: 30 minutes, plus overnight chilling times and proofing times
Cook time: 1 hour 45 minutes

For the orange-butter puree:
1 orange
6½ tablespoons (3¼ oz/90 g) butter (82 percent fat)
1 cup (7 oz/200 g) superfine (caster) sugar
5 tablespoons milk
1½ teaspoons ground cardamom
⅛ oz (4 g) ground mahleb

For the poolish:
5 tablespoons lukewarm water
1 oz (30 g) fresh yeast
scant ⅔ cup (2¾ oz/75 g) strong white flour

For the dough:
1 tablespoon granulated sugar
1 teaspoon (3 g) ground mastic
2 eggs
4 cups (1 lb 1 oz/490 g) strong white flour (with 14 g of protein)
½ teaspoon salt
oil, for greasing

To finish:
2 egg yolks, for egg wash
2½ tablespoons milk
slivered almonds, to decorate

***Tsoureki* is a sweet, enriched bread, traditionally made for Easter or during Christmas in some regions of Greece. It is a fragrant yeasted dough, with spices brought from the East and decorated with a dyed red egg in the middle (symbolizing the blood of Christ). It is a challenging dough, relying heavily on strong flour and a lot of kneading. As a result, it is suggested to use a stand mixer for this and let it do most of the work, otherwise the baker will be aching long before the dough is ready. Nevertheless, it will all be worth it when the kitchen is filled with the wonderful scent of warm bread, orange, and spices.**

To make the orange-butter puree: The day before baking, bring a small pot of water to a boil. Add the orange and cook for about 45 minutes, until soft. Let cool completely, then blend to a smooth puree in a food processor. This can be stored in the refrigerator for up to 3 days, or the freezer for 2 months.

In a pot, combine the butter, sugar, milk, cardamom, mahleb, and orange puree and heat gently until the butter melts and everything is combined. Store in the refrigerator overnight.

To make the poolish: The next day, in a large bowl, combine the lukewarm water with the yeast and flour. Mix until incorporated into a loose dough. Cover with plastic wrap (clingfilm) and proof in a warm place for 1 hour.

To make the dough: In a mortar, grind the sugar and mastic to a powder with a pestle and set aside.

In the bowl of a stand mixer fitted with the dough hook attachment, combine the poolish, eggs, and the butter-puree mixture. Add the flour, mastic mixture, and salt, and mix on low speed for about 5 minutes, or until the dough comes together. Increase the speed to medium–high and mix until the dough comes away from the edges of the bowl and is shiny and smooth. If the mixer is struggling, knead by hand to finish for 7–10 minutes.

Place the dough in a large, lightly oiled bowl, cover with plastic wrap, and proof in a warm place for 2 hours, until doubled in size.

Line a baking sheet with parchment paper and set aside.

Turn out the dough onto a counter, divide into 6 equal pieces of 7 oz (200 g) each, and roll each piece into a strand about 1 inch (2.5 cm) thick. Pinch together 3 strands at one end, then braid them together, and tightly pinch the tail ends together, then tuck the end pieces under the loaf. Repeat with the remaining 3 strands, then place the 2 loaves on the prepared baking sheet, cover with a clean dish (tea) towel, and proof in a warm place for 45–60 minutes.

Meanwhile, preheat the oven to 340°F (170°C/Gas Mark 3).

To finish: Beat together the eggs yolk with the milk. Brush the loaves with the egg wash and top with the slivered almonds. Bake for 40–60 minutes (if baking with the fan they will require less time). Remove from the oven and let cool. Store in an airtight container and enjoy for up to a week.

KA'AK ASFAR

Palestine

Submitted by Reem Kassis

Makes 8
Prep time: 30 minutes, plus proofing time
Cook time: 10–15 minutes

- 4 cups (1 lb 2 oz/500 g) all-purpose (plain) flour
- ½ cup (4 oz/115 g) unhulled sesame seeds, toasted (see notes)
- 4 tablespoons granulated sugar
- 3 tablespoons ground anise seeds
- 2 tablespoons nigella seeds
- 2 teaspoons salt
- 1½ teaspoons ground turmeric
- 1 teaspoon mahlab (optional)
- ½ cup (4 fl oz/120 ml) olive oil, plus extra for greasing, rolling, and brushing
- 1 tablespoon quick-rise yeast
- 2 teaspoons baking powder
- 1¼–1⅔ cups (10–14 fl oz/300–400 ml) warm water

This is a typical Palestinian bread that shows how culture can transcend religion; Christians and Muslims alike make it for their holidays and often share it with one another. This recipe comes from Palestinian food writer Reem Kassis, whose mother's family are Muslim and bake it on a set Thursday in April to distribute it throughout the village with boiled eggs—a tradition known in many villages as *khamees el-beid,* or "Thursday of eggs." On that day, they also visit cemeteries, offering the bread in memory of the dead and giving it to others as a quiet act of charity and remembrance. Around the same time each year, Palestinian Christians celebrate Easter by dyeing eggs and making this same bread, which they too share with friends and neighbors. A unique cultural practice, shaped by different faiths but deeply rooted in the same land and traditions. Traditionally this bread is eaten with boiled eggs, halloumi cheese, and sweet mint tea, but it can also be eaten on its own.

In a large bowl, combine the flour, sesame seeds, sugar, ground anise, nigella seeds, salt, turmeric, and mahlab, if using. Add the olive oil and work very well with your hands until fully combined and the mixture is crumbly.

Add in the yeast, baking powder, and 1 cup (8 fl oz/250 ml) of the water and knead, adding more water as necessary, until the dough comes together in a soft ball. The dough will be a little sticky because of the sugar and oil—you want to be able to just manage it. Grease the dough with some more oil, cover with a clean, damp dish (tea) towel, and proof for 1 hour, or until doubled in size.

Turn out the dough onto a greased counter and divide into 8 equal balls. Grease each ball with some more oil, cover, and let rest for 15 minutes.

Line a baking sheet with parchment paper and set aside.

Roll each ball into a circle approximately ½ inch (1 cm) thick. Use a mold or the prongs of a fork to decorate (see notes). Place on the parchment-lined baking sheet and set aside for approximately 15 minutes.

Preheat the oven to 400°F (200°C/Gas Mark 6). Bake for 10–15 minutes until the breads are lightly browned.

Remove from the oven and brush the top of each bread with some olive oil. Set aside to cool slightly, then serve warm or at room temperature. The breads will keep in an airtight container at room temperature for several days due to the oil content. They will freeze well for up to 3 months.

Notes

To toast the sesame seeds, place in a large skillet (frying pan) over low–medium heat for 7–10 minutes, stirring regularly, until golden brown, then set aside on a large sheet to cool.

Traditionally, the dough is rolled onto a wooden mold, and is then inverted to reveal a very nicely designed bread. This also serves to prevent the breads from rising. As these molds are difficult to come by, you can use the prongs of a fork to make a design all over each bread. Alternatively, mooncake molds are easier to purchase online or in Asian markets and can be used to stamp shapes into the dough.

VĂRZAR

Romania

Submitted by Diana Iovescu Tatucu

Serves 6–8
Prep time: 30 minutes, plus proofing time
Cook time: 30–35 minutes

This wild herb and sheep cheese bread is a rustic stuffed bread associated with countryside living and seasonal abundance in Romania. It is especially connected to early spring when fresh, wild greens emerge after winter. Often baked during Holy Week leading up to Easter (*Paște*), its vibrant green filling symbolizes renewal and rebirth. It also has fasting (*de post*) variations that are dairy-free, making it suitable during Lent. In addition to its ties to religious holidays, it is commonly prepared during harvest festivals and rural gatherings throughout spring and summer. Portable, nourishing, and adaptable, this bread embodies Romanian resourcefulness and deep connection to the land. Enjoyed warm or at room temperature, it's often served with a glass of kefir, *sana*, or *ayran*.

For the dough:
2 cups (16 fl oz/480 ml) milk, warmed
1 tablespoon granulated sugar
¼ oz (7 g) active dry yeast
scant 4 cups (1 lb 1 oz/480 g) all-purpose (plain) flour, plus extra for dusting
1 tablespoon salt
1 tablespoon olive oil

For the filling:
2 tablespoons butter or lard
handful each of assorted chopped greens (wild garlic/leurda, scallions [spring onions], leeks, sorrel, spinach, kale, Swiss chard, mustard greens—avoid lettuce)
handful of mixed fresh herbs (parsley, dill, basil), coarsely chopped
1 cup (5 oz/150 g) crumbled sheep milk feta or mozzarella

For topping (optional):
1 egg, beaten, for egg wash
sesame seeds

To make the dough: In a glass measuring cup, combine the warm milk, sugar, and yeast. Stir gently and let sit for 10 minutes until foamy.

Transfer to the bowl of a stand mixer fitted with the dough hook. Add the flour, salt, and olive oil. Mix on low speed until a dough forms and pulls away from the sides. Cover the bowl with a clean, damp dish (tea) towel and proof in a warm place for 1–1½ hours, or until doubled in size.

Meanwhile, to make the filling: In a large skillet (frying pan), heat the butter or lard over medium heat. Add the leeks and scallions (spring onions) and sauté for 2–3 minutes until softened. Add the remaining greens and cook for another 1 minute until wilted. Remove from the heat and stir in the herbs and crumbled cheese. Set aside.

Line a baking sheet with parchment paper and set aside. Once the dough has risen, punch it down to knock it back and turn it out onto a floured counter. Roll out into a rectangle and spread the filling evenly over the dough. Roll it up from the long end, like a jelly (Swiss) roll, and transfer to your prepared baking sheet. Let rise for another 30 minutes.

Preheat the oven to 400°F (200°C/Gas Mark 6).

For the topping, if using: Brush the roll with egg wash, sprinkle with sesame seeds, or dust lightly with flour. Bake for 25–30 minutes, until golden brown and risen.

Remove from the oven and let cool almost completely before slicing.

COZONAC

Romania

Submitted by Irina Georgescu

Makes 2
Prep time: 30 minutes, plus rising and optional chilling times
Cook time: 45 minutes

For the dough:
- 4⅔ cups (1 lb 5 oz/600 g) strong bread flour
- ½ oz (14 g) quick-rise dry yeast
- ⅞ cup (7 fl oz/200 ml) milk, warmed
- 2 eggs, plus 2 egg yolks (reserve whites for filling)
- ¾ cup (5½ oz/150 g) golden superfine (caster) sugar
- 1 tablespoon vanilla extract
- ⅔ cup (5½ oz/150 g) sour cream, at room temperature
- grated zest of 1 large orange
- 5½ tablespoons (2¾ oz/80 g) butter, melted
- sunflower oil, for greasing

For the filling:
- 2 egg whites
- 2½ cups (7 oz/200 g) ground walnuts
- 2 teaspoons powdered instant coffee (optional)
- 3 tablespoons unsweetened cocoa powder
- 2 tablespoons rum
- ¾ cup (5½ oz/150 g) superfine (caster) sugar

For the egg wash:
- 1 egg yolk, beaten with 1 tablespoon milk

This sweet, yeasted, and braided bread is a cherished part of many of Romania's major holiday traditions—especially Easter and Christmas—and its indulgence and richness is reflective of the seasons in which it is served. The name *cozonac* probably comes from the Greek word *kosona* and loosely translates to "cocoon." Historically, the braiding of bread (or dough) was linked to religious festivities, with the shaping forming part of a protective ritual.

The traditional filling of *cozonac* varies widely. One common mixture features ground walnuts, sugar, and egg whites leftover from the yolks used in the dough. Alternatively, cocoa powder could be used (or carob, as it was during the Communist era when cocoa powder was not available). Two further fillings commonly found are chunks of Turkish delight (*lokum*), and a poppyseed paste made with milk—suggestive of influences from both east and west.

To make the dough: In a large bowl or a stand mixer fitted with the paddle attachment, combine the flour and yeast. Add the warm milk and mix well.

In a separate bowl, whisk the eggs and yolks with the sugar and vanilla until foamy, then mix in the sour cream and orange zest. Add to the flour mixture and beat on medium speed for 5–8 minutes until thick strands of dough begin to separate. Add the butter 1 tablespoon at a time, incorporating well after each addition. Switch to a dough hook or knead by hand until the dough is smooth and pulls away from the sides of the bowl. Transfer the dough to a lightly oiled bowl, cover with a clean, damp dish (tea) towel, and let rest for 1½ hours in a warm place. This type of brioche dough doesn't double in size while resting.

Lightly oil two 4 × 8-inch (10 × 20-cm) loaf pans, line with parchment paper, and set aside.

Meanwhile, to make the filling: In a large bowl, whisk the egg whites until soft peaks form, then gently fold in the remaining ingredients and set aside. If not using instant coffee, increase the cocoa powder amount by 2 teaspoons.

If the dough is too soft to handle after proofing, punch it down to release the air and refrigerate for 30 minutes, covered in plastic wrap (clingfilm).

Turn out the dough onto a greased counter and divide it into 4 portions. Using your fingertips, stretch a piece of dough into a rectangle approximately 16 × 12 inches (40 × 30 cm), positioning the long side parallel to you. Spread a quarter of the filling evenly over the dough and roll it up into a long log. Repeat the process with a second portion of dough. Place one log over the other to form an 'X' shape. Twist the 2 logs of dough together, starting by crossing over one side of the 'X', then repeat with the other side. Lift the twisted bread and place it into the pan.

Repeat the stretching, filling, and twisting process with the remaining 2 pieces of dough and the remaining filling, then place into the other pan and cover both with a damp dish (tea) towel. Let proof in a warm place for 1½ hours.

Preheat the oven to 375°F (190°C/Gas Mark 5). Brush each loaf with the egg wash, then bake for 25 minutes. Lower the heat to 350°F (180°C/Gas Mark 4) and bake for another 20 minutes, until a toothpick (cocktail stick) inserted in the center comes out clean. If the tops brown too quickly, cover with a tent of aluminum foil.

Remove from the oven, place the loaves upside down on a wire rack, and let cool. Cover with a dish towel until completely cold, then slice and serve.

PORTER CAKE

Ireland

This Irish fruit cake eschews the traditional overnight tea-soaking of dried fruit for the same process but with a Guinness dry stout (a type of strong porter)—perhaps an adaptation from workers at its local brewery. This cake is often made several days ahead of serving, to allow its flavors to mature. Many families make two cakes and save one for Easter. Serve with salted butter or cheese—or both.

Submitted by Gareth Eoin Storey

Serves 8
Prep time: 15 minutes, plus soaking time
Cook time: 1½ hours

⅓ cup (1¾ oz/50 g) raisins
¾ oz (20 g) currants
⅓ oz (10 g) candied peel
⅞ cup (7 fl oz/200 ml) Guinness, warmed, plus generous ⅓ cup (3½ fl oz/100 ml)
neutral oil, for greasing
3⅔ cups (1 lb/450 g) self-rising flour
generous ½ cup (7¾ oz/220 g) black treacle or molasses
2 sticks (7¾ oz/220 g) butter, cold, cut into cubes
grated zest of 1 orange
grated zest of 1 lemon
pinch of ground cinnamon
pinch of ground ginger
1 egg, beaten
pinch of salt

In a small bowl, combine the raisins, currants, candied peel, and the ⅞ cup (7 fl oz/200 ml) warmed Guinness and let soak overnight.

The next day, preheat the oven to 325°F (160°C/Gas Mark 3). Lightly oil a 9-inch (23 cm) cake pan, line with parchment paper, and set aside.

In a large bowl, combine the fruit mixture, flour, treacle or molasses, butter, orange and lemon zests, cinnamon, ginger, egg, salt, and the remaining Guinness. Pour the batter into the prepared cake pan and bake for 1½ hours.

Remove from the oven and let cool for 10 minutes, then remove from the pan and cool on a wire rack.

SIMNEL CAKE

United Kingdom

Submitted by Anna Luntley

Serves 10–12
Prep time: 15 minutes, plus cooling time
Cook time: 1¾ hours

- 4 cups (1 lb 2 oz/500 g) self-rising flour
- ½ teaspoon fine salt
- 2¼ sticks (9 oz/250 g) butter, cubed, at room temperature
- ½ cup (4¼ oz/125 g) turbinado (demerara) sugar
- scant ⅔ cup (4¼ oz/125 g) superfine (caster) sugar
- 1 whole nutmeg, grated, or 3½ teaspoons ground nutmeg
- generous 1 cup (5¾ oz/170 g) golden raisins (sultanas)
- ⅓ cup (1½ oz/40 g) chopped dates
- 1½ oz (40 g) candied cherries or chopped dried apricots
- 1¼ cups (10 fl oz/300 ml) milk
- 2 eggs
- 1 lb 2 oz (500 g) marzipan
- 1 tablespoon apricot jam
- foiled-wrapped chocolate eggs, to decorate (optional)

Simnel cake is a lightly spiced fruit cake traditionally eaten around Eastertime or on Mothering Sunday (page 79). The name comes from the Latin *simila* and is a reference to the fine white flour with which it is traditionally made—and which would have been an expensive indulgence in medieval times when this recipe originated.

Today's cake now resembles a lighter version of the British Christmas cake, with the noted addition of marzipan layers and its distinctive eleven marzipan balls. This recipe comes from British baker Anna Luntley, whose Welsh ancestors baked it as a tea cake year-round to sell at market, and would dress it up with marzipan at Easter.

Preheat the oven to 325°F (160°C/Gas Mark 3). Line an 8-inch (20-cm) cake pan with parchment paper and set aside.

In a large bowl, combine the flour and salt. Add the cubed butter and rub into the flour mixture with your fingertips until the mixture resembles bread crumbs. Add the sugars, nutmeg, and fruits, and mix until they are evenly distributed.

In a separate bowl, combine the milk and eggs and gently beat to combine. Create a well in the dry ingredients and pour in the milk and egg mixture. Using a rubber spatula or large spoon, gently mix until you have a sticky mixture halfway between a dough and a batter. Spoon half of the mixture (about 1 lb 12 oz/800 g) into the bottom of the pan and smooth over.

Meanwhile, place half the marzipan between 2 sheets of parchment paper, and roll into an 8-inch (20-cm) circle. Gently place the marzipan onto the cake batter in your pan, then spoon the remaining batter on top of the marzipan and smooth over. Bake for 1½ hours, until golden and well risen, and a toothpick (cocktail stick) inserted in the center comes out almost clean.

Remove from the oven and allow the cake to cool in the pan.

Once completely cooled, remove the cake from the pan. Spread the top of the cake with the apricot jam. Place two-thirds of the remaining marzipan between 2 sheets of parchment paper and roll into an 8-inch (20-cm) circle. Gently lay this on top of the cake over the apricot jam.

Shape the remaining marzipan into 11 balls and place these in a circle around the edge of the cake, pressing down on each one gently to slightly flatten and secure. Set the broiler (grill) to medium heat, and place the cake under the broiler for a few minutes, until the marzipan starts to become a nice toasty brown color in places. Keep a close eye on it as this can happen quite quickly.

Remove from the broiler and let cool. Decorate with a heap of foil-wrapped chocolate eggs on top, if desired. It will keep for 7–10 days at room temperature so long as it is well wrapped or placed in an airtight container. It also freezes well.

PASCĂ

Romania

Submitted by Irina Georgescu

Makes 1 × 10-inch (25 cm) tart
Prep time: 30 minutes, plus proofing time
Cook time: 25–30 minutes

For the dough:
2⅓ cups (10½ oz/300 g) bread flour
3 tablespoons superfine (caster) sugar
¼ oz (10 g) fresh yeast
⅔ cup (5½ fl oz/165 ml) milk
2 egg yolks
pinch of salt
5 tablespoons (2½ oz/70 g) butter, melted

For the filling:
scant 1 cup 7 oz (200 g) curd cheese, twarog, or ricotta
⅔ cup (5½ oz/150 g) sour cream
2 tablespoons superfine (caster) sugar
2 egg yolks
zest of 1 large lemon
1 tablespoon vanilla extract
½ cup (2¾ oz/75 g) golden raisins (sultanas) soaked in 5 tablespoons warm rum for 30 minutes, then drained (optional)

For egg wash:
1 egg yolk, beaten with 1 teaspoon milk

Romanian *pască* is a distinctive and rich brioche tart filled with a mixture of curd cheese, sugar, eggs, and golden raisins (sultanas). Baked specifically for Easter, it is taken to church to be blessed during the service on Easter eve and enjoyed as a tradition to break Lent. In some families, like that of the recipe's contributor Irina Georgescu, the start of Easter begins at midnight with a slice of *pască*.

Curd cheese, known as *brânză de vaci* (cows' milk cheese), is a fresh, unpressed cheese that is young and crumbly with a tangy flavor. It is integral to the culinary tradition, especially at Easter, when it takes on a new meaning, symbolizing purity, as it's made with the first spring milkings.

Many folks prefer to do all their Easter baking, including *Cozonac* (page 102), on *Joia Mare*, or Holy Thursday, while others prepare theirs on Saturday evening so that the sweet bakes remain fresh throughout the day.

To make the dough: In the bowl of a stand mixer fitted with the dough hook attachment, combine the flour, sugar, yeast, milk, egg yolks, and salt. Knead on medium speed until the dough begins to pull away from the sides of the bowl. Add one-third of the melted butter and knead until well mixed, then repeat with the remaining butter. Cover with a clean, damp dish (tea) towel and proof in a warm place for 1½ hours, at around 70–72°F/21–22°C.

Lightly oil a 10-inch (25-cm) pastry ring or springform pan with the bottom removed, place it on a nonstick baking sheet lined with parchment paper, and set aside.

To make the filling: In a large bowl, combine the cheese, sour cream, sugar, egg yolks, lemon zest, vanilla extract, and golden raisins (sultanas), if using. Mix to combine.

Divide the dough into 2 pieces, and roll out one to fit in the pastry ring. Place it inside the ring, ensuring the dough touches the sides. Divide the remaining dough into 2 pieces. Roll these into 2 strands long enough to line the inside of the ring. Twist them together and position them inside the ring or pan, creating an attractive border around the sides. Cover with a clean dish (tea) towel while the oven heats.

Preheat the oven to 375°F (190°C/Gas Mark 5). Brush the edges of the dough with the egg wash, then pour in the filling. Bake for 25–30 minutes on a lower rack until the filling is soft and slightly wobbly in the center. If the dough darkens too much, tent with aluminum foil.

Remove from the oven, transfer to a wire rack, and let cool before serving.

HOT CROSS BUNS

United Kingdom

Submitted by Sam Luntley

Makes 12
Prep time: 30 minutes, plus soaking and proofing time
Cook time: 15–20 minutes

For the dough:
- 4¼ cups (34 fl oz/1 liter) boiling water
- 2 English Breakfast tea bags
- generous ¾ cup (4 oz/115 g) raisins
- ½ cup (4 oz/115 g) currants
- generous ¾ cup (4 oz/115 g) chopped dried figs
- ⅔ cup (4 oz/115 g) candied peel
- 2½ cups (11¼ oz/320 g) whole wheat bread flour
- 2⅔ cups (11¼ oz/320 g) brown spelt flour
- scant ¼ cup (1¾ oz/50 g) soft light brown sugar
- ⅓ oz (11 g) quick-rise dry yeast
- 1 tablespoon fine salt
- scant 1½ cups (11½ fl oz/340 ml) warmed milk
- 2 eggs
- 5 teaspoons sunflower oil
- 1¾ oz (50 g) sourdough starter (optional)
- grated zest of 1 orange
- 1 tablespoon (½ oz/15 g) apple pie spice

For the glaze:
- 1⅓ cups (10½ oz/300 g) turbinado (demerara) sugar

For the crossing paste:
- ¾ cup (3½ oz/100 g) strong white bread flour
- scant ½ cup (1¾ oz/50 g) confectioners' (icing) sugar

These lightly sweet, spiced buns have been traditionally baked for Good Friday, and Eastertime more generally, ever since the late sixteenth century, when Elizabethan law first decreed that they could be made only around certain holidays. The buns are marked with a cross, which is said to be an Anglo-Saxon pagan tradition and a reference to Eostre, a goddess of spring and the namesake of Easter in the United Kingdom. Serve these hot cross buns while still warm, or toast (if cold or over a day old) and spread with salted butter and a little bit of marmalade to bring out the flavor of the candied peel. Or make a bacon and egg sandwich. If you have any left after a few days, these are the perfect start to a bread and butter pudding.

To make the dough: In a large pitcher, combine the boiling water and the tea bags and leave to steep for 10 minutes.

Place the dried fruit in a large bowl and pour the tea over. Let soak for 30 minutes. In a separate medium bowl, combine the flours, sugar, yeast, and salt. Set aside.

In the bowl of a stand mixer fitted with the dough hook attachment, combine the warm milk, eggs, oil, and sourdough starter, if using, then add the dry ingredients on top. Mix on low speed for 10 minutes until the dough is coming away from the sides of the bowl and has good strength.

Drain the fruits, saving the liquid. Stir the orange zest and apple pie spice into the fruit. Add the fruit mixture to the dough and mix again until evenly incorporated. Place the dough in a large bowl, cover with plastic wrap (clingfilm), and proof in a warm place for 1–2 hours, or until doubled in size.

Once the dough has risen, punch it down to knock it back. At this point, you can chill it overnight and shape and bake your buns in the morning, if you wish.

When ready to bake, line a baking sheet with parchment paper and set aside.

Divide the dough into 12 equal pieces of 5 oz (140 g) each. Roll each piece into a ball and place on the prepared baking sheet. Proof in a warm place for 1½ hours, or until doubled in size.

Meanwhile, to make the glaze: In a medium pan, combine the saved tea liquor and turbinado (demerara) sugar. Place over low heat and stir to dissolve, then increase the heat and simmer for 2–3 minutes until you have a syrup. Set aside.

Preheat the oven to 400°F (200°C/Gas Mark 6).

To make the crossing paste: In a medium bowl, combine the strong white flour and confectioners' (icing) sugar. Beat in 5 tablespoons of water until you have a thick paste. Transfer the paste into a pastry (piping) bag. Pipe a cross on each risen bun. Bake for 15–20 minutes, turning halfway through, until the buns are golden brown.

Remove from the oven and brush each bun generously with the glaze. Let cool slightly, then serve warm or toasted.

KOULOURAKIA

Greece

Submitted by Ianthi Michalaki

Makes 70
Prep time: 45–60 minutes
Cook time: 15 minutes

⅛ oz (4 g) mastic
1½ cups (10½ oz/300 g) superfine (caster) sugar
6½ cups (1 lb 12 oz/800 g) all-purpose (plain) flour
¼ teaspoon baking powder
½ teaspoon salt
10½ tablespoons (5½ oz/150 g) sheep's milk butter
10½ tablespoons (5½ oz/150 g) cow's milk butter, 82% fat
1 tablespoon orange zest
2½ tablespoons fresh orange juice
½ teaspoon vanilla paste
2 eggs
½ teaspoon baking soda (bicarbonate of soda)

For the egg wash:
2 egg yolks
2½ tablespoons milk

***Koulourakia* (Κουλουράκια) originated with the Greek population of Izmir (Smyrni). After the burning of Smyrni in 1922, when many ethnically Greek refugees fled to Greece, they brought with them culinary traditions that were incorporated back into Greek cuisine. The Greeks of Izmir, being familiar with a wider range of spices and ingredients from across the Ottoman empire, introduced sugar and more delicate pastry techniques to local traditions. This recipe is usually made over Easter and produces a very aromatic cookie, which should be enjoyed with coffee or given as a gift to friends and family.**

Preheat the oven to 350°F (180°C/Gas Mark 4). Line two baking sheets with parchment paper and set aside.

Put the mastic and 5 teaspoons of the sugar into a mortar and grind to a powder using the pestle. In a separate bowl, combine the flour, baking powder, salt, and mastic-sugar mixture. Set aside.

In the bowl of a stand mixer fitted with the paddle attachment, cream together both the butters, the remaining sugar, the orange zest, and the vanilla paste until light and airy. Gradually add the eggs and mix for 2 minutes until fully incorporated. Clean the edges of the bowl with a rubber spatula and mix again for 30 seconds.

In a small bowl, combine the orange juice with the baking soda (bicarbonate of soda), then slowly pour into the batter, mixing on low speed. Add half of the dry ingredients and mix for about 30 seconds, until incorporated. Add the remaining dry ingredients and mix for another 30 seconds, until a dough is formed.

Turn out the dough onto a counter and knead together, then shape into a ball. Divide the dough into pieces of approximately ¾ oz (20 g) each. Shape each piece into a strand measuring 4–4½ inches (10–12 cm) long. Shape in any way you like, but traditionally they are shaped as a snail or small braid. Place on the prepared baking sheets, leaving sufficient space between them as they will expand in the oven.

In a small bowl, make the egg wash by beating together the egg yolks and milk, then brush this over the tops of the cookies. Bake for 8 minutes, then rotate the sheet and bake for another 7 minutes.

Remove from the oven and let cool. The cookies will keep up to 30 days in an airtight container.

SCARCELLE PUGLIESI

Italy

Submitted by Roberto Nitti

Makes 4
Prep time: 15 minutes, plus resting time
Cook time: 25–30 minutes

- 4 cups (1 lb 2 oz/500 g) all-purpose (plain) flour, plus extra for dusting
- 2 teaspoons baking powder
- ¾ cup (5½ oz/150 g) superfine (caster) sugar
- pinch of salt
- 2 medium eggs, plus 4 unpeeled, hard-boiled eggs
- generous ⅓ cup (3½ fl oz/100 ml) extra virgin olive oil
- 3½ tablespoons milk, plus extra for brushing
- 1 teaspoon vanilla extract
- grated zest of 1 lemon
- colored sprinkles, for decorating

***Scarcelle Pugliesi* are traditional Easter pastries from the Puglia region in southern Italy. Made from a slightly sweet, shortcrust-style dough (similar to pie dough) flavored with olive oil and lemon zest, these cookies are often shaped into symbolic forms—such as doves, hearts, baskets, or braids—that represent peace, rebirth, and celebration. A defining feature of *scarcelle* is the whole egg, sometimes dyed, that is nestled into the dough and baked in place, often secured with two small strips of dough crossed on top. After baking, they are typically decorated with sugar glaze and colorful sprinkles. Both a festive treat and a symbolic gift, scarcelle are often exchanged among family and friends during the Easter season as a gesture of goodwill and renewal.**

In a large bowl, sift together the flour and baking powder. Add the sugar and salt, then make a well in the center and add the 2 eggs, olive oil, milk, vanilla extract, and lemon zest. Mix with a fork, then knead by hand until a soft, smooth dough has formed. If it is too sticky, add a little flour, but do not overdo it to avoid making it too hard. Cover the dough with plastic wrap (clingfilm) and let rest for 30 minutes at room temperature.

Meanwhile, preheat the oven to 350°F (180°C/Gas Mark 4). Line a baking sheet with parchment paper and set aside.

Once the dough is ready, turn it out onto a lightly floured counter to ½ inch (1 cm) thick. Cut out 8 thin strips, then cut out 4 Easter shapes (bells, doves, bunnies, or nests). Nestle one of the hard-boiled eggs in the middle of each shape and cross with the dough strips to secure.

To make a braided version: Turn out the dough onto a lightly floured counter and divide into 12 equal parts. Roll into strands. Using 3 strands for each scarcella, braid together, then form into a circle, placing an egg in the center.

Place the scarcelle on the prepared baking sheet, brush them with the milk, and decorate with the colored sprinkles. Bake for 25–30 minutes, until golden brown.

Remove from the oven and let cool before serving. They will keep in an airtight container for 2–3 days.

PASTIERA NAPOLETANA

Italy

p. 114

Submitted by Agnese Negrini

Serves 12
Prep time: 1 hour, plus chilling and overnight resting
Cook time: 2 hours

For the dough:
- 2 sticks (7¾ oz/220 g) butter or lard
- ¾ cup (5½ oz/150 g) superfine (caster) sugar
- zest of ½ lemon
- pinch of salt
- 4 egg yolks
- 3¼ cups (14 oz/400 g) all-purpose (plain) flour, plus extra for dusting

For the filling:
- 2¼ cups (1 lb 2 oz/500 g) ricotta, drained
- 1½ cups (9 oz/250 g) granulated sugar (or up to 12–14 oz/350–400 g, if you would like it sweeter)
- 3 eggs, plus 1 egg yolk, lightly beaten
- grated zest of 1 lemon, plus juice, if needed
- grated zest of 1 orange
- a few drops (good-quality) orange blossom water
- pinch of ground cinnamon
- seeds of 1 vanilla bean (pod)
- generous pinch of salt
- 5 cups (1 lb 4 oz/560 g) cooked wheat berries
- ⅔ cup (5 fl oz/150 ml) milk
- 3 tablespoons butter
- ½ cup (3½ oz/100 g) candied fruits (optional)
- juice of 1 lemon (optional)

The Neapolitan *pastiera* is an Italian *crostata*, or baked tart, which is typically made in Naples at Eastertime, although nowadays can be found year-round in local bakeries.

Like many Italian bakes, the *pastiera* has a myth of origin rooted in antiquity: In a time when gods still walked among mortals and the world was still young, a siren named Partenope was living in the sea near Naples. At the arrival of spring, she would rise from the waters of the gulf to sing in celebration of the new season. To honor her presence of wonder and express their gratitude, the people of Naples offered her seven sacred gifts from the land, symbols of abundance and renewal: Golden wheat, fresh ricotta, eggs, sugar, spices, milk, and orange blossom water, the very scent of spring. Partenope carried these offerings to the depths of the sea, where the gods, moved by the devotion of the people, transformed them into a dessert unlike any other: A delicate shell of shortcrust pastry (similar to pie crust) enclosing a luscious filling of cooked wheat and ricotta, infused with the essence of the first, bright, warm days of spring.

The siren returned to the shore bearing this divine creation, gifting the first *pastiera* to the people of Naples. From that moment on, it became a cherished tradition to prepare this dessert each spring, as a tribute to the season's rebirth and a celebration of life itself, its golden crust like the warmth of the first rays of sunshine—a blessing after the long, dark months of winter.

To make the dough: In a large bowl, cream together the butter or lard, sugar, lemon zest, and salt until light and airy. Add the egg yolks and mix until combined. Add half of the flour and mix to combine, then add the remaining half and mix until just incorporated. Flatten into a disk and wrap securely in plastic wrap (clingfilm). Place in the refrigerator and chill thoroughly for at least 1 hour or overnight.

Meanwhile, to make the filling: In a medium bowl, combine the drained ricotta and sugar, and mix to combine. Add the beaten eggs and yolk, the lemon and orange zest, orange blossom water, cinnamon, vanilla seeds, and salt, and mix, trying to not incorporate any air. It's better to make this the day before, so that the egg mix can release some of the air that would make it "soufflé" during baking—you want to avoid any cracking on the surface of your cake.

The next day, in a pan over low heat, combine the wheat berries, milk, and butter, stirring often until combined. Let cool completely.

To make the pastry cream: Place the milk and scraped vanilla bean (pod) with its seeds into a pan over medium heat. Bring just to a simmer, then remove from the heat, cover with plastic wrap, and set aside for 30 minutes.

In a medium bowl, stir together the sugar, cornstarch (cornflour), and salt. Whisk in the egg yolks until the mixture is smooth and pale, then gradually pour in the warmed milk, whisking constantly, until all of it has been added.

Return the mixture to the original pan over medium heat and continue to whisk until the pastry cream begins to thicken, about 5 minutes. Remove from the heat and transfer the pastry cream to a bowl, then cover with plastic wrap, which should touch the surface of the cream to prevent a skin from forming. Refrigerate for at least 2 hours, until ready to use.

When ready to bake, combine the ricotta mixture and wheat berries in a bowl with 14 oz (400 g) of the pastry cream, and the candied fruits, if using. Add the lemon juice if it looks too dense.

For the pastry cream:
2 cups (8 fl oz/350 ml) milk
1 vanilla bean (pod), split and seeds scraped
⅓ cup (2¼ oz/65 g) granulated sugar
2 tablespoons cornstarch (cornflour)
¼ teaspoon salt
4 egg yolks

Preheat the oven to 300°F (150°C/Gas Mark 2). Lightly oil a 1-inch (5-cm) deep, 11-inch (28-cm) diameter tart pan, line with parchment paper, and set aside.

Turn the dough out onto a lightly floured counter and sprinkle with flour. Roll out to ⅛ inch (4 mm) thick and cut 7 strips of dough (about ½ inch/1 cm thick). Set the strips aside and use the remaining pastry to line the prepared pan. Pour the filling into the crust and decorate the surface with the reserved strips of pastry, crossing them over each other. Traditionally, there are 7 strips to represent the number of sacred gifts. Bake for 1 hour 40 minutes, or until the filling is slightly set and the surface is a deep golden brown.

Remove from the oven and let rest for at least 24 hours before serving.

MAZUREK

Poland

Submitted by Marta Orlikowska

Serves 10
Prep time: 20 minutes, plus chilling time
Cook time: 20 minutes

- 3 cups (14 oz/400 g) bread flour (preferably T500—wroclawska), plus extra for dusting
- generous ¾ cup (3½ oz/100 g) confectioners' (icing) sugar
- 1¾ sticks (7 oz/200 g) butter, chilled and diced
- 2 tablespoons sour cream, chilled
- 2 egg yolks, chilled
- 5 tablespoons black currant jam
- 2 × 12 oz (350 g) cans dulce de leche
- almonds, to decorate
- melted semisweet chocolate, to decorate

This filled shortcrust pastry is considered one of the most popular Easter desserts across Poland. Some say this cake's name may have its origins in the Masovians (old Mazurzy) tribe who inhabited, and gave their name to, the Mazovia region of central Poland, while others suggest it has to do with the popular traditional folk dance called the mazurka.

What distinguishes this cake from other festive desserts is its elaborate decoration of both dried fruit and nuts. The *mazurek* could be baked in many different ways: with the addition of orange, poppy seed, wine, apples—even whole wheat bread. Polish women used to treat their *mazurek*-making as something of a competition in terms of beautiful decoration and originality. This recipe focuses on the classic elements of *mazurki*: buttery thin dough, with a layer of black currant jam, and lots of dulce de leche.

In a large bowl, combine the flour, confectioners' (icing) sugar, diced butter, sour cream, and egg yolks. Knead the dough with your hands or in a stand mixer fitted with the dough hook attachment until it comes together. Flatten slightly, wrap with plastic wrap, and chill in the refrigerator for 1 hour.

Preheat the oven to 400°F (200°C/Gas Mark 6).

Remove the dough from the refrigerator and turn it out onto a lightly floured counter. Roll it out into a rectangle ¼–⅜ inch (5–7 mm) thick, slightly larger than the bottom of a 12½ × 8½-inch (32 × 22-cm) baking pan (ideally springform). Place the dough into the pan and use a small knife to cut off the excess dough. Fasten the sides of the pan, and press the rest of the dough against the sides of the pan to make a rim. Bake on the middle rack of the oven for 20 minutes.

Remove from the oven and let cool for 20 minutes. Once cool, spread a thin layer of jam on the pastry, then add the dulce de leche and smooth the top. Decorate with almonds and melted chocolate, as desired.

Left: *Pastiera Napoletana*, Easter (page 112)

SPIEGELEI-KUCHEN

Germany

Submitted by Tobias Beck

Serves 12–16
Prep time: 45 minutes, plus cooling times
Cook time: 40 minutes

For the sponge:
- 1¾ sticks (7 oz/200 g) butter, softened
- ¾ cup (5½ oz/150 g) superfine (caster) sugar
- 1 × ¼ oz (8 g) packet vanilla sugar (or 1 teaspoon vanilla extract)
- 4 eggs
- 2 cups (9 oz/250 g) all-purpose (plain) flour
- 2 teaspoons baking powder

For the topping:
- 2 × 3.4-oz (96-g) packets vanilla pudding powder (enough to each make about 2 cups/17 fl oz/500 ml pudding); you could also use 2 x 2.5 oz (70 g) packet of Dr. Oetker vanilla pudding, or 5 tablespoons custard powder
- 4¼ cups (34 fl oz/1 liter) milk
- 3 tablespoons superfine (caster) sugar (for pudding)
- 17 oz (480 g) canned apricot halves, drained and liquid reserved if unsweetened
- generous 2 cups (17 fl oz/500 ml) whipping cream

For the glaze:
- 2 × ½ oz (12 g) packets clear cake glaze (Tortenguss)
- 3 tablespoons superfine (caster) sugar

The *Spiegelei-Kuchen*, or "sunny-side-up cake," is a whimsical German creation that became popular in the 1980s and 1990s, during a wave of playful, colorful baking trends. It's not a traditional recipe in the historical sense, but rather a product of imaginative home bakers and food magazines. It's meant to surprise guests with a sweet that looks like breakfast eggs: Apricot halves mimic egg yolks within the "whites" of vanilla pudding and whipped cream—all layered on a light sponge. The cake is often served at Easter and spring gatherings, or as a cheerful surprise at potlucks. While not tied to any specific region, it reflects a long German tradition of creative *Blechkuchen* (sheet cakes) for both social and special occasions.

Preheat the oven to 350°F (175°C/Gas Mark 4). Line a large baking pan (approx. 12 × 16 inches/30 × 40 cm) with parchment paper and set aside.

To make the sponge: In a large bowl, cream together the butter, sugar, and vanilla sugar until pale and fluffy. Add the eggs one at a time, beating well after each addition.

In a separate bowl, mix the flour and baking powder, then fold into the batter. Spread the batter evenly in the prepared pan. Bake for 20–25 minutes until lightly golden and springy to the touch. Remove from the oven and let cool completely.

Meanwhile, to make the topping: Prepare the vanilla pudding according to the packet directions using the milk and sugar. Let cool slightly. In a bowl, beat the whipping cream until stiff peaks form, then stir into the pudding mix. Spread it evenly over the cooled cake base, smoothing the surface. Place the apricot halves cut-side down on the pudding layer, spacing them like sunny-side-up eggs, and let the pudding cool completely.

To make the glaze: Prepare the clear glaze according to the directions, using the sugar and a generous 2 cups (17 fl oz/500 ml) of water (or the reserved apricot juice). Let cool slightly, then carefully spoon or pour the glaze over the whipped cream to seal the surface. Chill the cake for at least 1 hour before serving.

EASTER SYRNIK

Ukraine

Submitted by Yuriy Kachak

Serves 6
Prep time: 20 minutes
Cook time: 45–50 minutes

- 6 tablespoons (3 oz/85 g) butter, melted, plus extra for greasing
- 1 lb 2 oz (500 g) twarog (European curd cheese)
- ⅔ cup (4½ oz/130 g) granulated sugar
- ¼ cup (1½ oz/40 g) fine semolina
- 3 eggs
- ½ cup (4 fl oz/120 ml) milk
- ¾ cup (3½ oz/100 g) raisins or 1 cup (3½ oz/100 g) fresh black currants or blueberries
- grated zest and juice of 1 lemon

Syrnik **comes from the Slavic word for curd cheese or quark—*syr*. In Eastern Europe a number of different curd-based desserts bear this name, like *syrniki*, which are a popular style of curd pancakes. This classic style of baked cheesecake (made from the same curd cheese) is popular at Eastertime in Ukraine.**

This recipe comes from Ukrainian baker Yuriy Kachak, of the Glasgow-based Deanston Bakery, who grew up making this cake, and prepares a fruit-topped variation of it there for his customers.

Preheat the oven to 325°F (160°C/Gas Mark 3). Grease and line a deep 8 × 8-inch (20 × 20-cm) square pan.

Place the twarog in the bowl of a food processor, then process until whipped. Transfer to a large bowl. Add the melted butter, sugar, and semolina, and mix to combine. Whisk in the eggs and milk. Add the raisins or fresh fruits and the lemon zest and juice, and mix to combine. Pour the batter into the prepared pan, then bake for 45–50 minutes.

Remove from the oven and let cool before serving. It will keep in the refrigerator for up to 5 days.

GALATOPITA

Greece

Submitted by Carolina Doriti

Serves 6–8
Prep time: 15 minutes
Cook time: 1 hour

Galatopita, meaning "milk pie," is a traditional Greek dessert with roots in antiquity. References to similar milk-based pies appear as early as the fifth century BCE, when ancient Greeks made custard-like candies from milk, flour, and honey. Evolving through Byzantine times into modern rural Greece, _galatopita_ became a seasonal dish, especially popular in spring when milk was abundant. It was traditionally baked in farming households using fresh goat or sheep milk, thickened with farina or flour, and lightly sweetened. While regional variations exist—some with phyllo (filo), others without—the pie's essence remains simple. It plays a role in religious and festive life, especially during Cheesefare Week (carnival; the last week before Lent) and Easter, when dairy is returned to the table after fasting. Today, _galatopita_ is still commonly prepared across Greece. It pairs well with fresh strawberries.

- 2 tablespoons (1 oz/28 g) butter, plus extra for greasing
- scant 1 cup (5½ oz/150 g) farina, plus extra for dusting
- 4¼ cups (34 fl oz/1 liter) milk (preferably sheep or goat's milk)
- 1 vanilla bean (pod), seeds scraped, or 1 teaspoon good-quality vanilla extract or powdered mastiha
- ¾ cup (5½ oz/150 g) superfine (caster) sugar
- grated zest of 1 lemon
- pinch of salt
- 3 large eggs, at room temperature
- ground cinnamon, for sprinkling
- confectioners' (icing) sugar or honey, for dusting or drizzling

Preheat the oven to 350°F (180°C/Gas Mark 4). Grease a 10½-inch (26-cm) round baking dish with butter, dust the bottom with farina, and set aside.

In a pan, heat the milk over medium heat. Add both the vanilla seeds and bean (pod), if using, to the milk. Simmer gently until the milk is hot and steamy, about 5 minutes (do not let it boil over). Remove the bean and gradually add the sugar and farina, stirring constantly with a whisk until the cream thickens, about 5 minutes. Remove from the heat, then stir in the butter, vanilla extract or mastiha, if using, the lemon zest, and salt. Mix well. Let the mixture cool slightly.

In another bowl, beat the eggs and slowly pour them into the batter, whisking constantly so they don't curdle.

Pour the batter into the prepared dish and smooth the surface (see note). Bake for 45–50 minutes, or until golden brown on top.

Remove from the oven and allow the pie to cool slightly. Sprinkle with cinnamon and confectioners' (icing) sugar or drizzle with honey. Serve either warm or chilled.

Note

For a light caramelized crust, you can sprinkle sugar over the top before baking and omit the confectioners' sugar in the serving.

HVEDER

Denmark

Submitted by Michael Craig

A Danish tradition of breaking fast in Lent, or in Denmark the *Store bededag* (Great Prayer Day: The fourth Friday after Easter), originated as one focused entirely on prayer and atonement, free from work, trade, and gambling. Bakers would prepare these buns the morning prior, selling them in the evening, so all Danes would have something to heat up and enjoy "fresh" on the day itself. Nowadays, these simple, cardamom-scented buns are enjoyed cut in half and toasted, with *tandsmør*, or "teeth butter"—butter spread so thick you can see teeth marks when bitten into.

Makes 15
Prep time: 30 minutes, plus proofing times
Cook time: 15–20 minutes

½ oz (15 g) fresh yeast
¾ cup (6 fl oz/175 ml) cold water
¾ cup (6 fl oz/175 ml) cold milk
2 eggs
5½ cups (1 lb 9 oz/700 g) strong bread flour
¼ cup (2 oz/55 g) granulated sugar
5 teaspoons ground cardamom
2 teaspoons salt
3½ tablespoons (2 oz/55 g) butter, softened

In the bowl of a stand mixer fitted with the dough hook, combine all the ingredients except for the butter. Knead the dough for about 10 minutes on medium speed until the dough is smooth. Continue mixing while adding the butter in small pieces until fully emulsified and the dough becomes shiny. Cover with a clean, damp dish (tea) towel and proof for 1–3 hours, or until doubled in size.

Line a baking sheet with parchment paper and set aside. Divide the dough into 15 equal pieces (approx. 3 oz/85 g each). Shape each piece into a circle. Place the buns 1–2 inches (3–5 cm) apart on the prepared baking sheet. Proof for another 2–3 hours, until doubled in size—they will proof into each other, taking the shape of a wheat spike.

Preheat the oven to 400°F (200°C/Gas Mark 6). Bake for 15–20 minutes, then remove from the oven, transfer them to a wire rack, and let cool before serving.

TORTA PASQUALINA

Italy

Submitted by Katie Smith

Serves 10
Prep time: 1 hour, plus chilling time
Cook time: 1 hour 30 minutes

For the pastry:

- 2 cups (9 oz/250 g) all-purpose (plain) flour, plus extra for dusting
- ⅔ cup (2¾ oz/80 g) whole wheat spelt flour
- ¼ teaspoon fine sea salt
- 2¼ sticks (9 oz/250 g) butter, cold, cubed
- ½ cup (4½ oz/130 g) crème fraîche or yogurt
- neutral oil, for greasing

For the filling:

- 14 oz (400 g) large leaf spinach
- 14 oz (400 g) chard
- 3 tablespoons olive oil
- 1 small white onion, finely diced
- 5½ oz (150 g) celery, finely diced
- ½ cup (1 oz/30 g) chopped parsley
- ½ oz (15 g) chopped marjoram
- ½ teaspoon grated nutmeg
- grated zest of 1 lemon, and juice of ½
- generous 1 cup (9 oz/250 g) ricotta
- scant 2 cups (5½ oz/150 g) grated Parmesan
- 6 large eggs
- salt, to taste

A chard and ricotta pie originating in Liguria, this dish is on many families' tables at Easter. The original recipe dates back to Ortensio Lando in the mid-1500s, who described a vegetable pie (then called *gattafura*) containing chard, spinach, ricotta, parmigiano, and eggs. There are many variations for the pastry; some use puff pastry, olive oil–rich doughs, or even phyllo (filo) pastry. This pie is best served cold or at room temperature—never hot! Italian chef Carla Tomasi always recommended adding fresh marjoram to her version.

To make the pastry: In a large bowl, combine the flours and salt. Add the cubed butter and rub the butter into the flour mixture with your fingertips until the mixture resembles bread crumbs. Add the crème fraîche or yogurt and mix to form a firm dough. Wrap in parchment paper and chill in the refrigerator for a minimum of 1 hour.

Preheat the oven to 375°F (190°C/Gas Mark 5). Lightly oil an 8-inch (20-cm) cake pan or pie pan.

Remove the dough from the refrigerator and break into 2 pieces—three-quarters for the bottom and one-quarter for the lid. Turn out onto a well-floured counter, and roll the larger piece of dough to 1/16 inch (2 mm) thick. Use this to line the pan, pressing into all corners and allowing the sides to slightly overhang. Line the dough shell with parchment paper and fill with ceramic baking beans or dried legumes. Bake for 15 minutes, or until the pastry is firm, then remove the beans and cook for about 10 minutes more, until golden brown, to blind bake. Remove from the oven and let cool.

Meanwhile, to make the filling: Separate the spinach and chard stalks from the greens and finely chop the stalks. In a large pan, heat the olive oil over medium heat. Add the onion and celery and cook for 10 minutes until tender. Add the chard and spinach stalks and cook for a few minutes until the water has evaporated and you have a reduced mixture. Remove from the heat and add the herbs, nutmeg, and lemon zest and juice.

Bring a pot of water to a boil. Add the spinach and chard greens and cook for 1 minute to blanch until wilted, then drain and rinse with cold water. Squeeze as much liquid as possible from the greens. Finely chop and add to the cooked onion mixture. Add the ricotta and Parmesan and stir to combine. Taste and season with salt as needed.

To assemble, spoon the filling into the blind-baked tart shell. With the back of the spoon, make 6 indents equally spaced apart to fit the eggs. Carefully crack an egg into each indentation.

Roll the remaining dough to form a lid for the pie. Fold the sides over to seal the pie, then crimp the edges with a fork. Use a knife to pierce a hole in the middle to allow the steam to escape.

Place the pie pan on a baking sheet and bake for 45 minutes to 1 hour, until the pastry top is golden.

Remove from the oven and let cool for at least 30 minutes before removing from the pan and slicing to serve.

ST. GEORGE'S DAY

It makes sense that April 23, the feast day of St. George, one of the world's most venerated saints, has many different traditions around the world, and especially across Europe. He is a patron saint in many countries: From England to Albania, Georgia (of course), and also across many regions of Spain, including Catalonia. It is there in Catalonia that one of the more unique traditions has emerged. Beyond being a day of regional pride, *diada de Sant Jordi*, as it's locally known, has become something like Valentine's Day, with many men gifting their partners a rose—symbolizing the rose bush said to bloom from the blood of the dragon George slew. Over time, April 23 also became celebrated as "The Day of the Book," a literary holiday, moved from October to the third week of April, when both William Shakespeare and Miguel de Cervantes died. It is for this reason that, after gifting their partners a rose, men will receive a book back in return. Because of the day's connection with Catalan identity, there is also much waving of the red and yellow *Senyera*—the region's iconic striped flag.

PAN MEINO

Italy

Submitted by Roberto Nitti

Makes 15
Prep time: 15 minutes
Cook time: 20 minutes

3 medium eggs
¾ cup (5½ oz/150 g) superfine (caster) sugar, plus extra for sprinkling
1 teaspoon vanilla extract
10½ tablespoons (5½ oz/150 g) butter, melted and cooled
pinch of salt
2 cups plus 2 tablespoons (10½ oz/300 g) finely ground cornmeal (polenta)
1½ cups plus 2 tablespoons (7 oz/200 g) all-purpose (plain) flour
4 teaspoons baking powder
elderflowers (optional), for sprinkling
confectioners' (icing) sugar, for dusting

***Pan meino* (also known as *pan de mej*) is a traditional sweet flatbread from Lombardy, in northern Italy, typically associated with the feast of St. George on April 23. Made with flour, sugar, butter, eggs, and infused with fragrant elderflower, this rustic, cookie-like bread has a golden crust and a tender, crumbly texture. The name *meino* comes from *miglio* (millet), once a common ingredient, though modern versions are usually made with wheat or polenta flour. Traditionally enjoyed with a cup of fresh cream or milk, *pan meino* is a simple yet aromatic treat that celebrates the arrival of spring and the blossoming of elder trees in the countryside.**

Preheat the oven to 350°F (180°C/Gas Mark 4). Line a baking sheet with parchment paper and set aside.

In a large bowl, combine the eggs, sugar, and vanilla extract and beat with an electric whisk to a creamy mixture. Incorporate the melted butter and pinch of salt into the mixture.

In a separate bowl, combine the ground cornmeal (polenta) with the flour and baking powder. Sift the flour mixture into the egg mixture. Knead by hand until you have a soft but workable dough.

Divide the dough into 15 equal pieces (about 2¼ oz/60 g), and shape each into a disk 3¼ inches (8 cm) in diameter. Place the pan de meino on the prepared baking sheet, and sprinkle with elderflowers (if using) and superfine (caster) sugar, and dust with confectioners' (icing) sugar.

Bake for 20 minutes, then remove from the oven and let cool before serving.

PAN DE SANT JORDI

Catalonia

Submitted by Alessandra Pili

Serves 6–8
Prep time: 45 minutes, plus proofing time
Cook time: 25–30 minutes

For the cheese dough:
⅓ oz (10 g) fresh yeast
⅛ oz (3 g) sourdough starter
½ cup (4 fl oz/120ml) warm water
1⅔ cups (7 oz/200 g) medium-strength flour
¾ cup (3 oz/80 g) grated Parmesan
½ teaspoon salt

For the sobrassada dough:
⅓ oz (10 g) fresh yeast
⅛ oz (3 g) sourdough starter
7 tablespoons warm water
⅓ cup (3 oz/80 g) sobrassada
1⅔ cups (7 oz/200 g) medium-strength flour
¾ teaspoon salt

For the walnut dough:
⅓ oz (10 g) fresh yeast
⅛ oz (3 g) sourdough starter
scant ½ cup (3¾ fl oz/110ml) warm water
1⅔ cups (7 oz/200 g) strong flour
¾ teaspoon salt
1½ teaspoons (¼ oz/8 g) butter
⅔ cup (2 oz/60 g) chopped walnuts

***El pan de Sant Jordi* was created by baker Eduard Crespo Almela in response to a commission from the Guild of Bakers of Barcelona in 1988. Although it's a relatively recent tradition, this bread has become a symbol of a very important day in the region—April 23, the day of Sant Jordi, the region's patron saint.**

The bread, available from many local bakeries, reflects the colors and stripes of the *Senyera*, the official flag of Catalonia, and is made from three different doughs: one with *sobrassada*, one with cheese, and one with walnuts.

To make the cheese dough: Dissolve the yeast and sourdough starter in the warm water. In a large bowl, combine the remaining ingredients with the yeast liquid and knead until it comes together. Cover with a clean, damp dish (tea) towel and let rest in a warm place for 25 minutes.

To make the sobrassada dough: Dissolve the yeast and sourdough starter in the warm water. In a large bowl, combine the remaining ingredients with the yeast mixture and knead until it comes together. Cover with a clean, damp dish towel and let rest in a warm place for 25 minutes.

To make the walnut dough: Dissolve the yeast and sourdough starter in the warm water. In a large bowl, combine the remaining ingredients with the yeast liquid and knead until it comes together. Cover with a clean, damp dish towel and let rest in a warm place for 25 minutes.

Turn out the cheese dough onto a clean counter and roll out to a ¼-inch (5 mm) thickness. Repeat for the sobrassada dough. Cut 5 yellow strips and 4 red ones.

Turn the walnut dough out onto a counter and roll out very thinly. Stack the colored strips in alternate colors in the center to form the Senyera, then wrap with the walnut dough. Cover and proof again until doubled in size.

Line a baking sheet with parchment paper. Slice the dough into 1¼-inch (3 cm) slices using a sharp serrated knife and lay on the prepared baking sheet. Cover and let rest while the oven heats.

Preheat the oven to 400–425°F (200–220°C/Gas Mark 6–7). Bake for 25–30 minutes until golden brown.

Remove from the oven and let cool before serving.

ANZAC DAY

Anzac Day celebrates the historic ANZAC (Australian and New Zealand Army Corps), an army corps of the British Empire created in December of 1914, almost five months into World War I, which served predominantly in the ill-fated Gallipoli campaign of the following year.

During the landing on the Gallipoli peninsula in modern-day Turkey, over 30,000 members of this company lost their lives. From April 25 of 1916, official annual remembrances were scheduled throughout the empire, but especially in Australia and New Zealand, and the holiday has continued into the present day. A modern tradition of Anzac Day is the drinking of a "gunfire breakfast" (black coffee or tea with rum), which is said to reflect a pre-battle "meal." While the corps-related and ubiquitous Anzac biscuits (cookies) have year-long popularity, they can often be made as a reminder of the tastes and tragedies of this period.

ANZAC BISCUITS

Australia and New Zealand

Submitted by Maxine Scheckter

Makes 12
Prep time: 20 minutes, plus cooling time
Cook time: 12 minutes

- 1½ sticks (6 oz/180 g) salted butter
- ¼ cup (2½ oz/70 g) golden syrup (see notes)
- 1⅓ cups (10½ oz/300 g) soft brown sugar
- 1 egg
- 1¾ cups (7¾ oz/220 g) all-purpose (plain) flour
- 1⅔ cups (5½ oz/160 g) rolled oats
- ½ cup (1½ oz/40 g) shredded coconut
- 1 teaspoon baking soda (bicarbonate of soda)

Despite their name, these rolled oat cookies actually predate the formation of the ANZAC (Australian and New Zealand Army Corps), which was established during World War I. The first recipe dates back at least to the 1820s, but they became especially popular at home during World War I for their commonly available ingredients and long shelf life, earning them the name "Anzac biscuits" as a patriotic nod to the sacrifice of the ANZAC during the ill-fated Gallipoli campaign.

These cookies, characterized not only by the rolled oats but also by the golden syrup and shredded coconut, are beloved and often made year-round, but they are eaten especially on Anzac Day (April 25).

Preheat the oven to 325°F (160°C/Gas Mark 3). Line 2 baking sheets with parchment paper and set aside.

In a pan over medium heat, melt the butter and whisk constantly until you have a nutty brown butter (see notes). Remove from the heat and set aside to cool for 15 minutes.

Once the butter has cooled, pour it into a bowl with the golden syrup and brown sugar. Whisk to combine, it may look split and oily at this stage, which is fine. Add the egg and whisk until smooth. Stir in the flour, rolled oats, coconut, and baking soda (bicarbonate of soda), and mix with a rubber spatula or by hand until you have a well combined dough.

Turn out the dough onto a counter and divide into 12 pieces, approximately 3 oz (85 g) each. Place 6 dough balls on each lined baking sheet. The dough balls can be placed in an airtight container and chilled for up to 1 week or frozen for up to 1 month at this stage.

Bake for 12 minutes, turning halfway through, until the cookies are golden brown.

Remove from the oven and let cool. The cookies will keep in an airtight container for up to 2 days.

Notes

Brown butter is not traditional, but it does make the biscuits even more delicious. If needed, it can be replaced with 10½ tablespoons (5½ oz/160 g) melted butter.

If you cannot find golden syrup, corn syrup or molasses can be substituted.

MAY

5

MAY

VE DAY

VE Day, more formally known as Victory in Europe Day, is a holiday celebrated on May 8 across Europe. It marks the surrender of Germany on this day in 1945, and is especially observed in former allied powers like the United Kingdom, but also in places like Germany, where it commemorates those locals who fought against fascism. Celebrations vary from country to country, but in the United Kingdom, where it is generally referred to as "VE Day," there are military processions, street parties with colorful bunting, and classically British dishes on long communal tables, as well as more solemn remembrances of those who lost their lives in the war.

VICTORIA SPONGE

United Kingdom

Submitted by Anna Luntley

Serves 6–8
Prep time: 20 minutes, plus assembly time
Cook time: 1 hour 10 minutes

- 4 eggs
- 1¾–2 cups (8–9 oz/225–255 g) self-rising flour
- 2–2¼ sticks (8–9 oz/225–255 g) butter, at room temperature, plus extra for greasing
- 1–1¼ cups (8–9 oz/225–255 g) superfine (caster) sugar
- 1 cup (8 fl oz/250 ml) heavy (double) cream
- 4 tablespoons strawberry jam
- handful ripe strawberries, hulled, then sliced or quartered
- confectioners' (icing) sugar, for dusting

The classic British sponge cake—often referred to as a Victoria sandwich cake—is a light, fluffy cake made with equal parts butter, sugar, and flour. This basic mixture, beaten together with eggs, is not only used for baking cakes but also as an essential component in numerous sweet desserts and pies.

A popular way to serve this British-style sponge is to sandwich it with fruit jam and sweetened whipped cream. This combination is said to have originated with Queen Victoria, who enjoyed her cakes split and spread with a layer of jam, thus earning the name "Victoria sandwich." While the Victoria sandwich has become an everyday feature of tearooms and cafes, it rises to center stage on the occasion of national celebrations in the United Kingdom, perhaps chief among them being VE Day (Victory in Europe Day), marking the end of World War II, and celebrated annually on May 8.

Weigh the eggs in their shells to determine the weight of your other cake ingredients—for example, if the eggs weigh 8 oz (225 g) in total, you will require 8 oz (225 g) each of butter, sugar, and flour.

Preheat the oven to 300°F (150°C/Gas Mark 2). Lightly oil an 8-inch (20-cm) loose-bottom or springform cake pan, and line with parchment paper.

Sift the flour into a bowl and set aside. In the bowl of a stand mixer fitted with the paddle attachment, cream together the butter and sugar until light and airy. Add the eggs one at a time, along with 1 tablespoon of the flour for each addition, and mix on medium speed until each egg is well incorporated. Remove the bowl from the mixer and, using a rubber spatula, gently fold in the remaining flour. Spoon the mixture into the prepared pan.

Bake for 1 hour 10 minutes, checking after 1 hour—the cake should be golden in color, gently risen, equal in texture all over, and a toothpick (cocktail stick) inserted in the center should come out clean.

Remove from the oven and set the cake aside on a wire rack until completely cool. While the cake is cooling, whip the cream to soft peaks.

Once cool, remove the cake from the pan and slice horizontally into 3 equal layers. Place the bottom third on a serving plate and spread with half the jam, followed by half the whipped cream and half the strawberry pieces dotted across the cream. Gently place the middle cake slice on top and repeat the process with the remaining jam, cream, and strawberries. Top with the final cake layer and dust liberally with confectioners' (icing) sugar to finish.

This cake is best eaten the day it is made but will also keep well, wrapped in plastic wrap (clingfilm), in the refrigerator for a couple of days, or the cake can be frozen before it is cut and filled.

Variation: This cake lends itself to playing with added flavors, such as a few drops of vanilla extract or rose water, to the cake batter or cream. The jam and berry flavors can be varied with the seasons, and it can be topped with buttercream frosting for a more celebratory cake.

CONSTITUTION DAY

May 17 is known throughout Norway as *Grunnlovsdagen* (Constitution Day), marking the signing of the kingdom's constitution and the broader realization of the nation's self-determination on this date in 1814. Since the sixteenth century, Norway had been the junior partner in a union with the Kingdom of Denmark, sharing a monarch and a government that were both based in Copenhagen. This union was split earlier in 1814 by the Treaty of Kiel, in which Denmark ceded Norway to the King of Sweden, Charles XIII. Despite sharing the same monarch, Norway's government would be distinct and self-governing.

Today, Constitution Day is widely celebrated by the wearing of Norway's traditional costume, the *bunad*, both in public and at private parties across the country. Throughout the day, there are marching bands, and a plethora of popular party food like ice cream and hot dogs, along with traditional Norwegian fare.

BLØTKAKE

Norway

Submitted by Per Theodor Tørrissen

Makes 1 × 9-inch (23-cm) cake
Prep time: 30 minutes
Cook time: 35 minutes

For the sponge cake (sukkerbrød):
butter, for greasing
5 eggs
¾ cup plus 2 tablespoons (6 oz/175 g) superfine (caster) sugar
1⅓ cups plus 1 tablespoon (6 oz/175 g) all-purpose (plain) flour
1 teaspoon baking powder

For the whipped cream:
3 cups (1 lb 9 oz/700 g) heavy (double) whipping cream
3 tablespoons confectioners' (icing) sugar

To assemble:
orange juice, for sprinkling
raspberry or strawberry jam
mixed berries (blueberries, strawberries, and raspberries, or other fruits/berries of your choice), for topping

This style of layered sponge-and-cream celebration cake is common throughout Scandinavia—known as *lagkage* (Denmark), *gräddtårta* (Sweden), and *täytekakku* (Finland). It is baked especially for birthdays and special occasions throughout the year—such as Constitution Day (May 17) in Norway. The first example of this cake can be found in a handwritten cookbook by a young Danish woman, Helle Schrøder, in 1692, who was preparing recipes for her future household. The lightness of the cake and its filling—sweetened whipped cream and fresh berries—make it especially popular in spring and summer.

Preheat the oven to 325°F (160°C/Gas Mark 3). Grease a 9-inch (23-cm) springform cake pan and line the base with parchment paper. Set aside.

To make the sponge cake: In a stand mixer fitted with the paddle attachment, cream the eggs and sugar together until the mixture becomes slightly stiff and lighter in color, about 5 minutes. Sift in the flour and baking powder and gently fold through the mixture using a rubber spatula. Pour the batter into the prepared cake pan, sit the pan on a baking sheet, and bake for 35 minutes, or until a toothpick (cocktail stick) inserted in the center comes out clean.

Remove from the oven and let cool, then remove from the pan.

Meanwhile, to make the whipped cream: In a stand mixer fitted with the whisk attachment, combine the cream and confectioners' (icing) sugar and whip on medium–high speed for 1–2 minutes.

To assemble: Cut the sponge cake into 3 even layers. Over the bottom layer, sprinkle a few drops of orange juice, then spread a layer of jam on top. Top the jam with whipped cream, spreading it out to the edges of the cake. Place the second layer of sponge on top and repeat with the juice, jam, and a little more of the whipped cream. Place the final layer of cake on top and cover completely with the rest of the whipped cream. Scatter the berries over the top, and serve.

WHITSUN

This holiday, known as Whitsun (from "Whit Sunday," meaning "white Sunday") in the United Kingdom, is in much of the rest of the world known as Pentecost. Rooted in the traditions (and calendar day) of the early Jewish harvest holiday Shavuot, Whitsun is celebrated on the seventh Sunday (forty-nine days) after Easter. On this day, worshippers commemorate the descent of the Holy Spirit to the Apostles, a key moment of divine inspiration for Jesus's disciples, which is said to have led directly to their work spreading Jesus's message and expanding the numbers of the Christian Church.

WHITSUN CAKE

England

Submitted by Anna Luntley

Makes 1 × 8-inch (20-cm) cake
Prep time: 2½ hours including proofing time
Cook time: 1 hour 5 minutes

For the cake:
⅔ cup (5 fl oz/150 ml) milk
10½ tablespoons (5½ oz/150 g) butter
1½ cups (7 oz/200 g) strong white bread flour
1¼ cups (5½ oz/150 g) all-purpose (plain) flour, plus extra for dusting
½ teaspoon fine salt
½ teaspoon superfine (caster) sugar
¼ oz (7 g) quick-rise dry yeast

For the filling:
1 cup (5½ oz/150 g) raisins
scant ½ cup (3½ oz/100 g) currants
scant 1 cup (7 oz/200 g) soft light brown sugar
7 tablespoons (3½ oz/100 g) melted butter
1 teaspoon ground cinnamon
1 teaspoon ground nutmeg
grated zest of 1 lemon (optional)
5 teaspoons whisky (optional)
1 egg yolk

For the topping:
1 egg
pinch of fine salt
1 tablespoon turbinado (demerara) sugar

These sweet, yeasted cakes hail from Lincolnshire in England's East Midlands, where they were baked for Whitsunday, elsewhere called the Holy Day of the Pentecost, in late May. Filled with a familiar mixture of warm spices and dried fruit, they were traditionally left to age for a few days after baking to let the flavors mature and mingle together.

The recipe below also includes a more seasonal take for this springtime cake, eschewing its traditional mincemeat-style filling for a seasonal fruit mixture. It tastes delicious as it is, accompanied by a cup of tea and a slice of strong Lancashire cheese, or served as a dessert warmed with vanilla ice cream or pouring cream.

To make the cake: In a small pan over low heat, warm the milk and half the butter until the butter is melted. Set aside.

In a large bowl, combine the flours, salt, superfine (caster) sugar, and yeast. Cube the remaining butter and add to the bowl. Using your fingertips, rub the butter into the flour mixture until the mixture resembles bread crumbs. Add the milk-butter mixture and bring together to make a sticky dough. Turn out the dough onto a lightly floured counter and gently knead until it becomes smooth and coherent. Put the dough into a clean bowl, cover with a clean, damp dish (tea) towel, and leave in a warm place to rise for 1 hour, or until doubled in size.

Meanwhile, to make the filling: In a medium bowl, combine the raisins, currants, light brown sugar, melted butter, cinnamon, nutmeg, lemon zest, if using, whisky, if using, and egg yolk and set aside.

To make the topping: Make an egg wash by beating together the egg with the salt. Set aside.

Line an 8-inch (20-cm) cake pan with parchment paper. It is best to do this by cutting a piece of parchment paper too large for the pan, loosely screwing this up into a ball, opening it out, and gently pushing it into the pan to create a loose lining. This way no butter can leak out of the pan while the cake is baking, and the dough will rise to fill the pan neatly. Set aside.

Once the dough has risen, turn out onto a lightly floured counter. Gently press out into a circle, knocking out some of the air. Divide the dough into 4 equal pieces. Roll out a piece of dough gently into an 8-inch (20-cm) circle. Place this into the bottom of the lined cake pan. Using a pastry brush, gently brush a ring of egg wash around the edge of the dough and spread one-third of the fruity filling over its surface leaving a border of about ½ inch (1 cm) of egg-washed dough showing at the edges. Roll another piece of dough to 8 inches (20 cm) and lightly place on top of the fruity filling, pressing down the edges onto the egg-washed border to seal. Egg wash the edge, add a fruity layer, roll out another piece, and place on top as above. Repeat another layer, finishing with your fourth piece of dough on top. Cover the pan with a clean, damp dish towel and proof in a warm place for 30 minutes–1 hour, until risen and mallowy to the touch.

Preheat the oven to 350°F (180°C/Gas Mark 4). Egg wash the top and sprinkle with the turbinado (demerara) sugar. Bake for 30 minutes, then reduce the temperature to 325°F (160°C/Gas Mark 3) and bake for another 30 minutes.

Remove from the oven and let cool completely before removing from the pan. To store traditionally, wrap well in parchment paper and/or aluminum foil and let rest to age for several days.

6

JUNE

FESTA JUNINA

Festa Junina, or *Festas de São João*, is a Brazilian harvest festival that lasts the whole month of June and celebrates rural farming traditions. In Brazil's austral growing season, June's midwinter conditions represent a prime month for the cultivation of many staple ingredients key to the Brazilian kitchen, with corn perhaps chief among them. Borrowing or melding some aspects of European Midsummer festivities, like the construction of a large bonfire, the month is filled with fireworks, folk dancing, and merriment, with three saints' days (St. Anthony, St. John, and St. Peter) serving as significant markers.

BRAZILIAN CORN CAKE

Brazil

Submitted by Hanny Guimarães

Serves 5
Prep time: 35 minutes
Cook time: 40 minutes

- sunflower oil, for greasing
- ⅔ cup (2¾ oz/80 g) fine cornmeal
- ½ teaspoon baking powder
- ¼ teaspoon salt
- ¼ cup (2¼ oz/60 g) yogurt
- 4 tablespoons milk
- 3 tablespoons (1½ oz/40 g) butter
- ¼ cup (2 oz/55 g) granulated sugar
- 1 egg, plus 1 egg yolk
- scant ½ cup (3½ oz/100 g) ricotta

Corn cake, or *bolo de milho*, plays a key role in Brazil's *Festa Junina*, a major occasion that celebrates the country's rural and agricultural heritage, and coincides with the annual corn harvest. During the festivities of *Festa Junina*, the cake is often made with fennel seeds and sometimes served with jelly toppings—especially guava jelly.

This recipe comes from Lida Padaria in São Paulo, whose method is quite labor intensive: They ferment, dry, and mill their own corn kernels, and serve it to customers as a proud reminder of the importance of this indigenous staple crop.

Once baked, the cake should be served warm. To reheat it, try pan-frying in butter—it results in a delicious crispy layer.

Preheat the oven to 350°F (180°C/Gas Mark 4). Lightly oil a 2¼ × 5½ × 3-inch (5.5 × 14 × 7.5-cm) loaf pan with sunflower oil, and line it with parchment paper.

In a medium bowl, combine the cornmeal, baking powder, and salt. Set aside. In a separate bowl, combine the yogurt and milk. Set aside. In the bowl of a stand mixer fitted with the paddle attachment, cream together the butter and sugar until light and airy. Add the egg, ensuring it is well incorporated before adding the yolk and continuing to mix until incorporated.

Add one-third of the dry ingredients and mix until just combined. Then, add half of the yogurt mixture. Add another third of the dry ingredients and the remaining yogurt mixture. Finish by adding the last third of the dry ingredients. The mixture should have a smooth consistency.

Using a rubber spatula, gently fold in the ricotta in small chunks, trying not to break it up too much. The goal is to have pieces of ricotta throughout the cake, rather than it being fully blended into the batter. Transfer the batter into the prepared pan.

Bake for 30 minutes, then rotate the pan and bake for another 10 minutes, until a toothpick (cocktail stick) inserted in the center comes out clean. Let cool before removing from the pan.

JUNETEENTH

Juneteenth (June 19) is a holiday that marks the end of slavery in the United States. The Emancipation Proclamation, issued in 1863, had freed (in legal terms) over three million enslaved Black people in the American south amid the nation's four-year civil war. Despite this issuance, the real end to the enslavement of people was a more gradual process, with the U.S. government enforcing its proclamation throughout the south in the months after the war had ended in April 1865. The formal abolishment of slavery, eventually enshrined in the United States Constitution, did not happen until the end of that year.

Juneteenth, which is a portmanteau of *June* and *nineteenth*, began as a holiday in Texas, which celebrated the enforcement of emancipation across the state that had occurred on June 19, 1865. Over time, the holiday's popularity spread across Black communities in the south, and by the middle of the twentieth century, into the north as part of the "great migration." Today, the holiday celebrates not only freedom from bondage but also progress and achievement. On the day, there is good food made and served, and much of it is either naturally or artificially colored red: a symbol of, and tribute to, the resilience of Black slaves across nearly 250 years.

RED VELVET BUNDT CAKE WITH CREAM CHEESE GLAZE

United States

p. 150

Submitted by Eden Westbrook

Serves 12
Prep time: 15 minutes, plus cooling time
Cook time: 55 minutes–1 hour 5 minutes

For the cake:
- 3 sticks (12 oz/340 g) butter, softened, plus extra for greasing
- 3 cups (13 oz/375 g) all-purpose (plain) flour, plus extra for dusting
- 3 cups (1 lb 5 oz/600 g) granulated sugar
- 5 large eggs, at room temperature
- 4 tablespoons unsweetened cocoa powder (not Dutch-processed)
- ½ teaspoon baking soda (bicarbonate of soda)
- ½ teaspoon kosher salt
- 1 cup (8 fl oz/250 ml) buttermilk (ideally full-fat, but low-fat also works), at room temperature
- 2 tablespoons beet (beetroot) powder or red food coloring
- 2 teaspoons vanilla extract
- 1 teaspoon distilled white vinegar

For the cream cheese glaze:
- ½ cups (4 oz/115 g) cream cheese, softened
- 1½ cups (6 oz/180 g) confectioners' (icing) sugar, sifted, plus extra if needed
- 1 teaspoon vanilla extract
- 3 tablespoons milk, plus extra if needed

Red velvet cake came from the old "velvet cakes" of the Victorian era: soft, smooth, tender cakes thanks to the addition of buttermilk and a little vinegar. The red hue first came from the cocoa reacting with the acid, but it really caught on once food coloring hit the shelves. Southern cooks made it into one of the region's many celebration cakes, and it's always on the dessert table on any occasion for Black Americans. On occasions like Juneteenth (June 19), the symbolism of red runs deep: the blood and sacrifice of ancestors, as well as resilience and joy. Red velvet cake was a staple on the festive table of this recipe's contributor, the Southern chef Eden Westbrook, and especially on Juneteenth.

Preheat the oven to 325°F (160°C/Gas Mark 3) with a rack in the center of the oven. Generously grease and flour a 12-cup Bundt pan, ensuring all crevices are covered, and set aside.

To make the cake: In a large mixing bowl with an electric hand mixer or stand mixer fitted with the paddle attachment on medium speed, cream together the butter and sugar until light and fluffy, about 5 minutes. Add the eggs one at a time and beat on low–medium speed, ensuring each egg is fully incorporated before adding the next.

In a separate bowl, whisk together the flour, cocoa powder, baking soda (bicarbonate of soda), and salt.

In another bowl, whisk together the buttermilk, beet (beetroot) powder, vanilla extract, and vinegar until smooth.

Add the dry and wet ingredients to the creamed butter mixture, alternating in 3 additions of dry and 2 additions of wet, beginning and ending with the dry ingredients. Mix each addition on low speed until just incorporated, scraping down the bowl as needed. Do not overmix—mix just until all the dry ingredients are absorbed by the batter. Pour the cake batter into the prepared Bundt pan, and gently smooth the top. Bake for 55 minutes–1 hour 5 minutes, or until a toothpick (cocktail stick) inserted in the center comes out clean.

Remove from the oven and cool the cake in the pan for 15 minutes, then carefully flip the cake onto a wire rack to cool completely.

Meanwhile, to make the cream cheese glaze: In a medium bowl with an electric hand mixer or clean stand mixer fitted with the paddle attachment, beat the softened cream cheese on medium speed until smooth with no lumps. Mix in the confectioners' (icing) sugar, vanilla extract, and milk until smooth and pourable. Adjust the consistency by adding more milk (thinner) or confectioners' sugar (thicker), if needed.

Generously drizzle the glaze over the cooled cake and let set for a couple of minutes before slicing and serving at room temperature. It will keep in an airtight container for up to 2 days.

Note: Adjust the beet powder slightly for a deeper or lighter red, adding up to 1 more teaspoon for a more vibrant hue, or reducing it slightly for a softer tone.

MIDSOMMAR

While the summer solstice is observed throughout much of Scandinavia, in Sweden, where it's known simply as *midsommar*, it has been elevated into a holiday of great significance. Here, in a part of the world, and at a time of year, when the sun barely sets at all, *midsommar* celebrates life, light, and the bounty of summer—with a feast of food both savory and sweet. The weaving (and wearing) of wildflower "crowns" (as well as folk dress) provides an extra burst of color and pageantry to the day, and traditional dances around the *midsommarstång* (maypole) will often last long into the evening or the early sun-lit hours of morning.

Left: *Red Velvet Bundt Cake with Cream Cheese Glaze*, Juneteenth (page 149)

JORDGUBBSTÅRTA

Sweden

Submitted by Cecilia Tolone

Serves 12
Prep time: 25 minutes
Cook time: 20–25 minutes

For the cake:
2¼ sticks (9¼ oz/260 g) butter, plus extra for greasing, if needed
3½ tablespoons (1¾ fl oz/50 ml) vegetable oil, plus extra for greasing, if needed
2¾ cups (12 oz/340 g) all-purpose (plain) flour
2 teaspoons baking powder
½ teaspoon salt
1⅔ cups (11½ oz/330 g) superfine (caster) sugar
4 eggs
⅓ cup (2¾ fl oz/80 ml) milk
2 teaspoons vanilla extract

For the vanilla whipped cream:
2¼ cup (1 lb 2 oz/500 g) heavy (double) cream
1 teaspoon vanilla extract or sugar
2 tablespoons confectioners' (icing) sugar (optional)

To assemble:
10½ oz (300 g) strawberries, hulled, and half of them quartered, to serve
edible flowers, to decorate (optional)

***Jordgubbstårta*—strawberry cake—is a classic Swedish cake served on *Midsommar*, a festival celebrating the summer solstice. The celebration's origins can be traced back to pagan times when it was a fertility rite dedicated to the Norse god Freyr. Today, the festivities are decidedly secular and include dancing around the *midsommarstång* (similar to a maypole), wearing traditional folk costumes, singing traditional songs, and enjoying an abundance of food and drink—including pickled herring, aquavit, and new potatoes.**

Strawberries are also at their peak around this time and as a result are synonymous with *Midsommar*. The actual cake base is *sockerkaka*, a classic Swedish cake similar to Victoria sponge, and it is very simply filled with a lightly sweetened whipped cream and fresh strawberries.

Preheat the oven to 375°F (190°C/Gas Mark 5). Grease 2 x 9-inch (23-cm) cake pans with butter or oil.

To make the cake: In a bowl, sift together the flour, baking powder, and salt. Place the butter and sugar in the bowl of a stand mixer fitted with the paddle attachment. Mix on high for 5 minutes. Add the eggs to the mixture. Mix on high for another 5 minutes, then scrape the sides of the bowl. Add half the sifted flour mixture to the batter. Mix gently just until combined. Add the milk, vegetable oil, and vanilla. Mix together gently until fully combined. Add the remaining half of the flour mixture and mix gently until fully incorporated, ensuring there are no streaks of milk or bits of flour left.

Pour the batter into the oiled cake pans. Bake for 20–25 minutes, or until a toothpick (cocktail stick) inserted into the center comes out clean.

Remove from the oven and let cool completely.

Meanwhile, to make the vanilla whipped cream: Pour the cream, vanilla, and confectioners' (icing) sugar into a bowl and whip until soft peaks form.

To assemble: Spread half the whipped cream over the first cake. Add most of the chopped strawberries. Place the second cake layer on top and spread a layer of whipped cream over it, then transfer the remaining cream to a piping (pastry) bag fitted with a star nozzle and pipe a border around the edge of the cake. Arrange the whole and remaining cut strawberries on top of the cake and decorate with edible flowers, if using.

ST. JOHN'S EVE

St. John's Eve, observed on June 23, during the summer solstice, is the eve of St. John the Baptist's feast day. Interestingly enough, this is one of the very few feast days that celebrates the birth of a saint—with many instead focusing on their death and martyrdom. Sometimes called the "summer Christmas," the main associated tradition with St. John's Eve is that of building and lighting bonfires. There are suggestions that this tradition either derives from, or is related to, earlier Midsummer festivities, for example those held in Scandinavia, which happen at nearly the same time. It is said that these bonfires represent the bright light that St. John brought into the world through Jesus Christ.

COCA DE SANT JOAN

Catalonia

Submitted by Alessandra Pili

Serves 6–8
Prep time: 1 hour, plus resting time
Cook time: 20–30 minutes

- oil, for greasing
- ½ oz (12 g) fresh yeast
- 5 tablespoons milk, warmed (use 4 tablespoons if using the anise liqueur)
- 2 cups (9 oz/250 g) strong flour
- 4 tablespoons (2 oz/55 g) butter, softened
- 1 whole egg, plus 1 egg, beaten, for egg wash
- ¼ cup (2 oz/55 g) granulated sugar
- pinch of salt
- grated zest of 1 lemon
- 1 tablespoon anise liqueur, or ¼ teaspoon ground anise
- 1¼ cups (7 oz/200 g) candied fruits (melon, orange, cherries), chopped
- ¼ cup (1 oz/25 g) pine nuts
- granulated sugar, for topping

The *coca de Sant Joan* is a typical sweet baked to celebrate the summer solstice, and is consumed during the night of *Sant Joan* (St. John's Eve, June 23). Tradition says that this sweet must have a canonical size—twice as long as it is wide—and should have rounded corners.

In its early days, the *cocas* were kneaded at home and then taken to bakers to be baked. With the birth of the first pastry stores in the nineteenth century, the recipe was sweetened with the addition of cherries and more candied fruits. In rural areas, there was a belief that it had to be eaten outdoors, as eating it under a roof would bring bad luck. It was once commonly accompanied by sweet or aged wine, but today these drinks have gradually been replaced by cava.

Today the most common *cocas* are filled with cream or marzipan, but creativity has opened the door to many more combinations.

Preheat the oven to 350°F (180°C/Gas Mark 4). Lightly grease a baking sheet with oil.

In a small bowl, combine the yeast and milk, then set aside for 5–10 minutes, until frothy. Add 3 tablespoons of the flour to the yeast mixture and whisk it until smooth. Cover with plastic wrap (clingfilm) and let rest in a warm place until doubled in size, about 30 minutes.

On a counter, place the remaining flour and make a well in the center. Add the butter, 1 whole egg, sugar, salt, lemon zest, yeast mixture, and anise liqueur. Work all the ingredients together by hand or with a fork, gradually incorporating the flour until the dough is soft but compact. Place on the prepared baking sheet and roll out to a ½-inch (1-cm)-thick oval shape. Brush with beaten egg and place the candied fruits on top. Cover loosely with plastic wrap and let rest again until doubled in size, about 1 hour.

Sprinkle with the pine nuts, then the sugar. Bake for 20–30 minutes until a skewer inserted into the center comes out clean.

Remove from the oven and let cool before serving.

JULY

7

JULY

INDEPENDENCE DAY (UNITED STATES)

American Independence Day marks the signing of the Declaration of Independence, which formalized the secession of the Thirteen Colonies from the British Crown on July 4, 1776. The symbolic birth of the nation is celebrated annually with patriotic songs, parades, barbecues, fireworks, sports, and summer get-togethers. The wearing of the flag's colors (red, white, and blue) is commonplace, as is the cooking or baking of seasonal dishes that share those colors. Along with Juneteenth (June 19), July 4 also represents one of the few major American holidays that occur this time of the year, and thus, it's hard not to associate the day itself with a celebration of summer-themed Americana—with the day's activities reading like a list of the country's favorite seasonal pastimes.

STRAWBERRY SHORTCAKE

United States

Submitted by Nicholas Andreadis

Serves 8
Prep time: 25 minutes, plus macerating time
Cook time: 12–14 minutes

For the strawberry filling:
- 3½ cups (1 lb/450 g) strawberries, hulled, some quartered, some halved
- 2 tablespoons granulated sugar

For the cookie dough:
- 5 tablespoons (2½ oz/70 g) cold butter
- 2 cups (8½ oz/240 g) all-purpose (plain) flour, plus extra for dusting
- 4 teaspoons baking powder
- 1 teaspoon fine salt
- 1½ tablespoons granulated sugar, plus extra for sprinkling
- ⅔ cup (5½ fl oz/160 ml) milk (or as needed)
- 1 cup (8 fl oz/250 ml) heavy (double) cream, cold, for whipping, plus extra for brushing

The recipe for this quintessential American dish comes from Greek-American baker Nicholas Andreadis, who was raised in Bristol, Rhode Island, and for whom this recipe conjures up fond childhood memories of early summer and especially the Fourth of July.

The town in which he was raised proudly hosts the oldest continuously celebrated Fourth of July parade in the country, and also makes their version of strawberry shortcake with an American cookie-style base, turning it into something of a breakfast or brunch dish.

This particular recipe was part of a family tradition, made on the morning of Independence Day before gathering to watch the parade—simple, celebratory, and unmistakably American.

To make the strawberry filling: Place the strawberries in a bowl, sprinkle with the sugar, and gently toss to coat. Let sit at room temperature for 20 minutes to macerate—this will draw out their juices and soften the berries.

To make the cookie dough: Cut the cold butter into small cubes (about ¼ inch/ 5 mm) and place it in the freezer while you prepare the dry ingredients. (Keeping the butter very cold helps create a flaky cookie.)

Preheat the oven to 425°F (220°C/Gas Mark 7). Line an 8-inch (20 cm) cake pan with parchment paper.

Meanwhile, in a large, cool mixing bowl, whisk together the flour, baking powder, salt, and sugar until evenly combined. Add the chilled butter to the dry ingredients. Using a pastry blender, your fingertips, or the paddle attachment of a stand mixer, work the butter into the flour until the mixture resembles coarse crumbs—somewhere between sand and small peas in texture. Slowly drizzle in the milk, a little at a time, mixing gently just until the dough comes together. You want it to hold together without being sticky. The exact amount may vary depending on the humidity, so go slowly and stop as soon as the dough forms.

Turn out the dough onto a lightly floured counter. Gently flatten it to about ¾ inch (2 cm) thick. Fold the 2 ends into the center like a letter. Turn the dough 90 degrees, flatten again to ¾ inch (2 cm), and fold once more. This gentle layering encourages additional layers and more flakiness.

Dip a 2-inch (5-cm) cookie cutter in flour and cut straight down—don't twist. Reflour the cutter before each cut. Place the cookies snugly in the lined cake pan so they're just touching; this helps them rise evenly and stay tender. Brush the tops with heavy (double) cream and sprinkle with granulated sugar. Bake for 12–14 minutes, or until the tops are golden brown.

While the cookies bake, whip the cold heavy cream by hand until it forms very soft peaks—just firm enough to hold its shape but still smooth and nearly pourable. The cream will set slightly as it sits.

Remove the cookies from the oven and while they are still warm, gently split them open with a fork (this keeps their crumb light and fluffy). Spoon some of the macerated strawberry juice over the bottom half, add a generous spoonful of berries, then a heavy dollop of whipped cream. Top with the other half of the cookie, add more cream, and decorate with the prettiest berries.

Note: If feeling extra festive, try decorating with fresh blueberries in the top left corner of each shortcake for a playful abstraction of the Stars and Stripes (the flag of the United States).

POTATO ROLL

United States

Submitted by Nicholas Andreadis

Makes 12
Prep time: 1 hour, plus resting, proofing, and overnight chilling times
Cook time: 45 minutes

For the potatoes:
2 (11 oz/315 g) Yukon Gold potatoes, peeled (reserve the peel), chopped into ½-inch (1-cm) cubes
3½ tablespoons butter

For the dough:
2½ tablespoons honey
¼ teaspoon ground turmeric
4⅓ cups (1 lb 3 oz/545 g) high-protein all-purpose (plain) flour or bread flour
2 teaspoons quick-rise dry yeast
milk, as needed
2 teaspoons fine salt
neutral oil, for greasing
1 egg, beaten, for egg wash

Most American summer gatherings revolve around the humble potato roll. These soft, golden buns are synonymous with July 4 celebrations, and in New England (where this recipe's author comes from) they are buttered, grilled, and piled high with lemony, mayo-dressed lobster meat.

The secret lies in the potato: it gives the roll a subtle sweetness, rich flavor, and an unbelievably soft, airy texture. While some things are hard to beat from the store's bread aisle, this handcrafted version is worth the endeavor.

To make the potatoes: Place the potatoes in a pot with the reserved peels. Cover with water and simmer for 15–20 minutes, until fork-tender. Strain, reserving 1 cup (8 fl oz oz/250 ml) of the cooking water. Mash the potatoes until smooth (use a ricer or fine-mesh sieve).

Combine 8½ oz (240 g) of the warm mashed potato with the butter. Mix together and let sit at room temperature, covered with a clean dish (tea) towel.

To make the dough: Add the reserved warm potato cooking water to the potato-butter mixture. Stir in the honey and turmeric until smooth and fully combined. Transfer to the bowl of a stand mixer fitted with the dough hook attachment. Add the bread flour and yeast. Mix on low speed for 2–3 minutes until the flour is fully incorporated. If the dough seems dry, add the milk 1 tablespoon at a time until the flour is fully incorporated but the dough is not wet. Cover with a dish towel and let rest for 20–30 minutes to allow the flour to hydrate.

After resting, add the salt. Knead the dough on low–medium speed for 8–10 minutes until smooth and elastic. The dough should clean the sides of the bowl and when stretched gently, it should form a thin, translucent sheet without tearing. Transfer the dough to a lightly oiled bowl, cover, and proof in a warm place for 1–2 hours, until increased in size by about 1½ times.

Once risen, cover tightly with plastic wrap (clingfilm) and refrigerate overnight. The next day, remove the dough from the refrigerator and let rest at room temperature for 2 hours. Meanwhile, line a baking sheet with parchment paper.

Divide the dough into 4 equal pieces, then divide each piece into 3 equal portions to make 12 pieces (each about 3½ oz/100 g). Flatten each piece slightly to release the excess gas. Gather the edges of the dough into the center, creating a tight, smooth ball with a rough seam underneath—like shaping a dumpling. Place seam-side down on the counter. Cup your hand loosely over the dough and roll in small, quick circles to create a smooth, round ball. Repeat with the remaining dough balls, then let all 12 rest, gently covered, on the counter for 10 minutes.

Gently flatten 1 dough ball. Roll the top edge down into the center, tucking as you go to build tension and form a log. Using both hands, roll it into a 6-inch (15-cm) log (a uniform cylindrical shape—not tapered at the ends). Place seam-side down on the prepared sheet. Repeat with the remaining dough.

Arrange the shaped buns in 2 rows of 6. They should be close enough that they'll touch once fully risen—this helps them bake evenly and stay soft. Cover loosely with a clean dish towel and proof in a warm spot for 30–45 minutes, or until noticeably puffy and doubled in size.

Preheat the oven to 325°F (160°C/Gas Mark 3). Once the buns have risen, gently brush the tops with the egg wash. Bake for 25 minutes, or until the buns are golden brown and the tops sound slightly hollow when tapped.

Remove from the oven and let cool slightly before serving.

INDEPENDENCE DAY (ARGENTINA)

In 1808, Napoleon's deposition of the Spanish King Ferdinand VII—in favor of his brother Joseph—caused unrest throughout much of Spain's global empire, as territories began to reckon with their own governance. This was especially true in the viceroyalty of the Río de la Plata (modern-day Argentina, Uruguay, Paraguay, and Bolivia), where in May of 1810, Criollo separatists seized power, and the ruling group, called the *Primera Junta*, exiled the Spanish viceroy, marking the beginning of a war that, at first, was for self-governing autonomy. On July 9, 1816, the viceroyalty's governing Congress of Tucumán officially declared independence from Spain, and within two years, it had defeated the last major Spanish threat to its independence.

Today, Argentina celebrates national holidays on both May 25 (*Día de la Revolución de Mayo*), which celebrates the *Primera Junta* and early self-autonomy, as well as July 9, *Día de la Independencia*, which marks the official split from Spain. Along with parades and fireworks, all manner of empanadas (and other traditional fare) is enjoyed.

PASTELITOS CRIOLLOS

Pampas and Argentina

Submitted by Julia Soria

Makes 12
Prep time: 1 hour, plus chilling time
Cook time: 25–30 minutes

For the dough:
- 4 cups (1 lb 2 oz/500 g) all-purpose (plain) flour, plus extra for dusting
- ⅔ cup (3¾ oz/110 g) lard, melted
- 2 teaspoons salt

For the lamination paste:
- ¾ cup plus 1 tablespoon (3½ oz/100 g) all-purpose (plain) flour
- scant ⅔ cup (3½ oz/100 g) lard, melted

For the syrup glaze:
- 1 cups (7 oz/200 g) superfine (caster) sugar
- peel of 1 orange
- 1 cinnamon stick

For the filling:
- 9 oz (250 g) set quince or sweet potato jelly, cut into 1¼-inch (3-cm) cubes

For baking:
- lard or neutral oil, for brushing
- 3–4 tablespoons granulated sugar, for sprinkling

The origins of *pastelitos criollos* date back to the early 1800s, during the country's struggle for independence. This led to the pastries becoming associated with the May Revolution in 1810—when Argentina formed its first autonomous government.

***Pastelitos* are cherished traditional candies (sweets) in Argentina, especially popular during patriotic celebrations such as May Revolution Day (May 25) and Independence Day (July 9).**

Today *pastelitos criollos* are commonly sold at school fairs, bakeries, and street stalls, where they symbolize festivity, family, and culinary heritage. They are known for their crisp, golden layers and sweet fruit filling. While frying remains the traditional and most widespread cooking method, producing a puffed, flaky texture, some modern versions offer a baked alternative, catering to lighter preferences or home kitchen convenience.

To make the dough: On a counter, place the flour and make a well in the center. Add the melted lard, salt, and scant 1¼ cups (9 fl oz/280 ml) water. Knead into a smooth dough. Cover with plastic wrap (clingfilm) and chill in the refrigerator for 30 minutes.

To make the lamination paste: In a bowl, combine the flour and melted lard and mix into a paste.

Remove the dough from the refrigerator and turn out onto a counter dusted with flour. Roll out to ⅛ inch (3–4 mm) thick, brush with the paste, dust with flour, and fold into thirds, as though folding a letter—fold the top third down and the bottom third up to cover it. Repeat this process twice to laminate, then wrap in plastic wrap and refrigerate for 30 minutes.

To make the syrup glaze: In a pan, combine the sugar, orange peel, cinnamon stick, and ½ cup (4 fl oz/120 ml) of water and simmer for 5 minutes. Remove from the heat and let cool.

Roll out the dough to ⅛ inch (3–4 mm) thick and cut into 3¼-inch (8-cm) squares. Place 1 cube of jelly on a dough square, then cover with another square, rotated 45 degrees to make a star shape. Pinch the edges to seal.

Preheat the oven to 400°F (200°C/Gas Mark 6), and line a baking sheet with parchment paper. Place the pastelitos on the prepared baking sheet and lightly brush with melted lard or oil. Bake for 20–25 minutes, flipping halfway, until golden and crispy.

Remove from the oven, then, brush with syrup, and sprinkle with sugar.

EMPANADAS CATAMARQUEÑAS

Argentina

Submitted by Julia Soria

Makes 12
Prep time: 30 minutes, plus chilling, cooling and resting times
Cook time: 40 minutes

For the filling:
- 5½ oz (160 g) potato, chopped (¼ × ¼ in/5 × 5 mm)
- ⅓ cup (1¾ oz/50 g) lard
- 1 cup (9 oz/250 g) minced onions
- 1 teaspoon ground cumin
- 1 teaspoon sweet paprika
- 9 oz (250 g) beef brisket or beef chuck, finely diced by hand (¼ × ¼ in/5 × 5 mm)
- ¼ cup (1 oz/25 g) green olives, quartered (optional)
- 3 tablespoons raisins, soaked in water (optional)
- ¼ cup (¾ oz/20 g) finely chopped scallions (spring onions)
- salt and freshly ground black pepper, to taste

For the dough:
- 2½ cups plus 2 tablespoons (12 oz/325 g) all-purpose (plain) flour, plus extra for dusting
- 1 tablespoon salt
- 1 tablespoon lard, melted
- ½–⅔ cup (4–5½ fl oz/120–160 ml) hot water

To glaze:
- 1 egg, beaten

In Catamarca, northwest Argentina, empanadas are known for being made with beef that's finely cut by hand, which makes the filling juicy and textured. They also traditionally include potatoes and raisins.

This recipe comes from Argentinian food writer Julia Soria, whose maternal grandmother Omelia was born in Pomán, a small town in the province of Catamarca. Soria's family always excluded the raisins, but it's unknown whether this came from a distaste for them within the family, or simply a differing recipe.

Omelia would make empanadas for every special occasion, especially for patriotic holidays like Independence Day on July 9 and the anniversary of the birth of the nation (the May Revolution) on May 25, and they would always be the first thing to disappear from the table. What stayed constant was her method: hand-cut beef, onions slowly sautéed until sweet, and potatoes, all wrapped in soft dough before being fried or, in this case, baked.

To make the filling: Put the chopped potatoes in a pan of water and bring to a boil. Boil until they are just shy of fully cooked—they should be slightly firm, or "al dente"—about 5 minutes. Drain, then chill in the refrigerator.

In a large skillet (frying pan), heat the lard over medium heat. Add the chopped onions and sauté for a few minutes, until translucent. Add the cumin and paprika, and cook for another 2 minutes. Increase the heat to medium–high and add the finely diced beef. Sear the meat, stirring occasionally, until it changes color but remains tender, about 5 minutes. Add the olives and raisins, if using. Remove the skillet from the heat and allow the mixture to cool to room temperature, then fold in the chopped potatoes and scallions (spring onions) and season to taste. Chill for at least 1 hour so the lard solidifies, making it easier to handle during empanada assembly.

Meanwhile, to make the dough: In a large mixing bowl, combine the flour and salt. Add the melted lard to the flour mixture and stir until well combined. Gradually pour in the hot water while mixing, until the dough comes together into a smooth, homogeneous ball.

Transfer the dough to a lightly floured counter and knead for 5–7 minutes, until it becomes soft and pliable. Cover the dough with a clean dish (tea) towel and let rest at room temperature for 30 minutes.

Preheat the oven to 400°F (200°C/Gas Mark 6). Line a baking sheet with parchment paper. Divide the dough into 12 equal portions. Roll each portion into a ball, then use a rolling pin to flatten each ball into a thin, even circle about 1/16 inch (1 mm) thick. These will be your empanada wrappers. Use the dough circles immediately with your desired fillings. If you are not using immediately, stack the dough circles with parchment paper between each to prevent sticking, and store them in an airtight container.

Place a portion of the filling onto each empanada dough disk. Brush a little beaten egg around the edge of the pastry, and fold the dough over to enclose the filling. Seal the edges by pressing with a fork or crimping. Arrange the empanadas on the prepared baking sheet and brush with beaten egg. Bake for 20–25 minutes, or until golden brown.

Remove from the oven and serve warm.

AUGUST

8

AUGUST

SAINT FANOURIOS DAY

There is very little known, through historical details or even myths, about the life of Fanourios, who might have been a persecuted soldier of ancient Rome, but whose cult of worship began no earlier than the fourteenth century, when an icon of him was discovered by a bishop in the ruins of an old church on the Greek island of Rhodes. Over time, Saint Fanourios became associated with the finding of lost or stolen items in exchange for a *tama*, or "offering"; one of the most likely reasons for this is the clear alliterative quality of his name, and the Greek verb φαίνω, or *faíno*, meaning "to look or reveal." Today, Saint Fanourios' feast day is celebrated mostly in Greece and Cyprus.

FANOUROPITA

Cyprus and Greece

Submitted by Carolina Doriti

Makes 1 × 11–12-inch (27–30-cm) cake
Prep time: 30 minutes
Cook time: 50 minutes

- 1 cup (8 fl oz/250 ml) light olive or sunflower oil, plus extra for greasing
- 4 cups (1 lb 2 oz/500 g) self-rising flour
- 1½ teaspoons baking powder
- 1½ teaspoons ground cinnamon, plus extra for dusting (optional)
- ¼ teaspoon ground cloves
- 1½ cups (10½ oz/300 g) granulated sugar
- grated zest of 2 oranges, plus 1½ cups (12 fl oz/350ml) orange juice
- 1 cup (5½ oz/150 g) raisins, soaked for 30 minutes, then drained and towel dried
- 1 cup (4¼ oz/120 g) chopped walnuts
- confectioners' (icing) sugar, for dusting (optional)

***Fanouropita* is a symbolic Greek cake baked in honor of Saint Fanourios, the patron saint of lost things. His icon was discovered in the fourteenth century in the ruins of a church on Rhodes—remarkably intact, depicting a young saint in Roman military dress. The inscription read *Ayios Fano*, later interpreted as Fanourios, from the Greek *faino* (φαίνω), meaning "to reveal." In gratitude or in hope of finding something lost, folks began baking this special offering.**

The cake is traditionally prepared by women, and with an odd number of ingredients, usually seven, nine, or sometimes eleven. (Both seven and nine are symbolic for Greek Christians: there are seven sacred mysteries, seven days of creation, and nine orders of angels.) Each ingredient carries symbolic meaning: oil for mercy, flour for life, spices for grace, and fruit or nuts for sweetness and abundance. While making the cake, tradition calls for a lit candle, burning incense, and the reading of a specific prayer. If the cake doesn't rise, it's considered a bad omen, but if it rises well, the news is good. It is then taken to church, blessed, and divided into forty pieces to be shared. On August 27, Saint Fanourios' feast day, churches across Greece are filled with the sweet, spiced aroma of these cakes, offered to be blessed in faith and hope for the lost to be found.

Preheat the oven to 350°F (180°C/Gas Mark 4). Lightly grease a round 11–12-inch (27–30-cm) cake pan with oil and set aside.

In a large bowl, combine the flour, baking powder, cinnamon, and cloves. In a separate large bowl, whisk the oil and sugar until the sugar dissolves. Add the orange zest and juice and mix well until combined. Start incorporating the flour mixture while mixing with a wooden spoon or rubber spatula—avoid overmixing as this will make the cake dense. Finally, fold in the raisins and walnuts. Pour the batter into the prepared pan and smooth the top. Bake for about 50 minutes, or until a toothpick (cocktail stick) inserted into the center comes out clean.

Remove from the oven and let cool completely, then dust with confectioners' (icing) sugar and cinnamon, if using.

SEPTEMBER

9

SEPTEMBER

ROSH HASHANAH

Rosh Hashanah, literally "the head of the year," is the Jewish New Year, and the first of what are called the "High Holy Days"—coming ten days before Yom Kippur, the day of atonement. Observed on the first of the month of Tishrei, it typically coincides with the start of fall (autumn) but comes nearly five weeks before the Jewish harvest holiday, Sukkoth. There is much symbolism in the foods eaten on the day, especially bakes, and there is an emphasis on sweetness—which is said to be reflected throughout the year. It is customary on this day to eat apples and honey together but also common to find them baked into cakes on the day.

ROUND CHALLAH

Ashkenazi Jewish

Submitted by Talia Jacobs

Makes 2 small or 1 large
Prep time: 45 minutes, plus resting and proofing times
Cook time: 25–35 minutes

- generous ⅓ cup (3½ fl oz/100 ml) warm water
- ¼ oz (7 g) active dry yeast
- 3½ cups (1 lb/440 g) strong white bread flour
- 2 eggs (7½ oz/100 g), plus 1 egg for egg wash
- ⅓ cup (2¾ fl oz/80 ml) vegetable or light olive oil, plus extra for greasing
- 3½ tablespoons (2½ oz/70 g) honey or ⅓ cup (2½ oz/70 g) superfine (caster) sugar
- 2 teaspoons sea salt
- sesame or poppy seeds, to decorate (optional)

Challah is the slightly sweet almost brioche-like braided bread that Jews traditionally eat for special occasions: from the weekly Shabbat dinner, to the biggest of holidays, Rosh Hashanah and Yom Kippur.

On Rosh Hashanah, challah, which is often baked as a long, thick braided loaf, is instead baked as a round to symbolize the cycle of the year at its beginning. It is eaten as part of a larger meal—always torn by hand, never cut—alongside, among many things, apples and honey, which represent the hope for a sweet new year.

In the bowl of a stand mixer fitted with the paddle attachment, add the warm water, yeast, and ½ cup (2¼ oz/60 g) of the flour. Mix to combine and set aside for 30 minutes, or until it starts to bubble and look active. Add the 2 eggs, oil, honey or sugar, and remaining flour and, using a dough hook, mix for 5 minutes. Let rest for 5 more minutes, then add the salt and continue mixing on low-medium speed for 5–10 minutes until it comes together into a smooth dough. If it feels too sticky add a touch more flour. Transfer the dough to an oiled bowl, cover with plastic wrap (clingfilm), and let rest somewhere warm for 1–2 hours, until doubled in size.

Line a baking sheet with parchment paper and set aside.

Punch down and halve the dough (for 2 small challahs), then divide into as many pieces as you are comfortable braiding. Stretch out each piece of dough and roll into fat little log shapes. Cover and let rest for 5 minutes. Roll each piece into a long, even strand, then braid the strands together. For a more elaborate finish, you can weave 4 strands together starting in the center, then alternating the direction in which you cross over the ends. Tucking the stray ends underneath. Put the loaves onto your prepared baking sheet and place in the oven with a shallow dish of steaming hot water to proof, until the dough no longer springs back when touched, then remove from the oven and set aside.

Preheat the oven to 350°F (180°C/Gas Mark 4). In a small bowl, beat the remaining egg and brush the top of each loaf. Sprinkle with sesame or poppy seeds, if using. Bake for 20 minutes, rotate, and bake for another 5–15 minutes depending on the size, until the loaf sounds hollow when tapped on the base.

Remove from the oven, let cool on a wire rack, and serve.

HONEY CAKE

Ashkenazi Jewish

Submitted by Talia Jacobs

Makes 2
Prep time: 20 minutes
Cook time: 30–45 minutes

scant 4 cups (15 oz/420 g) all-purpose (plain) flour
¾ cup (6 oz/180 g) soft dark brown sugar
3 teaspoons ground ginger
1½ teaspoons ground mixed spice
1 teaspoon ground cinnamon
1 teaspoon baking soda (bicarbonate of soda)
1½ teaspoons baking powder
pinch of salt
1¾ cups (14 oz/400 g) honey
¾ cup (6 fl oz/180 ml) neutral vegetable oil
¾ cup (6 fl oz/180 ml) strong black coffee, cooled
3 eggs
slivered (flaked) almonds, to finish (optional, for nut-free)

This dense, sticky honey cake—*lekach*—is one of the most iconic Jewish *simanim*, or holiday foods with symbolic meaning. It is most commonly made for the Jewish high holidays, especially Rosh Hashanah, the so-called "head of the year," as it is believed to bring a "sweet" new year.

In addition to the honey and sweet spices incorporated in the cake, it's also typical to include cooled brewed tea or coffee to deepen the flavor, and nearly every recipe uses oil instead of butter as the cooking fat. This allows the recipe to remain *parve* (including neither meat nor dairy), and thus suitable for those keeping kosher to eat following a large meaty dinner.

Preheat the oven to 325°F (160°C/Gas Mark 3). Line two 900 g (2 lb) loaf pans with parchment paper and set aside.

In a large mixing bowl, mix together the flour, sugar, spices, baking soda (bicarbonate of soda), baking powder, and salt. In a separate bowl, combine the honey, oil, coffee, and eggs and mix well. Make a well in the center of the dry ingredients and add the honey mixture. Using a whisk or spatula, mix until the batter just comes together—avoid over-mixing. Split the mixture between the two loaf pans, and sprinkle the tops with the slivered (flaked) almonds, if using.

Bake for 30–45 minutes, until a toothpick (cocktail stick) inserted in the center comes out clean.

Remove from the oven and let cool on a wire rack. Store in an airtight container for up to 1 week. They are best when 1–2 days old.

EXALTATION OF THE HOLY CROSS

This Christian feast day, celebrated on September 14, commemorates the cross on which Christ was crucified, as well as the third-century discovery of what is called the "true cross," and its presentation before worshippers at the Church of the Holy Sepulchre. It is considered a relatively solemn holiday, and the foods prepared to celebrate the day tend to be plainer fare with deeply packed religious significance—such as the incorporation of basil, which is said to have grown at the location where the cross was discovered.

BUCCELLATO

Italy

Submitted by Naomi Blair Gould

Serves 6
Prep time: 30 minutes, plus proofing time
Cook time: 30 minutes

- 2 cups (9 oz/250 g) strong white bread flour
- ¼ cup (2 oz/55 g) superfine (caster) sugar
- ¼ teaspoon fine sea salt
- ⅓ oz (10 g) fresh yeast
- ½ cup (4 fl oz/120 ml) plant-based milk, lukewarm
- 2 tablespoons plant-based butter, cubed, at room temperature
- ¾ teaspoon anise seeds
- ¼ cup (1½ oz/40 g) golden raisins (sultanas) or raisins, soaked in water for 30 minutes and drained
- neutral oil, for greasing
- maple syrup or simple syrup, for glazing

Buccellato is a sweet bread characterized by the addition of anise seeds and raisins. It has close associations with the religious festivity and procession celebrating _esaltazione della Santa Croce_ (the Exaltation of the Holy Cross), which happens every year in mid-September. The exaltation (and the bread) is of particular importance to the town of Lucca, in Tuscany, where there is even a saying that whoever visits without trying the bread might as well not have visited at all.

Buccellato is traditionally served either at breakfast or _merenda_, the Italian midafternoon snack with a coffee, or after dinner with a glass of wine or a sweet dessert wine. _Buccellato_ can be eaten fresh on the day it's baked, by the slice lightly toasted with butter, or alongside ricotta and rum or strawberries and cream.

The ancient original recipe is very basic, made with "poor man's" ingredients and therefore accidentally vegan, but these days it is often made with additions such as butter, milk, and egg, making it a richer brioche, although here it is made with plant-based ingredients.

In the bowl of a stand mixer fitted with the paddle attachment, or in a bowl using a wooden spoon, combine the flour, sugar, and salt.

In a separate bowl, crumble the fresh yeast into the milk and whisk together. If using a stand mixer, change the paddle attachment to a dough hook. Add the milk-yeast mixture into the dry ingredients, and knead on low speed for 10 minutes, slowly adding the butter until incorporated. Add the anise seeds and drained dried fruit, then knead until just incorporated. Shape the dough into a smooth, round ball. Place in a lightly oiled bowl, cover, and proof for 3 hours, until doubled in size.

Line a baking sheet with parchment paper and set aside. Divide the dough in half, being careful not to knock out the air. Shape each piece of dough into a baton shape and place on your prepared baking sheet. Score straight down the center of each baton with a bread lame or sharp knife. Let rest for 1 hour.

Meanwhile, preheat the oven to 350°F (180°C/Gas Mark 4). Bake for 30 minutes until golden brown. Transfer to a wire rack and glaze with the syrup. Let cool before serving.

Note: Another version of this bread is commonly baked in Sicily at Christmas time and is more elaborate in both ingredients and presentation in comparison to the rather simple Tuscan loaf. The Sicilian version is elegantly braided and embellished with bright candied fruit jewels, chocolate, and even candied pumpkin.

YOM KIPPUR

Yom Kippur, along with Rosh Hashanah, is one of the two holiest days of the Jewish calendar, and taking place two weeks after the latter, this holiday centers around atonement, repentance, and prayer. The holiday officially begins on the evening before, in a service called *kol nidrei*. It is also at this time that observant Jews will begin to fast, continuing to do so until sundown of the following day: drinking no liquid and eating no food. On Yom Kippur evening, as the first stars become visible in the night sky, the mood will turn joyous and celebrants will end their fast with a plentiful "break-fast" meal featuring a wide spread of traditional Jewish fare.

NOODLE KUGEL

Ashkenazi Jewish

Submitted by Myrna Schecter

Serves 6
Prep time: 25 minutes
Cook time: 1¼ hours

For the noodles:
8 tablespoons (4 oz/115 g) butter, melted, plus extra for greasing
12 oz (350 g) broad noodles (or use 1 lb/450 g if you want it to be a little firmer)
1 lb (450 g) cottage cheese
4 oz (115 g) Velveeta-style cheese, cut into small pieces
1 cup (8 oz/225 g) sour cream
¼ cup (2 oz/55 g) superfine (caster) sugar

For the custard:
4 eggs
½ cup (4 oz/115 g) superfine (caster) sugar
1¾ cups (14 fl oz/415 ml) milk
1 teaspoon vanilla extract

For the topping:
4 teaspoons granulated sugar
1 teaspoon ground cinnamon

A kugel, to Azhkenazi Jews, could be many different things. It is, in essence, a traditional layered casserole made from a base of either potatoes or noodles, incorporating sweet or savory ingredients such as onions and raisins, and baked for special occasions–especially the holidays.

Every kugel is different, but this one is my favorite. It is the one that my mother, Lisa, made for us growing up, and was (and is) very popular within our household. The recipe, which comes from my mother's cousin Myrna is a little sweet, a little savory, and a little creamy. It has a beautiful golden-brown and crispy top layer, but as kids our favorite part of it was the slightly controversial little dots of soft processed cheese distributed throughout the mix of noodles. It is also quite easy to put together, and is one of the first things I learned to cook.

Because of the versatility of the kugel, it could conceivably be eaten at any time of day. My mother made it most often as a side dish for the big Yom Kippur evening "break-fast," but I've eaten it just as often for breakfast or dessert, and as a kid, I'd often request it as a part of my birthday dinner.

Preheat the oven to 350°F (180°C/Gas Mark 4). Grease a 9 × 13-inch (23 × 33-cm) baking dish and set aside.

To make the noodles: Bring a pan of water to a boil and cook the noodles according to the packet directions until al dente, then drain, and transfer to a mixing bowl. Add the cottage cheese, Velveeta cheese, sour cream, sugar, and butter, and toss the noodles in the mix until well coated. Transfer the noodles to your prepared baking dish and set aside.

To make the custard: Beat together the eggs, sugar, milk, and vanilla extract. Pour over the noodles, lifting them slightly to ensure they can absorb the liquid.

In another bowl, mix together the sugar and cinnamon, and sprinkle generously over the noodles. Bake for 1¼ hours, until golden brown and crisped on top.

Remove from the oven, leave to cool slightly, then serve

CINNAMON BABKA

Ashkenazi Jewish

Submitted by Talia Jacobs

Makes 1 × 10-inch (25-cm) round cake
Prep time: 40 minutes, plus proofing time
Cook time: 40–55 minutes

For the dough:
- 3½ cups plus 2 tablespoons (1 lb/450 g) all-purpose (plain) flour, plus extra for dusting
- 3 tablespoons superfine (caster) sugar
- ⅛ oz (3.5 g) quick-rise yeast
- grated zest and juice of ½ lemon
- ½ teaspoon salt
- ½ cup (4 fl oz/125 ml) milk
- 2 eggs, plus 1 egg for egg wash
- 5 tablespoons (2¼ oz/65 g) butter, melted
- ½ teaspoon vanilla extract
- neutral oil, for greasing

For the filling:
- 1½ tablespoons ground cinnamon
- ½ cup (3½ oz/100 g) superfine (caster) sugar
- scant ½ cup (3½ oz/100 g) soft dark brown sugar
- 3½ tablespoons (2 oz/50 g) butter, softened

For the sugar syrup:
- 1 cup (7 oz/200 g) superfine (caster) sugar

Babka is a beautifully braided bread (or cake) that emerged in Eastern Europe in Ashkenazi Jewish communities of the early nineteenth century, apparently as a means of using up leftover dough from baking challah. The layers of the babka, whose name comes from the Polish *baba*, or "grandmother," were spruced up by the incorporation of a sweet filling like jam or chocolate. For this reason, the older, more traditional recipes are less indulgent than today's, and understandably more bread-like.

Today, the most popular recipes call for a chocolate (or rather, cocoa) filling, or one of cinnamon and sugar, although some bakers have started to experiment with different flavor combinations, including savory ones. It can also vary substantially in the thickness and amount of filling of its layers.

This recipe is very much coming from the older, more traditional "school" of babka. It comes from London-based baker Talia Jacobs, who modernized a recipe her mother, grandmother, and great-grandmother had used for decades. While babka is suitable for any special occasion, in Talia's family it was especially popular to serve as they broke the feast on Yom Kippur.

To make the dough: In the bowl of a stand mixer fitted with the dough hook attachment, add the flour, sugar, yeast, lemon zest, and salt. Make a well in the center and add the milk, 2 eggs, butter, vanilla, and lemon juice. Mix for 10–15 minutes until the dough comes together. If it is very sticky add a little more flour. Transfer to an oiled bowl, cover with a clean, damp dish (tea) towel, and proof until doubled in size.

Meanwhile, to make the filling: In a small bowl, mix together the cinnamon and sugars and set aside.

Grease a 10-inch (25-cm) round cake pan and line with parchment paper.

Punch down the dough, turn out onto a lightly floured counter, and roll out into a large rectangle. Brush the softened butter over the surface and sprinkle with the cinnamon sugar. Roll up into a long log shape, then slice down the center lengthwise. Twist the 2 strands over each other, swirl the twist into a round, and place in the center of the prepared cake pan. Cover with plastic wrap (clingfilm) and proof for 1½–2 hours, until the dough no longer springs back when poked.

Preheat the oven to 325°F (160°C/Gas Mark 3). In a small bowl, beat the remaining egg and brush the top of the babka. Bake for 40–55 minutes.

Meanwhile, to make the sugar syrup: In a pan over low heat, bring 1 cup (8 fl oz/250 ml) of water to a gentle simmer. Add the sugar and stir until it has dissolved completely. Set aside.

As soon as the babka comes out of the oven, pour the syrup over. Let cool before serving. The babka can be stored for 4 days at room temperature or frozen, well wrapped in plastic wrap and aluminum foil, for up to 1 month.

MID-AUTUMN FESTIVAL

The Mid-Autumn Festival, or Harvest Moon Festival, is an autumn harvest holiday celebrated on the fifteenth day of the eighth month of the Chinese lunisolar year—roughly late September or early October on the Gregorian calendar. This ancient Chinese holiday is rooted in traditions that date back 3,000 years, and centers around the arrival of the annual harvest moon, often considered the biggest and brightest full moon of the year.

Moongazing is of course an important part of festivities, as is the giving of thanks for a successful harvest, family meals, and the lighting of lanterns, which symbolize good fortune. The baking and enjoying of small traditional mooncakes is also synonymous with observance of the Mid-Autumn Festival. This is a traditional style of round pastry marked with elaborate stamps and decorations, and its many popular and regional fillings range widely, from savory salted egg yolk to sweeter fillings like red-bean paste.

In China it is one of the most significant holidays of the calendar year, but the day is also observed in Korea, where it's known as *Chuseok* (autumn eve), and Japan, where it's known as *Tsukimi* (moon viewing), as well as throughout East and Southeast Asia.

SAVORY MOONCAKES

China

Submitted by Jess Eng

Serves 20
Prep time: 1 hour, plus resting times
Cook time: 25–30 minutes

For the filling:
- 4 cups (1 lb/450 g) ground (minced) pork
- ¼ cup (1¾ oz/50 g) granulated sugar
- 1 tablespoon Fujian wine (or Shaoxing wine)
- 1 teaspoon soy sauce
- 1 teaspoon ground white pepper
- 1 teaspoon sweet potato starch or cornstarch (cornflour)
- 1 teaspoon black sesame seeds, crushed
- 1 teaspoon salted peanuts, crushed
- 1 scallion (spring onion), chopped

For the dough paste:
- 2 cups (10¼ oz/290 g) all-purpose (plain) flour
- ½ cup (3¾ oz/110 g) lard, or 1 stick (4 oz/115 g) butter

For the dough:
- 2 cups (7 oz/195 g) all-purpose (plain) flour, plus extra for dusting
- ⅓ cup (2 oz/55 g) lard, or 5 tablespoons (2½ oz/70 g) butter
- 1 tablespoon granulated sugar
- pinch of salt
- ¾ cup (6 fl oz/180 ml) hot water
- 1 egg beaten with 1 teaspoon water, for egg wash

When mooncakes come to mind, most picture beautifully patterned treats with glossy crusts and sweet lotus paste and salted duck egg fillings. That's because these Cantonese-style mooncakes are enjoyed during the Mid-Autumn Festival (typically early fall) and commonly enjoyed in Chinatowns around the world.

Mooncakes, however, aren't just for those with a sweet tooth. Savory versions, like this one from Fujian, are also beloved across China, and the varieties are near-endless. Some easily fit in the palm of your hand, while others resemble dinner-plate-size hockey pucks. The topping choices run the gamut too. In Fujian, vendors may add sesame seeds, chopped scallions (spring onion), and even peanuts for a bit of crunch. Traditional savory mooncakes are baked in a charcoal grill and stuffed with ground (minced) pork and spices, though a quick brush of egg wash makes them easy to bake in a home oven, too.

Their link to this holiday is rooted in legend: Chang'e was the wife of Hou Yi, a heroic archer who shot down nine of ten suns to save the Earth. As a reward, he was given an elixir of immortality, which Chang'e drank to prevent it from falling into the wrong hands, causing her to ascend alone to the moon. Heartbroken, Hou Yi placed her favorite foods on an altar each year, hoping to catch a glimpse of her. This tradition evolved into the Mid-Autumn Festival, where mooncakes are shared to honor the moon and their love.

To make the filling: In a medium bowl, mix the ground (minced) pork, sugar, wine, soy sauce, white pepper, starch, crushed sesame seeds, crushed salted peanuts, and the scallion (spring onion) until well incorporated. Set aside.

To make the dough paste: In a separate medium bowl, combine the flour with the lard or butter. Mix with your hands or a rubber spatula until a crumbly dough forms. Divide into 20 balls (about 1 tablespoon each), cover with plastic wrap (clingfilm), and let rest for 20 minutes.

Meanwhile, to make the dough: In a large heatproof mixing bowl, mix the flour with the lard, sugar, and salt. Slowly add the hot water while stirring. Once cool, knead the dough until it's smooth and elastic, adjusting with more flour or water as needed. Divide into 20 balls, cover with plastic wrap, and let rest for 20 minutes.

Flatten one ball of pastry dough in your palm, then wrap it around one ball of dough paste. Gently roll into a ball to seal the contents. Repeat with the remaining dough. Cover and let rest for 15 minutes.

On a lightly floured counter, roll each ball into a long, flat oval using a rolling pin. Roll the dough up from one of the shorter ends to form a log. Repeat for all. Cover with a clean, damp dish (tea) towel and let rest for 10 minutes.

Meanwhile, preheat the oven to 400°F (200°C/Gas Mark 6). Line a baking sheet with parchment paper and set aside.

Take one log and flatten it into a long oval. Roll the dough up again into a log. Turn it on its end and press the log down from the top until it resembles a spiral circle. Flatten into a 4-inch (10-cm) circle. Place a ball of meat filling in the center of each piece of dough. Pleat the dough up around the filling and pinch to seal. Flip seam-side down and gently flatten to about 1 inch (2.5 cm). Transfer the mooncakes to the prepared baking sheet. Brush the tops with the egg wash and bake for 25–30 minutes, or until golden brown.

Remove from the oven and let cool slightly before serving. They will keep for 4 days in the refrigerator or 4–5 months frozen.

YAKGWA

Korea

Submitted by Bitna Kang

Serves 4
Prep time: 15 minutes
Cook time: 30 minutes, plus soaking and draining times

For the syrup:
2 cups (16 fl oz/480 ml) rice syrup (jocheong)
1 oz (30 g) fresh ginger, sliced
1 cinnamon stick

For the dough:
1½ cups plus 2 tablespoons (7 oz/200 g) all-purpose (plain) flour, plus extra for dusting
½ teaspoon salt
½ teaspoon baking soda (bicarbonate of soda)
½ teaspoon ground cinnamon
4 tablespoons sesame oil
3 tablespoons soju (Korean distilled liquor)
4 tablespoons honey
2 tablespoons neutral cooking oil

To finish:
ground pine nuts, sesame seeds, or sliced jujubes

***Yakgwa* is a traditional Korean pastry that developed in Kaesong, the capital of Goryeo, and Hanyang, the capital of Joseon. The uniqueness of the *yakgwa* lies in its delicate texture. Folding and rolling the dough repeatedly to create pastry-like layers, adding the syrup, and soaking the syrup into every layer one-by-one, achieves a soft and sweet yet still crispy and chewy bite. The delicate balance of softness and crispness is the signature texture of *yakgwa*.**

Due to the effort and ingredients required to make *yakgwa*, it was historically served only in the royal palace, used during ancestral rites, or given as a special wedding favor. Nowadays, it remains a beloved dessert in Korea during holidays and celebratory events, such as *Chuseok*.

There are many different versions of *yakgwa* depending on how the dough is shaped: when pressed into a hand-carved wood mold called a *dasikpan*, it is called a *dasikgwa*. If the pieces are large, they are referred to as *daeyakgwa*, while smaller ones are called *soyakgwa*. When cut into squares, they are named *moyakgwa*.

In its traditional form, *yakgwa* dough is fried in oil at a low temperature. Modern variations are often oven-baked for a lighter flavor. Typically, it is garnished with pine nuts, sesame seeds, or sliced jujubes before serving. While *yakgwa* can be enjoyed on its own, it pairs beautifully with a scoop of vanilla ice cream or even with a glass of pinot noir or gamay wine.

To make the syrup: In a pan, combine the rice syrup, fresh ginger, and cinnamon stick with ⅔ cup (5 fl oz/150 ml) of water and bring the mixture to a boil, then reduce to low heat and simmer for 7 minutes. Set aside to cool.

To make the dough: In a large bowl, sift together the flour, salt, baking soda (bicarbonate of soda), and cinnamon. Pour the sesame oil over the mixture, and rub together with your fingers until the flour is evenly coated.

In a small bowl, mix the soju and honey. Working in 2 batches, add the soju-honey mixture to the flour and gently press together without kneading, to avoid forming gluten. The dough should be soft. Cover with plastic wrap (clingfilm) and let rest at room temperature for 30 minutes.

Preheat the oven to 350°F (180°C/Gas Mark 3). Line a baking sheet with parchment paper and set aside.

Turn out the dough onto a floured counter and roll out until ½ inch (1 cm) thick. Fold it in half, then roll it out again. Repeat this process 3 times, being careful not to use too much pressure. Cut the dough into 1¼ × 1½-inch (3 × 4-cm) pieces and use a fork to prick several holes in each piece. Place the pieces on the prepared baking sheet and brush the surface of each with the neutral cooking oil. Bake for 15 minutes.

Remove from the oven and immediately transfer the hot yakgwa into the cooled honey syrup. Let soak for 3 hours.

Set a wire rack over a baking sheet. Remove the soaked yakgwa from the syrup and place on the rack. Let drain for 1 hour.

To finish: Decorate with ground pine nuts, sesame seeds, or dried jujube slices before serving. They will keep in an airtight container for 5 days at room temperature, or up to 3 months frozen.

10

OCTOBER

CELEBRATION OF EL SEÑOR DE LOS MILAGROS

This Peruvian holiday celebrates a much venerated seventeenth-century painting of Jesus Christ (the "Lord of Miracles"), created by an enslaved Angolan named Benito living in Lima. In October 1655, an earthquake destroyed much of Lima, but the mural survived untouched, and was left similarly unscathed by subsequent earthquakes over the following century.

Every October, locals and visiting pilgrims and tourists alike take to the streets of Lima for celebrations that take over the city. The celebrants don purple robes, which are said to reflect the habit of a Mother of the Nazarene order, the same order that now cares for the mural. This highly popular religious celebration is also one of good food, with bright vibrant colors (such as purple) especially popular.

TURRÓN DE DOÑA PEPA

Peru

Submitted by Gastón Acurio

Serves 6
Prep time: 1 hour, plus chilling, cooling, and resting times
Cook time: 3¼ hours

For the turrón sticks:

- 8½ tablespoons (4¼ oz/120 g) butter
- 5¾ oz (165 g) vegetable shortening
- ½ oz (12 g) achiote shortening (optional—this colors the dough)
- 2 egg yolks
- generous 3¾ cups (1 lb 1 oz/480 g) pastry flour, plus extra for dusting
- 1½ teaspoons salt
- 4 teaspoons toasted anise seeds
- 2 teaspoons toasted sesame seeds
- 2¼ oz (60 g) anise infusion (boil 1 tablespoon of anise seeds in ½ cup/4 fl oz/120 ml of water for 1 minute, then let cool)
- colored sprinkles, for decorating

For the turrón honey:

- ½ orange (3 oz/85 g)
- 5½ oz (160 g) golden pineapple, peeled and diced
- 1 Granny Smith apple (5½ oz/155 g), cored and diced
- 1 peach (3 oz/85 g), pit (stone) removed and diced
- 1 quince (6 oz/175 g), cored and diced
- 1¾ cups (12 oz/360 g) granulated sugar
- 4¼ oz (125 g) chancaca (see note)
- ¼ oz (4 g) cinnamon stick
- 1 g whole cloves
- 1 teaspoon anise seeds
- 2 dried figs
- 1 fig leaf

In the eighteenth century, Josefa Marmanillo (also known as Doña Pepa), a freed slave, is said to have created this recipe with divine guidance after her miracle cure from paralysis. The layered nougat is made with sesame and anise, and then drizzled with a syrup made from *chancaca*, an unrefined sugar.

Each year, *turrón* is made to celebrate El Señor de los Milagros (October 28), and the image of street vendors selling it on every corner is considered a hallmark of the celebratory procession—along with women carrying candles, and passing clouds of incense.

This recipe comes from Peruvian chef Gastón Acurio, whose mother used to say that *turrón de Doña Pepa* wasn't something you ate—it was something you shared. Each piece, fragile and uneven, was offered the way blessings are: with open hands and heart. In Gastón's household, a tray of *turrón* would arrive every October wrapped in wax paper, with syrup shimmering, and the many candy sprinkles like the aftermath of a sacred celebration.

To make the turrón sticks: In the bowl of a stand mixer fitted with the paddle attachment, cream the butter and vegetable shortening, then add the achiote shortening and egg yolks. Add the flour, salt, toasted anise, and sesame seeds. Add the anise infusion and mix gently until combined. Turn out the dough onto a floured counter and knead by hand until it becomes smooth. Form into thin 12-inch (30-cm) long sticks. Place them on the lined baking sheet, leaving sufficient space between each as they will expand in the oven. Refrigerate for 1 hour.

Preheat the oven to 325°F (160°C/Gas Mark 3), and line a baking sheet with parchment paper. Bake for 45 minutes, or until golden brown, then let cool.

Meanwhile, to make the turrón honey: Peel the orange, then remove and discard the white part (the pith). Use only the orange pulp and the peel. Place 6 cups (50 fl oz/1.5 liters) of water in a pot along with the fruits (including the orange), sugar, chancaca, spices, and figs into a pot. Bring to a boil over medium heat and boil for 1½ hours, until the fruits start to break down. Strain, pressing it gently. Set aside the figs.

Place the strained liquid into a pot with the figs and fig leaf, bring to a simmer over low heat, and simmer for 1 hour. Check the temperature; it must reach 237°F (114°C) (soft-ball stage). Strain, reserving the candied figs, and let cool.

On a rectangular platter, place one-third of the baked turrón sticks close together and coat them with one-third of the turrón honey. Arrange another 2 layers of sticks on top, each layer coated with the honey. Decorate with colorful sprinkles and the reserved candied figs. Let rest for at least 4 hours. Trim the edges and serve.

Note: If you can´t find chancaca, you can replace it with piloncillo or panela.

DIWALI

Diwali is a festival of lights celebrated on the night of the first new moon of *kartika*, a lunar month in the Hindu calendar, and which roughly translates to a date in late October or early November. While the story behind the holiday varies based on the region of India it originates from, the central point is always the triumph of light over darkness, good over evil. For Hindus, this is one of the year's biggest holidays—lasting five days, it is a period to gather together at home, clean, and decorate homes with oil lamps and colorful rangoli-patterned artwork. Over the course of these several days, there will be gift exchanges, extensive firework displays—from the amateur to the professional—as well as a great deal of good food (especially sweets) representing prosperity and joy.

While Diwali is most significant for Hindus, it is also celebrated by Jains and Sikhs, as well as those who adhere to Buddhism in India, with the exact observances, customs, and story behind the day varying from one religion to another.

NANKHATAI

India

Submitted by Siddharth Chogle

Makes 12–15
Prep time: 20 minutes
Cook time: 12–15 minutes

- ½ cup (4 oz/115 g) ghee
- ½ cup (2¼ oz/60 g) confectioners' (icing) sugar
- ¼ teaspoon ground cardamom
- pinch of salt
- 1 cup (4¼ oz/125 g) all-purpose (plain) flour
- 2 tablespoons blanched almonds, chopped

***Nankhatai* is India's signature ghee shortbread, created in sixteenth-century Surat. After Dutch spice traders vacated a local bakery, it is said that Parsi baker Faramji Dotivala reworked the abandoned bread starter into an egg-free, crumbly cookie that suited the city's largely vegetarian merchants.**

The name *nankhatai* blends Persian *naan* (bread) with Afghan *khatai* (cookie), reflecting the port's busy trade routes. Made from wheat, chickpea, and semolina flours creamed with clarified butter, sugar, and cardamom, the cookie traveled quickly along caravan and rail lines to Delhi, Hyderabad, and Karachi. Today boxes of *nankhatai* are exchanged during Diwali, served with morning tea on Eid, and packed into winter wedding hampers, all symbols of buttery hospitality across South Asia.

Preheat the oven to 350°F (180°C/Gas Mark 4). Line a baking sheet with parchment paper and set aside.

In the bowl of a stand mixer fitted with the paddle attachment, beat the ghee with the confectioners' (icing) sugar on medium speed for 2 minutes, until smooth and light. Add the cardamom and salt and mix briefly. Sift in the flour. Mix on low speed just until the dough comes together—do not overwork. The texture should remain soft and short.

Divide the dough into 12–15 equal pieces. Roll each into a ball, place on the prepared baking sheet, and gently flatten to a 2-inch (5-cm) disc. Press a few chopped nuts into the center of each cookie, if using, and bake on the center rack of the oven for 12–15 minutes until the bases are pale-gold while the tops remain ivory; avoid overbrowning.

Remove from the oven and leave on the sheet for 5 minutes to firm, then transfer to a wire rack. The cookies will crisp as they cool and will keep in an airtight container for 7 days.

KAJU BADAAM PURI

India

Submitted by Siddharth Chogle

Makes 15
Prep time: 20 minutes, plus cooling time
Cook time: 25 minutes

- 4 teaspoons butter, plus extra for greasing
- ½ cup (2½ oz/70 g) cashew nuts
- ½ cup (2¾ oz/75 g) blanched almonds
- ¾ cup (3½ oz/100 g) confectioners' (icing) sugar
- ½ teaspoon ground cardamom
- ½ teaspoon saffron strands, loosely packed
- 1 tablespoon milk

***Kaju badaam puri*, a cashew-and-almond cookie from western India, gained popularity in candy stores during the late 1960s, when dry-fruit confections such as *kaju katli* became fashionable. To prepare this recipe, cooks reduce a paste of premium cashews, blanched almonds, sugar, fragrant cardamom, and costly saffron, roll it thin, and give each disk a brief, gentle bake that speckles the top yet keeps the center moist. Certain Ahmedabad makers later adopted a deep-fried, syrup-dipped twist, but the baked version still dominates festive trays. Using premium cashews, almonds, cardamom, and saffron not only delivers luxurious flavor but also symbolizes prosperity—making these crisp, nut-rich cookies an ideal gift for the Hindu festival of lights, Diwali, and signaling prosperity across Gujarat and Maharashtra today.**

Line a baking sheet with parchment paper and set aside. Grease a piece of parchment paper with butter and set aside.

In the bowl of a food processor, place the cashew nuts and grind to a coarse meal. Transfer to a bowl and set aside. Repeat with the blanched almonds.

Return the cashews and almonds to the food processor and add the confectioners' sugar, cardamom, and saffron. Pulse briefly until a fine, uniform powder forms.

In a heavy, nonstick pan, melt 1 tablespoon of the butter with 2 tablespoons of water over medium heat. Add the nut and sugar mixture and stir continuously for 10–12 minutes over low–medium heat, until it thickens and pulls away from the sides of the pan. Incorporate the remaining 1 teaspoon of butter and cook for 1 minute longer.

Spread the hot paste on the lightly greased sheet and let cool for about 10 minutes, until warm but comfortable to handle. Add the milk and knead briefly to form a smooth, pliable dough.

Preheat the oven to 350°F (180°C/Gas Mark 4). Divide the dough into 2 pieces. On a greased counter, roll each portion to ⅛ inch (3 mm) thick, forming a circle roughly 7 inches (18 cm) in diameter. Using a 2½-inch (6-cm) circle cutter, stamp out disks, rerolling scraps as necessary to yield about 15 pieces. Arrange the disks on the prepared baking sheet and bake for 10 minutes, then turn the disks over and bake for an additional 5 minutes, or until both surfaces display light golden speckles.

Remove from the oven, transfer the cookies to a wire rack, and let cool completely. Pack individually in waxed or cellophane wraps; they will keep for up to 10 days in an airtight container.

HALLOWEEN

Celebrated annually on October 31, Halloween as we know it today is centered around all manner of dark, macabre, and ghoulish stories, traditions, and culture. In Christianity, the holiday is rooted in the vigil held on the evening before All Hallows' Day (All Hallows' Eve—hence the modern holiday name), as well as older Celtic pagan traditions (Samhain), which marked the end of fall (autumn) and the coming of winter. Both holiday traditions have strong associations with the mourning of the dead and the thinning of the liminal space that separates the worlds of the dead and the living. Over the course of the last century, some Celtic traditions, like the carving of jack-o'-lanterns made from root vegetables (historically turnips, now pumpkins), and the wearing of costumes, have become a part of mainstream observance, as has the playing of games, and the telling of jokes or riddles. In the United States, trick-or-treating by costumed children was once rewarded with toys, fruit, or treats, but these days the focus is on chocolate bars and bags of candy—all things devilishly sweet.

BARMBRACK

Ireland

Submitted by Alice Mahon

Serves 8–10
Prep time: 20 minutes, plus overnight soaking time
Cook time: 1 hour–1 hour 10 minutes

2 cups (12 oz/350 g) mixed dried fruit
1¼ cups (10 fl oz/300 ml) hot, strong-brewed Irish breakfast tea
3½ tablespoons whiskey
grated zest of 1 orange
neutral oil, for greasing
2 cups (9 oz/250 g) all-purpose (plain) flour
2 teaspoons baking powder
1 teaspoon apple pie spice
pinch of salt
⅔ cup (5½ oz/150 g) soft brown sugar
1 egg

Barmbrack (*bairín breac*), meaning "speckled loaf," is a beloved Irish tea bread speckled with dried fruit and infused with warming spices. While enjoyed year-round, it holds special significance during Halloween, a festival with roots in the ancient Celtic celebration of Samhain. Traditionally, November 1 marked the time when spirits of the departed could pass into the next world, a belief that later influenced the Christian observance of All Saints' Day and eventually evolved into the Halloween we know today.

In Irish tradition, *bairín breac* was often baked with hidden tokens, each symbolizing a different fortune for the coming year. A coin foretold wealth, a ring signaled marriage, a pea suggested a year of independence, a matchstick warned of a troublesome marriage, and a piece of cloth hinted at financial hardship. Today, it's most common to include just a ring or a coin—if anything at all. Regardless of its fortune-telling past, this spiced, fruit-studded loaf is best enjoyed fresh from the oven, slathered with butter, and paired with a hot cup of tea.

In a bowl, combine the dried fruit with the tea, whiskey, and orange zest. Cover with plastic wrap (clingfilm) and let soak overnight.

Preheat the oven to 350°F (180°C/Gas Mark 4). Lightly oil a 2 lb (900 g) loaf pan, line with parchment paper, and set aside.

In a large bowl, whisk together the flour, baking powder, apple pie spice, and salt.

In a separate bowl, whisk together the sugar and egg until well combined. Add the soaked fruit along with its liquid and stir to combine. Fold in the dry ingredients until fully incorporated. Pour the batter into your prepared loaf pan. Bake for 1 hour–1 hour 10 minutes, or until a toothpick (cocktail stick) inserted in the center comes out clean.

Remove from the oven, place on a wire rack, and let cool before serving.

NOVEMBER

11

NOVEMBER

ALL SAINTS' DAY

All Saints' Day, or All Hallows' Day, originated in the early post-Roman period as a regular Christian festival commemorating all martyrs. Within a few centuries, Pope Gregory III expanded its celebrations to the veneration of all saints—even those who were not martyrs.

By the 800s, the Church implemented another lasting reform of the holiday: Moving its annual celebrations from mid-May to November 1. This date was already associated with the Celtic post-harvest festival known as Samhain, and a significant holiday that held strong associations with the remembrance of departed loved ones.

Today, the holiday is predominantly a Catholic holiday, with church services focusing on the model lives and sacrifices of the saints. Families may also spend some of the day visiting the graves of loved ones, often leaving flowers and candles in remembrance.

DINGLE PIES

Ireland

Submitted by Gareth Eoin Storey

Makes 4
Prep time: 1 hour, plus chilling time
Cook time: 2 hours 50 minutes

For the filling:
beef or lamb dripping, for frying
1 onion, chopped
2 carrots, chopped
1 lb 2 oz (500 g) boneless lamb, cut into small cubes
2 tablespoons all-purpose (plain) flour
1 teaspoon cumin seeds
4¼ cups (34 fl oz/1 liter) vegetable broth (stock)
¼ teaspoon freshly ground black pepper
¼ teaspoon ground white pepper
¼ teaspoon salt

For the pastry:
3⅔ cups (1 lb/450 g) all-purpose (plain) flour, plus extra for dusting
2¼ sticks (9 oz/250 g) butter
½ teaspoon salt

For the egg wash:
1 egg yolk
1 tablespoon milk

These spiced lamb pies are eaten in Dingle, a town in the County of Kerry (situated on Ireland's southwest coast), on All Saints' Day when folks spend time visiting cemeteries, going to church, and paying respect to the dead. Having the pies prepared in advance, to take along to eat as part of a picnic or as lunch on the go, or to heat in the oven upon returning home, was a great way to save time. The portability of the Dingle pie has also made it popular with fishermen headed to sea and shepherds going into the fields.

To make the filling: Heat the dripping in a pan over medium heat and pan-fry the vegetables for 5 minutes to brown, then remove. Add the lamb, and fry for 5 minutes until browned all over. Add the flour and cumin seeds, return the vegetables to the pot, and just cover with the broth (stock)—you may not need it all. Add the peppers and salt, bring to a simmer, and cook until tender, about 2 hours. Set aside and let cool.

Meanwhile, to make the pastry: Place the flour in a large bowl and set aside.

In a small pan over medium heat, melt the butter. Add ¾ cup (6 fl oz/175 ml) of water and bring to a boil. Pour the butter mixture into the flour, and mix until a loose dough forms. Cover the bowl with plastic wrap (clingfilm) and chill in the refrigerator until the meat mixture has fully cooled.

Preheat the oven to 425°F (220°C/Gas Mark 7).

To make the egg wash: Beat together the egg yolk with the milk. Set aside.

Remove the dough from the refrigerator. Turn out onto a counter and divide the dough into 4 portions, pinching off a third of each portion for the lids. Roll out the dough on a floured counter to about ¼ inch (5 mm) thick and put into 4-inch (10 cm) pie molds, ramekins, or cake molds. Fill each shell with the meat mixture. Roll out the lids, then place on top and brush with egg wash. Bake for 10 minutes, then reduce the oven to 350°F (180°C/Gas Mark 4) and bake for another 30 minutes.

Remove from the oven and serve warm.

CASTAGNACCIO

Italy

Submitted by Naomi Blair Gould

Serves 6–8
Prep time: 20 minutes
Cook time: 30–40 minutes

1 tablespoon extra virgin olive oil, plus extra for greasing and drizzling
1⅔ cups (7 oz/200 g) chestnut flour, sifted
¼ teaspoon fine sea salt
1 teaspoon superfine (caster) sugar (optional)
¼ cup (1 oz/30 g) pine nuts, lightly toasted
⅓ cup (1¾ oz/50 g) golden raisins (sultanas) or raisins, soaked in water for 30 minutes and drained
fresh rosemary sprigs, to decorate

Castagnaccio is a distinctly Tuscan fall (autumnal) cake made from chestnut flour and olive oil, and flavored with raisins, pine nuts, and fresh rosemary. The cake's use of this unique flour recalls the traditional importance of the chestnut to local peasant diets over many centuries, and although this cake has been enjoyed for hundreds of years, it has seen a resurgence in popularity since World War II. Today it is frequently prepared between All Saints' Day and All Souls' Day, a period of time that many regions of Italy call the "bridge of death," which they celebrate with traditional dishes.

This recipe comes from baker Naomi Blair Gould, who grew up in Tuscany, and for whom falling chestnuts always seemed to mark the start of fall. As a child, she and her sister would gather the fresh chestnuts in the woods, and take them home to toast and eat, or sell in the market.

Preheat the oven to 350°F (180°C/Gas Mark 4). Lightly oil or line an 8-inch (20-cm) nonstick cake pan.

In a medium bowl, combine the chestnut flour, sea salt, and superfine (caster) sugar, if using. Slowly pour 1¼ cups (10 fl oz/300 ml) of water into the dry ingredients while mixing to ensure no clumps form. Pour in the extra virgin olive oil and mix until combined. Stir half the toasted pine nuts and half the drained dried fruit into the batter. The batter should be a loose, smooth consistency.

Pour the batter into the prepared cake pan. Decorate with the remaining pine nuts and dried fruit, and the sprigs of rosemary. Finish by drizzling with extra virgin olive oil.

Bake for 30–40 minutes, until light golden brown, the sides start to come away from the edge of the pan, and cracks begin to appear across the surface. Do not overbake as you want the cake to be nice and soft inside. Let cool before serving.

Note: This recipe is naturally vegan and gluten-free, although many Tuscans serve their *castagnaccio* with fresh ricotta and chestnut honey—just like the Tuscan chestnut pancakes *necci*.

ALL SOULS' DAY

Whereas All Saints' Day focuses on the ultimate examples provided by Christian saints, All Souls' Day is a more intimate and solemn affair, grounded in the remembrance of departed loved ones, and especially family. Throughout the day, families plan outings to visit and say prayers for the souls of their dearly departed. While graveside, they will also commonly perform gestures of love, like sweeping aside dirt and leaves, refilling vases with fresh flowers and water, and leaving behind both gifts and candles (or lanterns).

SOUL CAKES

England

Submitted by Anna Luntley

Makes 18
Prep time: 15 minutes
Cook time: 12–15 minutes

- 1½ cups plus 2 tablespoons (7 oz/200 g) all-purpose (plain) flour, plus extra for dusting
- 1 teaspoon baking powder
- pinch of salt
- 7 tablespoons (3½ oz/100 g) cold butter, diced
- ¼ cup (1¾ oz/50 g) superfine (caster) sugar, plus extra for sprinkling
- scant ¼ cup (1¾ oz/50 g) turbinado (demerara) sugar
- ⅓ cup (2¾ oz/80 g) currants
- 1 teaspoon apple pie spice
- ½ teaspoon ground nutmeg
- 2 egg yolks
- 4 tablespoons milk, plus extra if needed

Despite their name, these are not cakes but British cookies, which have their roots in medieval Shropshire as part of Samhain celebrations. Originally called soulmass cakes or harcakes, they celebrated the Celtic end of harvest celebrations, which were later replaced by All Souls' Day.

Each cookie is marked with a cross and was originally exchanged in return for prayers to save the soul: a practice a little like modern trick-or-treating. Wealthier homes would bake them to give to the poor, and children would come calling to collect them, and offer their prayers in return. Perfect afternoon cup of tea cookies. Good for the soul.

Preheat the oven to 350°F (180°C/Gas Mark 4). Line 2 baking sheets with parchment paper and set aside.

In a large bowl, combine the flour, baking powder, and salt. Add the butter and rub in with your fingertips until the mixture resembles bread crumbs. Add the sugars, currants, and spices, and mix to evenly distribute.

In a small bowl or measuring cup, beat together the egg yolks and milk. Add to the bowl of dry ingredients and bring together to make a rough dough. If the dough feels too dry add a splash more milk—it should be a little sticky to the touch.

Turn out the dough onto a lightly floured counter and knead for a moment or two to bring together. Flour the counter again and roll the dough out using a well-floured rolling pin until it is about ¼ inch (5 mm) thick. Use a 2¾-inch (7 cm) cookie cutter to cut round cookies, then lay them out on the prepared baking sheets. Gather up the scraps, reroll, and cut again until you have used all of the dough.

Gently prick the surface of each circle with a fork. To follow tradition, lightly score each cookie with a cross using a blunt knife (being careful not to cut all the way through). Bake the cookies for 12–15 minutes, until golden brown.

Remove from the oven, then sprinkle liberally with superfine (caster) sugar and let cool completely on the sheets. They will keep well for a few days in an airtight container.

DÍA DE LOS MUERTOS

In the wake of the Spanish conquest of Mexico in the sixteenth century, a traditional Aztec festival celebrating the goddess of death, Mictecacihuatl, was also moved to the same two-day period that All Saints' Day and All Souls' Day occupy. This was done to more closely link the pagan and Christian holidays of death and remembrance. The lasting result of this "melding" is today's distinctly Mexican *Día de los Muertos*, a two-day celebration remembering the dead with colorful pageantry.

There are many ritual aspects to the celebration of this holiday, including an abundant cornucopia of colorful marigolds, hand-painted skulls (and faces), and candlelit family altars (*ofrendas*). Many families also remember their loved ones by cooking or baking some of their favorite foods and leaving them as gifts at their graves.

PAN DE MUERTO

Mexico

Submitted by Elena Reygadas

Makes 10
Prep time: 1 hour, plus proofing time
Cook time: 20–25 minutes

For the buns:
- ¾ cup (5 oz/145 g) superfine (caster) sugar
- 3¾ cups (1 lb 1 oz/475 g) all-purpose (plain) flour, plus extra for dusting
- ¼ oz (8 g) fresh yeast
- 1½ teaspoons salt
- ½ cup (4 fl oz/120 ml) milk
- a few drops orange blossom extract
- 3 medium eggs
- 1 tablespoon grated orange zest
- 8½ tablespoons (4¼ oz/120 g) butter, cubed

For decoration:
- 1¼ cups (3½ oz/100 g) clarified butter, melted and cooled
- ½ cup (3½ oz/100 g) superfine (caster) sugar, for coating

Pan de muerto has its origins in pre-Hispanic rituals, when offerings to the gods included breads like _papalotlaxcalli_, or "butterfly bread," made from an ancient grain called amaranth. Over time, in the wake of the Spanish conquest and subsequent introduction of wheat to the local diet, these sacred breads transformed into what we recognize today as _pan de muerto_. The bread's design, with symbolic bones and skulls, reflects the fusion of indigenous traditions and Catholic rituals.

Across Mexico, _pan de muerto_ takes on diverse forms. In Oaxaca, it is shaped into animals, flowers, and human figures, while in central Mexico, anthropomorphic breads known as _muertes_ are crafted. Puebla's _golletes_, Guanajuato's _yemitas_, and _fantasmas_ from other regions reflect local ingredients and cultural symbolism.

The circular shape of _pan de muerto_ represents the cycle of life and death, while decorations like bones and tears honor the deceased and express the sorrow of loss. Death was integrated into the Indigenous Mexican cycle of life, with the understanding that to die was to be reborn. Life was a stage of transition, and death was accepted as a natural and necessary passage.

This mystical worldview endures in Mexico's vibrant _Día de los Muertos_ celebrations, where ancient traditions and modern rituals intertwine, keeping the art of honoring the dead alive.

To make the buns: In the bowl of a stand mixer, combine one-third of the sugar with the flour, yeast, salt, milk, orange blossom extract, eggs, and orange zest. Mix on low speed for 3 minutes. Add the butter and continue beating for 5 minutes on low speed until it is fully incorporated. Add another third of the sugar and increase the speed to medium. Mix for 3 minutes. Add the final portion of sugar and beat for another 5 minutes, until the dough is smooth and elastic. Cover with plastic wrap (clingfilm) and let rest for 15 minutes.

Turn the dough out onto a lightly floured counter and divide into 10 equal portions of 2¾ oz (80 g) each. Reserve the remaining dough for decoration. Roll each portion of dough into a ball, cover, and proof for 30–50 minutes, or until doubled in size.

Meanwhile, line 2 baking sheets with parchment paper and set aside. Divide the reserved dough into 20 pieces of ¾ oz (20 g) each for the bones and 10 balls of ⅛ oz (4 g) each for the skulls. To form the bones, roll each ¾-oz (20-g) portion of dough into a strip, slightly pressing as you roll up and down to make thick and thin segments.

Place the proofed dough balls on your prepared sheets, leaving sufficient space between them. Brush each with some of the clarified butter, then arrange 2 bone-shaped strips in a cross on top, and place one of the skull dough balls in the center, pressing gently to secure it. Brush with more clarified butter, then let rest for 10–15 minutes.

Preheat the oven to 350°F (180°C/Gas Mark 4), and bake for 20–25 minutes, until golden brown. Let cool.

To decorate: Brush each pan de muerto with the remaining melted clarified butter and dust generously with the sugar.

BONFIRE NIGHT

Originally known as Guy Fawkes night, this holiday marks the failure of the so-called "gunpowder plot" of 1605. The plot, organized by several Catholic dissidents and spearheaded by York-born Guy Fawkes, sought to blow up Parliament and kill King James I, in an attempt to bring a Catholic monarch back onto the English throne.

The first observance of this day was held exactly a year after the plot was foiled, on November 5, 1606. Over time it became commonplace to build bonfires, and after crafting elaborate straw effigies of Fawkes, to cast them into the fire on this crisp November evening. Over time, however, the holiday has lost much of its original symbolism and developed something of a fall (autumnal) festival atmosphere, with fires, fireworks, and warming foods enjoyed all evening—and a spirit of mischief and merriment.

PARKIN

England

p. 210

Submitted by Sarah Lemanski

Serves 9
Prep time: 15–20 minutes, plus overnight soaking time
Cook time: 30–40 minutes

- 1 cup (4¼ oz/125 g) medium-cut oatmeal
- ½ cup (4 fl oz/120 ml) buttermilk (or milk)
- ¾ cup (3½ oz/100 g) all-purpose (plain) flour
- ½ cup (2¾ oz/75 g) whole wheat flour
- 2 teaspoons baking powder
- ½ teaspoon baking soda (bicarbonate of soda)
- scant 1 teaspoon sea salt
- 1 tablespoon ground ginger
- ½ teaspoon apple pie spice
- ¼ teaspoon ground nutmeg
- ⅛ teaspoon freshly ground black pepper
- 1¾ sticks (7 oz/200 g) butter
- scant ½ cup (3½ oz/100 g) soft dark brown sugar
- generous ½ cup (6 oz/175 g) golden syrup (see note)
- 2 tablespoons black treacle (or molasses)
- 1 tablespoon grated fresh ginger
- 2 eggs

Parkin is a form of oatmeal gingerbread common to Yorkshire and other parts of northern England where oats historically formed a significant part of local agriculture and diet. It is a fall (autumnal) cake, traditionally baked for Bonfire Night (November 5). Parkin should be baked at least a few days in advance of serving and left covered in a cool place, so that it will soften and the crumb will become sticky and moreish.

Combine the oatmeal with the buttermilk in a bowl, cover with plastic wrap (clingfilm), and leave in the refrigerator overnight.

The next day, preheat the oven to 325°F (160°C/Gas Mark 3). Line an 8 × 8-inch (20 × 20 cm) baking pan with parchment paper and set aside.

In a medium bowl, combine both the flours with the baking powder, baking soda (bicarbonate of soda), sea salt, ground ginger, apple pie spice, nutmeg, and black pepper.

Place the butter, sugar, syrup, and treacle in a pan, set over low heat, and melt but make sure it does not boil. Remove the pan from the heat and let cool slightly. Add the fresh grated ginger to the melted ingredients, followed by the oatmeal buttermilk mixture. Pour the melted ingredients into the dry ingredients and mix to combine. Add the eggs and stir until incorporated. Pour the batter into the prepared pan and bake for 30–40 minutes until the cake is well risen, even in color, and a toothpick (cocktail stick) inserted in the center comes out clean.

Remove from the oven and let cool on a rack. Once completely cool, serve the cake or wrap well in aluminum foil and store in an airtight container for 2–3 days, when it will become stickier and more flavorful.

Note: If you cannot find golden syrup, use corn syrup or molasses as a substitution.

ST. MARTIN'S DAY

November 11 marks the feast day of St. Martin of Tours, a fourth-century Pannonian (modern-day Hungary) of the Roman Empire, who left military service to join the faith, later rising to the bishopdom of Tours. Known for his generosity, he is famously said to have cut a cloak he was wearing in half to share with a beggar clad only in rags in winter. Fragments of the same cloak were housed in a shrine called a *capella*, which later gave its name to the English words chapel and chaplain. Historically, his feast day has been especially popular in German-speaking regions of Europe, although Martinmas was widely celebrated throughout England and Scotland until the time of the Reformation.

Left: *Parkin*, Bonfire Night (page 209)

ST. MARTIN'S CROISSANTS

Poland

p. 214

Submitted by Marta Orlikowska

Makes 26
Prep time: 1 hour, plus chilling, proofing, and cooling times
Cook time: 1 hour

For the poppy seed paste:
- 3⅓ cups (1 lb 2 oz/500 g) white poppy seeds
- 4¼ cups (34 fl oz/1 liter) boiling water
- 6 tablespoons (3 oz/85 g) butter
- 2 cups (14 oz/400 g) granulated sugar
- ¾ cup (3½ oz/100 g) raisins, finely chopped
- ⅔ cup (3½ oz/100 g) blanched almonds, finely chopped
- 1½ oz (40 g) candied orange peel, finely chopped
- 3½ cups (7 oz/200 g) sponge cake crumbs
- 3 eggs
- ½ teaspoon almond extract

For the dough:
- ¾ oz (20 g) fresh yeast
- scant ⅔ cup (4¼ oz/120 g) superfine (caster) sugar
- 8 cups (2 lb 4 oz/1 kg) all-purpose (plain) flour, plus extra for dusting
- 1⅔ cups (14 fl oz/400 ml) milk, warmed
- 2 eggs, plus 1 egg yolk at room temperature
- ⅓ teaspoon salt
- scant 2 cups (15 oz/420 g) butter, 8½ tablespoons (4¼ oz/120 g) melted, 1⅓ cups (10½ oz/300 g) frozen
- neutral oil, for greasing

***Rogal świętomarciński*—St. Martin's Croissant—is a sweet pastry from Poznań, in western-central Poland, where it originated as early as the 1860s.**

One legend attributes its popularity to the encouragement of a local priest in a small parish around the time of the Feast of St. Martin (also called Martinmas, held on November 11) in 1891. Allegedly, this priest passionately encouraged his congregation to follow the example of St. Martin, known for his charity, inspiring one pious parishioner, confectioner Jozef Melzer, to bake this delicious pastry with a sweet poppy seed filling, and to offer it to the poor for free.

The tradition surrounding its annual baking (and gifting), which began toward the end of the 1800s, was threatened by the economic hardships faced across Poland in the early twentieth century. Thankfully, the St. Martin's Croissant was not only saved from obscurity, but in 2008 was also recognized by the European Union as having a protected designation of origin (PDO). This recipe, inspired by the original, comes from Marta Orlikowska, whose father, also named Martin, would always bring them home, still warm, on St. Martin's Day.

To make the poppy seed paste: Rinse the white poppy seeds, then place in a pan and add the boiling water. Cover with a lid and cook over very low heat for 30 minutes. Drain the cooked poppy seeds in a large, thick strainer or in a sieve lined with gauze. Let cool, then grind the cooled poppy seeds 3 times in a spice grinder on the finest setting.

In a separate pot, melt the butter with the sugar. Add the raisins, blanched almonds, and candied orange peel. Pan-fry together over low heat for 2–3 minutes. Add the ground poppy seeds and pan-fry for another 10 minutes, stirring occasionally. Remove from the heat and set aside to cool. Add the crumbled sponge cake to the cooled mixture. Whisk in one egg at a time, mixing the mixture thoroughly between additions. At the very end, add the almond extract, then set aside in the refrigerator.

To make the dough: In a bowl, combine the yeast, 2 tablespoons of the sugar, 3 tablespoons of the flour, and a generous ⅓ cup (3½ fl oz/100 ml) of the warmed milk, then set aside for 5–10 minutes, until frothy.

In a separate bowl, beat the eggs and yolk with the remaining sugar until white and fluffy.

In a large bowl, combine the remaining flour with the salt. Add the remaining warm milk. Add the yeast mixture, melted and cooled butter, and beaten egg mixture. Mix together with a wooden spoon or rubber spatula. Transfer to the bowl of a stand mixer fitted with the dough hook and knead for at least 5 minutes until uniform, elastic, and smooth. Alternatively, knead the dough by hand. Transfer the dough to an oiled bowl, cover with plastic wrap (clingfilm), and proof for 30 minutes.

Coarsely grate the frozen butter and set aside. Turn the dough out onto a lightly floured counter. Punch down the dough and roll it out into the shape of a large rectangle. Spread the grated butter evenly over two-thirds of the rolled-out dough. Fold the third of the dough without butter into the middle, then fold the remaining third (with butter) into the center as well to form an envelope. Press the whole thing down slightly with your hands, then roll it out again into the shape of a smaller

For the icing:
- 1¾ cups (7 oz/200 g) confectioners' (icing) sugar
- 4½ tablespoons hot water (or warm milk)
- ⅔ cup (2¾ oz/80 g) almonds, chopped

rectangle. Repeat the folding process, then place the dough in a bowl, cover with plastic wrap, and refrigerate for 30 minutes. Repeat the rolling, folding, and refrigerating twice more.

Line 2 baking sheets with parchment paper and set aside.

Remove the dough from the refrigerator, then roll it out into a rectangle about ¼ inch (5 mm) thick. For ease, you can divide the dough into 2 parts: Chill one in the refrigerator, and roll the other out into a rectangle. Cut out long triangles (around 4 inches/10 cm at the base, and 10–12 inches/25–30 cm long; I cut out 13 triangles from 1 piece).

Transfer the poppy seed paste to a pastry (piping) bag with a ⅝-inch (1.5-cm) diameter nozzle. Squeeze out the poppy seed paste in 2 strips along the length of the triangles, thicker at the wider bottom, while thinner and connecting to each other at the thin tip of the triangle. Fold the bottom of the triangle in about 1¼ inches (3 cm), then make a cut in the center of the folded dough between the strips of poppy seed mixture. Split the dough slightly and bend to the sides. Continue to roll the croissant, then curve the ends inward to create a slight crescent shape. Repeat until you have used all the dough.

Place the croissants on the prepared baking sheet, allowing sufficient space between them. Cover with plastic wrap and proof for 30 minutes.

Meanwhile, preheat the oven to 350°F (180°C/Gas Mark 4). Bake the croissants on the middle rack for 20 minutes, or until risen and nicely browned.

If you split the dough into 2 parts, while the first batch of croissants is baking, prepare the second round from the second half of the dough. Remove from the oven and let cool.

To make the icing: Combine the confectioners' (icing) sugar in a bowl with the hot water or milk. While still hot, put the croissants on a wire rack, then glaze with the icing and sprinkle with chopped nuts.

Note: The dough can be prepared in the morning, and the croissants can be baked in the afternoon. If preparing the dough in the evening, it can be chilled in a well-wrapped dish (so that it does not dry out) in the refrigerator overnight. In the morning, roll, cut, shape, and bake the croissants. The filling can also be stored in the refrigerator in this way for 3–4 days.

THANKSGIVING

Thanksgiving is a fall (autumn) harvest holiday celebrated across North America: in Canada on the second Monday of October and in the United States on the fourth Thursday of November. Both versions are rooted in the same Anglo-Protestant tradition of celebrating "days of thanksgiving," a post-Reformation British custom of marking triumph over adversity through a day of prayer and giving of thanks.

The earliest notions of a Canadian Thanksgiving stem from Martin Frobisher's 1578 Arctic expedition, and his safe passage through to North America, while American Thanksgiving is rooted in a 1621 feast shared by English settlers and Indigenous Wampanoag, after a particularly successful harvest. Both origin stories, however, are largely symbolic—if not outright mythologized—in significance and serve more as a foundation for the modern holiday than as a reflection of what is being celebrated.

Today, in both countries, Thanksgiving is defined by the gathering of friends and family for a veritable feast and expressions of gratitude. The meal itself is a blend of Anglo-American culinary traditions, featuring many dishes derived from foods of the New World (western hemisphere), like pumpkins and sweet potatoes, as well as rich traditions from the Old World (eastern hemisphere)—roast poultry, tart jellies, and fruit pies.

Left: *St. Martin's Croissants*, St. Martin's Day (page 212)

BOURBON PECAN PIE

United States

p. 218

Submitted by Camille Cogswell

Serves 8–12
Prep time: 1 hour, plus overnight resting and chilling times
Cook time: 1 hour 15 minutes–1 hour 50 minutes

For the dough:
- 1½ cups (6½ oz/185 g) all-purpose (plain) flour, plus extra for dusting
- 1 tablespoon granulated sugar
- ¾ teaspoon kosher salt
- 10 tablespoons (5 oz/140 g) butter, well chilled and cubed
- 3–4 tablespoons ice-cold water

For the filling:
- 1 cup (8 fl oz/250 ml) dark corn syrup (see note)
- 1 cup (9 oz/225 g) soft brown sugar
- ½ teaspoon kosher salt
- 6 tablespoons (3 oz/85 g) butter
- 2 tablespoons bourbon whiskey
- 1 teaspoon vanilla extract
- 3 eggs
- 2 cups (7 oz/200 g) pecan halves
- whipped cream, to serve (optional)

This sweet, nutty, custardy pie is a staple of the American holiday table. While it originated at least as early as the late nineteenth century (as seen in an 1886 edition of *Harper's Bazaar*), it gained popularity in the south, Texas especially, before the end of the century. In the early 1900s, common recipes specified Karo brand corn syrup, and later, Karo embraced this by putting a standardized recipe for pecan pie on the back of their syrup bottles. The popularity of the pie skyrocketed.

While the pecan pie is perhaps rooted in earlier traditions of sugar or syrup-based custard pies, like the British treacle tart, it is distinctly American. Pecans are themselves indigenous to North America, and the common incorporation of bourbon—a veritable Southern export—underscores its regional affiliation.

While pecan pies are today popular enough to be baked and eaten all year round, they are an emblematic feature of the Thanksgiving spread, as well as Christmas dessert tables.

To make the dough: In the bowl of a food processor, combine two-thirds of the flour with the sugar, salt, and cold butter cubes. Pulse until the mixture is the size of fine pebbles. Transfer this mixture into a bowl and toss in the remaining flour by hand to incorporate. Add 2 tablespoons of the cold water and gently and evenly distribute the liquid with a claw-like hand and lightly rubbing the mixture between your fingers to break up clumps. Do not mix or knead the mixture (see note). Incorporate 1 tablespoon of water at a time until there are no more clumps: the mixture should look like a crumble but when you take a spoonful of dough and squeeze it in your palm, it should hold its shape. Compress the dough between your hands in the bowl to form a ball, then flatten that into a disk about 1 inch (2.5 cm) thick, pressing closed any cracks on the sides. Wrap in plastic wrap (clingfilm) and refrigerate for at least 6 hours, preferably overnight.

Unwrap the dough and place onto a lightly floured work counter. Roll out the dough with a rolling pin to a circle just under ¼-inch (6-mm) thick, and 10½-inch (29-cm) in diameter. If any cracks appear while rolling, just press them closed with your fingertips.

Line a 9½-inch (24-cm) pie pan with the dough, pressing it well into the bottom and corners. Crimp the edges as desired. Prick the bottom of the crust with a fork about a dozen times, and chill in the refrigerator or freezer for at least 2 hours, preferably overnight.

Preheat the oven to 350°F (180°C/Gas Mark 4).

To blind bake your pie shell: Take a piece of foil slightly larger than the pie pan and spray one side with baking spray, then press the greasy side down into the bottom and sides of the crust, with 2 inches (5 cm) of overhang around the whole pan. Curl the overhanging foil over the edges of the pan to fully cover the crust. Fill the pan at least halfway with dry beans, rice, or pie weights. Put the pan on a baking sheet in the center rack of the oven and bake for 30–40 minutes, rotating halfway through, until the edges start to look dry and mostly cooked.

Carefully remove the foil and weights. If the crust has puffed up in the center, prick it with a fork a couple of times. Return to the oven and continue baking for 5–10 minutes more, until the crust loses its wet sheen and is just barely starting to take on a golden color. If the crust is still a little puffy in the center, put a small flat plate on top of it for a couple of minutes while it's still hot out of the oven to flatten it. Let cool completely.

Meanwhile, to make the filling: In a medium mixing bowl, combine the corn syrup, brown sugar, and salt. Set aside.

In a small pan over medium heat, melt the butter, stirring occasionally, until it becomes frothy and you can see the milk solids turning golden brown. Immediately pour the brown butter into the mixing bowl, on top of the sugars. Whisk to combine. Add the bourbon, vanilla, and eggs to the bowl and whisk together well until smooth and homogenous. Spread the pecan halves evenly on the bottom of the baked pie shell. Pour the rest of the mixture on top to completely cover the pecans.

Place the pie pan on a baking sheet and bake in the center of the oven for 45–60 minutes, rotating the sheet halfway through baking, until the filling has puffed up, is set on the edges, and still wobbles slightly in the center when you nudge the tray.

Remove from the oven and let cool completely. Serve alone or with whipped cream.

Note: If you can't find dark corn syrup, use light corn syrup and substitute 2 tablespoons of the light corn syrup with molasses.

When adding the water to the dough, imagine that you are tossing a salad. The less you "work" your dough, the less your chances of crust shrinkage later.

APPLE PIE

United States

Submitted by Carri Thurman

Makes 1 × 9-inch (23-cm) pie
Prep time: 30 minutes, plus chilling time
Cook time: 50 minutes–1 hour

For the butter crust:
- 1¾ cups (8 oz/225 g) all-purpose (plain) flour, plus extra for dusting
- 1 stick (4 oz/115 g) butter, cold and cubed
- 2 tablespoons granulated sugar
- ½ teaspoon salt
- scant ½ cup (3½ fl oz/105 ml) cold water, with a splash of white vinegar

For the filling:
- 4 Granny Smith apples, peeled, cored, and sliced ½ inch (12 mm) thick
- ⅓ cup (3 oz/85 g) soft brown sugar
- 3 tablespoons all-purpose (plain) flour
- 1 teaspoon ground cinnamon
- 3½ tablespoons (2 oz/55 g) butter, melted

To finish:
- 1 egg, for egg wash
- 2 tablespoons turbinado (demerara) sugar, for sprinkling
- vanilla ice cream, to serve

Though the apple pie has its roots in medieval Europe, where it is still enjoyed, in modern times it has emerged as a symbol of American culinary quintessence, and a staple of the American holiday table, especially at Thanksgiving. Apples are one of the fall (autumn) fruits that hold up well in storage through the fall and winter, making them a favorite ingredient to use for holiday baking.

To make the butter crust: In the bowl of a food processor, combine the flour, butter, granulated sugar, and salt. Pulse until the butter is incorporated into the flour, about 4 times. This can also be done by hand by grating the cold butter into the dry ingredients and rubbing the butter into the flour mixture until your butter is as fine as bread crumbs. Transfer the dough to a bowl and add the water and vinegar mixture, folding it in until it just comes together in a ball. Divide the dough into 2 equal pieces and flatten into disks. Wrap securely in plastic wrap (clingfilm) and chill thoroughly for at least 1 hour. The dough can be stored for 1 week in the refrigerator or 1 month in the freezer.

Place 1 disk of dough on a lightly floured counter and sprinkle with flour. Roll out to ⅛ inch (3 mm) thickness and use it to line a 9-inch (23-cm) pie pan.

To make the filling: In a large bowl, combine the sliced apples with the brown sugar, flour, and cinnamon. Toss until the apples are well coated. Drizzle in the melted butter and fold together until everything is combined. Transfer the apple mixture into the pie crust.

Roll out the second disk of dough to ⅛ inch (3 mm) thickness, and use it to top the pie. Pinch the edges of the crust together to seal and cut a few small vents in the top.

Preheat the oven to 350°F (180°C/Gas Mark 4). Line a baking sheet with parchment paper.

To finish: Make the egg wash by beating together the egg with equal parts water. Brush over the top of the pie crust, then sprinkle with the turbinado (demerara) sugar. Place the pie pan on the prepared sheet and bake for 50 minutes, or until golden and bubbly. Let cool before serving with vanilla ice cream.

Left: *Bourbon Pecan Pie*, Thanksgiving (page 216)

PUMPKIN PIE

United States and Canada

Submitted by Carri Thurman

Makes 1 × 9-inch (23-cm) pie
Prep time: 30 minutes
Cook time: 1 hour 50 minutes

- 1 small sugar pumpkin or large butternut squash
- 2 eggs
- ½ cup (4 oz/115 g) soft brown sugar
- 1 cup (8 fl oz/250 ml) heavy (double) cream
- ½ teaspoon salt
- 1 teaspoon ground cinnamon
- 1 teaspoon ground ginger
- ¼ teaspoon ground cloves
- ⅛ teaspoon freshly ground black pepper
- 1 x butter crust dough disk (page 219)
- all-purpose (plain) flour, for dusting
- sweetened whipped cream, to serve

Sweet pies made using pumpkin have been popular since the introduction of the squash (to Europe) in the sixteenth century. Early versions called for layers of sliced pumpkin and a mix of dried fruit and spices, and it was these versions that were popular in England and were even made in the colonies before independence.

This distinctly North American pie, made with a filling more akin to a spiced pumpkin custard, was included in the publication of *American Cookery*, one of the first American cookbooks, in 1796, and its popularity grew exponentially over the coming decades.

Today, pumpkin pie is seen as one of the hallmarks of fall (autumnal) celebrations, especially Thanksgiving (both American and Canadian), which has its origins in harvest festivals celebrated by some of the first pilgrims to the continent in the early 1600s.

Preheat the oven to 350°F (180°C/Gas Mark 4). Line 2 baking sheets with parchment paper.

Cut the pumpkin in half and place it face down on one of the prepared baking sheets. Roast for 1 hour, or until soft. Remove from the oven, leaving the oven on, and let cool. Scoop out the seeds and discard. Scoop out the flesh and set aside, discarding the skin. You should have about 1 lb (450 g) of roasted pumpkin flesh.

In the bowl of a food processor or blender, combine the roasted pumpkin with all the other ingredients, except the dough. Blend until smooth.

Place the disk of dough on a lightly floured counter and sprinkle with flour. Roll out to ⅛ inch (3 mm) thickness and use it to line a 9-inch (23-cm) pie pan. Place the pan on the prepared baking sheet and pour in the filling. Bake for 40–50 minutes, turning once halfway through to ensure even baking. Let cool thoroughly before slicing. Serve with sweetened whipped cream.

DECEMBER

12

DECEMBER

FEAST OF SINTERKLAAS

Nicholas of Myra was a third-century Greek-born bishop whose numerous miraculous deeds earned him sainthood, as well as a large worshipful following in the centuries after his death in 343 AD. Over time, Saint Nicholas became especially well known for legends of his selfless generosity and acts of secret gift-giving, and by the twelfth century, nuns in France had begun to celebrate his feast day with gift-giving, especially to children in need. For centuries, his feast day has been a major holiday in many parts of Europe, especially the Netherlands and Belgium, where parades, special foods, traditional bakes, and of course gift exchanges, are a big part of the day. The stories of Saint Nicholas (*Sinterklaas* in Dutch) then traveled with Dutch immigrants to the United States, where they eventually became the foundation for the modern holiday figure of Santa Claus.

SPECULAAS

Belgium and The Netherlands

Submitted by Barbara Serulus

Makes 35–40
Prep time: 20 minutes, plus resting time
Cook time: 15–20 minutes

- 1¾ sticks (7 oz/200 g) butter, softened
- 1¼ cups (8 oz/225 g) soft brown sugar
- pinch of salt
- zest of ½ lemon
- 1⅔ cups (7oz/200 g) all-purpose (plain) flour
- 1⅔ cups (7oz/200 g) white buckwheat flour
- 1 teaspoon baking powder
- 3 tablespoons speculaas spices (see notes)
- 3½ tablespoons milk

In the Low Countries (Belgium and The Netherlands), *Sinterklaas* (Saint Nicholas Day), held every year on December 6, is a hugely popular part of the holiday season. On the evening of December 5, kids leave their shoes by the door or fireplace, along with a little gift for *Sinterklaas* or his helpers. *Sinterklaas* is said to arrive in the night, and tucks gifts and especially candies (chocolates, marzipan, mandarins, and of course, speculaas cookies) into the shoes.

The speculaas itself is traditionally made using a distinct spice mixture (so ubiquitous as to be widely available premixed), as well as a specific kind of brown sugar common to Belgium, called *kandij cassonade*, which is a more-or-less caramelized white sugar. The cookies can be quite large, and baked in a wooden mold (said to be the origin of the name, which is believed to derive from the Latin *speculum* or "mirror") as in a traditional setting, but is typically baked much smaller for home kitchens. Recipes for speculaas vary regionally, from thin and crispy to thicker and softer versions, but the flavors remain the same.

In a large mixing bowl, beat together the butter, sugar, salt, and lemon zest until light and fluffy, about 2 minutes. Add the flour, buckwheat flour, baking powder, and speculaas spices, and stir with a wooden spoon. Mix in the milk until the dough comes together. Shape the dough into two flat disks and wrap them in plastic wrap (clingfilm). Let them rest in the refrigerator for at least 1 hour.

Preheat the oven to 350°F (180°C/Gas Mark 4). Line a baking sheet with parchment paper and set aside.

Transfer the dough to a lightly floured counter and roll out to about ¼ inch (5 mm) thick. Cut out shapes with your choice of cookie cutters and place on the lined baking sheet. You don't need to leave much space in between, as they won't spread much. Gather any scraps into a ball and repeat until all the dough is used. Do the same with the second disk.

Bake for 15–20 minutes, until firm around the edges, then transfer to a wire rack to cool. They will keep for at least a week stored in an airtight container.

Notes: White buckwheat flour is used here. There is also a darker whole wheat (wholemeal) version, but that's not what we want for this recipe.

If you don't have a ready-made speculaas spice mix, you can make your own blend with 8 teaspoons of ground cinnamon, 2 teaspoons each of ground nutmeg and ground ginger, and 1 teaspoon each of ground cloves, ground white pepper, and ground cardamom.

ST. LUCIA'S DAY

St. Lucia's Day is a festival of lights celebrated across Scandinavia on December 13. While this holiday technically commemorates the martyrdom of the fourth-century figure Lucia of Syracuse, it has become better known as a celebration of light in the darkest time of the year. In much of Scandinavia, especially Sweden, young girls dress in robes of white, wearing wreaths that feature candles or electric lights. There are processions and songs, like "Sankta Lucia," as well as a great deal of baking, much of which centers around the use of saffron for flavor and color, on account of the flame-like glow it provides to pastries and buns.

LUCIA BUNS

Sweden

Submitted by Alice Mahon

Serves 8–10
Prep time: 40 minutes, plus overnight chilling and proofing times
Cook time: 20 minutes

For the water roux (tangzhong):
scant ½ cup (1¾ oz/50 g) all-purpose (plain) flour

For the dough:
½ teaspoon saffron strands, crushed
1 tablespoon hot water
⅞ cup (7 fl oz/200 ml) milk
6 tablespoons granulated sugar
1 oz (30 g) fresh yeast
3½ cups (1 lb/450 g) strong white bread flour, plus extra for dusting
1 teaspoon salt
7½ tablespoons (3¾ oz/110 g) butter, at room temperature
1 egg, beaten, for egg wash
8–10 raisins, to decorate

In Scandinavia, the festival of Saint Lucia is a beloved tradition that brings light to the dark winter days leading up to Christmas. Celebrated on December 13, Saint Lucia is seen as a bearer of hope and warmth during the year's longest nights. A highlight of the celebration is the Lucia procession, where Saint Lucia, wearing a glowing crown of candles, leads a group of attendants dressed all in white in a moving display of light and song.

No Saint Lucia celebration is complete without Lucia buns (*lussekatter*)—soft, saffron-scented yeasted buns shaped into elegant "S" spirals and decorated with raisins. There are many different beliefs about the origins of these festive treats. Some believe their golden color symbolizes light conquering darkness, while the distinctive shape represents an ancient sun symbol. Another theory links them to the seventeenth-century German tradition of *Döfvelskatt*, or "devil's cat," where a Christ-like child rewarded good children with sweet buns, while the devil, appearing as a cat, visited the naughty ones. The bright yellow hue of the buns was thought to ward off evil, making these festive treats not just delicious but also rich in tradition and meaning.

To make the water roux: In a pan over medium–high heat, bring a generous ⅓ cup (3½ fl oz/100 ml) of water to a boil. Remove from the heat and quickly whisk in the flour until a smooth paste forms. Transfer to a bowl, cover with plastic wrap (clingfilm), ensuring that the plastic wrap is in direct contact with the surface of the roux to prevent a skin from forming, and let cool to room temperature. Once cooled, refrigerate until completely chilled, ideally overnight.

To make the dough: Add the saffron to a small bowl and add the hot water. Let sit for 3–5 minutes to steep, until the liquid turns a dark red. Let cool.

In the bowl of a stand mixer fitted with the dough hook attachment, combine the milk, sugar, yeast, and 5½ oz (150 g) water roux, and mix for 1 minute until well combined. Add the flour, salt, saffron water, and butter, then knead on medium–high speed for 10–15 minutes until the dough becomes smooth and elastic.

Alternatively, to mix by hand: In a large mixing bowl, whisk together the milk, sugar, yeast, and water roux until fully combined. Add the flour, butter, saffron, and salt, then mix by hand until a rough dough forms. Transfer the dough to a lightly floured counter and knead for 8–10 minutes until smooth and elastic.

Line a baking sheet with parchment paper and set aside. Gently punch down the dough, then turn it out onto a lightly floured counter and divide into 3½-oz (100-g) pieces. Roll each piece into a smooth, even strand about 4 inches (10 cm) long. Once all the pieces are rolled out, return to the first one and curl both ends in opposite directions toward the center, creating a tight "S" shape. Repeat with the remaining pieces.

Place the shaped buns on the prepared baking sheet, leaving about ¾ inch (2 cm) of space between each (use 2 sheets if needed). Cover them loosely with plastic wrap or a clean dish (tea) towel and let them proof in a warm place for approximately 1 hour, until doubled in size and light to the touch.

Preheat the oven to 350°F (180°C/Gas Mark 4). Once risen, brush the buns with the egg wash and press a raisin into the center of each swirl. Bake for 12–15 minutes, or until they turn lightly golden.

Remove from the oven and let cool before serving.

PIG SLAUGHTER

Until the advent of canned foods, frozen goods, and factory farms, common folk would have had little access to meat throughout the year except on special occasions like feast days or holidays. In the approach to winter, as resources to feed livestock dwindled, families would slaughter some of their animals to provide for their own home by salting, smoking, or otherwise preserving meat from the butchered animal, as well as storing its fat for cooking.

In Hungary, the ritual pig slaughter, called *disznótor*, would typically happen around Christmas, and involve an elaborate ceremony around the butchering of the animal, incorporating elements of folk belief, *pálinka*-drinking, and sausage-making. In addition to using the lard to cook savory dishes, it could also be incorporated into the baking of pastries or cakes. And although it might not be as common as it once was, in rural communities, it still retains some of its festive charm.

HÁJAS TÉSZTA

Hungary

p. 232

Submitted by Lilla Szőcs

Serves 25
Prep time: 30 minutes, plus chilling and resting times
Cook time: 30 minutes

- 2⅓ cups (14 oz/400 g) pork leaf lard, cleaned and ground
- 1 tablespoon white vinegar
- 5⅔ cups (1 lb 9 oz/700 g) all-purpose (plain) flour, plus extra for dusting
- generous ⅓ cup (3½ fl oz/100 ml) white wine
- generous ⅓ cup (3½ fl oz/100 ml) sparkling water
- 3 tablespoons tejföl (full-fat soured cream)
- 2 eggs
- pinch each of granulated sugar and salt
- 2 cups (1 lb 2oz/500 g) thick plum jam
- confectioners' (icing) sugar, for dusting

***Hájas tészta* is a yeasted or puff pastry-like dough made using pork leaf lard—the soft fat from the pig's abdominal cavity. It is then filled with various flavorings, most commonly plum jam. The result is a layered, tender, sweet-and-savory pastry that is crisp on the outside and soft on the inside.**

***Disznótor* (the "funeral of the pig") is a longstanding agricultural tradition in Hungary marking the slaughter of a pig before Christmas time. Once the pig is dispatched, the cooking (and drinking) begins—every part of the animal is put to use, and the resulting dishes are preserved to stock the pantry for the winter. It was a task that required many folks for the cooking that followed. If a household could afford to do it twice, they were considered well-to-do.**

The pork fat obtained was later used for baking pastries, as it was cheaper and more readily available than butter. The dishes prepared in this way, like lard pastry, could even be served on New Year's Eve.

In a bowl, combine the pork leaf lard with the vinegar and let sit.

In a large bowl, combine the flour, white wine, sparkling water, tejföl, eggs, sugar, and salt. Knead until the dough comes together. Turn out the dough onto a counter and roll out into a rectangle about the size of a baking sheet (roughly 16 × 12 inches/ 40 × 30 cm), then spread the soaked pork fat evenly over the surface.

Divide the dough into thirds horizontally. Fold one-third into the center, then fold the remaining third over that, as though folding a letter. Then rotate and fold it in half to create a square. Wrap the dough in plastic wrap (clingfilm) and chill it in the refrigerator for 30–40 minutes. Repeat this rolling, folding, and chilling process twice more.

Line a baking sheet with parchment paper and set aside.

Remove the dough from the refrigerator and turn it out onto a lightly floured counter. Roll out into a rectangle about ¼ inch (5 mm) thick. Cut it into smaller rectangles, approximately 3¼ × 2½ inches (8 × 6 cm).

Place about 1 tablespoon of thick plum jam in the center of each, then either fold them in half or bring the 2 long edges together over the top and press to seal. Place on the prepared baking sheet, then let rest for 30 minutes.

Preheat the oven to 375°F (190°C/Gas Mark 5). Bake for 30 minutes, then remove from the oven, dust with confectioners' (icing) sugar, and serve.

CHRISTMAS

Christmas, which takes place on December 25 (or January 7 in some Orthodox traditions), marks the birth of Jesus Christ, and is perhaps the most widely celebrated winter holiday in the world. The Christmas "season" begins for many people with the start of Advent (from the Latin *adventus,* meaning "arrival") on the fourth Sunday prior to the holiday, and it is in this period that people begin to decorate their homes for the occasion. For many, the season is defined by elaborate decorations and homeliness: nativity scenes portraying Christ's birth in a manger, colorful electric lights, or fir trees wreathed in tinsel and hanging ornaments.

While the modern holiday is undeniably Christian in nature, much of the symbolism that underlies it is rooted in pre-Christian tradition: Candles and fires, evergreen trees and greenery, and perhaps even the Christmas ham, may all derive from the ancient winter solstice holiday known as yule. This Germanic holiday, once widely celebrated throughout, was effectively merged with Christmas after the conversion of its pagan population in the tenth century, and throughout Scandinavia that is still apparent in the holiday's name: *Jul*. Outside of Scandinavia, the term "yule" is also sometimes a stand-in for Christmas, as in the case of the yule log burning on an open fire—another tradition derived from ancient pagan roots.

In many countries, the holiday's festivities properly commence on Christmas Eve (December 24 or January 6), but in some cultures, like throughout much of Central and Eastern Europe, it is Christmas Eve that is the main celebration and day of gift-giving. Regardless, both December 24 and 25 are filled with gatherings of family and friends, the exchange of presents, and hearty festive meals. Many traditional Christmas recipes, bakes especially, include ingredients that were historically considered rare or expensive: sweet spices, butter, dried fruits, and sugar. It's no surprise, then, that there are so many baking traditions incorporating all of these ingredients in abundance.

Left: *Hájas Tészta*, Pig Slaughter (page 231)

GINGERBREAD HOUSE

Germany and United States

Submitted by Shaina Loew-Banayan

Serves 12
Prep time: 2–5 hours, depending on the complexity of the structure
Cook time: 15–20 minutes

For the dough:
4 sticks (1 lb/450 g) butter, at room temperature
2 cups (1 lb/450 g) soft light brown sugar
3 eggs
scant ½ cup (6 oz/180 g) molasses
1½ teaspoons salt
10 cups (2 lb 12 oz/1.25 kg) all-purpose (plain) flour
1½ teaspoons baking soda (bicarbonate of soda)
4 tablespoons ground ginger
4 teaspoons ground allspice
4 teaspoons ground cinnamon
1 tablespoon ground nutmeg
1 tablespoon ground black pepper

For the icing:
4 egg whites
pinch of salt
1 teaspoon cream of tartar
4 cups (1 lb/450 g) confectioners' (icing) sugar
food coloring (optional)

Gingerbread has been popular in Europe since medieval times—especially in Britain and across Central and northern Europe. Large elaborate molds were made for shaping the dough into decorative cookies depicting figures, religious scenes, or animals.

Gingerbread houses, popularized in Germany following the publication of *Hansel and Gretel* in 1812, were brought to the United States through waves of German immigrants.

This recipe comes from chef Shaina Loew-Banayan, whose family made a gingerbread house every year around Christmas. Each year they chose a different iconic structure to build: from Versailles to the Parthenon, and even a giant ferry in honor of the one they'd take to visit their grandmother.

Much of the enjoyment of the gingerbread house is in its making: it's less about aesthetic accuracy than it is about fun. The cookies can be made in advance so that the house-making becomes the main spectacle—and one for all ages.

To make the dough: In the bowl of a stand mixer fitted with the paddle attachment, cream together the butter and sugar on medium speed for about 2 minutes. Add the eggs and molasses and continue mixing for another minute. Add all the remaining ingredients at once, mixing on low to incorporate fully.

Divide the dough in half for ease of handling later on. Wrap each half in plastic wrap (clingfilm) and chill in the refrigerator for about 1 hour.

Preheat the oven to 350°F (180°C/Gas Mark 4). Line a baking sheet(s) with parchment paper and set aside.

Transfer the chilled dough to a work counter, and roll out to ¼ inch (5 mm) thickness. Cut out your desired shapes (see notes), then use a spatula to carefully transfer the shapes to your prepared baking sheet(s).

Bake for 15–20 minutes. They should be darker once baked and will firm up completely upon cooling. Let cool on a wire rack.

To make the icing: In the bowl of a stand mixer fitted with the whisk attachment, whisk the egg whites, salt, and cream of tartar until foamy. Add the sugar and beat until the volume increases 2 or 3 times. The icing should look thick and glossy.

If using the icing just for building, put it in a pastry (piping) bag. If you wish to decorate with it, thin it out with enough water to achieve your preferred consistency, adding food coloring if you wish to.

When the cookies are cool, decorate them as desired. If you are making a house, use your icing as mortar to glue first the sides and then the roof of the house together. Use piped icing to decorate the house or to glue on candy or other decorative items.

Notes: If making a gingerbread house, draw up some blueprints for your building. Make sure all measurements make sense. It is helpful to revisit high school geometry if you want to have a nice roof. And if you can't do math so well, you can later rely on icing to fill gaps. So double the amount of icing if you want to go really crazy with decorating.

CHRISTMAS CAKE

United Kingdom

Submitted by Neil Buttery

Serves 8
Prep time: 50 minutes, plus (3–4 weeks) maturing time
Cook time: 2–3 hours

The British Christmas cake is a dense and heavily spiced fruit cake that epitomizes the idea of turning your best and most luxurious ingredients into a showstopping dessert. The cake, which derives from Christmas pudding, and by extension, medieval sweet-and-savory "plum pottage," is filled with a cornucopia of dried fruit, nuts, and sweet spices. The mixture is then (traditionally) allowed to rest for days if not weeks and get a regular "feeding" of brandy, which deepens the flavor. A few days before serving, some people spread the top of the cake with a layer of apricot jam, and then the final coat, a layer of royal icing, is draped over the top. The icing, which will harden over a few days, is for some more about preservation—and can be broken off before eating if desired.

For the cake:
- generous 5 cups (2 lb/900 g) mixed dried fruit (such as currants, raisins, and golden raisins [sultanas])
- scant 1 cup (4¼ oz/125 g) whole roasted almonds, plus extra to decorate
- ¾ cup (4¼ oz/125 g) chopped candied mixed peel, plus extra to decorate
- ½ cup (4¼ oz/125 g) candied cherries, rinsed, plus extra to decorate
- 2⅓ cups plus 1 tablespoon (10½ oz/300 g) self-rising flour
- 1½ teaspoons mixed spice
- grated zest of 1 lemon
- 2¼ sticks (9 oz/250 g) salted butter, softened
- generous 1 cup (9 oz/250 g) soft dark brown sugar
- 1 teaspoon vanilla extract
- 1 tablespoon blackstrap molasses
- 6 eggs
- ½ cup (4 fl oz/120 ml) brandy, plus extra for feeding

For the royal icing:
- 3 egg whites
- 5 cups (1 lb 5 oz/600 g) confectioners' (icing) sugar, sifted
- 1 teaspoon glycerine
- 2 teaspoons lemon juice

Preheat the oven to 275°F (140°C/Gas Mark 1). Line an 8-inch (20-cm) round cake pan with parchment paper.

To make the cake: Put the dried fruit, almonds, candied mixed peel, and cherries into a large bowl and mix together. Sift in the flour, add the mixed spice and lemon zest, and stir through until everything is coated in the flour.

Put the butter and dark brown sugar into another large bowl and, using a wooden spoon, beat them together until they are pale and fluffy. Stir in the vanilla extract and molasses. Beat the eggs into the butter and sugar mixture, one at a time, then mix through well. Add the fruit and flour and mix together with enough brandy to slacken the mixture to a dropping consistency. Pour the batter into the prepared cake pan, shaping a small indent in the center so that when it bakes, it rises with a reasonably flat top. Bake in the oven for 2–3 hours, but check it after 2½ hours. If a skewer inserted into the center comes out clean, it's done. Let cool in the pan.

Keep the cake in an airtight container to mature for 3–4 weeks, "feeding" it every week by pouring 2–3 tablespoons brandy evenly across the cake.

To make the royal icing: Whisk the egg whites in a large bowl to soft peaks using electric beaters. Fold the sugar into the egg whites, a spoonful at a time. When all the sugar has been incorporated, stir in the glycerine and lemon juice and whisk for 10 minutes, or until the mixture becomes very stiff. The mixture is ready when it starts to hold its shape.

Cover the top of the cake with the royal icing using a palette knife dipped in hot water (or you could ice the top and sides). Smooth and neaten the icing, then leave for at least 3 days so that the royal icing can firm up. Decorate with cherries, almonds, and candied peel and serve in slices.

Variation: If desired, a classic combination is to layer jam and marzipan underneath the icing. Bring 2 tablespoons of apricot jam and 1 tablespoon of water to a boil in a small saucepan over medium heat. Strain it through a fine-mesh sieve into a small heatproof bowl, then brush it over the top and sides of the cake.

Using at least 1 lb 2 oz (500 g) ready-to-roll marzipan, roll out a third into a circle, about ⅛–⅙ inch (3–4 mm) thick. Use the cake pan as a guide for the size of the marzipan circle. Put the disk onto the top of the cake. Measure the height of the cake and roll out the remaining marzipan, cutting into rectangles of the appropriate width for the sides. Adhere the marzipan to the side of the cake, then let dry for 2 days before adding the icing to the cake.

BÛCHE DE NOËL

France

Submitted by Marie Kerkeling

Serves 8
Prep time: 45 minutes, plus chilling time
Cook time: 25 minutes

For the vanilla sponge cake:
butter, for greasing
4 extra-large eggs
½ cup (3½ oz/100 g) superfine (caster) sugar
⅔ cup (2¾ oz/80 g) all-purpose (plain) or T55 flour
pinch of fleur de sel
1 teaspoon vanilla extract
confectioners' (icing) sugar, for dusting

For the chocolate buttercream (crème au beurre):
2 cups (7 oz/200 g) superfine (caster) sugar
8 egg yolks
3½ sticks (14 oz/400 g) butter, softened
1 cup (4¼ oz/120 g) unsweetened cocoa powder

For decoration:
confectioners' (icing) sugar, for dusting (optional)
fresh raspberries

The *bûche de Noël* comes from the old European tradition of burning a large "Yule log" during winter solstice to bring back light and warmth. This was especially common in Celtic areas and southern France, including Provence. On Christmas Eve, families would burn the log together, placing wine, bread, salt, and candle wax around it. They would tell stories or play games to guess what the new year might bring.

As houses got smaller and fireplaces disappeared, folks started making cakes shaped like logs instead. This tradition really took off in nineteenth-century France, especially during the Belle Époque, when talented pastry chefs turned it into the dessert we know today. Today's versions still look like real logs, with chocolate bark and little meringue mushrooms. The *bûche de Noël* remains a favorite Christmas tradition, and now pastry chefs can get as creative as they want; the only rule is keeping that long log shape as a nod to the original custom.

Preheat the oven to 350°F (180°C/Gas Mark 4). Line a 16 × 12-inch (40 × 30-cm) baking pan with parchment paper and grease it lightly with butter. Set aside.

To make the vanilla sponge cake: In a medium bowl, beat together the eggs and sugar with an electric mixer for 5–6 minutes until thick, pale, and tripled in volume.

In a separate bowl, sift together the flour and salt. Gently fold this into the egg mixture along with the vanilla extract. Spread the batter evenly in the prepared pan. Bake for 12–15 minutes until golden and springy to the touch. Be careful not to overcook it, or it will crack when rolled.

Remove from the oven and immediately invert the cake onto a clean dish (tea) towel dusted with confectioners' (icing) sugar. Remove the parchment paper and allow the cake to cool.

Meanwhile, to make the chocolate buttercream: In a small pan, combine ⅔ cup (5½ fl oz/160 ml) of water with the superfine (caster) sugar. Warm over medium heat until the syrup reaches 244°F/118°C on a candy thermometer. At the same time, in the bowl of a stand mixer fitted with the whisk attachment, whisk the egg yolks.

When the syrup is ready, slowly pour the hot syrup into the yolks while whisking constantly. Continue whisking until the mixture cools to room temperature (otherwise, the butter will melt when added). Gradually beat in the softened butter until the mixture is smooth and fluffy. Sift the cocoa powder and gently fold it into the buttercream.

To assemble: Ensure the buttercream is at room temperature for easy spreading. If it seems too soft, chill briefly before using. Spread half of the chocolate buttercream evenly over the surface of the cake using an offset spatula.

Roll the cake tightly using the dish towel to help and chill in the refrigerator for at least 2 hours. Remove the cake from the refrigerator and place seam-side down on a serving plate. Trim both edges with a large sharp knife. Spread the remaining buttercream all over the cake. Use a fork or a pastry (piping) bag fitted with a fluted tip (douille cannelé) to create a bark-like texture. Dust with confectioners' sugar to resemble snow, if desired, and decorate with the berries. The cake can be made a day ahead and refrigerated.

MINCE PIES WITH BRANDY BUTTER

United Kingdom

Submitted by Sam Jacobson

Makes 12
Prep time: 1½ hours, plus chilling time
Cook time: 45 minutes

For the mincemeat filling:

- 3½ tablespoons (1¾ oz/50 g) butter
- scant ¼ cup (1¾ oz/50 g) soft brown sugar
- 3½ tablespoons brandy (or whisky)
- ½ cup (4¼ oz/125 g) currants
- scant 1 cup (4¼ oz/125 g) raisins
- ¾ cup (3½ oz/100 g) golden raisins (sultanas)
- ½ cup (3½ oz/100 g) candied peel
- 1 tablespoon grated fresh ginger
- ¼ teaspoon each ground nutmeg, cardamom, and cloves
- 2 pinches of salt
- grated zest and juice of 1 satsuma
- 1 Granny Smith apple (or other tart apple), diced very small or grated

For the shortbread:

- 2 sticks (8 oz/230 g) salted butter, softened
- ⅓ cup (2½ oz/70 g) superfine (caster) sugar, plus extra for sprinkling
- ⅓ cup (2½ oz/70 g) soft brown sugar
- 1 egg yolk
- 1 teaspoon vanilla extract
- generous 2 cups (9¼ oz/260 g) all-purpose (plain) flour

For the brandy butter:

- 1⅓ cups (10½ oz/300 g) butter
- 2¼ cups (9 oz/250 g) confectioners' (icing) sugar
- 1 tablespoon vanilla extract
- ⅓ cup (3½ fl oz/100 ml) brandy

In the United Kingdom, mince pies can be said to herald the arrival of the festive Christmas season. As the name suggests, these little pies were once made with ground (minced) meat, but in the early nineteenth century it became popular to prepare its sweetly spiced dried fruit filling weeks or months in advance in order to allow its flavors to deepen. As a result, folks began to leave out the beef entirely, which eventually became the prevailing decision. Serve with a good slather of brandy butter and a mug of mulled wine.

To make the mincemeat filling (ideally do this a couple of days ahead): In a pan over low heat, melt the butter with the brown sugar and brandy. Add the dried fruit, candied peel, ginger, spices, salt, and satsuma zest and juice. Cook for 15–20 minutes, stirring frequently, to allow the fruit to absorb the liquid. If you feel it needs more liquid, you can add a little more citrus juice (or brandy). Stir in the apple very close to the end, so that it maintains its integrity and does not break down.

Let the filling cool, then transfer to a bowl or jar, pressing down firmly to ensure that any remaining liquid is soaked up. Store in the refrigerator until needed.

To make the shortbread: In the bowl of a stand mixer fitted with the paddle attachment, beat the butter until well creamed. Add both sugars and continue to beat until well combined (30 seconds–1 minute). Stop the mixer and stir in the egg yolk and vanilla extract, pausing to scrape down the sides, then continue to mix until smooth. With the mixer off, add half the flour and mix for just a few seconds, then stop and add the rest, then mix just until combined.

Gather the dough into a ball, wrap in plastic wrap (clingfilm), and set aside in a cool place. If not using the same day, it may be refrigerated. If doing this, remove it from the refrigerator and allow it to come to room temperature before use.

Preheat the oven to 350°F (180°C/Gas Mark 4).

To assemble the pies: Prepare either 1-inch (2.5-cm) deep, 3-inch (7.5-cm) diameter disposable foil pie pans or a small muffin pan. On a smooth, well-floured counter, evenly roll out the dough to about ⅛ inch (3 mm) thickness. Using a 4-inch (10-cm) cookie cutter, cut out 12 circles. Using a bench scraper, gently lift these off the counter one at a time and place on top of the pans or muffin cups. Carefully press the dough circles into the pans—the sides should reach the top and if there are any cracks in the bottom, simply press down to spread the dough out a little and eliminate them or, if necessary, plug the crack with a tiny bit of extra dough.

Fill the pies to the top with the mincemeat filling. Then, using a 3-inch (7.5 cm) cutter, cut 12 circles of dough. Lift these up, lightly spray one side with water, and place sprayed side down on top of the pies, pressing down to seal. If there is enough dough leftover, cut out some stars or other decorations, spray with water and place on top, sprayed-side down. Spray the top of each pie lightly with water, and sprinkle generously with sugar. Bake for 20–25 minutes, or until the crust is golden brown.

Remove the pies from the oven and let cool slightly.

Meanwhile, to make the brandy butter: Beat the butter and sugar together with the vanilla extract until light and creamy. Add the brandy a little at a time and continue beating until fully incorporated and smooth. (Rest assured—you can add more brandy if needed!) Chill in the refrigerator until needed but bring to room temperature before serving to allow it to soften and spread well on the mince pies. To serve, spread the desired amount of brandy butter on top of the pies.

PIONONO

Argentina

Submitted by Julia Soria

Serves 8–10
Prep time: 25 minutes, plus resting time
Cook time: 20 minutes

- 1½ tablespoons (¾ oz/20 g) butter, melted, plus extra for greasing
- 4 eggs
- 6 tablespoons granulated sugar, plus extra for dusting
- 1 tablespoon vanilla extract
- ⅔ cup (2¾ oz/80 g) all-purpose (plain) flour
- filling of choice (see below)

The *pionono* is a cherished dessert in Argentina, especially during festive occasions like Christmas and New Year. This light, rolled sponge cake is a staple on the Argentine holiday dessert table, often accompanying other traditional desserts such as *pan dulce* and *turrón*. While clearly inspired by the European Swiss roll (jelly roll), the Argentine version has been adapted to local tastes, in both texture and flavor.

Given that the holidays fall during the height of summer in Argentina, fillings tend to be lighter and fresher than the rich creams or chocolate often found in European versions. Dulce de leche remains the classic choice, but cream cheese, fruit preserves, and savory cheeses are also common, reflecting regional variety and the influence of both sweet and savory traditions.

Preheat the oven to 400°F (200°C/Gas Mark 6). Line a 16 × 12-inch (40 × 30-cm baking pan and grease with butter.

In a metal bowl, combine the eggs and sugar. Place over a pan of simmering water to create a bain-marie (do not allow the base of the bowl to touch the water) and whisk constantly until the mixture reaches 105°F (40°C)—it will feel warm to the touch.

Remove from the heat and beat with an electric mixer until it triples in volume and the mixture falls off the beaters like ribbons. Stir in the vanilla extract, then sift in the flour and gently fold it into the mixture using a rubber spatula with slow, sweeping motions. Add the melted butter, folding carefully so as not to deflate the batter. Pour the batter into the prepared baking pan and bake for 10–12 minutes, or until golden and springy to the touch.

Remove from the oven and immediately invert the sponge onto a clean dish (tea) towel or parchment paper dusted with sugar. Peel the parchment paper off the bottom of the sponge, cover with the pan to keep in the moisture, and let rest for 5 minutes.

While still warm and pliable, gently roll up the sponge from one of the short edges. Let cool rolled to set its shape.

To assemble, unroll the sponge, spread with your filling of choice (see below), and roll tightly again. Chill slightly before serving.

Suggested Fillings

For classic dulce de leche: Spread 1–1½ cups (10–14 oz/300–400 g) of thick dulce de leche evenly across the sponge.

For dulce de leche and cream cheese: Blend ¾ cup (7 oz/200 g) of dulce de leche with scant ½ cup (3½ oz/100 g) of cream cheese for a sweet-salty balance.

For blue cheese and cream cheese: Mix 2¼ oz (60 g) of blue cheese with ⅔ cup (5 oz/140 g) of cream cheese until smooth. If desired, add a touch of honey or pear preserve for contrast. This version is ideal for a savory take, served as an appetizer.

STOLLENKONFEKT

Germany

Submitted by Luisa Weiss

Makes 36
Prep time: 20 minutes
Cook time: 1 hour

For the dough:
7 tablespoons (3½ oz/100 g) butter (ideally high-fat, European-style), at room temperature
6 tablespoons granulated sugar
1 cup (9 oz/250 g) quark, drained if necessary
grated zest of 1 lemon
½ teaspoon vanilla extract
1 tablespoon dark rum
2⅓ cups plus 1 tablespoon (10½ oz/300 g) all-purpose (plain) flour
¼ teaspoon salt
¾ teaspoon ground cinnamon
½ teaspoon ground cloves
⅛ teaspoon ground cardamom
1½ teaspoons baking powder
½ cup (2¾ oz/75 g) blanched almonds, chopped
1 cup (5½ oz/150 g) raisins

For the Vanillezucker:
1 vanilla bean (pod), quartered
2 cups (14 oz/400 g) granulated sugar

For the topping:
7 tablespoons (3½ oz/100 g) butter
¾ cup plus 1 tablespoon (3½ oz/100 g) confectioners' (icing) sugar

A simpler version of the more elaborate and painstaking German *Christstollen* (or simply "stollen"), the richly spiced marzipan-filled yule-tide fruit bread. *Stollenkonfekt* are made using bite-size portions of the same sort of quark-based dough, spiced with cardamom, cinnamon, and cloves, studded with almonds and raisins, and thickly cloaked in *Vanillezucker* (vanilla-scented confectioners' [icing] sugar). While you can make a very nice vanilla sugar by simply plunging a vanilla bean (pod) into a jar of sugar and leaving it there (for a really long time), you can also make a slightly fancier version by processing the vanilla and sugar together until the bean is broken down and the sugar is speckled with flecks of vanilla seed. The sugar is more intensely flavored than regular supermarket variety vanilla sugar.

***Stollenkonfekt* actually improve with a few days rest before tasting or serving but won't last as long as a whole loaf of stollen might. Still, they should keep well for at least a week or two when kept in an airtight container. Serve decoratively with other Christmas cookies.**

Preheat the oven to 350°F (180°C/Gas Mark 4). Line 2 baking sheets with parchment paper and set aside.

To make the dough: In the bowl of a stand mixer fitted with the whisk attachment, whisk the butter and sugar together until light and airy. Add the quark, lemon zest, vanilla extract, and rum, and beat until well combined.

In a separate bowl, whisk together the flour, salt, cinnamon, cloves, cardamom, and baking powder. Add to the quark mixture and beat together until just combined. Briefly beat in the chopped almonds and raisins. Using your hands, pinch off golf ball-size pieces of dough and, without overhandling them, form them into 2-inch (5-cm) ovals or rectangles. Place them on the prepared baking sheets, leaving 1 inch (2.5 cm) between them. Place 1 of the baking sheets in the oven and bake for 30 minutes, or until pale golden brown.

Meanwhile, to make the Vanillezucker: Place the quartered vanilla bean (pod) and sugar in the bowl of a food processor. Process until the vanilla bean is finely ground and well distributed, and the sugar is powdery. Transfer to an airtight container until ready to use; it will keep for months.

To make the topping: Melt the butter in a small pan. In a separate small bowl, whisk together the confectioners' (icing) sugar and 3 tablespoons of Vanillezucker.

Remove the stollen bites from the oven, and slide in the second batch. Let the first batch cool briefly, just until you can handle them. Dip each piece into the melted butter, then toss in the confectioners' sugar mixture and place back on the baking sheet to set.

Cook the second batch for 30 minutes and dip as above. Let cool completely. Store in airtight containers separated by pieces of parchment paper for at least 1 day. They are best if allowed to rest for 3–4 days before serving.

Just before serving, dust again with a fresh layer of sifted confectioners' sugar. They will keep in an airtight container for at least 10 days and up to 3 weeks.

DORTHEA'S CARAWAY COOKIES WITH TROLL CREAM

Norway

Submitted by Åshild Blyseth

Makes 50
Prep time: 1½ hours, plus chilling time
Cook time: 8–10 minutes

For the cookies:
3 eggs
1¼ cups (9 oz/250 g) superfine (caster) sugar
2 cups (9 oz/250 g) all-purpose (plain) flour, plus extra for dusting
1 tablespoon baking powder
1⅓ cups (10½ oz/300 g) butter, at room temperature
caraway seeds, for sprinkling

For the troll cream:
5 cups (1 lb 2 oz/500 g) lingonberries
1 cup (7 oz/200 g) superfine (caster) sugar
2 teaspoons vanilla sugar
2 egg whites

This is a local Norwegian shortcrust pastry cookie baked every year for Christmas. The main flavoring comes from caraway, which grows wild in the Nordland region of north Norway. These cookies are named after a local woman in the old fishing village of Bardal, Dorthea, who was known for making the best version of these caraway Christmas cookies. This was her recipe.

They are served with the cream of the trolls, which is made from lingonberries that grow wild in the forests of Norway. Lingonberries are a traditionally well-used berry in Norwegian cuisine. Troll cream pairs wonderfully with caraway cookies.

To make the cookies: In a large bowl, whisk the eggs and sugar until light and fluffy. Sift half of the flour and baking powder over the mixture.

In a separate bowl, rub the butter into the other half of the flour and baking powder until it resembles bread crumbs. Mix together with the egg-sugar mixture, a little at a time, until combined, then wrap the dough in plastic wrap (clingfilm) and chill in the refrigerator for at least 30 minutes.

Line a baking sheet with parchment paper and set aside.

Turn out the dough onto a well-floured counter and roll out to a thickness of ⅛ inch (2–3 mm). Using a cookie cutter, cut out circles, or cut into diamond shapes, and place on the prepared baking sheet with plenty of space between them. Sprinkle the cookies with the caraway seeds, then chill for 1 hour before baking.

Preheat the oven to 375°F (190°C/Gas Mark 5). Bake for 8–10 minutes. The cookies should remain light in color. Remove from the oven and let cool.

To make the troll cream: Reserve a small handful of lingonberries for decoration, if desired, then whip all the ingredients together until you get a firm, pink foam. Transfer to a bowl, decorate with the reserved berries, if using, and serve alongside the cookies.

The cookies will keep for up to 5 days in an airtight container at room temperature.

MELOMAKARONA

Greece

Submitted by Ianthi Michalaki

Makes 45–50
Prep time: 40 minutes, plus overnight chilling time
Cook time: 17–20 minutes

For the syrup:
- 3¼ cups (1 lb 7 oz/650 g) granulated sugar
- 3½ tablespoons glucose syrup
- scant ½ cup (3½ oz/100 g) honey

For the cookie dough:
- scant 1 cup (8 fl oz/250 ml) sunflower oil
- 2 teaspoons orange zest, plus ⅔ cup (5 fl oz/150 ml) fresh juice (see notes)
- 2 teaspoons cognac
- ⅔ cup (2¾ oz/80 g) confectioners' (icing) sugar
- 1 tablespoon ground cinnamon
- 1 teaspoon ground cloves
- 3¼ cups (14 oz/400 g) all-purpose (plain) flour
- 4 teaspoons baking powder
- scant ⅔ cup (3½ oz/100 g) farina

For the topping:
- scant ½ cup (3½ oz/100 g) honey, for drizzling
- 1¾ cups (7 oz/200 g) finely chopped walnuts

Perhaps the most iconic Greek cookie, the *melomakarona* (Μελομακάρονα) varies widely across Greece: In some parts a softer or crumblier cookie, in others a greater emphasis on spice, but everywhere across the country, Greeks will agree that the signature flavor of this Christmas treat comes from its soaking in honey.

These cookies often herald the beginning of the Christmas season and are made in most homes and bakeries at the beginning of December. Their long shelf life allows them to be displayed in the living room throughout the following weeks in decorative Christmas tree-shaped platters—ones that make an appearance only once a year. They are usually medium size and oval shaped, but smaller versions have become more popular in recent years. A smaller cookie bakes more evenly whereas a bigger size has a softer center that requires less syrup, to avoid getting soggy. Also, with a bite-size cookie, it's easier to lose track of how many you've eaten.

To make the syrup: The night before serving, combine 1⅔ cups (14 fl oz/ 400 ml) of water with the sugar and glucose syrup in a pan. Bring to a boil and cook for 5 minutes. Take off the heat, add the honey, and stir to dissolve. Let the syrup cool to room temperature, then cover with plastic wrap (clingfilm) and store in the refrigerator overnight.

The next day, to make the cookie dough: Preheat the oven at 350°F (180°C/Gas Mark 4). Line a baking sheet with parchment paper and set aside.

In the bowl of a stand mixer fitted with the paddle attachment, combine the oil, orange zest and juice, and cognac, and mix until incorporated, about 30 seconds. Add the confectioners' (icing) sugar and spices and mix until combined.

In a separate bowl, combine the flour, baking powder, and farina. Add the dry ingredients into the wet, and mix until a loose dough comes together.

Working quickly, divide the dough into ¾-oz (20-g) pieces and shape into circles. Place on the prepared baking sheet, leaving sufficient space between each as they will expand in the oven. Bake for 17–20 minutes, until golden brown.

Remove the syrup from the refrigerator and have at hand. Remove the cookies from the oven and, while still hot, dunk each in the bowl of cold syrup and soak for 30 seconds, or a bit longer for a softer cookie. Place on a wire rack to drain, then drizzle honey over the tops and decorate with the chopped walnuts.

Store them in layers on top of each other, to keep them from drying out and allow the excess honey and syrup to be absorbed. They are best eaten the day after they're made, but will keep for up to 2 weeks in an airtight container at room temperature.

Notes: The cookie dough needs to be processed and cooked quickly. The longer it is left to sit, the more likely the oil will start separating from the dough.

For better absorption, it helps if the liquids are at room temperature or lukewarm. If the juice is chilled, warm it in the microwave for 30 seconds beforehand.

SARAH BERNHARDT COOKIES

Scandinavia, Central and Eastern Europe

Submitted by Diana Iovescu Tatucu

Makes 30–35
Prep time: 40 minutes, plus cooling and chilling times
Cook time: 25 minutes

For the meringue base:
3 egg whites
pinch of salt
1 cup (7 oz/200 g) granulated sugar
2½ cups (7 oz/200 g) finely ground walnuts

For the chocolate cream filling:
4 egg yolks
¾ cup (5½ oz/150 g) granulated sugar
1¾ sticks (7 oz/200 g) butter, softened
3½ oz (100 g) semisweet (dark) chocolate (at least 50 per cent cocoa solids), melted and slightly cooled
1 teaspoon vanilla extract

For the chocolate glaze:
5½ oz (150 g) dark chocolate
3½ tablespoons (2 oz/50 g) butter

These delicate and decadent cookies were created in Denmark by Johannes Steen in the early 1900s as a tribute to the popular French actress Sarah Bernhardt. Though she never baked them herself, her name became associated with luxurious almond- or nut-based confections layered with silky chocolate cream and glazed in more chocolate.

The recipe eventually spread through cultural exchange to Romania, where they are lovingly called *tobite* or *Saraberne*, and are typically found on Christmas or holiday dessert platters. Made with a chewy walnut meringue base and a rich chocolate buttercream, these cookies are an indulgent bite-size treat perfect for celebrations. Their texture—a crisp shell, creamy center, and glossy coating—is pure elegance.

Preheat the oven to 300°F (150°C/Gas Mark 2). Line a baking sheet with parchment paper and set aside.

To make the meringue base: Beat the egg whites with the pinch of salt until foamy. Gradually add the sugar, beating until stiff peaks form. Gently fold in the ground walnuts with a spatula. Pipe or spoon small rounds onto the prepared baking sheet. Bake for 25 minutes, or until lightly golden and set, then let cool completely.

Meanwhile, to make the chocolate cream filling: In a heatproof bowl set over simmering water (bain-marie), whisk the egg yolks with the sugar until thickened and pale. Set aside and let cool.

In a separate bowl, beat the butter until fluffy. Gradually mix in the cooled egg yolk mixture. Add the melted dark chocolate and vanilla and beat until smooth. Refrigerate for 30 minutes until slightly firm.

To assemble: Pipe or spread the chocolate cream onto the flat side of half the meringue bases. Top with another meringue to sandwich. Chill in the refrigerator to firm up before glazing.

Meanwhile, to make the glaze: In a pan over low heat, melt the chocolate and butter together until smooth. Remove from the heat, then dip the tops of the sandwich cookies into the glaze, place on parchment paper, and allow to set fully before serving.

BUTTERBREDELE

France

Submitted by Sarah Lemanski

Makes 15–20
Prep time: 25 minutes, plus chilling time
Cook time: 11–12 minutes

For the dough:
9 tablespoons (4¼ oz/125 g) butter, at room temperature
⅔ cup (4¼ oz/120 g) superfine (caster) sugar
scant ½ teaspoon fine sea salt
4 egg yolks
2 cups (9 oz/250 g) all-purpose (plain) flour
grated zest of 1 lemon or orange, or seeds from ½ fresh vanilla bean (pod), or ½ teaspoon ground cinnamon (optional)

For the egg wash:
1 egg yolk
1 teaspoon milk

***Butterbredele* are Christmas cookies that hail from Alsace, in northeastern France, along the border with both Germany and Switzerland. They come from a wide "family" of cookies called *Bredele*, or "little cakes" in German, which are commonly baked and distributed over the Christmas period with *Butterbredele* both one of the simpler and most popular. As the name suggests, this is a moreish butter cookie, sometimes spruced up with a little added zest or spice, and cut into star shapes before baking and frosting, dusting with confectioners' (icing) sugar, or enjoying plain.**

Preheat the oven to 350°F (180°C/Gas Mark 4). Line a baking sheet with parchment and set aside.

To make the dough: Using a hand mixer or stand mixer fitted with the paddle attachment, beat the butter until soft and creamy. Add the sugar and salt and beat on high speed until the mixture is light and fluffy. Scrape down the sides of the bowl and the paddle from time to time to ensure that all the mixture reaches the same whipped texture. Add the egg yolks in 2 additions, beating on low–medium speed until incorporated. Add the flour and your chosen flavoring, if desired, and beat on low–medium speed until fully incorporated. The dough should look even in texture with no dry streaks. Place the dough between 2 sheets of parchment paper and roll out to ¼ inch (5 mm) thick. Chill in the refrigerator for at least 1 hour.

Once the dough has chilled, cut out circles using a cookie cutter of your choice, and place on the prepared baking sheet. Re-roll any off cuts until all the dough is used. Chill in the refrigerator or freezer until very firm.

To make the egg wash: In a small bowl, beat together the egg with the milk. Brush each cookie to evenly coat. Bake for 11–12 minutes, turning halfway, until lightly golden and firm to the touch (adjust according to the size of your cookies).

Remove from the oven and let cool on a wire rack. The Bredele will keep in an airtight container for up to 2 weeks.

ZIMTSTERNE

Germany, Switzerland, and France

Zimtsterne **are traditional German Christmas star-shaped cookies made with almond meal, cinnamon, and a crisp meringue glaze. Popular in Germanic regions (Germany, Switzerland, and Alsace, France), they date back to at least the sixteenth century, alongside other festive cookies. Typically made a few weeks before Christmas, they keep well through the holiday season and are often prepared as a family activity, especially with children.**

Submitted by Marie Kerkeling

Makes about 60
Prep time: 45 minutes, plus chilling time
Cook time: 25 minutes

For the dough:
- 3¼ cups (14 oz/400 g) almond meal (ground almonds)
- 2¼ cups (9 oz/250 g) confectioners' (icing) sugar
- 1 teaspoon ground cinnamon
- 2 egg whites
- 2 tablespoons Amaretto
- all-purpose (plain) flour or cornstarch (cornflour), if gluten-free, for dusting

For the meringue topping:
- generous 1 cup (4¼ oz/125 g) confectioners' (icing) sugar
- 1 egg white

To make the dough: In a bowl, mix the almond meal, confectioners' (icing) sugar, and cinnamon together. Add the egg whites gradually to avoid making the dough too wet. The texture should be similar to modeling clay. Mix in the Amaretto. Wrap the dough in plastic wrap (clingfilm) and refrigerate for 30 minutes.

Preheat the oven to 250°F (120°C/Gas Mark ½). Line a baking sheet with parchment paper and set aside.

To shape the stars: Turn out the dough onto a lightly floured (or starched) counter and roll it out to about ¼ inch (5 mm) thick. Use a star-shaped cutter to cut out stars and place them on the prepared baking sheet.

To make the meringue topping: Whisk the confectioners' sugar and egg white until stiff peaks form. Gently spread the meringue over each star with a teaspoon, going all the way to the edges. Use a paring knife to cleanly finish the points, if desired. Bake for 25 minutes.

Remove from the oven and let cool completely. Stored in an airtight container, they will keep well for a few weeks.

PFEFFERNÜSSE

Germany

Submitted by Luisa Weiss

Makes 48
Prep time: 20 minutes
Cook time: 20 minutes

For the lebkuchengewürz:

5 tablespoons ground cinnamon
1½ tablespoons ground cloves
1 teaspoon ground allspice
1 teaspoon ground cardamom
1 teaspoon ground ginger
1 teaspoon ground mace
¾ teaspoon ground anise seeds

For the dough:

½ cup (5½ oz/160 g) honey
¼ cup plus 2 tablespoons (2¾ oz/75 g) granulated sugar
⅛ teaspoon white pepper
1 teaspoon baker's ammonia
1 tablespoon rum, slightly warmed
2½ cups (11 oz/310 g) all-purpose (plain) flour, plus extra if needed
1 teaspoon unsweetened cocoa powder
¼ teaspoon salt
1 egg

For the glaze:

¾ cup plus 1 tablespoon (3½ oz/100 g) confectioners' (icing) sugar
1 tablespoon freshly squeezed lemon juice, or more if needed

Every fall (autumn), German grocery stores start stocking specialty items just for the Christmas baking season. Little cardboard display cases are set out that are fully stocked with bars of baking chocolate, packages of potash and baker's ammonia, candied citron and orange peel, vials of flavor extracts, and spices like anise and cardamom, as well as spice mixtures for stollen and *lebkuchen*. When January rolls around, the picked-over stands are packed up and put away again.

***Pfeffernüsse*, which translates to "pepper nuts," are little domed cookies made with a lebkuchen spice mixture, as well as a hint of white pepper for a pleasing warmth, and a little cocoa powder for color. *Pfeffernüsse* differ slightly from region to region, and this recipe from Offenbach in west-central Germany, has a wonderful texture—soft yet chewy, with a thin sugar glaze offering only the faintest bit of resistance.**

The cookies come out of the oven plump and crisp, but "ripen" over the course of a few days in an airtight container, becoming chewier and developing a more complex flavor profile. If kept properly cool and airtight, they should remain good for at least a couple of weeks.

***Lebkuchen* spice—a mixture of all the usual suspects in wintertime baking—is called for in many German Christmas recipes. If you make a batch of it in early fall, you'll be well-equipped for the holiday season.**

To make the lebkuchengewürz: Combine all the ingredients in a bowl and mix well to combine. Store in a glass jar with a tight-fitting lid. Kept in a dark, cool place, the mix will stay fresh for 1 year.

Preheat the oven to 375°F (190°C/Gas Mark 5). Line 2 baking sheets with parchment paper and set aside.

To make the dough: In a small pan over medium-high heat, warm the honey and granulated sugar, stirring until the sugar has completely melted. Remove from the heat and stir in 2 teaspoons of lebkuchengewürz and the white pepper. Set aside.

In a small bowl, stir the baker's ammonia into the warm rum to dissolve, then stir this into the honey mixture.

In a separate bowl, stir together the flour, cocoa powder, and salt. Stir this mixture into the honey mixture, then add the egg. Stir or knead until well combined. The dough will be quite sticky. You may have to add a little flour as you knead, but don't add much flour or the cookies will be stiff and dry. You should be able to pluck off a piece of the dough and roll it into a ball that holds its shape.

Turn out the dough onto a counter and roll into 1-inch (2.5-cm) balls. Place on the prepared baking sheets, leaving ½ inch (12 mm) between them. Place one of the baking sheets in the oven and bake for 10 minutes, until the cookies are domed and dry to the touch but not brown.

Meanwhile, to make the glaze: In a bowl, whisk together the confectioners' sugar, lemon juice, and 1 tablespoon of water. Remove the cookies from the oven and let cool slightly on a wire rack.

While the cookies are still hot, paint the tops and edges thinly with the glaze. As you work, the glaze may stiffen slightly—whisk in a few drops of water or lemon juice to loosen it. Repeat with the second baking sheet of cookies and the glaze.

Allow the cookies to cool completely before storing in a tin, then wait 2–3 days before eating. The cookies will keep in the tin at room temperature for several weeks.

PEPPARKAKOR

Sweden

Submitted by Cecilia Tolone

Makes 50
Prep time: 1 hour, plus chilling time
Cook time: 7 minutes

- 10½ tablespoons (5½ oz/150 g) butter, room temperature
- 1 cup (7 oz/200 g) superfine (caster) sugar
- ⅔ cup (7 oz/205 g) golden syrup (see notes)
- 1¼ teaspoons ground ginger
- 1 teaspoon ground cloves
- 2 tablespoons ground cinnamon
- ½ teaspoon ground anise
- 1 teaspoon vanilla sugar or vanilla extract
- ¼ teaspoon salt
- ⅔ cup (5 fl oz/150 ml) heavy (double) cream
- 5 cups (1 lb 6 oz/625 g) all-purpose (plain) flour
- 1 teaspoon baking soda (bicarbonate of soda)

In Sweden, *pepparkakor*—ginger thins—are the Christmas cookie par excellence. Every bakery and grocery store sells them; every home kitchen prepares them.

The most common shape you'll find for the store-bought varieties are fluted circles or hearts. For homemade cookies, the most common shapes are hearts and—perhaps surprisingly—pigs (a tradition said to date from pagan times). When baked into larger shapes, the *pepparkakor* sometimes get a thin coat of frosting, but the traditional smaller sizes don't have this. Unlike American or British gingerbread cookies, these are always thin and crisp.

In a bowl, combine the butter, sugar, golden syrup, ginger, cloves, cinnamon, anise, vanilla sugar, and salt in a bowl. Stir in half of the cream. Once fully combined, add the other half and stir. Add the flour and baking soda (bicarbonate of soda) to the bowl, and mix until completely homogeneous. Divide the dough into 4 portions. Wrap each portion in plastic wrap (clingfilm) and refrigerate for at least 24 hours (see notes).

Preheat the oven to 375°F (190°C/Gas Mark 5). Line a baking sheet with parchment paper and set aside.

Take one piece of dough at a time from the refrigerator and roll it out very thinly. It's easiest to roll out while still cold. The dough should be so thin you can read through it. Stamp out your desired shapes and place them on the prepared baking sheet. Bake for about 7 minutes, or until they turn a beautiful golden brown.

Remove from the oven and let cool on a wire rack before enjoying. Once baked, these cookies can last for a couple weeks in a cookie tin stored in a cool, dry place.

Notes: The dough is best prepared ahead of time and allowed to rest in the refrigerator for at least 24 hours, but the dough can sit in the refrigerator for over a month without a problem. If well-wrapped, it keeps in the freezer even longer.

If you absolutely cannot find golden syrup, the best alternative is honey, although it will affect the taste. Maple syrup, agave, and glucose will not work in this recipe.

MANTECADOS

Spain

Submitted by Simone and Inés Ortega

Makes 50
Prep time: 20 minutes, plus resting time
Cook time: 15 minutes

butter, for greasing
6½ cups (1 lb 10 oz/750 g) all-purpose (plain) flour, plus extra for dusting
3 tablespoons superfine (caster) sugar
2⅓ cups (14 oz/400 g) lard
juice of ½ lemon

To decorate:
confectioners' (icing) sugar
ground cinnamon

***Mantecados* are a dense and lightly sweet form of shortbread cookie, which originated in Andalusia but are now popular all across Spain. They, like the similarly named (but entirely distinct) *mantecadas,* are a lard-based pastry, as their etymological root *manteca* (meaning lard or cooking fat from a pig) suggests.**

***Mantecados* are associated with Christmas, and are often purchased wrapped in a twist of tissue paper. Part of the excitement of enjoying the *mantecado* is in the anticipation of its unwrapping, something that many Spaniards retain from childhood. Of course, when these warm cookies come out of the oven, they'll provide plenty of anticipation in and of themselves.**

Preheat the oven to 300°F (150°C/Gas Mark 2). Grease a baking sheet with butter and set aside.

Sift the flour onto a marble slab, make a well in the center, and add the sugar, lard, and lemon juice. Knead together until you have a smooth dough, then let rest for 10 minutes.

On a lightly floured work counter with a floured rolling pin, roll out the dough to about ⅜ inch (8 mm) thick. Stamp out small circles or ovals with a 2-inch (5-cm) cookie cutter and place onto your prepared baking sheet (some people prefer to make a hole in the middle of each one). Bake for 15 minutes, but do not allow them to brown.

Remove the cookies from the oven, leave to cool slightly, then sprinkle with the confectioners' (icing) sugar and ground cinnamon. The cookies will keep for up to 1 week in an airtight container at room temperature.

KOURABIEDES

Greece

Submitted by Ianthi Michalaki

Makes 20–25
Prep time: 1 hour, plus chilling time
Cook time: 18–20 minutes

- 9 tablespoons (4¼ oz/125 g) butter (82 percent fat)
- 9 tablespoons (4¼ oz/125 g) sheep or goat's milk butter
- ½ vanilla bean (pod), seeds scraped
- 4½ cups (1 lb 2 oz/520 g) confectioners' (icing) sugar
- 1¼ teaspoons baking soda (bicarbonate of soda)
- 1 egg yolk
- 2 cups plus 1 tablespoon (9¼ oz/ 260 g) all-purpose (plain) flour
- scant 1 cup (4¼ oz/125 g) roasted almonds, chopped into small pieces

If *melomakarona* (page 246) is the standout star of the Christmas season, *kourabiedes* is its understated, elegant cousin. *Kourabiedes* is a refined shortbread-like cookie with a light buttery texture and subtle aroma that wins over its fans. But with its charms as subtle as they are, it is also easy to mess up. Excellent *kourabiedes* are a result of good ingredients and correct sizing. When shaped too big or if the almonds are used whole, the cookie crumbles after the first bite. This recipe works great for a small, bite-size cookie and will require a lot of willpower to not consume them all within a day.

In the bowl of a stand mixer fitted with the paddle attachment, cream together both butters and the vanilla seeds until light and airy.

In a separate bowl, combine 3 tablespoons of the confectioners' (icing) sugar with the baking soda (bicarbonate of soda). Add this to the butter mixture and mix until incorporated. Add the egg yolk and mix for 30 seconds. Scrape down the edges of the bowl and mix again for another 30 seconds. Add half of the flour and half the almonds, and mix on low speed for 15–20 seconds. Follow with the remaining flour and almonds and mix until the dough just comes together.

There are 2 ways to shape the cookies: Traditionally, small portions of 1 oz (30 g) are rolled into balls by hand. Place the shaped cookies in the refrigerator for 10 minutes until firm. Alternatively, while the dough is still soft, place it between 2 sheets of parchment paper and roll out to a thickness of approximately ½ inch (12–15 mm). Chill it in the refrigerator for 10 minutes until firm, then cut out bite-size circles or squares with a cookie cutter. Reroll the trimmings, or shape them by hand.

Preheat the oven at 350°F (180°C/Gas Mark 4). Line a baking sheet with parchment paper and set aside. Place the chilled cookies on the prepared baking sheet. Bake for 18–20 minutes, until golden brown.

Remove from the oven and let cool, then gently toss the cookies in the remaining confectioners' sugar until evenly coated. To serve, dust with more confectioners' sugar if the first layer has been absorbed.

GUBANA

Italy

Submitted by Chiara Barla

Serves 8
Prep time: 1 hour, plus soaking, overnight chilling, and proofing times
Cook time: 45–60 minutes

For the filling:
3¼ cups (1 lb/440 g) raisins
4 tablespoons grappa
grated zest of 1 lemon
grated zest of 1 orange
⅔ cup (2¾ oz/80 g) coarsely chopped walnuts
½ cup (1¾ oz/50 g) coarsely chopped hazelnuts
¼ cup (1 oz/30 g) pine nuts, toasted
1 oz (30 g) semisweet (dark) chocolate, coarsely chopped (optional)
2 teaspoons ground cinnamon

For the dough:
4 cups (1 lb 2 oz/500 g) strong flour, plus extra for dusting
¾ oz (20 g) fresh yeast
generous ⅓ cup (3½ fl oz/100 ml) milk
2 medium eggs, plus 2 egg yolks (reserve 1 egg white)
5½ tablespoons (2¾ oz/80 g) butter
1½ teaspoons salt
1 cup (7 oz/200 g) granulated sugar

Originating from the border regions of northeastern Italy, *gubana* stands as a beautiful culinary bridge between Italian and Slovenian traditions, with deep roots in religious celebrations and festive occasions such as Christmas and Easter, as well as weddings. Its name likely comes from the Slovenian word *guba*, meaning "fold," a nod to the sweet's characteristic spiral shape.

This recipe comes from Italian chef and baker Chiara Barla, who hails from the opposite end of northern Italy. She discovered *gubana* later in life—thanks to a close friend from a small town near the Slovenian border, whose family owns a hotel and restaurant there, and who prepared this for her one Christmas. Rich, aromatic, and bursting with flavor, it was the perfect treat—especially paired with a glass of grappa to ward off the winter chill.

To make the filling: The evening before baking, put the raisins, grappa, and lemon and orange zest in a bowl. Soak for at least 4 hours.

Combine the walnuts, hazelnuts, pine nuts, chocolate, if using, and cinnamon in a bowl. Add the soaked raisins and mix thoroughly until the mixture is moist and well blended. Cover and refrigerate overnight to let the flavors melt.

The next day, to make the dough: In the bowl of a stand mixer fitted with the paddle attachment, combine the flour with the yeast. Gradually add the milk, whole eggs and yolks to the dry ingredients while mixing on the lowest speed. Add the butter and salt and continue kneading until you obtain a smooth, homogeneous dough. Shape into a ball, place in a bowl, cover with a clean, damp dish (tea) towel, and proof in a warm, draft-free area for about 3 hours.

Line a baking sheet with parchment paper and set aside.

Once the dough has risen, turn it out onto a lightly floured counter and roll out into a circle about ¼ inch (5 mm) thick. Spread the prepared filling evenly over the dough surface. Roll the dough tightly into a log. To achieve the characteristic spiral shape of gubana, coil the log into a snail-like spiral. Place the shaped gubana on the prepared baking sheet, cover with a clean dish (tea) towel, and proof for another 2 hours in a warm, draft-free place.

Preheat the oven to 350°F (180°C/Gas Mark 4).

In a small bowl, beat the reserved egg white lightly with a fork. Brush the surface of the gubana with the egg white and sprinkle generously with the sugar. Let it rest for 10 minutes.

Bake the gubana for 45–60 minutes, then remove from the oven and let cool on a wire rack. For the best flavor, consume the following day, when all the aromas have fully developed.

PANDOLCE GENOVESE

Italy

Submitted by Chiara Barla

Serves 8
Prep time: 30 minutes, plus proofing and overnight resting times
Cook time: 1 hour

- 2 cups (9 oz/250 g) strong flour, plus extra for dusting
- ¼ oz (10 g) fresh yeast
- ⅓ cup (2¾ oz/75 g) granulated sugar
- 2 teaspoons honey
- 6½ tablespoons (3¼ oz/90 g) butter
- ½ teaspoon salt
- 1 vanilla bean (pod), seeds scraped
- grated zest of 1 orange
- 1 oz (30 g) candied citron
- 2 oz (60 g) candied orange peel
- generous ¾ cup (4¼ oz/120 g) raisins
- 1 tablespoon fennel seeds
- ¼ cup (1 oz/30 g) pine nuts
- 1 teaspoon orange blossom water

***Pandolce* is a traditional Ligurian dessert with roots tracing back to ancient Persia. The modern version is credited to Andrea Doria, the legendary sixteenth-century Genoese statesman, who challenged local bakers to create a sturdy, long-lasting, nourishing sweet for sailors on long sea voyages. Families would prepare their own dough and bake it in communal wood-fired ovens.**

This recipe comes from Italian chef and baker Chiara Barla, whose first memory of making and eating *pandolce* were the ones her aunt baked in a wood-fired oven, shortly after baking bread for the household. This was a ritual that always marked the beginning of the festive holiday season.

In the bowl of a stand mixer fitted with the dough hook attachment, combine half of the flour, 7 tablespoons of water, and the yeast. Mix until well combined, cover with a damp dish (tea) towel, and let rest at room temperature for 2 hours, allowing the dough to proof.

After the initial proof, gradually incorporate the remaining flour into the dough. Once fully absorbed, add the sugar and honey, mixing until smooth. Next, add the butter in 3 additions, waiting for each portion to be fully incorporated before adding the next. Add the salt, vanilla seeds, and orange zest, mixing until just combined. Finally, gently fold in the candied fruit, raisins, fennel seeds, pine nuts, and orange blossom water. Mix only until evenly distributed—avoid overworking the dough. Let the dough rest for 30 minutes.

Line a baking sheet with parchment paper. Turn out the dough on a clean, lightly floured counter and shape it into a round loaf. Transfer to the prepared baking sheet. Cover with a clean dish towel and let rest overnight (or for 12 hours) at room temperature.

The next morning, preheat the oven to 350°F (180°C/Gas Mark 4). Score a shallow triangle on the top of the loaf. Bake for 1 hour, or until golden and fully cooked through.

Remove from the oven and let cool on the baking sheet before serving.

MÁKOS GUBA

Hungary

Submitted by Lilla Szőcs

Serves 6
Prep time: 30 minutes, plus resting and proofing times
Cook time: 30 minutes

For the kifli:
1 oz (25 g) fresh yeast
1 cup (8 fl oz/250 ml) milk, lukewarm
1 tablespoon confectioners' (icing) sugar
1 teaspoon salt
1 egg
4 cups (1 lb 2 oz/500 g) all-purpose (plain) flour
3½ tablespoons (1¾ oz/50 g) butter

For the mákos guba:
generous 2 cups (17 fl oz/500 ml) milk
3½ tablespoons (1¾ oz/50 g) butter, plus extra for cooking
1½ cups (7 oz/200 g) ground poppy seeds
honey, for drizzling

One of the unique characteristics of Hungarian food culture is its incorporation of sweet, dessert-like main courses. One such example is the famous Hungarian Christmas dish called *mákos guba* (known as *Mohnpielen* in German and *makówki* in Polish), which originated in Hungarian peasant culture and eventually found its way onto fine dining menus.

In peasant households, this dish was simple and cheap to prepare, using stale *kifli* (crescent rolls) and pantry staples. The recipe was born out of practicality: It was a quick, affordable way to feed many hungry mouths. It's a sweet-salty comfort food, made of fluffy sliced *kifli* soaked in milk (or in the modern version, vanilla custard or vanilla sauce), then sprinkled with honey and ground poppy seeds.

Traditionally, special *guba* rolls are baked for this dish, though some families use store-bought *kifli*, stale pretzels, or even sweet, braided bread (*kalács*). It is usually served at Christmas, after the traditional fish soup (*halászlé*). The following authentic recipe comes from a household in Baja in southern Hungary, passed down by Aunt Cila, who has prepared *guba* this way with her family for generations.

Line a baking sheet with parchment paper and set aside.

To make the kifli: In a bowl, combine the yeast, lukewarm milk, and sugar, then set aside for 5–10 minutes, until frothy.

In a separate bowl, combine the salt, egg, and flour, then pour in the milk with the activated yeast. Knead until the dough starts to come together, then add the butter and continue to knead until smooth. Cover with plastic wrap (clingfilm) and proof in a warm place for 40–50 minutes.

Turn out the dough onto a counter and divide into 8 portions. Roll each piece into a strand about ¾ inch (2 cm) thick and long enough to fit across a baking sheet. Place them on the prepared sheet with about 2 fingers' width between each. Proof for another 20 minutes.

Preheat the oven to 350°F (180°C/Gas Mark 4). Bake for 20–25 minutes, then remove from the oven.

To make the mákos guba: In a pan, combine the milk with the butter and bring to a boil. Slice the kifli into circles. Melt a little butter in a pan over medium heat and lightly toast them for 5 minutes. Remove from the heat, pour over the hot milk mixture, and let sit to allow them to soak it up. Sprinkle with ground poppy seeds and drizzle with honey. Serve warm.

POMPE À L'HUILE

France

Submitted by Agnese Negrini

Serves 6
Prep time: 1 hour, plus proofing and multiple overnight resting times
Cook time: 15–20 minutes

For the preferment:
- scant 4 cups (1 lb 2 oz/500 g) bread flour with a high-protein content
- 1/16 oz (2 g) fresh yeast

For the dough:
- 5⅓ cups (1 lb 9 oz/700 g) bread flour
- 1 cup (7 oz/200 g) superfine (caster) sugar
- 1½ oz (45 g) fresh yeast
- 4 teaspoons fine sea salt
- 1½ cups (12½ fl oz/370 ml) extra virgin olive oil, chilled, plus extra for oiling topping
- flaky salt, to decorate

***Pompe à l'huile* (literally "oil pump") is part of southern France's Christmas traditions and usually served as one of *lei tretze dessèrts* (the thirteen desserts), the classic sweet ending to Provençal Christmas dinner.**

The *pompe à l'huile* is a soft, simple, and fragrant brioche made with extra virgin olive oil but without any eggs—instead, high-quality flour and proper fermentation do all the magic. The simplicity of the ingredients, from the aroma to the soft crumb and remarkable fluffiness, is something that becomes quickly addictive. Traditionally hunks of the bread are broken off by hand rather than being cut and are eaten along with dried fruits or nuts. Due to the high percentage of oil, it can keep for a few days.

To make the preferment: In a medium bowl, combine 1 cup (8 fl oz/250 ml) of room-temperature water with the flour and yeast. Let rest for 8–12 hours, or ideally overnight. Line a baking sheet with parchment paper and set aside.

To make the dough: In the bowl of a stand mixer fitted with the dough hook attachment, combine the preferment with 1½ cups (12 fl oz/360 ml) water, and the flour, sugar, and yeast. Mix on low speed until the dough becomes smooth and stretchy. Add the fine salt and continue mixing until fully incorporated. Gradually pour in the olive oil. The dough should feel silky, elastic, and slightly translucent. With lightly oiled hands, gently fold the dough and shape into a ball. Place it in a lightly oiled bowl, cover with plastic wrap (clingfilm), and proof until doubled in size.

Gently deflate the dough. Turn it out onto a counter and divide into pieces of 12–14 oz (350–400 g) each. Shape each piece into a ball and place on the prepared baking sheet. Lightly oil the surface of the dough and cover with plastic wrap, then place in the refrigerator and let rest overnight.

The next day, your brioches should be nicely risen and airy. If they still seem underproofed, let them rest at room temperature for an additional 1–2 hours.

Gently press down each brioche and make a small cross-shaped incision in the center. Let them rest again for another 30 minutes.

Meanwhile, preheat the oven to 425°F (220°C/Gas Mark 7).

Place a small oven-safe dish of water on the bottom rack of the oven for the first 10 minutes of baking, or if your oven allows, use the 10–20% steam setting. Bake for 15–20 minutes, or until the brioches are light golden and baked through.

Remove from the oven, brush with a bit of extra virgin olive oil for shine, and decorate with a sprinkle of flaky salt.

PAIN D'EPICES

France

Submitted by Victoria Effantin and Cécile Khayat

Serves 8–10
Prep time: 30 minutes, plus resting time
Cook time: 50–55 minutes

- ¼ cup (3½ oz/100 g) molasses
- generous 2 cups (1 lb 1 oz/475 g) chestnut honey
- 5 teaspoons flower honey
- 1½ cups (12 fl oz/350 ml) milk
- 6 eggs
- scant 4 cups (1 lb/450 g) rye flour
- ⅓ cup (1¾ oz/50 g) whole wheat flour
- 2 tablespoons baking powder
- 2 tablespoons ground cinnamon
- 1½ teaspoons ground nutmeg
- 1½ teaspoons ground ginger
- 2 teaspoons ground coriander
- oil, for greasing

The *pain d'épices*, a dense and sticky spiced loaf, can take many different forms: from cookies to cakes, or even a kind of bread. *Pain d'épices* originally comes from Alsace, along France's border with Germany and Switzerland, but at Christmas time it is available everywhere across the country in France, and the warming smell of it brings to mind fond memories of local Christmas markets. This recipe was provided by Mamiche Bakery in Paris, where the style sits somewhere between the bread and cake varieties, which means it is sweet, soft, and sticky. They do this so it can be served however the celebrant likes: with foie gras for Christmas dinner (traditional), or as a sweet treat with a cup of tea.

In a pan over low heat, melt the molasses, chestnut honey, and flower honey together. In a medium bowl, combine the milk and eggs. Pour the melted honey and molasses mixture into the bowl with the milk and eggs.

In a separate bowl, combine the rye flour, whole wheat flour, baking powder, and spices and whisk to combine.

Lightly oil a clafouti mold, line with parchment paper, and set aside. Pour the batter into the greased mold, then level the batter evenly and smooth the surface. Let rest for 30 minutes before baking.

Meanwhile, preheat the oven to 340°F (170°C/Gas Mark 3). Bake for 50–55 minutes, until a toothpick (cocktail stick) inserted in the center comes out clean.

Remove from the oven, then unmold and wrap in parchment paper while still warm. Let rest until the next day, then serve.

VÖRTBRÖD

Sweden

Submitted by Cecilia Tolone

Serves 8–10
Prep time: 30 minutes, plus cooling, resting, and proofing times
Cook time: 30 minutes

- 1⅔ cups plus 2 tablespoons (15 fl oz/450 ml) stout or porter beer (see notes)
- ¼ oz (10 g) fresh yeast, or ½ teaspoon (⅛ oz/4 g) dry yeast
- 2¼ cups (9¾ oz/275 g) all-purpose (plain) flour
- scant 1 cup (3¾ oz/105 g) fine rye flour
- 2 tablespoons butter, at room temperature, plus 1 tablespoon, melted, for brushing
- ¼ cup (2¼ oz/60 g) bread syrup (brödsirap) (see notes)
- 1½ teaspoons ground cardamom
- ½ teaspoon ground cloves
- ⅛ oz (3 g) ground bitter orange peel (pomeransskal) (see notes)
- 1½ teaspoons ground cinnamon
- 1 teaspoon salt
- ⅓ cup (1¾ oz/50 g) raisins (optional)

***Vörtbröd* is a heavily spiced bread traditionally served on the *Julbord*, or Christmas table. It is named after wort (*vört*), which is the liquid extracted from the mashing process during the brewing of beer or whisky. This bread is lightly sweet, a little bitter, and delicious with a bit of Christmas ham. This recipe contains quite a few Sweden-specific ingredients, but sometimes regional dishes need regional ingredients. Please read the notes section below for substitutions, but be aware that so much of the flavor and appearance of this bread comes from the combination of beer and syrup used. The more substitutions that are made, the bigger the difference in flavor will be.**

Pour the beer into a large pot (the beer will foam up tremendously) and bring to a boil. Continue cooking until reduced by half, or there is about scant 1 cup (7½ fl oz/225 ml) of liquid. Remove from the heat and let cool to room temperature.

In the bowl of a stand mixer fitted with the whisk attachment, whisk the yeast into the cooled beer until dissolved. Add ⅔ cup (3 oz/85 g) of the all-purpose (plain) flour and ½ cup (2¼ oz/60 g) of the fine rye flour and mix by hand until a homogenous, loose batter forms. Cover with a clean dish (tea) towel and let rest for 30 minutes.

Fit the dough hook attachment to the mixer, then add all the other ingredients, including the remaining flours but not the raisins, to the bowl. Mix on slow speed for 5 minutes. Scrape down the sides, add the raisins, if using, and mix on slow speed for another 5 minutes. Let rest in the bowl, covered with a dish towel, for 40 minutes.

Turn out the dough onto a counter and shape into a ball. Let rest on the counter for 20 minutes to relax.

Line a baking sheet with parchment paper and set aside.

Form the dough into a ball. This dough is quite stiff so it shouldn't need extra flour while shaping. Place on the prepared baking sheet, cover with a clean dish towel, and proof for about 45 minutes.

Meanwhile, preheat the oven to 400°F (200°C/Gas Mark 6). Bake the dough for about 30 minutes, until it sounds hollow when tapped on the base.

Remove from the oven and brush with butter. Serve warm.

Notes: Unless you make beer yourself, it can be really difficult to get your hands on wort. Even in Sweden where every bakery sells *vörtbröd* at Christmas time it is next to impossible to find. Most bakeries don't even use it; they use a product called *bagerivört*, or "bakery wort," a syrup specially produced for this bread. To get as close to the real thing, the liquid in this bread comes exclusively from beer. It is very important to use a stout or porter for this. Cecilia Tolone, who contributed this recipe, recommends Carnegie Stout because Swedish bread needs Swedish beer, but if in doubt use Guinness. Do not use any sort of lager or IPA.

To get the sweetness but also the desired maltiness, use bread syrup (*brödsirap*), also called malt syrup in the United States. If you can't find malt syrup, the best substitutes would be *mörksirap*, molasses, or even honey.

The final special ingredient is *pomeransskal*: dried and powdered bitter orange peel. The best substitute would be the zest of half an orange.

BIBINGKA

Philippines

Submitted by Florence Mae Maglanoc

Serves 6
Prep time: 15 minutes
Cook time: 25–30 minutes

banana leaves, for lining
butter, for brushing
1¾ cups (9 oz/250 g) rice flour
1 teaspoon baking powder
½ cup (3½ oz/100 g) granulated sugar
¼ teaspoon salt
⅞ cup (7 fl oz/200 ml) coconut milk
2 eggs
1 salted egg, sliced
scant ½ cup (1¾ oz/50 g) grated cheese of your choice

***Bibingka* is a festive rice cake traditionally baked in clay pots lined with banana leaves and topped with salted eggs and cheese. It is strongly associated with Filipino Christmas celebrations and is commonly eaten after attending *simbang gabi* (Christmas midnight mass). This recipe has been adapted for modern kitchens and oven baking.**

Preheat the oven to 350°F (180°C/Gas Mark 4). Line 6 individual baking pans (4½ inches/11.5 cm wide) with softened banana leaves and brush with butter.

In a bowl, mix the rice flour, baking powder, sugar, and salt.

In a separate bowl, whisk together the coconut milk, a generous ⅓ cup (3½ fl oz/100 ml) water, and eggs. Add to the dry ingredients and stir until smooth. Pour the batter into the prepared pans. Top with slices of the salted egg and the grated cheese. Bake for 25–30 minutes, or until golden and set.

Remove from the oven, brush with butter, and serve warm.

FRESH COCONUT CAKE

United States

Submitted by Camille Cogswell

Serves 12–16
Prep time: 1½ hours, plus cooling time
Cook time: 45–55 minutes

For the cake:
- 11 tablespoons (5½ oz/160 g) butter, at room temperature, plus extra for greasing
- 2¾ cups (12 oz/340 g) cake or all-purpose (plain) flour, plus extra for dusting
- 1⅓ cups (9 fl oz/270 ml) buttermilk
- 3 eggs, at room temperature
- 2¼ teaspoons vanilla extract
- 1¾ cups (12 oz/340 g) granulated sugar
- ¾ teaspoon kosher salt
- 1½ tablespoons baking powder

For the shredded coconut:
- 1 whole coconut

For the meringue frosting:
- 7 egg whites
- 1¾ cups (12 oz/340 g) granulated sugar
- ½ teaspoon kosher salt
- ¼ teaspoon cream of tartar
- ½ teaspoon vanilla extract

Coconut cake originated in the southern United States as early as the 1830s. Fresh coconut was considered a luxury, with its preparation a notoriously arduous task usually completed by enslaved Black women. This process, and the resulting iconically beautiful cake, were decades later detailed by early Black cookbook writers like Malinda Russell (1866) and Abby Fisher (1881). Today, this luscious, layered coconut cake is popular for any special occasion in the south and beyond, but it is perhaps baked most commonly around Christmas time, when its snowy-white presentation feels especially apt.

Traditionally, the cake was made with a "7-minute icing" where eggs and sugar were whisked together (later with an electric handheld mixer) over a pot of simmering water for 7 minutes. In order to make the recipe as consistent and successful as possible using common modern kitchen appliances, it has here been adapted to incorporate a stand mixer, and to cook the icing to a temperature point instead of using a time.

To make the cake: Preheat the oven to 350°F (180°C/Gas Mark 4). Lightly grease, line, and flour the bottom of 3 × 8-inch (20-cm) cake pans. Set aside.

In a small bowl, combine 4 tablespoons of the buttermilk, the eggs, and the vanilla and whisk together.

In the bowl of a stand mixer fitted with the paddle attachment, combine the flour, sugar, salt, and baking powder. Stir together with a spoon. Add the soft butter and the remaining buttermilk. Mix on low speed until the dry mixture is moistened, then increase the mixer speed to medium–high and mix for 1½ minutes. Scrape down the sides of the bowl with a flexible rubber spatula. Add one-third of the egg mixture to the bowl and mix on medium speed until fully incorporated. Repeat with another third of the egg mixture, scrape down the bowl, then incorporate the last third of the egg mixture. Remove the bowl from the stand and with a few turns of your spatula, make sure that the batter is smooth and homogenous.

Split the batter evenly between the three cake pans. Bake in the middle of the oven for 30–40 minutes, until each cake springs back to a gentle touch and is starting to pull away from the sides of the pan. Remove the pans from the oven and let cool completely before running a small spatula or butter knife around the sides of the pans and unmolding the cakes. The cakes can be baked up to a day in advance and held at room temperature, covered with parchment paper.

To make the shredded coconut: Preheat the oven to 400°F (200°C/Gas Mark 6). With a skewer, press into each of the 3 eyes of the coconut until you find the one that is soft. Poke the pick into this eye and twist it around to widen the hole. Pour the coconut water into a container and set aside in the refrigerator. Place the coconut in a baking pan and bake for 15 minutes. Remove the pan from the oven and let the coconut cool completely.

Place the cooled coconut onto a wooden cutting board and hit it hard with a hammer or mallet to crack it into a few large pieces. Using a spoon, carefully wedge the edge of it between the husk and the flesh of each piece of coconut, separating them. Discard the coconut husk.

Using a vegetable peeler, carefully peel the brown skin from the white coconut flesh. Discard the skin. Grate the white coconut flesh into shreds in a downward motion, then chill in the refrigerator until you are ready to assemble the cake. The coconut can be shredded up to a day in advance.

To make the meringue frosting: In a heatproof stand mixer bowl, combine the egg whites, sugar, salt, and cream of tartar. Place the bowl over a pot of simmering water, ensuring that the bowl doesn't touch the water. Stir the mixture constantly with a flexible rubber spatula and frequently check the temperature with an instant-read thermometer. When it reaches 175°F (80°C), roughly 5 minutes, remove the bowl from the pot of water and immediately attach it to the stand mixer with the whisk attachment. Add the vanilla extract, and whisk on medium–high speed until the bowl is only barely warm to the touch and a fluffy, shiny meringue that holds stiff peaks has formed. Use immediately; keep the mixer going on low–medium speed until you're ready to start frosting your cake.

To assemble the cake: Remove the parchment and trim the tops of each cake with a serrated knife so that you're left with 3 even, 1-inch- (2.5-cm)-thick, flat layers. Sprinkle the reserved coconut water evenly on top of the trimmed cake layers.

Place one cake on a serving plate, and spread one-quarter of the frosting evenly to the edges with a small flat spatula. Sprinkle about ¼ cup (3 oz/85 g) of freshly shredded coconut onto the frosting, then put another cake round on top. Add another quarter of the frosting onto the next cake layer and repeat the spreading and sprinkling of coconut. Place the last cake layer upside down on top of the others.

Spread the remaining frosting evenly over the top and sides of the cake. Working over a tray, press the remaining coconut gently into the sides and top of the cake to stick to the frosting. The cake is best served the day that it's made. Leftovers will keep up to 1 week in the refrigerator but retain their best quality in the first 3 days.

LINZERTORTE

Austria

Submitted by Till Gurka

Serves 16
Prep time: 20 minutes, plus chilling time
Cook time: 40 minutes

The *Linzertorte* has the distinction of being the world's oldest cake to be named after a place—the city of Linz in northern Austria. The earliest recorded recipe dates back to 1696 in a Viennese cookbook, though some sources suggest even earlier versions from the mid-seventeenth century. This iconic pastry features a tender, spiced nut dough (often made with almond meal/ground almonds or hazelnuts) filled with red currant or raspberry jam, topped with a distinctive lattice crust. Traditionally baked for festive occasions, especially Christmas, the *Linzertorte* is cherished for its ability to improve with age—resting for several days allows the flavors to meld beautifully. It is best served in thin slices, accompanied by coffee or tea, and enjoyed slowly to appreciate its rich history and delicate balance of sweet and tart notes.

- 2¼ sticks (9 oz/250 g) butter
- 1¼ cups (9 oz/250 g) superfine (caster) sugar
- 3½ oz (100 g) marzipan
- 1 egg
- 2 cups (9 oz/250 g) all-purpose (plain) flour
- 1 teaspoon baking powder
- 2 teaspoons unsweetened cocoa powder
- 1½ teaspoons ground cinnamon
- ¼ teaspoon ground cloves
- ¼ teaspoon salt
- 1½ cups (9 oz/250 g) ground roasted hazelnuts
- scant 1 cup (9 oz/250 g) red currant jelly
- apricot jam, for glazing
- toasted sliced almonds, to decorate

Cream the butter and sugar together in a bowl until smooth. Add the marzipan and egg and knead into the butter mixture.

Sift the flour, baking powder, cocoa, cinnamon, cloves, and salt into the bowl, with the ground roasted hazelnuts. Mix to combine, and briefly knead everything into the butter mixture. Chill the dough in the refrigerator for 1 hour.

Preheat the oven to 375°F (190°C/Gas Mark 5).

Remove the dough from the refrigerator and separate into 2 pieces—one 1 lb 2 oz–1 lb 5 oz (500–600 g) for the bottom, and the other a 10½ oz (300 g) piece for the edge and lattice. Roll out the large piece of dough to fit a 9-inch (23 cm) cake pan, then line the pan with the dough.

Roll out the smaller piece of the remaining dough and cut strips for the lattice, one slightly thicker. Use the thicker strip to line the edge of the pan. Arrange the thinner strips overlapping into a lattice shape.

Spread a thin layer of red currant jelly on the bottom of the pie shell and finally place the lattice on top. Bake for approximately 40 minutes. Remove from the oven, then glaze with apricot jam and decorate the edge by sprinkling over the sliced, roasted almonds.

BOLO DE MEL

Madeira

Submitted by João Rodrigues

Serves 8
Prep time: 45 minutes, plus soaking time
Cook time: 50 minutes–1 hour

- 7 tablespoons (3½ oz/100 g) butter, plus extra for greasing
- 4 cups (1 lb 2 oz/500 g) all-purpose (plain) flour, plus extra for dusting
- ¾ cup (3½ oz/100 g) raisins
- 1 cup (8 fl oz/250 ml) Madeira
- 2 eggs
- generous 1 cup (9 oz/250 g) brown sugar (preferably dark muscovado or similar)
- ¾ cup (10½ oz/300 g) molasses
- 1¼ cups (5 ½ oz/150g) lard
- 1 teaspoon ground cinnamon
- ½ teaspoon ground cloves
- ½ teaspoon ground nutmeg
- 1 teaspoon baking soda (bicarbonate of soda) (or baking powder)
- grated zest of 1 lemon
- grated zest of 1 orange
- generous ¾ cup (3½ oz/100 g) chopped walnuts
- generous ¾ cup (3½ oz/100 g) chopped almonds
- whole almonds and walnuts, to decorate (optional)

One of Madeira's most famous culinary exports, the *bolo de mel* (honey cake) is an iconic Portuguese Christmas cake, which originated in the sixteenth century, capitalizing on luxurious spices from India and the local production of cane molasses (here called *mel-de-cana*) from the sugar cane, the latter of which was also a significant part of local culinary traditions.

Despite being a Christmas cake, tradition dictates it should be prepared roughly two weeks prior on December 8 (the Feast of the Immaculate Conception) and allowed to mature in an airtight container. This cake is not to be cut with a knife but rather broken by hand and served, of course, with Madeira wine.

Place the raisins and wine in a bowl. Let soak for 30 minutes.

Meanwhile, in a separate bowl, beat the eggs with the brown sugar until you have a pale, fluffy cream.

In a pan over low heat, gently heat the molasses together with the butter and lard, stirring until everything is melted and well combined. Remove from the heat and let cool slightly.

In a large mixing bowl, sift together the flour with the cinnamon, cloves, nutmeg, and baking soda (bicarbonate of soda). Make a well in the center and pour in the beaten egg mixture, followed by the melted molasses and butter mixture. Carefully mix everything together until the batter is smooth and uniform. Finally, add the citrus zest, the drained raisins (with a little drizzle of the wine, if desired), and the chopped walnuts and almonds. Fold everything in gently.

Preheat the oven to 325°F (160°C/Gas Mark 3). Grease and flour a 10-inch (25 cm) cake pan and line the base with parchment paper. Pour the batter into your prepared pan. Bake for 50 minutes–1 hour, or until a toothpick (cocktail stick) inserted into the center comes out almost clean—this is a cake that is meant to remain moist.

Remove from the oven and let cool completely before unmolding. Wrap in parchment paper and store for several weeks, during which it will become even more flavorful. When it is time to serve, decorate with whole almonds and walnuts, if desired, and tear it into generous pieces by hand.

PAVLOVA

Australia and New Zealand

Submitted by Maxine Scheckter

Now known the world over, this iconic dessert originated in Australia and New Zealand, where Anna Pavlova, a famous Russian prima ballerina of the early 1900s, famously toured in 1926. The pavlova was created in her honor to celebrate her lightness on stage. Served with pouring cream and seasonal fruit (especially strawberries), this is a favorite on Christmas Day—a light and soothing abatement from the summer heat.

Serves 12
Prep time: 45 minutes, plus cooling time
Cook time: 1½ hours

For the meringue:
6 egg whites
scant ½ cup (10 oz/280 g) superfine (caster) sugar
1 teaspoon white vinegar
1 teaspoon vanilla extract, or ¼ teaspoon vanilla bean paste
2 teaspoons cornstarch (cornflour)
14 oz (400 g) fresh seasonal fruit (such as strawberries, kiwi, and mixed berries), sliced, to serve

For the vanilla cream:
⅔ cup (5 fl oz/150 ml) whipping cream
⅔ cup (5 fl oz/150 ml) mascarpone cream
¼ cup (1 oz/30 g) confectioners' (icing) sugar
½ teaspoon vanilla extract, or ⅛ teaspoon vanilla bean paste

Preheat the oven to 230°F (110°C/Gas Mark ¼). Line a baking sheet with parchment paper and set aside. If desired, trace a 10-inch (25-cm) circle on the underside of the parchment paper as a guide for spreading the pavlova mix.

To make the meringue: In the bowl of a stand mixer fitted with the whisk attachment, whisk the egg whites on medium speed until the egg whites are at least doubled in size. Add the superfine (caster) sugar and continue to whisk on medium-high speed for at least 15 minutes, until you have a stiff-peaked and shiny meringue. The meringue cannot be overwhisked with this amount of sugar so you can leave this whisking for up to 30 minutes. Add the vinegar, vanilla, and cornstarch (cornflour), then whisk on low speed until well combined.

Scoop the pavlova batter into a 10-inch (25-cm) circle on the prepared baking sheet. Use an offset or frosting spatula to swirl the meringue decoratively as desired, leaving a flat circle in the center to be filled with the vanilla cream and fruit later. Bake for 1½ hours.

Remove from the oven and let cool before transferring to a serving platter. If desired, the pavlova can be stored in an airtight container for up to 2 days, but it may go slightly soggy depending on the humidity in the kitchen.

To make the vanilla cream: In the bowl of a stand mixer fitted with the whisk attachment, combine the cream, mascarpone, confectioners' (icing) sugar, and vanilla and whip to a medium peaked cream.

Spoon on top of the pavlova and spread over the top decoratively. Place the fruit on top of the cream, making sure it is generous and plentiful. Serve immediately, within a few hours at most.

BAATH CAKE

India

Submitted by Siddharth Chogle

Makes 12
Prep time: 25 minutes, plus cooling and standing time
Cook time: 50 minutes–1 hour

- 1 tablespoon ghee
- 1½ cups (8½ oz/240 g) farina (fine semolina)
- 5 egg yolks
- 1¼ cups (8 oz/225 g) superfine (caster) sugar
- 1 teaspoon vanilla extract
- ½ teaspoon ground cardamom
- ¼ teaspoon freshly grated nutmeg
- ½ cup (4 oz/115 g) butter, softened
- 1 cup (3½ oz/100 g) fresh grated coconut
- 4 tablespoons coconut milk
- neutral oil, for greasing
- 3 egg whites
- ½ teaspoon salt

Christmas in Goa feels incomplete without *baath* cake, a moist farina and coconut loaf rooted in the region's Portuguese colonial history. In the sixteenth century, Portuguese cooks introduced *bolo de coco* (a traditional coconut cake); local Goan bakers swapped in fresh coconut, ghee, and *rava* (a local form of farina or semolina), then slowly baked the batter in clay ovens until a mahogany crust formed. By the eighteenth century the recipe had secured a place on every Advent checklist, sliced into bars to anchor the season's *kuswar*, a festive sweet assortment. *Kuswar*—its name adapted from the Portuguese *consoada* (to comfort)—is still carried to neighbors, friends, and, most importantly, households that are grieving or facing hardship, transforming a plate of candies into an act of solidarity. *Baath's* gentle cardamom aroma, week-long keeping quality, and resistance to humid weather make it the perfect traveler and a delicious emblem of Goa's Iberian-Konkan heritage.

In a heavy pan over medium–low heat, melt the ghee. Add the farina and stir for 3–4 minutes until aromatic but still pale. Spread on a baking sheet to cool completely.

In a stand mixer fitted with the paddle attachment, beat the egg yolks and sugar on medium–high speed until thick and pale, and the batter falls off the paddle like ribbons, about 4 minutes. Add the vanilla, cardamom, nutmeg, and softened butter, and mix just to combine. Fold in the grated coconut, followed by the cooled farina and the milk to obtain a cohesive batter. Cover and let stand for 30 minutes at room temperature.

Preheat the oven to 325°F (160°C/Gas Mark 3). Line and lightly oil an 8-inch (20-cm) round (or 7-inch/18-cm square) pan.

Whisk the egg whites to medium peaks; fold one-third into the rested batter to loosen, then fold in the remainder in 2 additions, retaining maximum aeration. Finally, fold in the salt. Transfer the batter to the prepared pan and level the surface. Bake on the center rack for 45–55 minutes, until the top is deep golden and a toothpick (cocktail stick) inserted in the center comes out clean.

Remove from the oven, cool for 15 minutes in the pan, then unmold onto a wire rack and cool completely. Wrap well and let sit to mature overnight; flavor and texture improve as the farina softens.

Slice into 7-inch (18-cm) squares and serve. They will keep in an airtight container for up to 7 days.

BLACK CAKE

Jamaica

Submitted by Rawlston Williams

Makes 2 × 9-inch (23-cm) cakes
Prep time: 45 minutes, plus fruit soaking time
Cook time: 2½ hours

For the fruit mixture:
- generous 2 cups (11¼ oz/320 g) raisins
- 1 cup (5¾ oz/170 g) prunes
- 1 cup (5 oz/145 g) dried currants
- 1 cup (5½ oz/150 g) candied cherries
- 1 cup (5½ oz/150 g) mixed candied peel
- 1 cup (8 fl oz/250 ml) dark rum, plus more (optional) for brushing
- 1 cup (8 fl oz/250 ml) port wine

For the cake:
- 2 sticks (8 oz/230 g) butter, at room temperature, plus extra for greasing
- 1 cup (7¾ oz/220 g) soft dark brown sugar
- 6 eggs
- 2½ cups plus 2 tablespoons (12 oz/325 g) all-purpose (plain) flour
- 1 teaspoon baking powder
- 1 teaspoon ground cinnamon
- ½ teaspoon freshly grated nutmeg
- 1 teaspoon vanilla extract
- ½ cup (4 fl oz/120 ml) dark molasses
- 3 tablespoons browning

Black cake is a rum-laced fruit cake that is traditionally made for Christmas and weddings across the Caribbean. It derives originally from the British Christmas pudding and Christmas cake, but over time has become entirely Caribbean through its use of local ingredients, spices, and "browning"—what is essentially a burnt sugar mixture. For black cake, the incorporated dried fruit is first soaked in a rum and wine mixture—ideally for at least a week and anywhere up to a year or longer—before the cake is made. One of the crucial differences is that the fruit is typically then blended (completely or partially) with the soaking liquor before it's incorporated into the cake batter. This amounts to a smoother textured cake, dense but moist.

To make the fruit mixture: In a large glass jar or container, combine the raisins, prunes, currants, cherries, and mixed peel. Pour the rum and port wine over the fruits, ensuring they are fully submerged. Cover the jar tightly and let the fruits soak for at least 1 week, or up to several months.

When ready to use, blend all or part of the fruit with ¼–⅓ cups (2–3 fl oz/60–80 ml) of the soaking liquid, depending on your preferred texture. Reserve the remaining soaking liquid.

Preheat the oven to 300°F (150°C/Gas Mark 2). Grease and line two 9-inch (23-cm) round cake pans and set aside.

To make the cake: In a large bowl, cream the butter and brown sugar until light and fluffy. Add the eggs one at a time, beating well after each addition.

In a separate bowl, sift together the flour, baking powder, cinnamon, and nutmeg. Gradually mix the dry ingredients into the butter mixture, then fold in the fruit, vanilla extract, molasses, browning, and another ¼–⅓ cup (2–3 fl oz/60–80 ml) of the soaking liquid. Stir until everything is fully combined, then divide the batter between the prepared pans and level the top. Bake for about 2½ hours, or until a toothpick (cocktail stick) inserted in the center comes out clean.

Remove from the oven and let the cake cool completely in the pans. Once cooled, brush or pour additional rum over the surface, if desired, then wrap tightly and store. The flavor continues to improve over time, and the cake will keep for weeks or even months if stored properly.

MAJA BLANCA

Philippines

***Maja blanca* is a soft, creamy pudding made from coconut milk and sweet corn, said to derive from the Spanish *manjar blanco* (a variation of the medieval European dessert *blancmange*). It's a festive dish usually served during Christmas, town fiestas, or *merienda* gatherings.**

Submitted by Florence Mae Maglanoc

Serves 8
Prep time: 10 minutes, plus chilling time
Cook time: 20 minutes

neutral oil, for greasing
3⅓ cups (27 fl oz/800 ml) coconut milk
1¼ cups (10 fl oz/300 ml) evaporated milk (optional, for richness)
½ cup (7 oz/200 g) granulated sugar
1 cup (4¼ oz/120 g) cornstarch (cornflour)
1¼ cups (7 oz/200 g) canned corn kernels

For the topping:
1 cup (5½ oz/160 g) sweetcorn kernels, drained well if canned
2 tablespoons butter, melted
3 tablespoons brown sugar
1 tablespoon condensed milk
pinch of salt

Lightly grease an 8 × 8 inch (20 × 20 cm) baking pan or line with parchment paper.

In a pot, combine the coconut milk, evaporated milk, if using, and sugar. Bring to a gentle simmer.

In a small bowl, dissolve the cornstarch (cornflour) in a small amount of water to make a slurry. Gradually add to the pot while stirring continuously. Add the corn kernels and continue stirring until the mixture thickens and becomes glossy.

Pour into the prepared pan. Level the top and let cool to room temperature. Chill for at least 2 hours, or until set.

Meanwhile, to make the topping: Preheat the oven to 400°F (200°C/Gas Mark 6) and line a baking sheet with parchment paper.

Pat the sweetcorn dry with kitchen towel, then transfer to a bowl and combine with the melted butter, brown sugar, condensed milk, and salt until well coated. Spread the mixture on a small lined baking sheet or ovenproof dish in an even layer. Bake for 12–18 minutes, stirring once halfway through, until the sweetcorn is sticky and caramelized around the edges. Let cool for a few minutes so the topping thickens slightly.

Spoon over the chilled maja blanca and serve. Or for a deeper color, place it under the broiler (grill) for 1–2 minutes before serving, keeping a close eye on it so it does not burn.

KLAPPERTAART

Indonesia

Submitted by Petty Pandean-Elliott

Serves 8
Prep time: 30 minutes, plus chilling time
Cook time: 1 hour

1 lb 2 oz (500 g) young coconut flesh
generous ¾ cup (3½ oz/100 g) slivered almonds or kacang kanari or pili nuts
2 teaspoons ground cinnamon, for dusting

For the spiced raisins:
8 whole cloves
1 short cinnamon stick
1 cup plus 2 tablespoons (3½ oz/100 g) raisins

For the vanilla custard:
6 egg yolks
½ cup (3½ oz/100 g) granulated sugar
2 teaspoons cornstarch (cornflour)
1 cup (8 fl oz/250 ml) milk
1 vanilla bean (pod), seeds scraped
1 cup (8 fl oz/250 ml) heavy (double) cream
2 tablespoons dark rum

Klappertaart is a Dutch-Indonesian dessert from Manado in North Sulawesi, Indonesia, where it is traditionally made with young coconut flesh, custard, rum, and spiced raisins, along with local almonds known as _kacang kenari_ (Java almonds or pili nuts). When baked, this mixture creates a rich, custard-like pudding with a firm texture. The creamy richness of the coconut is beautifully balanced by the warmth of cloves and cinnamon, which bring depth and a subtle spiced aroma that enhances the tropical flavors. The contrast of textures—soft coconut strands, juicy spiced raisins, and silky custard—makes each bite even more enjoyable.

This recipe comes from Indonesian chef Petty Pandean-Elliott, whose mother and grandmother always served this pudding during Christmas and New Year celebrations. Nowadays, you can find _klappertaart_ in Jakarta, the capital city of Indonesia, and other major cities across Indonesia's 17,000 islands. You can also substitute _kacang kenari_ or pili nuts with roasted slivered (flaked) almonds.

To make the spiced raisins: In a pan, bring a generous ⅓ cup (3½ fl oz/100 ml) of water to a boil with the cloves and cinnamon stick. Add the raisins and simmer for 6–8 minutes until the water evaporates, leaving juicy and fat raisins. Remove the cloves and cinnamon stick and set aside to cool.

Preheat the oven into 350°F (180°C/Gas Mark 4).

To make the vanilla custard: In a mixing bowl, beat together the egg yolks, sugar, and cornstarch (cornflour) until creamy. Combine the milk and vanilla bean (pod) and seeds in a pan and heat gently until steaming. Slowly pour the hot milk into the egg mixture, stirring all the time until combined. Stir in the cream and the rum.

Pour the custard mixture back into the pan and stir over low heat until the mixture thickens sufficiently to coat the back of a wooden spoon. Remove the vanilla bean pieces.

Put the young coconut into a square 8-inch (20-cm) baking dish at least 3 inches (7.5 cm) deep. Add the raisins and custard, gently mixed well. Sprinkle with the almonds or pili nuts and ground cinnamon. Bake in the oven for 45 minutes, or until the top is slightly brown.

Remove from the oven and let cool to room temperature. Chill in the refrigerator for at least 2 hours before serving.

BEJGLI

Hungary

Submitted by Lilla Szőcs

Makes 4
Prep time: 45 minutes, plus resting and chilling times
Cook time: 25–30 minutes

For the dough:
- 1¾ oz (50 g) fresh yeast
- ⅓ cup (3 fl oz/90 ml) lukewarm water or milk
- 8 cups (2 lb 4 oz/1 kg) all-purpose (plain) flour, plus extra for dusting
- 1⅓ cups (5½ oz/150 g) confectioners' (icing) sugar
- 2 egg yolks
- 4½ sticks (1 lb 2 oz/500 g) butter or margarine
- ⅞ cup (7 fl oz/200 ml) tejföl (full-fat soured cream) or full-fat, thick yogurt

For the poppy seed filling:
- 3 cups (14 oz/400 g) ground poppy seeds
- 3 cups (12 oz/350 g) confectioners' (icing) sugar
- 1–2 tablespoons lemon zest

For the walnut filling:
- 5 cups (14 oz/400 g) ground walnuts
- 3½ cups (14 oz/400 g) confectioners' (icing) sugar
- 1–2 tablespoons lemon zest
- 1 tablespoon rum

For the topping:
- 3 egg yolks, beaten
- 3 egg whites, beaten

In Hungary there is no Christmas party without *bejgli*. Traditionally homemade, it can also be found at bakeries around Christmas time. Filled with rich ground poppy seeds or walnuts, this pastry is a holiday staple that is popular with young and old alike. The true origin of the pastry remains a subject of debate: Some theories suggest it came from Silesia and reached Hungary through German (Bavarian or Austrian) influence. Others argue that it was introduced during the period of Ottoman rule.

Poppy seed rolls resembling today's *bejgli* became widely known in the nineteenth century, and their first recorded mention appears in István Czifray's 1830 cookbook, where they were referred to as "*Pozsonyi finom mákos kalács*" (Pozsony's fine poppy seed loaf).

The choice of filling has its roots in folk beliefs and traditions: The walnut version is believed to protect the family from misfortune, while the poppy seed is thought to bring abundance, wealth, and happiness. For young women, eating poppy seed *bejgli* is said to help them find a husband in the coming year, a tradition that yields mixed success but is, nonetheless, absolutely delicious.

To make the dough: In a small bowl, combine the yeast and lukewarm water or milk, then set aside for 5–10 minutes, until frothy. In a large mixing bowl, sift together the flour and confectioners' (icing) sugar. Add the yeast mixture along with the egg yolks. Crumble in the butter or margarine, mix to a rough dough, then tip onto a clean counter and knead until it comes together into a smooth, firm dough. Divide into 4 equal parts, wrap each portion in plastic wrap (clingfilm), and refrigerate for 1 hour.

To make the poppy seed filling: In a pan, mix the ground poppy seeds with the confectioners' sugar. Add just enough water for the mixture to come to a paste-like, spreadable consistency, then add lemon zest to taste. Cook over medium heat for about 5 minutes until creamy and smooth, and the texture is no longer gritty.

To make the walnut filling: Combine all the ingredients in a pan with just enough water for the mixture to come together, then cook gently over medium heat for 10–15 minutes, until thickened.

Line a baking sheet with parchment paper and set aside. Put another piece of parchment paper on the counter and dust with flour.

Remove the dough from the refrigerator, turn it out onto a counter, and roll out one portion on the flour-dusted parchment into a rectangle roughly 14 × 9½ inches (35 × 24 cm). Try to roll it thin enough to be pliable but not so thin that it tears. Spread the filling of your choice evenly over the dough piece, aiming for a layer that is about as thick as the dough itself. Use the parchment paper under the dough rectangle to help lift and guide it, then roll gently and evenly into a neat log. Place on the prepared baking sheet, and repeat rolling and filling with the remaining dough portions, making sure there's at least a finger's width of space between them, as they will expand in the oven. Brush each roll with the beaten egg yolk, then poke the tops gently with a fork. Proof for 30 minutes until the yolk has dried.

Brush with the beaten egg white to give the baked rolls their signature marbled finish, then proof again in a warm place, covered, for another 20–30 minutes.

Meanwhile, preheat the oven to 400°F (200°C/Gas Mark 6). Bake for 15 minutes, then reduce the temperature to 340°F (170°C/Gas Mark 3) and continue baking for another 10–15 minutes, until the tops are golden. Remove from the oven and let cool before slicing. The bejgli will keep for 2–3 days in an airtight container at room temperature, or up to 2 weeks in the refrigerator.

PAN DE JAMÓN

Venezuela

Submitted by Ricardo Chaneton

Serves 8
Prep time: 1 hour, plus resting time
Cook time: 30 minutes

For the pan de jamón:
1 egg
5 tablespoons superfine (caster) sugar
¼ oz (8 g) fresh yeast
1 teaspoon Venezuelan beer
2 teaspoons salt
6⅓ cups (1 lb 13 oz/830 g) bread flour
4½ tablespoons milk
7 tablespoons (3½ oz/100 g) butter, softened
2¼ cups (9 oz/250 g) pitted green olives
20 slices cooked ham
4¼ oz (120 g) bacon
¼ cup (1½ oz/40 g) raisins, soaked in Venezuelan rum, then drained and chopped

For the egg wash:
1 egg
pinch of salt

For the sugar glaze:
¾ oz (20 g) papelón (if you can't find papelón, use brown sugar instead)

***Pan de jamón* is a traditional Venezuelan Christmas bread that was created in Caracas in 1905. Pioneered by bakery owner Gustavo Ramella, it's made by rolling leftover ham in bread dough and baked until golden and crispy. Over time, the recipe has evolved to incorporate ingredients like raisins, green olives, and nuts, making it a must-have holiday staple. Enjoyed throughout the holiday season, especially on December 24 and 31, it's served during family meals, for a sit-down dinner, breakfast, or even as an afternoon snack.**

To make the pan de jamón: In a mixing bowl, combine the egg, sugar, yeast, beer, and salt with a generous 1 cup (9 fl oz/260 ml) of water. Add half of the bread flour, and slowly mix together. Slowly add the other half of the bread flour. Add the milk and softened butter until a dough comes together. Divide into 3 portions, then wrap in plastic wrap (clingfilm) and let rest for 1 hour.

To make the egg wash: Mix together the egg and salt with ½ tablespoon of water. Set aside.

Line a baking sheet with parchment paper.

Roll the dough into a rectangular shape, place the olives in a line along a shorter edge and roll the edge just over the olives. Line the ham and bacon on the dough, then sprinkle the chopped raisins on top of the meat. Continue rolling it up, leaving 3¼ inches (8 cm) unrolled at the end of the dough.

Cut the unrolled dough into strips ⅝ inch (1.5 cm) wide. Brush the dough with egg wash, then cross the strips over the rolled loaf. Place on the prepared baking sheet. Brush the loaf all over with egg wash and let sit for 15–30 minutes.

Preheat the oven to 340°F (170°C/Gas Mark 3). Bake the dough for 30 minutes.

Meanwhile, to make the sugar glaze: Combine the papelón and 2 teaspoons of water in a saucepan and heat until the papelón has dissolved.

Remove the bread from the oven and immediately brush the sugar glaze all over it. Let cool, then serve.

KASTENGEL

Indonesia

Submitted by Petty Pandean-Elliott

Makes 80
Prep time: 20 minutes, plus chilling time
Cook time: 25–30 minutes

Kastengel are Indonesian savory snacks or cookies—the name derives from the Dutch words _kaas_ (cheese) and _stengels_ (sticks)—that come from the long period of Dutch colonial rule over Indonesia. They are still frequently enjoyed after a meal or with a cup of coffee or tea, during Christmas gatherings, and at the end of Ramadan (or _Idul Fitri_, as it is known in Indonesia).

This recipe comes from chef Petty Pandean-Elliott, who grew up in Manado, and whose grandmother and mother made them frequently for their family when she was a child—using processed cheese when fresh cheese was hard to come by. These days local cheesemakers, especially in Java and Bali, are creating more artisanal options. A harder cheese keeps the cookies crunchy (hence the Parmesan and extra-mature Cheddar in this recipe), and the dough can be frozen so that the cheese sticks can be enjoyed on a whim.

- 1⅓ cups (10½ oz/300 g) salted butter, room temperature
- 4 egg yolks
- scant 2¼ cups (12 oz/350 g) all-purpose (plain) flour, plus extra for dusting
- 6 tablespoons cornstarch (cornflour)
- 6 cups (7 oz/200 g) grated Parmesan, plus extra for sprinkling
- scant 1 cup (3½ oz/100 g) grated extra-mature Cheddar

In the bowl of a stand mixer fitted with the paddle attachment, beat the butter for 2–3 minutes. Add 2 of the egg yolks and mix. Add the flour, cornstarch (cornflour), and both cheeses and mix for another 1–2 minutes at low speed until combined. Do not overmix. Transfer the dough to a cutting board and shape it into a log, about 2 inches (5 cm) in diameter. Chill in the refrigerator for 2–3 hours.

Preheat the oven to 340°F (170°C/Gas Mark 3). Line 2 baking sheets with parchment paper and set aside.

Remove the dough from the refrigerator and cut it into 1¼-inch- (3-cm)-thick slices. On a counter lightly dusted with flour, roll each piece of dough with your hands to a ¾-inch- (2-cm)-diameter "rope". Flatten the top of the dough and cut it into 2¾-inch (7-cm) lengths. Arrange the cookies on the prepared baking sheet.

Put the remaining 2 egg yolks in a small bowl and beat. Brush the egg wash over the cookies, then sprinkle with Parmesan cheese. Bake for 25–30 minutes, until golden brown.

Remove from the oven and let cool for 5 minutes on the baking sheet, then transfer the cheese sticks to a wire rack and let cool completely. They will keep in an airtight container for 4 weeks.

TOURTIÈRE

Canada

Submitted by Allisa Murphy

Makes 1 × 9-inch (23-cm) pie
Prep time: 45 minutes
Cook time: 1 hour 15 minutes

For the pastry:
2⅓ cups plus 1 tablespoon (10½ oz/300 g) all-purpose (plain) flour, plus extra for dusting
½ teaspoon salt
¼ teaspoon baking powder
scant ½ cup (2¾ oz/75 g) lard
5½ tablespoons (2¾ oz/75 g) butter, cold
5 tablespoons cold water

For the filling:
2⅔ cups (10½ oz/300 g) ground (minced) pork
2⅔ cups (10½ oz/300 g) ground (minced) beef, lamb, or game
1 teaspoon fennel seeds
½ onion, diced
2–3 carrots, diced
½ bulb of fennel, diced
½ whole nutmeg, finely grated
generous ⅓ cup (3½ fl oz/100 ml) beef broth (stock), ale, or cider
10½ oz (300 g) Maris Piper potatoes, boiled and lightly mashed
3–4 shakes Worcestershire sauce
1 tablespoon wholegrain mustard
1 egg, beaten, for egg wash
salt and freshly ground black pepper

During the often dreary days between Christmas and New Year, *tourtière* is eaten at lunch time with friends and family. It is like a big warm hug: Showing up at someone's home to rejoice in the season of giving by eating this double-crusted meat pie, full of potato, carrot, and warm spice. French Canadian in its history, the name likely derives from the French word for the dish, *tourte*, traditionally featuring cubed game meat (more modern adaptations use ground (minced) pork, beef, or lamb) cooked in ale, cider, or beef broth (stock) to add a deep well of flavor. The *tourtière* is then bound together with lightly mashed potato and seasoned with nutmeg and fennel seed. It may be simple food—enjoyed alongside a brightly dressed salad, brown sauce, or homemade ketchup—but it is a perfect bridge between the celebrations of days passed and parties yet to come.

To make the pastry: In a large bowl, combine the flour, salt, and baking powder. Add the lard and butter, and rub between your fingers until the mixture resembles bread crumbs. Add the cold water, and gently knead into a ball. Wrap the dough in plastic wrap (clingfilm) and place in the refrigerator.

To make the filling: Heat a skillet (frying pan) over medium heat, then add the ground meats and fry for 5–7 minutes until mostly cooked through—increase the temperature if the meat releases a lot of liquid. Add the fennel seeds and season with salt and pepper, then cook for a few more minutes until the meat is fully cooked through. Add the onion, carrots, fennel, and nutmeg, and sauté for 5 minutes, or until the vegetables are tender. Add the liquid (broth [stock], ale, or cider), and cook for 10–15 minutes, or until the majority of the liquid has reduced. Remove from the heat.

Add the mashed potatoes to the pot, along with the Worcestershire sauce, wholegrain mustard, and more salt and pepper to taste. Set this mixture aside and let cool to room temperature.

Turn out the pastry onto a lightly floured counter and roll out to ⅛ inch (3 mm) thick. Cut a circle for the bottom by placing a 9-inch (23-cm) pie dish in the center of the rolled-out dough, and tracing around it with the tip of a knife, including enough pastry to fill the sides of the dish. Place the pastry into the bottom and up the sides of the dish and add the filling.

Gently knead the remaining dough together, then let rest for 5–10 minutes before rolling out again to a slightly smaller circle for the lid.

Preheat the oven to 375°F (190°C/Gas Mark 5). Brush the egg wash along the edges of the inside of the lid and secure it onto the top of the tart with any desired crimping style, or just a simple pinch, joining together the bottom pastry with the top. Brush the entire lid with egg wash, and cut an "X" in the center of the pastry to let out any residual steam while baking.

Bake for 20 minutes, then check the pie—if it is browning too quickly, reduce the temperature to 340°F (170°C/Gas Mark 3). Bake for another 20–25 minutes, or until the crust is a deep golden brown.

Remove from the oven and serve hot.

NEW YEAR

It may seem surprising, but the Western holidays of New Year's Eve and New Year's Day, as celebrated from the evening of December 31 into January 1, are relatively modern in their observances and traditions, dating back to the advent of the Gregorian calendar in 1582. Before this time, the New Year began not in January but in March, with its closer links to the natural rebirth of the landscape, the first shoots of spring, and the restart of the agricultural cycle.

Modern celebrations involve parties that center around counting down the hours to midnight, culminating in the ringing of bells—either in person or now streamed in live from different cities or countries around the world. Parties with friends and family, complete with celebratory food, and especially drinks, are commonly held, as are fireworks to mark the very first moments of the new year.

In some countries, New Year's celebrations were historically even more important than the biggest of holidays, like Christmas. In Scotland, where it is known by its older Scots name of Hogmanay, rituals like "first footing" are observed. This tradition sees neighbors take their first steps into the homes of friends and family on January 1, often with gifts like cakes or breads in hand.

KRANSEKAGE

Norway and Denmark

Submitted by Alice Mahon

Serves 10–15
Prep time: 1 hour, plus resting time
Cook time: 10–12 minutes

For the kransekage:
1 lb 4 oz (550 g) marzipan
grated zest of 1 orange
1¼ cups (4¾ oz/135 g) confectioners' (icing) sugar
1 egg white
1 drop almond extract

For the icing:
1¾ cups (7 oz/200 g) confectioners' (icing) sugar
2 egg whites

***Kransekage*, meaning "wreath cake," is a beloved confection from Norway and Denmark, traditionally enjoyed during festive occasions. Once a symbol of wealth and exclusivity when marzipan was a rare luxury, it has now become a staple of celebrations, most notably on New Year's Eve.**

This elegant cake is made from a rich marzipan-based dough, shaped into rings of varying sizes, baked, and carefully stacked from largest to smallest, creating a beautifully tiered centerpiece. In addition to being a highlight of New Year's festivities, *kransekage* is also a wedding tradition, where each ring is said to represent the number of children the couple will have.

While the traditional stacked *kransekage* is the most well-known version, modern variations include smaller, bite-size bars, sometimes dipped in chocolate for an extra indulgent touch. If the idea of constructing the full cake feels daunting, you can instead shape the dough into small 3½-oz (100-g) bars, decorating them just as beautifully—chocolate is optional but highly recommended! Just remember: the smaller bars will require a shorter baking time.

Line a baking sheet with parchment paper and set aside.

To make the kransekage: In the bowl of a stand mixer fitted with the paddle attachment, combine the marzipan, orange zest, sugar, egg white, and almond extract, and mix on low speed until fully incorporated.

Divide the dough into portions according to length and weight in the list below. Roll each piece into a long strand, ensuring the length corresponds to its weight.

14 inches (35 cm) / 4 oz (115 g)
12½ inches (32 cm) / 3¾ oz (105 g)
11½ inches (29 cm) / 3¼ oz (95 g)
10½ inches (26 cm) / 3 oz (85 g)
9 inches (23 cm) / 2¾ oz (75 g)
8 inches (20 cm) / 2¼ oz (65 g)
6½ inches (17 cm) / 2 oz (55 g)
5½ inches (14 cm) / 1½ oz (45 g)

Roll the last piece, which should be around 1¾ oz (50 g) into a round ball—the kransekage "topper."

To shape the rings: Using a damp hand, gently flatten one end of each strand to create a concave triangle shape. Bring the ends of each strand together to form a ring, pressing lightly to seal the join. Place the rings on the prepared baking sheet, working in batches if necessary. Let sit for 30 minutes before baking.

Preheat the oven to 400°F (200°C/Gas Mark 6). Bake the rings, in batches if needed, for 10–12 minutes, until lightly golden. The smaller rings will bake slightly faster than the larger ones, so keep an eye on them. Allow the rings to cool completely before assembling.

To make the icing: In a medium bowl, mix the confectioners' (icing) sugar and egg whites until smooth. Transfer to a pastry (piping) bag and cut a small hole at the tip. Pipe a zigzag pattern onto each ring and allow the icing to set.

To assemble the tower: Starting with the largest ring at the bottom, stack the rings in descending order to form a tower, and finish with the topper ball.

BLACK BUN

Scotland

This dark and richly spiced Scottish pastry-wrapped fruit cake is baked every year around New Year's Eve, or Hogmanay as it is called in Scotland. It is one of the most common and traditional gifts given by "first-footers," the first entrants to a home on New Year's Day. The cake, if stored in a dark and cool place, will keep for weeks, and is lovely when served with a cup of tea and a thin wedge of a nice Scottish cheese.

Submitted by Anna Luntley

Serves 8–10
Prep time: 1 hour, plus chilling time
Cook time: 2 hours

For the pastry:
¾ cup plus 1 tablespoon (3½ oz/100 g) all-purpose (plain) flour, plus extra for dusting
¾ cup (3½ oz/100 g) whole wheat all-purpose (plain) flour
½ teaspoon baking powder
2 pinches of superfine (caster) sugar
3 pinches fine sea salt
7 tablespoons (3½ oz/100 g) cold, diced butter, plus extra for greasing
5 tablespoons ice-cold water
1 egg, for egg wash
granulated sugar, for dusting

For the filling:
1¼ cups (5½ oz/150 g) all-purpose (plain) flour
⅓ cup plus 1 tablespoon (1¾ oz/50 g) almond meal (ground almonds)
4 cups (1 lb 9 oz/700 g) mixed dried fruit (see note)
1 teaspoon apple pie spice
½ teaspoon ground black pepper
2 teaspoons grated fresh ginger
scant ½ cup (3½ oz/100 g) dark soft brown sugar
½ teaspoon baking soda (bicarbonate of soda)
grated zest of 1 orange and ½ lemon
1 egg
3½ tablespoons milk
4 teaspoons marmalade
1 tablespoon black treacle (or molasses)
2 tablespoons brandy or whisky

To make the pastry: In a large bowl, sift together the flours, baking powder, superfine (caster) sugar, and 2 pinches of salt. Add the butter and rub it into the flour mixture with your fingertips until the mixture resembles coarse bread crumbs. Slowly add the ice-cold water and mix into the dough, being careful not to overwork it. Wrap the dough in plastic wrap (clingfilm) and chill in the refrigerator for at least 30 minutes.

To make the filling: In a large bowl, combine the flour, almond meal, dried fruit, spices, sugar, baking soda (bicarbonate of soda), and orange and lemon zest.

In a separate small bowl, lightly beat together the egg, milk, marmalade, and treacle to combine. Add to the bowl of dry ingredients, along with the brandy or whisky and mix to combine. Set aside.

Preheat the oven to 325°F (160°C/Gas Mark 3). Prepare a 2-lb (900-g) loaf pan by generously brushing it with melted butter to completely coat the bottom and all sides. Set aside.

Remove the chilled pastry from the refrigerator and turn out onto a lightly floured counter. Cut off one-quarter of the pastry and set aside—this will be the top. Roll the remaining pastry into a rectangle about 1/16 inch (2 mm) thick—large enough to line the bottom and sides of the loaf pan. Gently press the pastry into your loaf pan, leaving an overhang of about ½ inch (1 cm). Trim off any excess as necessary and set aside. Spoon the fruit cake mixture into the pastry shell.

Roll out the remaining pastry to about 1/16 inch (2 mm) thick, then cut into a rectangle to fit the top of the pan.

To make the egg wash: Beat together the egg with the remaining pinch of salt. Lightly brush the edge of pastry in the pan with the egg wash and place the rectangular piece on top, pinching the edges to seal. Brush the top of the pastry with egg wash.

If there are any excess pastry scraps, roll these out and cut leaves, petals, or any additional decoration as you wish. Add to the top of the pie, brush with egg wash, and dust the top with granulated sugar. Bake for 2 hours, turning after 1 hour, until golden brown.

Remove from the oven and let cool in the pan before serving. This cake will keep well for many weeks in an airtight container.

Note: Currants and golden raisins (sultanas) are the most traditional dried fruit to include, but you can also include raisins, figs, prunes, dates, and candied peel.

VASILOPITA

Greece

Submitted by Ianthi Michalaki

Serves 8–10
Prep time: 45 minutes, plus cooling time
Cook time: 1 hour 10 minutes

- neutral oil, for greasing (optional)
- 1½ cups (6¾ oz/190 g) self-rising flour
- 1 teaspoon ground cinnamon
- ½ teaspoon ground nutmeg
- pinch of salt
- 7 tablespoons (3½ oz/95 g) butter (82 percent fat), at room temperature
- 1⅓ cups (9½ oz/270 g) superfine (caster) sugar
- 1½ teaspoons orange zest
- 5 egg yolks
- 2½ tablespoons milk
- ⅓ cup (2½ oz/70 g) whole natural yogurt
- ¼ cup (1 oz/30 g) pecan halves, finely chopped
- 5 egg whites
- confectioners' (icing) sugar or frosting, to decorate

Vasilopita (which translates literally as "Basil's pie", but is more commonly known as "King's Cake") is a mainstay of New Year's festivities in Greece. Every year on New Year's Day the cake is served up among family and friends in a manner both spiritual and symbolic: The first few pieces are cut for the home, then for Christ, and then for each member of the family. A gold coin, hidden inside the cake, is said to bring good luck to its finder for the rest of the year.

Despite its modern association, _Vasilopita_ actually originated as part of the celebrations for Saint Basil's Day (also January 1) and was made as a savory pie (like it still is in Epirus). After the 1920s, in the wake of the vast Greek–Turkish population exchange, it changed, as cakes and fine pastry were popularized throughout the country. _Vasilopita_ took the form of a sweet, enriched dough that was—similar to _tsoureki_—decorated with almonds, a version still popular today in the regions of northern Greece. In the rest of the country and most homes, _Vasilopita_ is a fragrant cake with nuts, dusted commonly with confectioners' (icing) sugar and decorated with the numbers of the new year on top.

This recipe, provided by Ianthi Michalaki, a Greek baker in Athens, comes from her grandmother but has been tweaked by Michalaki over the years.

Preheat the oven to 350°F (180°C/Gas Mark 4). Lightly oil a 9-inch (23-cm) cake pan, or line with parchment paper, and set aside.

In a medium bowl, sift the flour and spices together. Add the salt and set aside.

In the bowl of a stand mixer fitted with the paddle attachment, cream the butter, 1 cup (7 oz/200 g) of the sugar, and the orange zest until light and airy. Change to the whisk attachment and add the egg yolks, mixing on low speed. Once all the yolks have been incorporated, clean the edges of the bowl with a rubber spatula and mix again on medium–high speed for 1–2 minutes until increased in volume. Add 2½ tablespoons of water, the milk, and yogurt, and mix briefly until incorporated. Add half of the dry ingredients, and mix for about 30 seconds, until just incorporated. Add the remaining dry ingredients and mix for another 30 seconds, until just incorporated. Gently fold in the pecans with a rubber spatula.

In a clean bowl, combine the egg whites and remaining sugar and whisk to soft peaks. Fold this meringue gently into the cake batter. Transfer the batter into the prepared pan and bake for 1 hour and 10 minutes, until a toothpick (cocktail stick) inserted in the center comes out clean.

Remove from the oven and let cool for 30 minutes before removing from the pan. Once completely cool, flip it over and hide a coin inside. Decorate with confectioners' (icing) sugar or frosting. The cake freezes very well wrapped in plastic wrap (clingfilm) and keeps for up to 5 days if uncut and well wrapped.

SAUERKRAUT & CUMIN STRUDEL

Romania

Submitted by Diana Iovescu Tatucu

Serves 6–8
Prep time: 30 minutes, plus resting time
Cook time: 1 hour

For the dough:
2 cups (9 oz/250 g) all-purpose (plain) flour, plus extra for dusting
½ teaspoon salt
1 egg
generous ⅓ cup (3½ fl oz/100 ml) warm water
2 tablespoons sunflower oil or melted butter, plus extra for brushing

For the filling:
1 tablespoon sunflower oil
1 teaspoon cumin seeds
1 onion, finely chopped
1 lb 2 oz (500 g) sauerkraut, finely chopped and drained
freshly ground black pepper

Sauerkraut and cumin strudel is a savory pastry that hails from the multicultural heart of Romania—particularly Transylvania and Banat, where German, Hungarian, and Romanian influences have long intertwined. This dish reflects Austro-Hungarian culinary traditions, brought by Saxon settlers and adapted over generations. It is especially associated with winter holidays such as Christmas (*Crăciun*) and New Year (*Revelion*), when fermented foods like sauerkraut are a staple on the cold-weather table. The cumin adds a distinct warmth and fragrance, balancing the sharpness of the cabbage. This strudel is often served as a snack, appetizer, or side dish during festive meals, sometimes accompanying pork roasts or hearty bean soups. Baked until crisp and golden, it is a reminder of the resourcefulness of rural kitchens and a celebration of preserved winter flavors.

To make the dough: In a bowl, mix the flour and salt. Add the egg, water, and oil or melted butter. Knead until a smooth, elastic dough forms (8–10 minutes). Cover with a clean dish (tea) towel and let rest for 30 minutes at room temperature.

Meanwhile, to make the filling: Heat the oil in a pan over medium heat. Add the cumin seeds and let them sizzle for 30 seconds. Add the chopped onion and cook for 10 minutes until soft and translucent. Stir in the sauerkraut and cook for 10–15 minutes, stirring occasionally, until the moisture has mostly evaporated. Season with black pepper and let cool.

Preheat the oven to 375°F (190°C/Gas Mark 5). Line a baking sheet with parchment paper and set aside.

Turn out the dough onto a floured counter and roll it out into a thin rectangle. Spread the sauerkraut filling evenly over the surface, leaving a border. Starting at a long edge, roll up the dough tightly into a log and seal the ends. Place on the prepared baking sheet and brush with oil or melted butter. Bake for 35–40 minutes, until golden brown and crisp.

Remove from the oven and let cool slightly before slicing and serving.

ALL YEAR

ALL YEAR

BIRTHDAYS

The earliest birthday feasts date back to ancient Egypt, Persia, and Greece, but we wouldn't quite recognize them. That's because these occasions originated as celebrations of gods or, occasionally, divinely appointed figures such as monarchs. It would not be until the early modern age (*c.* 1600) that celebrating your own birthday, or the birthday of a friend or family member, began to gain traction. Even the tradition of lighting candles was one that, for centuries in western Europe, was more closely linked to prayer and worship than secular festivity. This began to change with the spread of Protestantism, and by the eighteenth and nineteenth centuries, the rise of the middle class brought with it an emphasis on marking the occasion of personal milestones with a party or festivity of some kind.

Nowadays we completely personalize our birthday celebrations, but the ritualistic, almost spiritual roots of modern birthday trends, including a candlelit cake, song, or some of our favorite foods, are still visible throughout much of Western-rooted culture.

VANILLA BIRTHDAY CAKE WITH CHOCOLATE FROSTING

United States

Submitted by Nicholas Andreadis

Serves 16
Prep time: 1 hour
Cook time: 30–35 minutes

For the sponge:
2½ cups (1 lb 2 oz/500 g) superfine (caster) sugar
7 tablespoons (3½ oz/100 g) butter, softened
⅔ cup (5 fl oz/150 ml) vegetable oil
4 large eggs
1 egg yolk
1⅓ cups (11¼ fl oz/320 ml) milk
1½ teaspoons vanilla extract
4 cups (1 lb 2 oz/500 g) cake flour
1 tablespoon baking powder
½ tablespoon fine salt

For the buttercream:
2 cups (11½ oz/325 g) chocolate pellets (at least 75 percent cocoa solids)
splash of cognac or brandy (optional)
5½ sticks (1 lb 6 oz/625 g) butter
5 cups (1 lb 10 oz/750 g) confectioners' (icing) sugar
½ teaspoon vanilla extract
½ teaspoon salt
sprinkles, to decorate (optional)

This recipe conjures images of classic Americana: backyard birthday parties on Kentucky bluegrass lawns bordered by white picket fences, games of pin the tail on the donkey, latex bounce houses, clowns, and face painters. And at the center of it all, a sheet cake, candles flickering atop a thick layer of chocolate buttercream, topped with rainbow sprinkles and set over a yellow-hued, vanilla-scented sponge. This is the quintessential American birthday cake—simple, celebratory, and joyfully devoured by all.

This cake recipe was the standard for early birthdays for its author, Nicholas Andreadis. Now an adult, he suggests adding a nip of cognac or brandy to the buttercream—just enough to enhance the jammy, fruity notes of a truly good single origin chocolate.

Preheat the oven to 325°F (160°C/Gas Mark 3). Line the bottom and sides of a 9 × 13-inch (23 × 33 cm) cake pan with parchment paper and set aside.

To make the sponge: In a stand mixer fitted with the paddle attachment, combine the sugar, butter, and vegetable oil. Mix on medium speed until just combined—the mixture should look grainy and glossy, like wet sand. Scrape down the sides and bottom of the bowl to make sure all the sugar is incorporated.

In a small bowl, whisk the eggs. Slowly pour the eggs and egg yolk into the mixer while it's running on low–medium speed. Mix until fully incorporated and slightly thickened. Scrape the bowl down again to ensure all the egg is fully blended in.

In a microwave-safe cup, combine the milk and vanilla extract. Warm slightly (20–30 seconds); it should feel warm to the touch, not hot. Set aside.

Onto a piece of parchment paper, sift together the cake flour, baking powder, and salt. With the mixer on low speed, add one-third of the dry mixture to the bowl. Mix gently until mostly incorporated. Slowly stream in half of the warm milk mixture while the mixer runs. Add another third of the dry ingredients and mix again gently. Add the remaining milk mixture and mix until combined. Add the final third of the dry ingredients and fold by hand with a rubber spatula. The batter may look slightly uneven or separated at first, but as you fold, it will come together smoothly. Pour the batter into the prepared pan. Use an offset spatula to spread it evenly, creating a slight dip in the center to encourage it to rise flat. Bake on the center rack for 30–35 minutes, until the top is golden, the edges start to pull slightly from the sides, and a toothpick (cocktail stick) inserted into the center comes out clean.

Remove from the oven and let cool in the pan on a wire rack.

Meanwhile, to make the buttercream: Set a heatproof bowl over simmering water, add the chocolate, and stir until it is 80 percent melted. Remove from the heat and stir to finish melting. Stir in the cognac or brandy, if using.

In the bowl of a stand mixer fitted with the paddle attachment, combine the butter and confectioners' (icing) sugar. Start on low speed , then once combined, increase the speed and add the vanilla extract and salt. Whisk until pale, fluffy, and spreadable—this may take up to 5 minutes on medium–high speed.

Add a heaping spoonful of the whisked butter mixture to the melted chocolate and mix until fully combined. Add the chocolate mixture back into the main bowl with the rest of the buttercream. Beat until fully combined and smooth.

To assemble: Place the cooled cake onto a cake board or serving platter using a small dollop of buttercream to hold it in place. Add large dollops of buttercream on top of the cake and use an offset spatula to spread it evenly across the surface. Decorate with sprinkles.

PINE BARK CAKE

Norway

Submitted by Máret Rávdná Buljo

Serves 8
Prep time: 30 minutes
Cook time: 30–45 minutes

For the cake:
4 eggs
generous 2 cups (15 oz/425 g) granulated sugar
3 cups (24 fl oz/700 ml) kefir
1½ cups (12 oz/350 g) melted butter
generous 2 cups (10½ oz/300 g) whole wheat flour, sifted
½ cup (4 oz/120 g) pine bark flour, sifted
4 tablespoons unsweetened cocoa powder
2 teaspoons baking soda (bicarbonate of soda)
4 teaspoons vanilla sugar
½ teaspoon salt

For the frosting:
generous 2 cups (8½ oz/240 g) confectioners' (icing) sugar
2 teaspoons vanilla sugar
3 tablespoons unsweetened cocoa powder
3 tablespoons pine bark flour
3½ tablespoons brewed coffee, cooled
jelly candies or similar, to decorate

This recipe comes from Sámi cultural activist and chef Máret Rávdná Buljo, who champions the usage of traditional ingredients and elements of Sámi food culture in modern cooking and baking environments. This recipe, utilizing pine bark flour (made from sustainably foraged, cleaned, baked, and then ground pine bark) has become a popular birthday cake in Lofoten where she and her family live, with the "mystery ingredient" becoming a favorite even among kids.

Preheat the oven to 350°F (180°C/Gas Mark 4). Line a baking sheet with parchment paper and set aside.

To make the cake: In a bowl, combine the eggs and sugar and whisk until fluffy. Add the kefir and melted butter, and gently stir everything together. Fold in the flours, cocoa powder, baking soda (bicarbonate of soda), vanilla sugar, and salt until evenly incorporated. Pour the cake batter onto the prepared baking sheet, and bake on the second lowest rack for 30–45 minutes.

Remove from the oven and set aside to cool before applying the frosting.

To make the frosting: In a bowl, combine the confectioners' (icing) sugar, vanilla sugar, cocoa powder, and bark flour. Add the coffee and stir together. Spread the frosting over the cake. Decorate with jelly candies, or candies of your choice. Let the frosting set before serving.

DOBERGE CAKE

United States

Submitted by Lisa Donovan

Serves 12–16
Prep time: 1½ hours
Cook time: 15 minutes per batch

For the cakes:
- ¾ cup (6 oz/170 g) butter, plus extra for greasing
- 3½ cups (15 oz/420 g) cake flour, sifted, plus extra for dusting
- 4 eggs, separated
- 2 cups (14 oz/400 g) superfine (caster) sugar
- 3 teaspoons baking powder
- 1 cup (8 fl oz/250 ml) milk
- 1 teaspoon vanilla paste
- 1 teaspoon rum or bourbon
- juice of ½ lemon
- salt

For the filling:
- 2 cups (14 oz/400 g) superfine sugar
- 4 tablespoons all-purpose (plain) flour
- 4 tablespoons cornstarch (cornflour)
- 2 tablespoons unsweetened cocoa powder
- 4 cups (32 fl oz/945 ml) milk
- 4 eggs, at room temperature
- 1 tablespoon (½ oz/14 g) butter, melted
- 4 tablespoons semisweet (dark) chocolate, melted
- 1 tablespoon vanilla paste

For the frosting:
- 2 sticks (8 oz/225 g) butter
- 2 cups (8 oz/225 g) confectioners' (icing) sugar, sifted
- 1 cup (4¼ oz/120 g) good-quality unsweetened cocoa powder
- 1 oz (30 g) chocolate (at least 70 per cent cocoa solids), melted
- 1 teaspoon vanilla paste

The Doberge cake is a southern United States adaptation of the Budapest-born Dobos torte, originally invented by József Dobos in 1885. The Hungarian version features thin layers of sponge cake intricately layered with chocolate buttercream, a grand affair, fitting of the patisserie trends of late nineteenth-century Austro-Hungaria.

In the 1930s, Beulah Ledner, a New Orleans-based baker, and the child of Hungarian immigrants, adapted the Dobos torte, increasing the height and size of the cake, and substituting buttercream for American-style "pudding" or custard. The final result was a more home-style cake that suited American tastes, and became a hit across the city, and the wider region.

Today, the Doberge cake is a popular bake for all kinds of special celebrations including birthdays and Mardi Gras. This recipe is an adaptation of Beulah Ledner's own, by southern pastry chef and food writer Lisa Donovan. While the cake component always remains a classic vanilla sponge, the pudding or custard mixture can vary between chocolate, lemon, or caramel—in this case, chocolate.

Preheat the oven to 375°F (190°C/Gas Mark 5). Grease and flour as many 9-inch (23-cm) cake pans as will fit in the oven for even baking (you will need 8 layers of this cake) and set aside.

To make the cakes: In the bowl of a stand mixer fitted with the whisk attachment, whisk the egg whites until very stiff. Transfer to a separate bowl and set aside.

In the same bowl (no need to rinse), using the paddle attachment, cream the butter, sugar, and ½ teaspoon of salt until fluffy and smooth. Add the egg yolks, one at a time, and blend until smooth, scraping the bottom and sides of the bowl frequently.

Sift the flour and baking powder into a bowl together. Add the dry mixture alternately with the milk in thirds—scraping the bottom and sides of the bowl and beating well after each addition—until you have added all the flour and milk. Add the vanilla, rum, and lemon juice and mix to combine. Remove from the stand mixer and, using a spatula, gently fold in the beaten egg whites.

Pour one-eighth of the batter into each prepared pan, spreading evenly over the bottom. Give each pan a gentle thump to release any air pockets, then bake for 12–15 minutes. If necessary, repeat the process until you have 8 thin cake layers. Let cool, then cover loosely with a clean dish (tea) towel to prevent them from drying out.

To make the filling: In a saucepan, combine the dry ingredients, then add the milk, eggs, melted butter, melted chocolate, and vanilla paste, and whisk everything together. Cook over low heat until dispersed and steaming hot and thick. Press through a fine-mesh sieve to remove any lumps, then cool over an ice bath. Cover with plastic wrap (clingfilm) directly on top of the mixture to prevent a skin from forming and chill in the refrigerator.

To make the frosting: In the bowl of a stand mixer fitted with the paddle attachment, cream the butter and sugar together until fluffy. Add the cocoa powder and blend well, then add the melted chocolate and vanilla. Season with salt. If the frosting is too thick, add a little hot water until the consistency is right.

To assemble the cake: Alternate the cake layers with the chocolate custard filling. Chill well, then coat with the chocolate butter cream frosting over the top and sides.

UBE CAKE

Philippines

Ube cake is a vibrant purple chiffon cake made with *ube halaya* (purple yam jam) and ube extract. It has become a favorite in Filipino celebrations like birthdays and holidays due to its striking color and nostalgic flavor.

Submitted by Florence Mae Maglanoc

Serves 8
Prep time: 20 minutes
Cook time: 30–35 minutes

For the cake:
½ cup (4 fl oz/120 ml) vegetable oil, plus extra for greasing
1½ cups plus 2 tablespoons (7 oz/200 g) cake flour
2 teaspoons baking powder
5 egg yolks
1 cup (7 oz/200 g) granulated sugar
¾ cup (6 fl oz/180 ml) coconut milk
generous ⅓ cup (3½ oz/100 g) ube halaya (purple yam jam)
1 teaspoon ube extract
7 egg whites
½ teaspoon cream of tartar
whipped cream, for topping (optional)
maraschino cherries, for decorating

For the ube buttercream:
1⅓ sticks (5 oz/150 g) butter
2⅔ cups (10½ oz/300 g) confectioners' (icing) sugar
1 teaspoon ube extract
1 tablespoon milk or coconut milk, plus extra if needed

Preheat the oven to 340°F (170°C/Gas Mark 3). Grease and line 2 round 9-inch (23 cm) cake pans.

To make the cake: In a bowl, combine the cake flour and baking powder.

In a separate bowl, whisk together the egg yolks, ½ cup (3½ oz/100 g) of the sugar, the oil, coconut milk, ube halaya, and ube extract until smooth. Add this to the dry ingredients.

In another bowl, beat the egg whites with the cream of tartar until foamy. Gradually add the remaining ½ cup (3½ oz/100 g) sugar and beat until stiff peaks form. Gently fold this meringue mixture into the ube batter. Divide between the pans and bake for 30–35 minutes, until a skewer inserted into the center comes out clean.

While the cake is baking, make the ube buttercream: In the bowl of a stand mixer fitted with the paddle attachment, beat the butter and confectioners' (icing) sugar together until light and fluffy. Add the ube extract and the milk and continue to beat to create a spreadable buttercream. You may need to add a little more milk, if desired.

Remove the cake from the oven and let cool completely, then spread the ube buttercream or whipped cream all over the cake. If desired, you can use a pastry (piping) bag fitted with a star nozzle to decorate. Top with the cherries, and serve.

ORANGE SODA CAKE

Hungary

Submitted by Lilla Szőcs

Serves 12
Prep time: 1 hour
Cook time: 35 minutes

For the sponge cake:
1 tablespoon sunflower oil, plus extra for greasing
6 tablespoons all-purpose (plain) flour, plus extra for dusting
7 eggs, separated
7 tablespoons superfine (caster) sugar
1 tablespoon baking powder
2 tablespoons unsweetened cocoa powder

For the cottage cheese cream:
2¼ cups (1 lb 2 oz/500 g) cottage cheese (túró)
¾ cup (6 oz/180 g) margarine
1¾ cups (7 oz/200 g) confectioners' (icing) sugar
1 tablespoon vanilla sugar
grated zest of 1 lemon

For the orange jelly:
5 tablespoons Dr. Oetker's vanilla instant pudding powder
4 tablespoons granulated sugar
3 cups (24 fl oz/700 ml) carbonated orange soda
1 tablespoon lemon juice

Ever since soft drinks have existed, people around the world have been making cakes with them—Americans, Germans, and Hungarians alike. In Hungary, one particular version made with orange-flavored soda (usually Fanta) evokes strong nostalgia among the millennial generation.

In the 1960s, at a time when Hungary was still struggling with a shortage of ingredients after the war, the *üdítő szelet*—orange soda cake—was born. "Imperialist" soft drinks had not yet entered the country, so instead, production of local "socialist" beverages began, which were considered trendy in their own right. While it might be hard to imagine today, soft drinks were once regarded as valuable commodities—older generations still recall their first sips and how difficult it was to get hold of them (especially the real Western sodas).

It is likely that the soda cake recipe was born out of a need to avoid waste, making use of the precious drink by incorporating it into baking. The recipe has changed very little over the years, and is still most often made of chocolate sponge, cottage cheese, and jelly (Jell-O)—despite the fact the brand of soft drinks (mostly orange-flavored) varies depending on availability.

Preheat the oven to 350°F (180°C/Gas Mark 4). Lightly grease an 11-inch (28-cm) cake pan with oil and dust with flour.

To make the sponge cake: In a large bowl, whisk the egg whites into stiff peaks. Gradually add the sugar. Then mix in the egg yolks, followed by the sunflower oil.

In a separate bowl, combine the baking powder, cocoa powder, and flour. Gently fold this mixture into the egg foam. Pour the batter into your prepared pan, then bake in the oven for 15–20 minutes, until a skewer inserted into the center comes out clean. Remove from the oven and let cool.

Meanwhile, to make the cottage cheese cream: Either press the cottage cheese through a fine-mesh sieve or blend it with a stick blender until smooth. Transfer to a bowl, then add the margarine, confectioners' (icing) sugar, vanilla sugar, and lemon zest to the pureed cheese and mix well. Once the sponge cake has cooled, spread the cottage cheese cream over the cake.

To make the orange jelly (do this at the very last moment, as it sets very quickly once it starts to cool): In a pan, combine the vanilla pudding powder, sugar, orange soda, and lemon juice, stirring over a low heat until it starts to thicken. Remove from the heat and leave to cool slightly. Once lukewarm, spread over the cottage cheese cream layer, then refrigerate for at least 2 hours before serving.

PRINSESSTÅRTA

Sweden

p. 308

Submitted by Cecilia Tolone

Serves 10–12
Prep time: 30 minutes, plus chilling time
Cook time: 30 minutes

For the marzipan:
3¼ cups (14 oz/400 g) almond meal (ground almonds)
2⅔ cups (10½ oz/300 g) confectioners' (icing) sugar
2 egg whites
almond extract (optional), to taste
few drops red food coloring
few drops green food coloring

For the raspberry jam:
1½ cups (9 oz/250 g) raspberries
1 cup (7 oz/200 g) granulated sugar
lemon juice, to taste

For the pastry cream:
generous 1 cup (17 fl oz/500 ml) milk
1 vanilla bean (pod), seeds scraped
6 egg yolks
½ cup (3½ oz/100 g) granulated sugar
7 tablespoons cornstarch (cornflour)
2 tablespoons (1 oz/28 g) butter

For the cake:
4 tablespoons (2¼ oz/65 g) butter, melted, plus extra for greasing
4 eggs, plus 5 egg yolks
scant ¾ cup (5 oz/140 g) superfine (caster) sugar
1 cup plus 2 tablespoons (5 oz/140 g) all-purpose (plain) flour

Prinsesstårta—princess cake—is a traditional Swedish dessert that originated in the early twentieth century. It was created by Jenny Åkerström, a teacher who notably tutored three princesses of the Swedish royal family in the early 1900s. The original name for the cake, _gröntårta_, or "green cake," came from its distinctively colored marzipan topping, but it was later renamed _prinsesstårta_, due to its popularity among the princesses.

Originally, it did not contain any jam, and some Swedes still like to argue that a true princess cake is made with just vanilla pastry cream and whipped cream. Nowadays, however, raspberry jam is almost ubiquitous.

In Sweden today, princess cake is the go-to cake for celebrations of all kinds: it is eaten at everything from birthdays to christenings to graduations. It is common now to use different colored marzipan and decorate the top according to the party theme, but green is the classic.

To make the marzipan: In the bowl of a food processor, combine the almond meal (ground almonds) and confectioners' (icing) sugar. Mix until the confectioners' sugar is evenly distributed and the almond meal is slightly finer. Add 1 egg white and mix. Add a drop of almond extract, if using. Scrape the sides, add the second egg white, and mix until a homogeneous dough forms. If the marzipan is dry, add 1–2 tablespoons of water.

Break off a small piece of the marzipan, add a drop or so of red dye to it to color it pink, then add a few drops of green dye to the rest to color it light green. Wrap the colored marzipan separately in plastic wrap (clingfilm) and set aside.

To make the raspberry jam: In a pot, combine the raspberries and sugar. Place over low heat and gently bring to a simmer. Simmer for about 10 minutes, stirring often. Once the jam is thick, turn off the heat and add the lemon juice to taste. Pour the jam into a heatproof container, let cool, then chill in the refrigerator.

To make the pastry cream: Bring the milk and vanilla bean (pod) and scraped seeds to a boil in a pan.

In a separate bowl, whisk the egg yolks, sugar, and cornstarch (cornflour) together. Add the hot milk mixture, whisking continuously, to temper the eggs. Return the mixture to the pot and bring to a boil, stirring continuously. Boil for 1 minute until thick and glossy. Remove from heat, add the butter, and stir until combined. Strain the cream, let cool slightly, then chill in the refrigerator.

Preheat the oven to 340°F (170°C/Gas Mark 3). Line a 9-inch (23-cm) cake pan with parchment paper and brush all over with melted butter.

To make the cake: Prepare a double boiler. In the bowl of a stand mixer, whisk the eggs, egg yolks, and sugar. Place the bowl over the simmering water and whisk continuously until the mixture reaches 130°F/55°C on a candy thermometer. Transfer to the bowl of a stand mixer fitted with the whisk attachment and whisk until light, fluffy, and just warm but no longer hot. Gradually sift and fold in the flour. Fold in the melted butter in 2 additions. Pour the batter into the prepared pan and bake for 20 minutes.

Remove from the oven and allow the cake to cool completely.

Meanwhile, whip the heavy (double) cream until soft peaks form. Mix about ⅓ cup (3½ fl oz/100 ml) of the pastry cream with two-thirds of the whipped cream to create diplomat cream. Reserve the leftover whipped cream.

For the diplomat cream:
generous 1 cup (17 fl oz/500 ml) heavy (double) cream

To assemble:
confectioners' (icing) sugar, for dusting

To assemble: Cut the cake horizontally into 3 layers. Spread the raspberry jam over the bottom layer, then place another cake layer on top and spread with the pastry cream. Spread the diplomat cream over the pastry cream, and smooth into a dome. Place the last cake layer over the diplomat cream and press it down a little to help keep the dome shape. Roll out the light green marzipan and drape it over the cake, smoothing and trimming any excess. Transfer to a cake plate and dust with confectioners' sugar.

Take the small piece of red marzipan and divide it into 6 equal pieces. Shape one into a small cone, then gently flatten the remaining 5 pieces. Carefully wrap the flattened pieces at intervals around the cone, to create the shape of a rose with petals. Decorate the cake with the marzipan rose and serve with the reserved whipped cream, if desired.

WEDDINGS

The earliest recorded evidence of a wedding (with ceremony and contract) comes from ancient Mesopotamia around 4,000 years ago. In the same era, in nearby Babylon, legal codes like the Laws of Eshunna demonstrate the importance of food to the wedding—stating that a wedding without a feast would not be valid. The notion of a "cake" to celebrate this occasion stems back at least as far as ancient Rome, where it was common to bake what is called a *mustaceum*, a simple bread sweetened with grape must (hence the name) and baked on bay leaves.

In medieval and even early modern times, many cultures deepened that association between baking and weddings, but whether sweet or savory, these "bride's pies" or "bride's cakes" remained quite plain. As the wider culture surrounding baking developed, and ingredients like eggs, butter, and sugar became cheaper, these cakes became richer and sweeter.

Our notion of the elaborate multitiered wedding cake, crowned in white icing, seems to be a late nineteenth- or early twentieth-century tradition that derives from the style of cakes featured at two weddings: Queen Victoria's in 1840, and then, some forty years later, her youngest son Leopold's in 1882. Today, there is of course less dogma surrounding what to eat at a wedding, but the underlining idea remains the same: Celebrating the union of two individuals with an auspicious centerpiece.

Left: *Prinsesstårta*, Birthdays (page 306)

NAAN KHAMEI

Iran

Submitted by Shiva Shirazi Gombart

Makes 12–16
Prep time: 30 minutes
Cook time: 25 minutes

For the choux pastry:
3½ tablespoons milk
3½ tablespoons (1¾ oz/50 g) butter
1 teaspoon sugar
½ cup plus 1 tablespoon (2¾ oz/75 g) bread flour
2–3 eggs
scant ½ teaspoon salt

For the filling:
⅞ cup (7 fl oz/200 ml) heavy (double) cream (minimum 45% fat)
½ tablespoon rosewater
¼ cup (1 oz/25 g) confectioners' (icing) sugar, plus extra for dusting
1 oz (25 g) ground pistachios

This Persian cream puff is the Iranian adaptation of French choux pastry. The technique of making these hollow pastry shells with a filling was introduced to Iran during the Qajar or early Pahlavi era (late nineteenth century into early twentieth century), when French culinary influence grew in Iran's urban circles, especially the capital, Tehran. By the 1970s, *naan khamei* had become an essential in bakeries and traditional pastry stores.

These pastries, filled with rosewater-infused cream and topped with pistachios and confectioners' (icing) sugar, are typically served during *bale boroun* ceremonies (a traditional pre-wedding event where the bride officially accepts the proposal and the families set the date for the wedding). They're also very popular during *Nowruz* and engagement parties, symbolizing sweetness and new beginnings. *Naan khamei* is often enjoyed with a cup of warm tea.

Preheat the oven to 425°F (220°C/Gas Mark 7). Line a baking sheet with parchment paper and set aside.

To make the choux pastry: Heat 4 tablespoons of water with the milk, butter, and sugar in a pan until the butter is fully melted and the mixture starts to boil. Add the flour immediately and stir with a rubber spatula until a thick dough forms. Keep stirring for a couple of minutes or until a thin film forms at the bottom of the pan. If you have a thermometer, the temperature of the dough should be 167°F (75°C). Transfer the dough to the bowl of a stand mixer fitted with the paddle attachment and mix the dough until it cools down slightly.

Meanwhile, break the eggs into a small bowl, add the salt, and mix until just combined. Slowly stream the egg mixture into the dough, little by little, continuing to mix until the batter becomes shiny and forms a "V: shape when you lift the paddle attachment.

Transfer the dough to a pastry (piping) bag and, depending on the desired size (12 medium or 16 small), pipe the dough onto the prepared baking sheet, leaving at least ¾–1¼ inches (2–3 cm) between each choux, as they will expand. Bake for 15 minutes, then reduce the oven temperature to 375°F (195°C/Gas Mark 5) and bake for another 10 minutes, or until the choux pastries are golden brown. Set aside to cool while you prepare the filling.

To make the filling: In a bowl, whip the cream, rosewater, and confectioners' (icing) sugar until firm. Cut the choux pastries in half, fill them with the rose cream, and sprinkle generously with the ground pistachios. Replace the tops and dust generously with confectioners' sugar. Serve immediately.

HJÓNABANDSSÆLA

Iceland

Submitted by Anna Luntley

Serves 10–12
Prep time: 30 minutes
Cook time: 1¼ hours

For the cake:
- 3½ tablespoons set honey
- 10½ tablespoons (5½ oz/150 g) butter
- scant 1 cup (7 oz/195 g) soft light brown sugar
- 1 cup plus 2 tablespoons (5 oz/140 g) almond meal (ground almonds)
- ⅔ cup (2¼ oz/60 g) oat flour
- 2½ cups (9 oz/250 g) oats
- ½ teaspoon baking soda (bicarbonate of soda)
- ½ teaspoon salt
- 1 lb 2 oz (500 g) rhubarb, chopped into ½-inch (1-cm) pieces
- seeds from ½ vanilla bean (pod)
- 2 tablespoons cornstarch (cornflour)
- ⅔ cup (2¾ oz/80 g) slivered (flaked) almonds

To serve:
- confectioners' (icing) sugar, for dusting (optional)
- whipped cream (optional)

***Hjónabandssæla* translates as "happy marriage," and this cake is said to be a poetic allusion to the harmony and balance of its main ingredients, oats and rhubarb, rather than referring to the occasion when it is baked.**

This recipe for happy marriage cake comes from British baker Anna Luntley, who often enjoyed this cake at a local cafe while working in Iceland. After returning to the United Kingdom, she started to regularly make the *hjónabandssæla* at her own bakery, where many folks also began ordering it for their own weddings in lieu of a more traditional wedding cake.

Anna's version swaps the rhubarb jam of the original for fresh rhubarb to create a more distinct flavor profile and a more luscious but less sweet bake overall. It is an easy recipe to play with the flavors, swapping in seasonal fresh fruit (or jam or jelly) as the months and weather change.

Preheat the oven to 350°F (180°C/Gas Mark 4). Line an 8 × 11-inch (20 × 27-cm) baking pan with parchment paper and set aside.

To make the cake: In a medium pan over low heat, combine the honey, butter, and ⅔ cup (4¼ oz/120 g) of the soft light brown sugar.

Meanwhile, in a large bowl mix together the almond meal (ground almonds), oat flour, oats, baking soda (bicarbonate of soda), and salt. Set aside.

In another bowl, combine the chopped rhubarb with the remaining soft light brown sugar, the vanilla seeds, and the cornstarch (cornflour). Mix well to coat the rhubarb and distribute the vanilla seeds. Set aside.

By this time the sweet honey mixture in the pan should be melted. Stir to combine, and if necessary increase the heat a little, stirring constantly until you have a bubbling and uniform pot of caramelly goodness. Remove from the heat and pour over the oat and almond mixture. Mix well to coat the oats.

Weigh 14 oz (400 g) of this mixture into the prepared pan and spread out into an even layer—this is easiest with wet fingers and a confident touch— steal a little more mix from the bowl if necessary to fully cover the bottom of the pan. Bake for 15 minutes, until golden.

Meanwhile, add the slivered (flaked) almonds to the remaining oat mixture and stir to combine.

Remove the pan from the oven, then sprinkle the rhubarb mixture across the bottom, scraping out the juices, too. Top with the remaining oat and almond mixture to cover the rhubarb, pressing down lightly. It is fine for some little bits of rhubarb pink to be still showing. Return the pan to the oven and bake for another 45–60 minutes, until the oats are caramelized and any bits of rhubarb are bubbling and turning a deep reddish brown.

Remove from the oven and let cool before serving. When ready to serve, dust with confectioners' (icing) sugar and top with whipped cream, if desired.

TORTA DELLE ROSE

Italy

Submitted by Agnese Negrini

Serves 6
Prep time: 2 hours, plus proofing time and optional overnight resting and chilling
Cook time: 45 minutes

For the preferment:
1¼ cups (5½ oz/155 g) strong baking flour (at least 11% protein)
¼ oz (8 g) fresh yeast
neutral oil, for greasing

For the brioche:
½ cup (4½ fl oz/130 ml) milk
1 extra-large egg yolk
⅓ cup (2¾ oz/75 g) honey
2¾ cups (12 oz/350 g) strong bread flour (at least 11% protein)
seeds of 1 vanilla bean (pod)
grated zest of 1 mandarin
grated zest of 1 lemon
scant ½ teaspoon salt
4 tablespoons (2¼ oz/60 g) butter

For the filling:
8½ tablespoons (4¼ oz/120 g) butter, at room temperature
½ cup (3½ oz/100 g) granulated sugar
chopped nuts, dried fruits, or spices (optional)

For the egg wash:
2 egg yolks, beaten with 4 teaspoons cream or milk

To decorate:
apricot jelly, thinned with a little water

The *torta delle rose*, or "rose cake," is a beautiful brioche-like dessert with its roots in the Italian Renaissance. It is said that the *torta delle rose* was created in 1490 to celebrate the marriage of Isabella d'Este, a highly influential noblewoman from Ferrara, to Francesco II Gonzaga, the Marquis of Mantua. To honor this union, the court's pastry chefs crafted a dessert resembling a bouquet of blooming roses, a tribute to Isabella's beauty.

Made from a rich, buttery dough, the *torta delle rose* is rolled out, generously spread with a mixture of butter and sugar, then sliced into ribbons, which are later rolled up. These spirals of dough are arranged side by side in a pan so that, as they rise and bake, they bloom into golden "roses," caramelized on top and irresistibly soft inside.

This recipe comes from chef Agnese Negrini, whose Mantuan family would often bake this in their wood-fired oven and serve it for festive occasions. Served warm, the buttery aroma quickly spreads through the room. These days, Agnese makes the *torta* for weddings or big celebrations at the restaurant she works at, and especially in spring and summer, when the romantic and floral motifs of the cake are particularly relevant.

Decadent *zabaione*, vanilla custard, or whipped cream with fresh strawberries all make for great accompaniments, and the buttery filling can be flavored as you wish: Jam, chocolate, dried fruit, or nuts all make wonderful additions.

To make the preferment: In a medium bowl, combine a generous ⅓ cup (3½ fl oz/100 ml) of water with the flour and yeast and mix until fully combined. Transfer to a lightly oiled bowl, cover with a clean, damp dish (tea) towel, and proof for about 1 hour, or until doubled in size.

To make the brioche: In the bowl of a stand mixer fitted with the dough hook attachment, combine the preferment with 3 tablespoons of water and the milk, egg yolk, honey, and flour. Mix on low speed until the dough starts to come together, then add the vanilla and mandarin and lemon zests. Continue mixing until the dough becomes smooth and elastic. Add the salt and mix until fully dissolved. Gradually incorporate the butter, making sure each addition is fully absorbed before adding more. The dough should be soft and glossy with good elasticity. Shape it into a ball, cover, and proof for about 1 hour, or until doubled in size.

Line a 9-inch (23-cm) round cake pan with parchment paper and set aside.

To make the filling: In a bowl, cream together the butter and sugar.

Gently deflate the dough and roll it out into a rectangle, roughly 20 × 12 inches (50 × 30 cm). Spread the surface of the dough with the butter-sugar filling, and add any nuts, dried fruits, or spices, if using. Starting from the long side, roll the dough up tightly to form a log. If it feels too soft or sticky to slice cleanly, refrigerate for 15–20 minutes.

Slice the log into 6 equal pieces to form your "roses." Place one rose in the center of your prepared cake pan, and the rest evenly spaced around it. Cover loosely with plastic wrap (clingfilm) and proof until doubled in size.

Preheat the oven to 350°F (180°C/Gas Mark 4). Brush the egg wash over the surface of the cake. Bake the cake for 45 minutes, until golden brown and fragrant. If the top browns too quickly, loosely tent it with aluminum foil.

Remove from the oven, and while the cake is still warm, brush the surface with the thinned apricot jelly. Let cool, then tear off individual "roses" to serve.

ROGEL CAKE

Argentina

Submitted by Julia Soria

Serves 10–12
Prep time: 45 minutes, plus chilling time
Cook time: 20 minutes

For the dough:
4¾ cups (1 lb 5 oz/600 g) all-purpose (plain) flour
1 teaspoon fine salt
2 eggs, plus 9 egg yolks
3½ tablespoons corn oil
water or milk (optional), if needed

For the Italian meringue:
1½ cups (10½ oz/300 g) superfine (caster) sugar
4 egg whites, at room temperature

To assemble:
2¾ cups (1 lb 12 oz/800 g) dulce de leche (preferably repostero—the thick spreadable type)

The *rogel* cake is a traditional Argentine cake, beloved for its combination of crisp pastry, rich dulce de leche, and glossy meringue. While its exact origin is debated, a popular story is that it originated in a suburb of Buenos Aires in the 60s as the creation of a baker named Rogelia, and later adapted and popularized by María "Charo" Balbiani. Over time the cake evolved into a local favorite, featured at weddings, birthdays, and festive gatherings.

To make the dough: On a counter, sift together the flour with salt, then form a well in the center. Add the egg yolks, whole eggs, and oil, and mix with your fingers to form a smooth dough that pulls away from the counter. If needed, add a little water or milk. Divide the dough into 6–8 equal pieces, cover with a clean dish (tea) towel, and let rest for 30 minutes–1 hour in the refrigerator.

Preheat the oven to 375°F (190°C/Gas Mark 5). Line 2 baking sheets with parchment paper and set aside.

Remove the dough from the refrigerator and roll each piece into a thin circle (8½ × 9½ inches/22 × 24 cm). Place on the prepared baking sheets (you will need to bake in batches) and prick with a fork. Bake for 6–10 minutes, flipping halfway through. Remove from the oven and let cool on a wire rack.

Meanwhile, to make the Italian meringue: In a pan, heat the sugar and a generous ⅓ cup (3½ fl oz/100 ml) water to 250°F/120°C.

In a large bowl, whisk the egg whites to soft peaks. Slowly pour the sugar syrup into the egg whites in a thin stream, whisking continuously.

To assemble: Stack the baked disks with generous layers of dulce de leche in between. Press lightly to secure. Cover the top of the cake with the meringue, using a spoon or pastry (piping) bag for texture. If you have one, use a blowtorch to color the meringue. Serve immediately.

PATYR NON

Uzbekistan

Submitted by Malika Sharipova

Serves 2
Prep time: 45 minutes, plus resting and proofing times
Cook time: 15–20 minutes

- ⅛–¼ oz (5–7 g) active dry yeast (or 1 oz/25 g fresh yeast)
- 1 teaspoon granulated sugar
- generous 1 cup (8 fl oz/250 ml) milk, warmed
- 4 cups (1 lb 2 oz/500 g) wheat flour
- 1 teaspoon salt
- 1 tablespoon plain or Greek yogurt
- 1 whole egg, plus 1 egg yolk, beaten, for egg wash
- 2 tablespoons butter, plus 7 tablespoons (3½ oz/100 g) melted butter, or a mix of melted lamb fat and butter (for traditional flavor)
- sesame seeds, for topping

In Uzbekistan, *non* (bread) is sacred down to the last crumb. It's an important symbol of hospitality, life, and respect, and is never cut with a knife, but rather is torn by hand. If bread or its crumbs fall on the ground, it's immediately collected and offered to birds or animals. Bread is also used in various rituals, weddings, and seeing-off ceremonies. Traditions include biting off a piece before leaving home: This bitten bread is then hung up on the wall until the person returns.

***Patyr non* is a holiday and festival bread. Enriched with butter or cream, it is both layered and flaky. Traditionally it was made in Andijan and Kashkadaryo (in eastern and southern Uzbekistan) for weddings and special gatherings.**

In a bowl, dissolve the yeast and sugar in warm milk. Let stand for 10 minutes, until bubbly.

In a large bowl, mix the flour and salt. Make a well, add the yeast mixture, yogurt, whole egg, and the 2 tablespoons of butter. Knead together for 8–10 minutes until soft, smooth, and slightly sticky. Cover with a clean, damp dish (tea) towel and proof in a warm place for 1½–2 hours, or until doubled in size.

Line 2 baking sheets with parchment paper.

Divide the dough into 2–4 equal portions (depending on the desired size). Roll each portion into a very thin sheet (as thin as phyllo [filo] if possible), and brush generously with the melted butter. Roll the sheet into a log, then coil it into a spiral, like a snail shell. Gently flatten the coil with your palm or a rolling pin into a thick circle (about ⅝–¾ inch/1.5–2 cm thick). This creates laminated layers, which will bake into flaky, buttery textures. Place the shaped breads on the prepared baking sheets. Cover with a clean dish towel and let rest for 20–30 minutes.

Meanwhile, preheat the oven to 425°F (220°C/Gas Mark 7) with a baking stone or steel if available.

Lightly score the top of the bread with a knife or a traditional chekich stamp, if you have one. Brush with the egg wash and sprinkle with the sesame seeds. Transfer carefully to the baking stone, and bake for 15–20 minutes until deep golden, puffed, and crisp outside.

Remove from the oven. For extra color and shine, brush with a little butter as soon as it comes out. Let cool slightly before serving.

HAMBASHA

Ethiopia and Eritrea

Submitted by Ayda Biru

Serves 16
Prep time: 40 minutes, plus resting and proofing times
Cook time: 35–40 minutes

- 1 tablespoon active dry yeast
- 16 cups (4 lb 8 oz/2 kg) unbleached baking flour, plus extra for dusting
- 1 cup (8 fl oz/250 ml) warm water
- 1 teaspoon lemon zest
- 1 teaspoon salt
- 1 teaspoon ground fenugreek
- 1 tablespoon nigella seeds (tikur azmud)
- 1 tablespoon baking powder
- 2 tablespoons honey or granulated sugar
- 4 tablespoons vegetable oil, plus extra for greasing

***Hambasha*, known as *ambasha* in Amharic, is a round bread beloved in both Eritrean and Ethiopian households, especially in the Tigray region. The two regions share deep cultural and culinary ties due to their shared border and historical connection. Traditionally served during weddings, holidays, baptisms, funerals, or alongside a coffee ceremony, *hambasha* is most often paired with *ye kemem chai* (spiced tea with cardamom, cloves, and other warming spices).**

Distinctive for its appearance, *hambasha* is typically circular, divided into eight equal sections resembling a wheel, and often embellished with decorative patterns pressed into the surface before baking. These designs not only make it visually striking but also create natural cutting points for sharing.

This recipe was submitted by Ayda Biru, whose mother prepared it every Saturday so it could be enjoyed fresh on Sundays after church—often served as *buna kurse* (a snack during the coffee ceremony). For her, it was a favorite childhood memory to prepare the dough with her mother and siblings, each of them carving a section of the traditional wheel pattern.

To activate the yeast starter: In a medium bowl, add the yeast, 1 cup (4¼ oz/125 g) of the flour, and the warm water. Mix well, cover with a clean dish (tea) towel, and let sit for 30–45 minutes until bubbly and foamy.

In a stand mixer or large bowl, mix the remaining flour with the lemon zest, salt, fenugreek, nigella seeds, baking powder, honey or sugar, and vegetable oil. Stir well to combine. Add 3 cups (24 fl oz/700 ml) of water and the yeast mixture to the flour mixture. Mix on low-medium speed, kneading for about 10 minutes, until the dough becomes soft, smooth, and elastic. Leave the dough in the bowl, cover with a clean dish towel, and proof for 2 hours in a warm, draft-free spot.

Gently knead or swirl the dough around in the bowl with your hands for about 3 minutes to help redistribute the yeast and improve the texture. Do not add any water. Proof for another 2–4 hours.

Lightly oil your hands and gently stretch out the dough into a thin, flat circle as if preparing a pizza. Return the stretched dough to the bowl, cover again, and proof for 30 minutes.

Preheat the oven to 350°F (180°C/Gas Mark 4). Lightly oil a 12-inch (30-cm) cake pan.

Transfer the dough to a floured counter and lightly stretch the dough again. Using the handle of a spoon, mark a cross to divide the circle into 4, then divide each section again to create 8 wedges. Use the spoon and a fork to create alternate decorative patterns on the surface. Transfer the patterned dough into the prepared baking pan, placing it with the decorated side facing upward so the pattern remains visible after baking. Bake for 35–40 minutes, or until golden brown on top and cooked through.

Remove from the oven and let cool before serving.

KOUGLOF

France

Submitted by Marie Kerkeling

Serves 8–10
Prep time: 30 minutes, plus soaking and proofing times
Cook time: 40–45 minutes

generous ½ cup (2¾ oz/80 g) raisins
2 tablespoons kirsch or rum (or your favorite alcohol)
1 oz (25 g) fresh yeast, or 1 tablespoon (⅓ oz/10 g) quick-rise dry yeast
⅔ cup (5 fl oz/150 ml) milk, lukewarm
2 eggs
5 tablespoons superfine (caster) sugar
½ teaspoon fine salt
2¾ cups (12 oz/350 g) all-purpose or T55 flour, plus extra for dusting
3½ tablespoons (1¾ oz/50 g) butter, softened, plus extra for greasing
⅓ cup (1¾ oz/50 g) blanched almonds
confectioners' (icing) sugar, for dusting

***Kouglof* (or *Kugelhopf/Kougelhopf*) is a yeast-risen cake with roots in Austria and southern Germany, later becoming iconic in Alsace. Its tall, fluted shape is baked in a distinctive mold with a central chimney. Traditionally enriched with butter, almonds, and raisins soaked in kirsch, it became a celebratory cake for weddings and baptisms. According to legend, Marie Antoinette helped popularize it in France after bringing Viennese tastes to Versailles. In Alsace, both sweet and savory versions developed (of which this recipe represents the former), and the cake is now enjoyed fresh or dry, as part of both festive and everyday traditions. The old traditional tins are pieces of art in their own right, many featuring distinctive regional patterns.**

Soak the raisins in the kirsch or rum for 30 minutes. Drain and set aside.

In a small bowl, dissolve the yeast in the lukewarm milk. Let sit for 5–10 minutes until slightly foamy.

In a separate bowl, mix the eggs with the sugar and salt until the sugar is mostly dissolved. Set aside.

In a large mixing bowl, combine the flour, yeast-milk mixture, and egg-sugar mixture. Mix until a rough dough forms, then knead for 5–7 minutes until smooth and elastic. Add the butter, a few pieces at a time, kneading until fully absorbed and the dough is soft, glossy, and slightly sticky. Cover and proof in a warm spot for 1½ hours, or until doubled in size.

Grease and flour a Kougelhopf mold (or bundt pan). Press one almond into each groove at the bottom. Add the drained raisins to the dough and gently fold them in. Place the dough into the mold and level it out. Proof again for about 1 hour, until the dough has reached almost to the top.

Preheat the oven to 350°F (180°C/Gas Mark 4). Bake for 40–45 minutes. If the top darkens too quickly, cover with aluminum foil halfway through.

Remove from the oven, let cool slightly, then turn out while still warm. Let cool completely before dusting with confectioners' (icing) sugar to serve. They are best eaten the same day but can also be eaten sliced and toasted the next few days.

PERDE PILAVI

Turkey

Submitted by Cemre Torun

Serves 6–8
Prep time: 15 minutes
Cook time: 1¾ hours

For the chicken and rice filling:
1 × 3 lb 5 oz (1.5 kg) chicken
1 each: celery stalk, carrot, onion, roughly chopped
1 teaspoon coriander seeds
1 bay leaf
1 teaspoon black peppercorns
5½ tablespoons (2¾ oz/80 g) butter
6 tablespoons pine nuts
1½ cups (10½ oz/300 g) medium-grain rice, washed and dried
2 tablespoons currants
2 teaspoons salt
1 teaspoon freshly ground black pepper
1 teaspoon each dried mint, dried oregano, and ground cinnamon

For the cake pan:
butter, at room temperature, for greasing and brushing
scant ½ cup (1¾ oz/50 g) slivered (flaked) or ⅓ cup (1¾ oz/50 g) blanched almonds

For the dough:
2 medium eggs
¼ cup (2¼ oz/60 g) plain yogurt
4 tablespoons (2¼ oz/60 g) butter, at room temperature
4 tablespoons olive oil
2¾ cups (12 oz/350 g) all-purpose (plain) flour, plus extra for dusting
1 teaspoon salt
1 teaspoon baking powder

This rich and fragrant rice dish is favored at weddings. *Perde* (meaning "drape" or "curtain" in Turkish) symbolizes the sanctity of the newly weds' home, and each of the recipe's ingredients are symbolic: the currants represent health, the spices signify the good and bad times in life, and the almonds and pine nuts are for the couple's future children. Overall, the dish symbolizes the building of a new home together. Some versions (in traditional recipes) use rooster or partridge, and some also include chicken liver.

To make the chicken and rice filling: Place the chicken in a large pot, add the celery, carrot, onion, coriander seeds, bay leaf, and peppercorns, and cover with cold water. Cook over medium heat for 45 minutes, or until the chicken is cooked through. Remove the chicken from the pot and set aside to be used in the filling. Strain the broth (stock) and keep warm. Remove the chicken bones and skin, then roughly shred and reserve.

Melt the butter in a heavy-bottom pot, then add the pine nuts and sauté over medium heat for a few minutes until lightly golden. Add the rice and stir for a minute or so until well-coated and lightly toasted. Stir in the currants, salt, pepper, herbs, spices, and 2¾ cups (22 fl oz/650 ml) of the chicken broth. Cover the pan and gently simmer for 10–15 minutes, until the rice is almost cooked through. It should be slightly moist, so that it doesn't dry too much when cooked for the second time in the dough. Remove from the heat, mix in the shredded chicken, then cover the pot with a clean dish (tea) towel, secure with the lid, and set aside.

Preheat the oven to 350°F (180°C/Gas Mark 4). Generously grease a 7-inch (18-cm) cake pan with the butter and sprinkle the almonds around the bottom and sides, using the butter to help them stick. Set aside.

To make the dough: Place the eggs, yogurt, butter, and oil in a bowl and whisk until smooth.

In a separate bowl, sift the flour, salt, and baking powder and mix. Add the dry ingredients gradually to the wet ingredients and mix until you have a smooth dough.

On a lightly floured counter, roll out the dough slightly larger than your cake pan, leaving plenty of pastry to hang over the edges to be able to enclose the filling. Place the dough in the cake pan, then fill with the cooled rice filling. Fold the hanging pastry over to enclose the filling, trim the excess, and brush with butter. Bake for 35–40 minutes, or until the dough is golden brown.

Remove from the oven and let cool for 15 minutes, then invert onto a serving plate, and serve.

Note: There is a special pot for this rice, but it would be impossible to find outside of Turkey. The closest alternative could be a deep cake pan or a 7-inch (18-cm) Charlotte mold.

PASTEL DE NOVIA

Argentina

Submitted by Julia Soria

Serves 10
Prep time: 45 minutes, plus resting time
Cook time: 60 minutes

In the sugar-cane towns of southern Tucumán, Argentina, *pastel de novia*, or "bride's pie," was the region's wedding "cake" long before layer cakes reached the rural northwest of the country. For every marriage, neighbors pooled a range of ingredients—chicken, dried peaches, raisins, wine, lard, spices—and expressed their collective abundance in one monumental, sweet-savory pie. The meringue-topped Tucumán bride's pie has a flaky shell and spiced filling which echoes the Hispano-Arab meat pie carried across the Atlantic by Spanish conquerors, while nineteenth-century Syrian-Lebanese love for dried fruit and warm seasonings added further depth to the recipe. You'll still find this pie baked for family celebrations and sold on Saturdays in the local markets of Tucumán.

For the dough:
- 4¾ cups (1 lb 5 oz/600 g) all-purpose (plain) flour
- scant ½ cup (3¼ oz/90 g) granulated sugar
- 2 teaspoons baking powder
- 1 tablespoon ground cinnamon
- 2 egg yolks
- scant ⅔ cup (3½ oz/100 g) lard, melted
- ½ cup (4 fl oz/120 ml) sweet wine (Port or Marsala)

For the filling:
- 2 tablespoons lard
- 2 tablespoons granulated sugar
- 2 cups (7 oz/200 g) finely sliced onion
- 2¾ oz (75 g) red bell pepper, chopped
- 1 cup (5 oz/140 g) grated carrot
- 1 lb 2 oz (500 g) cooked chicken
- ⅓ cup (1½ oz/40 g) green olives, sliced
- ¾ cup (3½ oz/100 g) raisins
- ¾ cup (5½ oz/150 g) dried peaches (pelones), rehydrated and diced
- 1 tablespoon sweet paprika (pimentón)
- 1 teaspoon ground cumin
- 2 tablespoons white wine (optional)
- 2–4 tablespoons chicken broth (stock)
- 2 medium hard-boiled eggs, chopped
- neutral oil, for greasing
- salt and freshly ground black pepper

For the meringue:
- 2 egg whites
- ¼ cup (1¾ oz/50 g) superfine (caster) sugar

To make the dough: In a large bowl, whisk together the flour, sugar, baking powder, cinnamon, and a scant ½ teaspoon of salt. Add the egg yolks, melted lard, and wine, and stir. Work in a generous ⅓ cup (3½ fl oz/100 ml) of water gradually until a soft dough forms. Wrap tightly in plastic wrap (clingfilm) and place in the refrigerator to rest for 30 minutes.

Meanwhile, to make the filling: In a wide pan, heat the lard and sugar over medium heat until melted and a light caramel color, about 5 minutes. Add the onion and pepper and sauté for 1 minute, then add the carrot and sauté for 1 minute. Shred the cooked chicken, then add with the olives, raisins, diced peaches, paprika, cumin, and wine, if using. Moisten with the broth and simmer for 5 minutes until glossy but spoonable. Remove from the heat, and let cool, then fold in the chopped hard-boiled egg.

Preheat the oven to 350°F (180°C/Gas Mark 4). Lightly oil a 10½-inch (26-cm) pie pan.

Remove the dough from the refrigerator and remove one-third, so you have 2 pieces. Roll out the larger piece of dough to ¼ inch (5 mm) thick, and large enough to cover the bottom and sides of the pan. Place the dough in the pan and spoon in the filling.

Roll out the remaining piece of dough to ¼ inch (5 mm) thick and large enough to cover the top of the pie. Place on top and crimp together the edges to seal, then pierce the top of the dough once or twice. Bake for 25–30 minutes, until golden.

Meanwhile, to make the meringue: In a large bowl, whisk together the egg whites and sugar to soft peaks.

When the pie has finished baking, remove it from the oven, quickly spread a thin layer of the meringue mixture over the hot pie, then return it to the oven for another 5–10 minutes to color.

Remove from the oven, let cool for 10 minutes, then serve slightly warm.

FUNERALS

Baking can be an act of solace and remembrance, as well as love for the bereaved. In many cultures around the world, funerals are followed immediately or in the days to come, by reception lunches or catered gatherings—like an Irish wake or the Jewish *shiva*—which often include special bakes that can feed a crowd of gathered mourners. These are bakes that aren't designed to lift a mood exactly, but rather bring some comfort and care to those who need it.

ZWARTE PRUIMENVLAAI

The Netherlands and Belgium

Submitted by Sarah Lemanski

Serves 10
Prep time: 40 minutes, plus overnight resting time
Cook time: 35–40 minutes

Zwarte pruimenvlaai*, or "black plum tart," is a variation of the traditional *vlaai* style of tart that hail from Limburg, a fruit-growing region situated across the Netherlands and Belgium. *Vlaai* are usually made from a yeasted pastry dough filled generously with a mixture of cooked fruit (like cherry, apricot, or plum), custard, a rice or semolina porridge, or even quark. Before being baked, *vlaai* are commonly topped with either an intricate lattice pastry or streusel-like crumb layer called *kruimels*.

Until the twentieth century, *vlaai* were made and served almost exclusively for special occasions, often made with seasonal fruit mixture or regional specialties. The *zwarte pruimenvlaai* is a combination commonly baked for funerals, likely due to the dark color of its filling. Another traditional form of *vlaai*, the *bakkemoezenvlaai*, is made from dried pears, which reach a similarly deep and richly dark color.

For the pastry:
- generous ⅓ cup (3½ fl oz/100 ml) milk
- 2½ cups (10½ oz/300 g) all-purpose (plain) flour
- 2 tablespoons superfine (caster) sugar
- ½ teaspoon sea salt
- ½ oz (14 g) fresh yeast or ¼ oz (7 g) quick-rise dry yeast
- 1 extra-large egg
- 3 tablespoons (1½ oz/45 g) butter, melted
- neutral oil, for greasing

For the filling:
- 2¼ cups (1 lb 2 oz/500 g) dried pitted plums (prunes)
- 1¼ cups (10 fl oz/300 ml) boiling water
- 2 × 2-inch (5-cm) strips of lemon peel
- 1 tablespoon lemon juice
- 1 sprig fresh rosemary
- 1 spent vanilla bean (pod)
- 4½ teaspoons soft light brown sugar
- ¼ teaspoon fine sea salt

To finish:
- butter, for greasing
- splash of milk
- turbinado (demerara) sugar, for dusting
- confectioners' (icing) sugar, to serve

To make the pastry: In a small saucepan, bring the milk to barely a simmer. Pour into a measuring cup and let cool.

Meanwhile, in the bowl of a stand mixer fitted with the dough hook, combine the flour, sugar, and sea salt.

Once the milk is cool, add the yeast, then the egg, and finally the melted butter. Add to the dry ingredients and mix on medium–low speed for 5 minutes, until incorporated. The dough will look sticky. Increase the speed to medium–high and continue to mix for 5–7 minutes, until the dough looks more cohesive and uniform. It may still seem loose and slightly sticky but should be smoother. Place the dough in an oiled bowl, cover, and place in the refrigerator to rest overnight.

To make the filling: Place the prunes in a heatproof bowl with the boiling water, lemon peel, juice, rosemary, and vanilla bean (pod), then cover and leave overnight.

The following day, remove the lemon peel, rosemary, and vanilla bean from the prunes. Transfer to the bowl of a food processor, add the sugar and salt, and process until a thick but spreadable puree forms. If the puree looks too runny, transfer to a pan and cook out any residual water until you can trace a line through the mixture and clearly see the base of the pan. Let cool.

Preheat the oven to 425°F (220°C/Gas Mark 7). Grease a 10-inch (25-cm) loose-bottom tart pan with butter and set aside.

Remove the dough from the refrigerator and divide into two portions: one should be one-third of the dough, the other two-thirds. Roll the larger piece out to a little more than the diameter of the pan, large enough to ensure the dough will come up the sides. Place the dough in the pan and gently press it into the edges, then up the sides, leaving a little overhang around the top edge. Using a fork or knife, lightly prick holes (dock) the base of the tart, then set aside to rest for 5–10 minutes, in which time it should start to puff slightly.

Fill the tart with the prune puree, smoothing to make an even layer.

Roll the second piece of dough to a fraction wider than the diameter of the pan. Divide it into ¾-inch- (2-cm)-wide strips, then weave into a lattice with alternate vertical and horizontal strips on top of the pie, until the surface is covered. Press around the edge of the tart to adhere the strips to the overhang of dough lining the base. Alternatively, use a lattice roller to create the lattice effect. Trim off the excess dough neatly and press to secure the top and bottom crusts. Brush the lattice with milk and add a sprinkle of turbinado (demerara) sugar. Bake for 35–40 minutes, then remove and let cool. Dust with confectioners' (icing) sugar and serve.

CHOCOLATE RUGELACH

Ashkenazi Jewish

Submitted by Talia Jacobs

Makes 48
Prep time: 45 minutes, plus proofing time
Cook time: 20–25 minutes

For the dough:
- ¾ cup (6 fl oz/180 ml) warm milk
- 2 eggs, plus 1 egg for egg wash
- ¼ oz (7 g) quick-rise dry yeast
- scant 4 cups (1 lb 1 oz/480 g) all-purpose (plain) flour, plus extra for dusting
- 5 tablespoons granulated sugar
- ½ teaspoon salt
- 6 tablespoons (3 oz/90 g) butter, plus extra for greasing

For the filling:
- 2⅓ sticks (9½ oz/270 g) butter
- 5½ oz (150 g) semisweet chocolate
- ⅔ cup (2½ oz/70 g) unsweetened cocoa powder
- 1½ cups (6 oz/180 g) confectioners' (icing) sugar
- 1 teaspoon salt
- 2 teaspoons ground cinnamon

For the sugar syrup:
- 1 cup (7 oz/200 g) superfine (caster) sugar
- ½ teaspoon orange blossom water

***Rugelach*, which means "little horns" in Yiddish, are traditional Azhkenazi Jewish crescent pastries that originated in Eastern Europe—most likely Poland—as early as the medieval period, and are believed to share an origin with other crescent-shaped bakes from Central and Eastern Europe, such as the Austrian *kipfel* and the Hungarian *kifli*. Despite this, rugelach are quite distinct from these bread-like relatives, and much closer to the *schnecken*, a German-Jewish style of cinnamon or fruit-and-nut pastry. Much like *schnecken*, rugelach were also traditionally made using a pastry base that incorporated sour cream—and more recently cream cheese. The pastry is then rolled up with fillings that range from cinnamon and sugar to chocolate (or cocoa), and ground nuts, or jams.**

Rugelach are very much a quintessential "party" food in that they are most commonly prepared or purchased to feed large gatherings of friends and family. While they can be found on many holiday tables, they are also a staple of the Jewish *shiva*, the ritual week-long mourning period, where they'll sit beside bagels and catered deli platters.

To make the dough: In the bowl of a stand mixer fitted with the dough hook attachment, add the milk, 2 eggs, yeast, flour, sugar, and salt, and mix until a smooth ball of dough forms. Gradually mix in small pieces of the butter until they are fully incorporated. Mix until the dough has a nice sheen and is coming away cleanly from the bowl. Transfer to a greased bowl, cover with a damp dish (tea) towel, and let it rest in a warm spot until doubled in size.

Meanwhile, to make the filling: In a pan on low heat, gently melt the butter and chocolate together. Add the cocoa powder, sugar, salt, and cinnamon, and mix to form a smooth paste.

Line a baking sheet with parchment paper and set aside.

Turn out the dough onto a lightly floured counter and roll into a large rectangle, about 1/16–⅛ inch (2–3 mm) thick. Spread one-third of the filling over half the dough, then fold over the other half to cover. Gently roll out the dough into a large rectangle, spread another one-third of the filling, fold over, and roll out again until very thin. Spread the remaining filling all over the large rectangle and, using a large knife, divide into 4 rectangles. From each of those, cut 12 long triangles with a base width of 2 inches (5 cm). Roll up each triangle starting from the widest side to create a croissant shape and place onto the prepared baking sheet. Repeat with the remaining dough. Cover the sheets with a dish towel and proof for 1 hour.

Preheat the oven to 340°F (170°C/Gas Mark 3).

In a small bowl, beat the remaining egg and brush over the tops of the rugelach. Bake for 20–25 minutes, until golden brown.

Meanwhile, to make the sugar syrup: Combine the sugar, orange blossom water, and 1 cup (8 fl oz/250 ml) of water. Set aside.

As soon as the rugelach come out of the oven, pour the sugar syrup over the top. Let cool, then serve. Store in an airtight container for up to 1 week.

IRISH WAKE CAKE

Ireland

Submitted by Katie Smith

Serves 10
Prep time: 30 minutes
Cook time: 45–50 minutes

1½ cups (6½ oz/180 g) all-purpose (plain) flour
1 teaspoon baking powder
½ teaspoon fine salt
5½ oz (160g) butter, softened
3½ oz (100 g) cream cheese, softened
scant 1½ cups (9¾ oz/280 g) superfine (caster) sugar
3 eggs
3½ oz (100g) currants, soaked in 3 tablespoons hot water or whiskey
1 cup (3½ oz/100 g) confectioners' (icing) sugar, sifted
generous 2 tablespoons lemon juice

The Irish wake cake can be found on the buffet table at a church hall, at the kitchen table at a wake, or as a carefully packaged gift for a grieving family. A soft, cream cheese pound cake with the addition of whiskey-soaked currants, it's the perfect cake to encourage friends and family to sit down and eat during a time when food is often the least of their worries.

Preheat the oven to 340°F (170°C/Gas Mark 3) and line a 2-lb (900-g) loaf pan with parchment paper.

Combine the flour, baking powder, and salt together in a large bowl.

In the bowl of a stand mixer, beat together the butter, cream cheese, and superfine (caster) sugar until fluffy and well combined, ensuring you scrape the bottom of the bowl. Add the eggs, one by one, mixing thoroughly in between each addition.

With the mixer on the lowest setting, fold through the dry ingredients and soaked currants until a loose cake batter forms and there are no visible dry flour streaks. Pour into the prepared pan and bake for 45–50 minutes, until golden and a skewer inserted in the middle of the cake comes out clean.

While the cake cools, prepare the icing: Mix together the confectioners' (icing) sugar and lemon juice until smooth and loose. Pour this over the warm cake and allow to set for 1 hour before slicing.

FIKA

In Sweden, coffee and cake have been inextricably linked for well over a hundred years. By the late nineteenth century, the connection had developed enough to spark the maxim *sju sorters kakor* (seven kinds of cake), which reminded hosts of the appropriate number of bakes to offer their guests.

The term *fika*, a slang inversion of the Swedish word *kaffe* (coffee), has been in use since the early 1900s. It reflects not a simple break but more of a rhythmic pause that provides structure. The popularity of *fika* has gradually led to it becoming an essential aspect of culture, and in recent decades it has evolved into ritualized social traditions like *fredagsfika*, where workplaces cap their weeks with a small social gathering centered around baked goods.

CARDAMOM BUNS

Sweden

Submitted by Flora Manson

Serves 14
Prep time: 50 minutes, plus proofing time
Cook time: 20–25 minutes

For the tangzhong:
6 tablespoons milk
¼ cup (1¼ oz/35 g) strong white bread flour

For the dough:
5 tablespoons milk
¼ oz (8 g) quick-rise dry yeast
⅓ cup (2½ oz/70 g) superfine (caster) sugar
2 eggs
3½ cups (1 lb/460 g) strong white bread flour, plus extra for dusting
3 teaspoons ground cardamom
¾ teaspoon fine sea salt
9 tablespoons (4½ oz/130 g) butter, at room temperature

For the butter filling:
¾ cup (5¾ oz/170 g) butter, at room temperature
scant ½ cup (3½ oz/95 g) superfine (caster) sugar
½ teaspoon fine sea salt

For the cardamom sugar:
5 teaspoons ground cardamom
¼ cup (2 oz/55 g) superfine (caster) sugar
pinch of fine sea salt

For the egg wash:
1 egg, whisked

Green cardamom arrived in Sweden via eastern trade routes in the medieval period, but it wasn't until the early 1900s that it was used as a flavoring in soft and enriched sweet buns like *kardemummabuller* (cardamom buns). Today, intricately braided *kardemummabullar* are ubiquitous with coffee across all of Scandinavia and beyond. But at home in Sweden, it is something even more serious, through the ritualized national tradition of *fika*. This recipe comes from Flora Manson, a Scottish baker based in Sweden, whose love for *kardemummabullar* transcends borders.

To make the tangzhong: Add the milk, flour, and 4½ tablespoons of water to a pot and whisk until smooth. Set the pot over medium heat, whisking gently while the mixture heats and thickens. Once the mixture is a very thick, smooth paste, remove from the heat and let cool for a few minutes.

To make the dough: Add the slightly cooled tangzhong to the bowl of a stand mixer fitted with the paddle attachment, then add the milk, yeast, and sugar and whisk until smooth and combined. Add the eggs, flour, ground cardamom, and salt and briefly mix to produce a shaggy dough, then swap to the dough hook and mix on medium speed for 5 minutes, until the dough is smooth and pulls away from the sides of the bowl. With the mixer running on medium speed, add the butter 1 teaspoon at a time, allowing each addition to mix for about 15 seconds before adding the next. Continue to mix until smooth and the dough passes the "windowpane test"—you can stretch a small piece of dough until it's thin and translucent without tearing—10–12 minutes. Remove the dough from the bowl and knead slightly into a smooth ball. Place the dough back into the bowl, cover with plastic wrap (clingfilm) and proof in a warm place for 1½ hours, until doubled in size.

To make the butter filling: Combine the butter, sugar, and salt until smooth.

To make the cardamom sugar: Combine the ground cardamom, sugar, and salt.

Line two large baking pans with parchment paper.

Punch the dough down, then turn out onto a floured counter and shape it into a rectangle with your hands. Roll out the dough to 12 × 14 inches (40 × 35 cm) with a thickness of ⅛ inch (3 mm). Use a bench scraper or palette knife to spread the butter filling across the dough, right to the edges, then sprinkle over two-thirds of the cardamom sugar. Fold the top third of the dough down to cover two-thirds of the dough, then fold the bottom half up to cover it. Flour the counter again, then roll the dough out to 12 × 16 inches (30 × 40 cm). Trim the ends of the dough to make sure they are straight, ensuring the finished dough measures 14 inches (35 cm) in width. Use your fingers to seal the sides and top of the dough, then cut the dough into 5½ x 1-inch- (14 × 2.5-cm)-wide strips.

To shape the buns: Pick up a strip of dough at one end with your thumb and middle finger. Drape the dough, laminated butter-side facing up, across the index, middle, and ring fingers of your other hand. Wrap the dough around your fingers twice, forming an "X" shape, then wrap the remaining dough across the middle of the "X" and tuck the end inside the bun. Place on the prepared baking pan and shape the rest. Cover the unbaked buns loosely with lightly greased plastic wrap, then leave in a warm place to proof for 1–1½ hours, or until doubled in size.

Preheat the oven to 375°F (190°C/Gas Mark 5).

Bake the buns for 12–15 minutes, rotating the trays after 6 minutes, until lightly golden on top and bottom. As soon as the buns are removed from the oven, brush with the egg wash and sprinkle over the remaining cardamom sugar.

KAFFE UND KUCHEN

The German tradition of *Sonntagskuchen* (Sunday cake), and more broadly, of *Kaffe und Kuchen* (coffee and cake), is rooted in the arrival of coffee to the country in the seventeenth century. Over time, *Kaffe und Kuchen* became a recognized afternoon meal, especially on Sundays, when throughout much of the German-speaking world, a home-baked cake or torte would be served alongside a cup of coffee.

The popularity of this tradition had become widespread by the 1950s, with successful marketing campaigns by baking brands like Dr. Oetker establishing the almost moral role that the *Sonntagskuchen* played in the life of the ideal family. Now, decades later, *Kaffe und Kuchen* is a ritual that brings together family and friends around the familiarity of fine bakes and good coffee.

DONAUWELLE

Germany

Submitted by Tobias Beck

Serves 18
Prep time: 45 minutes, plus cooling and chilling times
Cook time: 35–40 minutes

For the sponge:
2¼ sticks (9 oz/250 g) butter, softened
1 cup (7 oz/200 g) granulated sugar
1 × ¼ oz (8 g) packet vanilla sugar (or 1 teaspoon vanilla extract)
5 eggs
2⅓ cups plus 1 tablespoon (10½ oz/ 300 g) all-purpose (plain) flour
2 teaspoons baking powder
2 tablespoon unsweetened cocoa powder
2 tablespoons milk
sour cherries from a jar, drained thoroughly (drained weight approx. 12–14 oz/ 350–400 g)

For the buttercream:
3.4-oz (96-g) packet vanilla pudding powder; you could also use 2.5-oz (70 g) packet of Dr. Oetker vanilla pudding, or 3 tablespoons custard powder
generous 2 cups (17 fl oz/500 ml) milk
2 tablespoons confectioners' (icing) sugar
2¼ sticks (9 oz/250 g) butter, softened

For the chocolate glaze:
7 oz (200 g) semisweet (dark) chocolate (or couverture)
2 tablespoons neutral oil

This layered plain-and-chocolate sponge cake is a staple of the German cake culture that originated in the 1960s—the name comes from "Donau," the German name for the Danube river, and "Welle," meaning wave, due to the wave-like decoration in the chocolate glazing. By the 1970s and 1980s it was so widespread that it became available as a ready-made cake batter. During the partition of Germany, in the German Democratic Republic (East Germany) it was called *Schneewittchenkuchen* (Snow White cake) due to its distinctive colored layers.

This cake holds a lot of nostalgia for the recipe's contributor, Berlin-based chef Tobias Beck, whose grandmother would make it for his birthday. It is often also served for the almost ritualistic German tradition of *Kaffee und Kuchen*, a regular occasion for meeting friends and family over coffee and cake. Serve with filter coffee.

Preheat the oven to 350°F (180°C/Gas Mark 4). Line a 12 × 16-inch (30 × 40 cm) baking pan with parchment paper and set aside.

To make the sponge: In a large bowl, cream together the butter, sugar, and vanilla sugar until light and fluffy. Add the eggs one at a time, beating well after each addition.

In a separate bowl, mix the flour and baking powder, then gradually fold this into the wet mixture. Spread two-thirds of the batter evenly on the prepared pan. Mix the remaining third with the cocoa powder and milk, then spread it carefully over the light batter. Distribute the drained cherries evenly on top, pressing them lightly into the batter. Bake for 35–40 minutes, until golden and firm. Remove from the oven and let the cake cool completely in the pan.

Meanwhile, to make the buttercream: Cook the vanilla pudding according to the packet directions using the milk and sugar. Cover with plastic wrap (clingfilm) directly on the surface to prevent a skin from forming. Let cool to room temperature (do not refrigerate).

Beat the softened butter until creamy, then gradually add the cooled pudding, one spoonful at a time, beating continuously until smooth and fluffy. Spread evenly over the cooled cake and chill for 30 minutes.

Meanwhile, to make the chocolate glaze: Melt the chocolate with the oil in a heatproof bowl set over a pan of simmering water, then let cool slightly. Pour over the buttercream and spread evenly, using a fork to create wave-like patterns in the glaze before it sets. Let set before serving.

SPECIAL OCCASIONS

Many baked goods bring a certain specialness to an occasion, even if they lack a strong and distinct connection with any one holiday or type of event. What these sorts of bakes share are their cultural resonance, and how they bring families and friends together. They suggest, by their very presence, that this is not a normal day, meal, or moment. In some households these recipes may have developed their own special significance or associations, but across their wider respective communities, they are a mainstay of all festive occasions.

TORTA LARANJA

Portugal

Submitted by João Rodrigues

Serves 8
Prep time: 20 minutes
Cook time: 25 minutes

- 3½ tablespoons (1¾ oz/50 g) melted butter, plus extra for greasing
- generous ⅓ cup (1½ oz/40 g) cornstarch (cornflour)
- 1¾ cups (12 oz/350 g) superfine (caster) sugar, plus extra for sprinkling
- 8 eggs
- grated zest and juice of 2 large oranges

Oranges (*laranjas*) from China were introduced to Europe by the Portuguese in the fifteenth century—which is why they are often still called "Portuguese" in several countries across Europe. Many orange tree groves were planted in the Algarve, so in the convents—where nuns were already producing heavenly egg-focused desserts—they started to make the base for this cake by mixing orange juice and zest with the eggs.

Today, this "rolled" cake is baked for celebratory occasions of all kinds, with some in the Algarve making it especially for both Christmas and Easter.

Preheat the oven to 350°F (180°C/Gas Mark 4). Line a jelly roll (Swiss roll) pan (15 × 10 inches/38 × 25 cm) with parchment paper, grease with butter, and set aside.

In a bowl, mix together the cornstarch (cornflour) and the sugar.

In a separate bowl, beat the eggs with the juice and zest of the oranges and the melted butter. Add the sugar and cornstarch mixture and beat well. Pour the batter into the prepared baking pan and bake for about 25 minutes, or until a toothpick (cocktail stick) inserted into the center comes out clean.

Remove from the oven, sprinkle with sugar, and let cool slightly.

Put a clean piece of parchment paper on the counter and sprinkle some sugar over it. Invert the cake onto the parchment paper and carefully peel away the lining paper. Use the parchment paper to roll the cake into a log. Wrap the parchment paper around the outside of the roll and let cool completely. When ready to serve, remove the parchment paper.

BÁNH BÒ NUÓNG

Vietnam

Submitted by Marie Kerkeling

Serves 8
Prep time: 30 minutes, plus resting time
Cook time: 50–60 minutes

- 1¾ oz (50 g) cut 1¼-inch (3-cm) pandan leaves (or 1½ teaspoons pandan extract)
- 1 cup (8 fl oz/250 ml) coconut milk
- 9 eggs
- 1¾ cups (12 oz/360 g) white sugar
- ½ teaspoon salt
- 1 tablespoon melted coconut oil or neutral oil, plus extra for greasing
- 2 cups (9 oz/250 g) tapioca starch
- 2 tablespoons rice flour
- 1 tablespoon baking powder (ideally a single-acting brand)

***Bánh Bò Nuóng* originates from the Chinese *bái táng gāo*, but Vietnamese cooks adapted it by adding coconut milk and pandan, ingredients widely used in Vietnam. Its natural green color has led folks to commonly refer to it as "green cake." The name means "baked cow cake," but don't worry, there's no beef in it—in this instance *bò* is just a poetic way of describing how the batter rises slowly in the oven, forming the signature honeycomb texture. Over time, it has become a classic at family gatherings and festivals, spreading across Vietnam and into Vietnamese communities abroad.**

These days, it's a favorite cake found in bakeries and cafés, most often served at room temperature with hot tea or *cà phê sữa đá*. The rich coconut flavor pairs especially well with strong Vietnamese coffee.

Preheat the oven to 340°F (170°C/Gas Mark 3). Place an empty 9-inch (23 cm) cake pan in the oven to warm to help prevent sticking and aid in forming a nice crust.

In a blender, blend the cut pandan leaves with the coconut milk until smooth. Strain through a fine-mesh sieve or cheesecloth (muslin) to remove the pulp. Set aside.

In a large bowl, gently beat the eggs (avoid overwhisking to prevent bubbles). Add the sugar, salt, pandan-coconut milk mixture, and melted coconut oil. Stir gently until the sugar is dissolved.

In a separate bowl, sift together the tapioca starch, rice flour, and baking powder. Gradually whisk the tapioca starch mixture into the wet mixture. Whisk just until smooth, but do not overmix. Let the batter rest for 10–15 minutes to reduce bubbles, which helps maintain the honeycomb texture.

Lightly grease the warmed pan with neutral oil. Pour in the batter and immediately bake in the center of the oven for 50–60 minutes, or until the cake is golden brown, puffed up, and a toothpick (cocktail stick) inserted in the center comes out clean.

Remove from the oven and allow the cake to cool in the pan for 10 minutes before inverting it onto a wire rack. Cool completely before slicing to reveal the signature honeycomb structure.

BOLO PODRE

Portugal

Submitted by Leopoldo Calhau

Serves 10
Prep time: 20 minutes
Cook time: 45 minutes

- 1 cup (8 fl oz/250 ml) olive oil, plus extra for greasing
- 5 eggs, separated
- scant ½ cup (2¾ oz/75 g) superfine (caster) sugar
- ¾ cup (9 oz/250 g) honey
- 1 teaspoon brandy
- 2 cups (9 oz/250 g) all-purpose (plain) flour
- ⅛ oz (5 g) royal baking powder
- 2 teaspoons ground cinnamon

The deceptively named *bolo podre* (literally "rotten cake") is a lightly sweet, moist, and aromatic cake made with honey and olive oil that hails from the Alentejo region of Portugal, just southeast of Lisbon. The cake likely derives from the rich Portuguese tradition of convent sweets—a wider legacy wherein Portuguese nuns crafted desserts using a base of excess egg yolks.

This particular recipe comes from Lisbon-based chef Leopoldo Calhau, who has spent the last several years exploring and cooking dishes from his home region of Alentejo. It can be prepared for special occasions of any kind, but is perhaps most commonly served at Christmas time.

Preheat the oven to 350°F (180°C/Gas Mark 4). Grease a 9-inch (23cm) springform cake pan with olive oil and line the bottom with parchment paper.

In a bowl, beat the egg yolks with the sugar until pale in color. Add the honey, olive oil, and brandy and mix until combined.

In a separate bowl, mix together the flour, baking powder, and cinnamon. Add this little by little to the wet mixture, stirring to combine between each addition.

In another bowl, beat the egg whites until stiff, then fold these into the batter in 3 parts.

Pour the batter into the prepared pan and bake for 45 minutes, or until a skewer inserted into the center comes out clean. Cover the top of the pan with foil if the cake is browning too quickly.

Remove from the oven and let cool before serving.

RIMETEA WALNUT-FILLED CRESCENT COOKIES

Romania

Submitted by Irina Georgescu

Makes 16
Prep time: 30 minutes, plus chilling time
Cook time: 5–8 minutes

For the dough:
- 1½ cups (6 oz/180 g) all-purpose (plain) flour, plus extra for dusting
- 7 tablespoons (3½ oz/100 g) butter
- 1 egg, plus 1 egg yolk (save the white for the filling, below)
- 3 tablespoons superfine (caster) sugar
- pinch of salt
- confectioners' (icing) sugar, for dusting

For the filling:
- 1½ cups (6 oz/175 g) walnut pieces
- 2 tablespoons superfine (caster) sugar
- 2 tablespoons all-purpose (plain) flour
- 2 tablespoons (1 oz/30 g) butter, softened
- drop of almond extract (optional)
- pinch of salt
- 1 egg white

These crescent-shaped cookies are one of the most popular sweet treats in Romania. They are often paired with a cup of coffee or tea, or even a shot of plum brandy. They are a frequent gift for neighbors, especially because gift-giving (often through homemade treats) is seen as an essential part of visiting friends and loved ones. The host is expected to reciprocate and never return the plate empty, often sending it back filled with even more cookies, fruit, freshly baked bread, or shelled walnuts. Naturally, they are also baked for Christmas, Easter, and almsgiving.

Being such a popular recipe, every family has its own version and favorite twist or filling, but regardless of the flavoring, the texture of the crescents is irresistible when done right.

This recipe is inspired by Rimetea, a charming village in Transylvania shaped by its local Székely population (ethnic Hungarians living in Romania) and renowned for its walnut-filled cookies.

To make the dough: Combine the flour and butter in a large bowl and rub the butter into the flour mixture with your fingertips until it resembles coarse bread crumbs. Alternatively, you can use a food processor and pulse about 4 times for 2 seconds each. Add the egg, egg yolk, and sugar, then bring the dough together by kneading gently and briefly. Wrap in plastic wrap (clingfilm) and chill it in the refrigerator for 30 minutes.

To make the filling: Blend together the walnuts, sugar, flour, butter, almond extract, if using, salt, and egg white, until the mixture has the consistency of a smooth paste that doesn't easily fall off a spoon. Chill in the refrigerator for 1 hour.

Preheat the oven to 400°F (200°C/Gas Mark 6). Line a baking sheet with parchment paper and set aside.

Turn out the dough onto a well-floured counter and roll out into a square approximately 14 inches (35 cm) in size. You can also trim the pastry after rolling it to achieve the desired shape. Cut the pastry into 16 even squares. Place a teaspoon of the filling in the center of each square. Bring 2 parallel sides together in the middle, then press the ends and fold them over (they won't meet in the center). Turn the pastry seam-side down and gently press to shape it into a package with the ends tucked underneath. Alternatively, you can roll them like a croissant. Place on the prepared baking sheet and repeat with the remaining squares. Bake for 5–8 minutes on the middle rack of the oven, until they turn a pale golden color.

Remove from the oven, let cool, then dust with confectioners' (icing) sugar before serving.

PIZZA EBRAICA

Italy

Despite its name, this Italian "pizza" is in fact a sweet cookie full of dried fruits, candied peel, and nuts, which has a deep-rooted history in the Jewish Ghetto of Rome—itself nearly 500 years old. Pasticceria il Boccione on the Via del Portico d'Ottavia has been making these for over 200 years using a secret recipe, and queues form every day to get a taste of this Roman classic.

Submitted by Katie Smith

Makes 24
Prep time: 40 minutes
Cook time: 20–30 minutes

For the almond paste:
- 3 tablespoons almond meal (ground almonds)
- ¼ cup (1 oz/30 g) confectioners' (icing) sugar

For the dough:
- ½ cup (2¾ oz/75 g) raisins
- ⅓ cup (2¾ oz/75 g) candied cherries
- scant ½ cup (2¾ oz/75 g) candied peel, finely chopped
- ⅓ cup (3 fl oz/85 ml) olive oil
- ⅓ cup (3 fl oz/85 ml) white wine
- ¾ cup plus 1 tablespoon (3½ oz/100 g) almond meal (ground almonds)
- 1½ cups (6¾ oz/190 g) all-purpose (plain) flour
- ⅔ cup (4¼ oz/120 g) superfine (caster) sugar
- ⅔ cup (3½ oz/100 g) skin-on almonds, toasted and roughly chopped
- scant ½ cup (1¾ oz/50 g) pine nuts, toasted
- pinch of salt

To make the almond paste: In the bowl of a food processor or blender, combine the almond meal (ground almonds) and confectioners' (icing) sugar. Mix in ½ teaspoon of water to form a paste. Set aside.

To make the dough: Soak the raisins, cherries, and peel in the olive oil and wine for at least 30 minutes.

Preheat the oven to 400°F (200°C/Gas Mark 6). Line 2 baking sheets with parchment paper.

In a large bowl, combine the almond meal, flour, sugar, almonds, pine nuts, salt, and almond paste. Add the soaked fruits and any liquid remaining. Mix to form a stiff dough.

Roughly divide the dough into 2 portions, then shape each into a flat rectangle about ¾ inch (2 cm) thick. Transfer to the prepared baking sheets, then, using a sharp knife, score indents in the dough to achieve your desired shapes or sizes—a common size is to score 12 rectangles in each piece of dough.

Bake for 20–30 minutes, until dark golden. Let cool before cutting slices along the scored lines.

OMM ALI

Egypt

Submitted by Moustafa Elrefaey

Serves 6–8
Prep time: 20 minutes
Cook time: 50 minutes–1 hour

- 4 sheets of rokkak (or 1 sheet of puff pastry)
- 1 tablespoon butter, for greasing
- ½ cup (2¼ oz/60 g) chopped nuts (typically a mix of pistachios, almonds, and hazelnuts)
- ¼ cup (1¼ oz/35 g) golden raisins (sultanas)
- ¼ cup (¾ oz/20 g) shredded coconut
- 4¼ cups (34 fl oz/1 liter) milk
- ¾ cup (5½ oz/150 g) granulated sugar
- 1 teaspoon vanilla extract or ½ teaspoon mastic gum, crushed (optional)
- ¾ cup (6 fl oz/180 ml) heavy (double) cream

Rich, warm, and steeped in both cream and folklore, *Omm Ali* is one of Egypt's most beloved desserts—a celebratory bread-like pudding of indulgent golden layers traditionally served during feasts, holidays, and special gatherings. Its name, meaning "Ali's mother," is wrapped in a legend that dates back to the thirteenth century during the Mamluk era. According to popular lore, the dish was created to celebrate the death of Shagaret al-Durr, the wife of Sultan As-Salih Ayyub, and political rival to Omm Ali, the first wife of the next sultan, Izz al-Din Aybak. Legend has it that after Shagaret al-Durr was killed, Omm Ali commissioned her kitchen staff to prepare a celebratory dessert and distribute it to the people of Cairo. The recipe—layered with pastry, sugar, milk, and nuts—was so well received that it became a festive staple ever since. *Omm Ali* is more than just a historical curiosity; it's a deeply comforting dish made from *rokkak*—a dry, unleavened Egyptian pastry somewhat similar to phyllo (filo) or lavash. Traditionally, *rokkak* is baked until crisp, then broken into shards and soaked in warm milk and sugar before being layered with a generous mix of nuts, raisins, and coconut. In modern kitchens, puff pastry is often used as a convenient substitute, offering similar flaky richness, though purists still favor the textural integrity of *rokkak*.

Served warm and often finished under the broiler (grill) for a beautifully browned top, *Omm Ali* is a dish of generosity, joy, and legacy—passed down and adapted through centuries, yet welcomed at the table like an old friend.

Preheat the oven to 350°F (180°C/Gas Mark 4) and line a baking sheet with parchment paper.

If using rokkak, place on the lined baking sheet and lightly toast the sheets in the oven for 15 minutes, until crisp and golden. Break into medium pieces. If using puff pastry, roll out, then place on the baking sheet and bake according to the package directions until golden, then break into pieces.

Grease a deep baking dish with butter. Layer the broken rokkak or puff pastry pieces in the dish. Sprinkle the nuts, raisins, and coconut evenly over the top.

In a pan, heat the milk, sugar, and vanilla or mastic until just before boiling. Stir to dissolve the sugar completely. Pour the hot milk mixture over the layered rokkak and nuts and let soak for 5 minutes. Pour the heavy (double) cream evenly over the top. Bake for 20–25 minutes, or until bubbling and golden on top. For a caramelized finish, place under the broiler (grill) for 2–3 minutes at the end.

Remove from the oven and serve immediately for the best taste, though it can also be enjoyed at room temperature. No decoration is necessary—Omm Ali is delightful in its simplicity.

BUTTER TARTS

Canada

Submitted by Allisa Murphy

Makes 12
Prep time: 30 minutes, plus chilling and freezing times
Cook time: 25–35 minutes

For the dough:
- 3 cups (13 oz/375 g) all-purpose (plain) flour, plus extra for dusting
- ⅔ cup (2¾ oz/75 g) confectioners' (icing) sugar
- 1 teaspoon salt
- 2 sticks (8 oz/225 g) butter, cold and cubed
- 3 egg yolks
- 3 tablespoons ice water

For the filling:
- 3 egg yolks
- ⅔ cup (5½ oz/150 g) turbinado (demerara) or soft light brown sugar
- ½ cup (5½ oz/150 g) maple syrup
- 9 tablespoons (4½ oz/130 g) butter
- 1¼ cups (10 fl oz/300 ml) heavy (double) cream
- 3 tablespoons cornstarch (cornflour)
- 1½ teaspoons salt, or to taste
- 1 cup (5½ oz/150 g) raisins (optional)
- 1½ cups (6 oz/175 g) chopped and toasted pecans (optional)
- whipped cream, to serve

The origins of the butter tart are much debated among its enthusiasts, who claim it has roots in either French or British (or both) gastronomy. But ask the same folks if they can imagine a more quintessentially Canadian dessert, and they'll be hard pressed to find one.

Despite its relative simplicity, there are many variations of butter tarts around the country, so much so that it has become personalized to individual tastes: Some like the tart filling to be runny or gooey, some throw in nuts or raisins, some let the maple syrup really sing. What most can agree on, however, is their love for these deep-filled and delicate individual pastries.

While you can find butter tarts in Canadian bakeries year-round, they enjoy a special popularity in southern Ontario, where they are a ubiquitous sight on dessert tables at most festive gatherings and celebrations. Enjoy with a dollop of freshly whipped cream, or just as they are.

To make the dough: In a food processor or a large bowl, mix together the flour, confectioners' (icing) sugar, and salt. Add the butter, and pulse if using a food processor, or if working by hand, rub together until the mixture resembles bread crumbs.

In a separate bowl, whisk together the egg yolks with the ice water. Add the wet ingredients into the dry mixture, and gently bring together. Turn the dough out onto a counter and knead gently, until no dry patches remain. Roll the dough into a log and wrap in plastic wrap (clingfilm). Place in the refrigerator for 2 hours, or ideally overnight.

Once the dough is firm, slice into 12 circles each weighing 1¾ oz (50 g). On a lightly floured counter, roll out each disk so that it fits the holes of a 12-cup muffin pan. Remove any excess flour with a pastry brush, and give each disk a slight pleat to fit comfortably in the pan. Look out for any cracks in the dough, as this will prevent any sticking once filled and baked. Place the pan of pastry shells in the freezer while you prepare your filling.

To make the filling: Place the egg yolks in a large bowl and set aside.

In a double boiler, combine the sugar, syrup, butter, and cream, and bring to a simmer so that all the butter and sugar has melted, whisking continuously. When the sugar has dissolved, add the cornstarch (cornflour) and continue to whisk for 2 minutes, until incorporated. Season with the salt to taste.

Slowly incorporate the butter and sugar mixture into the egg yolks, adding a little bit at a time so as not to scramble the egg. Transfer to a measuring cup and let cool to room temperature. At this stage, the mixture can be stored in the refrigerator until needed—if doing so, whisk before using (the fat will rise to the top).

Preheat the oven to 350°F (180°C/Gas Mark 4). Remove the tart shells from the freezer. Place the raisins or chopped toasted pecans, if using, in the tart shells, then pour in the filling to just below the tops of the shells, taking care not to let any of the mix run down the sides. Bake for 15 minutes, then check. They are done if the pastry is golden brown and has begun to ooze a little of its butter around the edges, and the filling is a dark golden color with a slight, unified wobble and bubbly surface. If they are not done, bake for another 5–10 minutes.

Remove from the oven and let cool before removing from the pan. Serve with whipped cream.

JAGODZIANKI

Poland

Submitted by Maksymilian Smółka

Makes 9
Prep time: 1 hour, plus proofing time
Cook time: 14–16 minutes

For the dough:
- 3⅔ cups (1 lb 1 oz/475 g) T500 (bread) flour
- ⅔ cup (5 fl oz/155 ml) milk
- 2 medium eggs
- 1½ teaspoons salt
- ⅓ cup (2¼ oz/65 g) superfine (caster) sugar
- ½ oz (12 g) fresh yeast
- 7½ tablespoons (3¾ oz/110 g) butter, softened, cubed
- 4 cups (2 lb 4 oz/1 kg) wild blueberries, cleaned

For the crumble:
- 1½ cups (7 oz/200 g) T500 (bread) flour
- 7 tablespoons (3½ oz/100 g) butter
- ½ cup (3½ oz/100 g) granulated sugar
- scant ½ teaspoon salt

For the egg wash:
- 1 egg, beaten

These sweet buns filled with wild blueberries became a popular treat in the Mazovia region of Poland in the mid-twentieth century. During so-called indulgences in parish churches, it was a tradition to invite friends over and, as they departed, give them *jagodzianki* as a parting gift. Today, *jagodzianki* have become a beloved summer staple, with folks often standing in long lines to get them. They are highly seasonal, as the wild blueberry harvest in Poland usually lasts from late June to July, depending on the weather and the region. When *jagodzianki* are available, it's a sign that summer has started. Social media goes wild and everyone shares their favorite recipe.

This recipe comes from Polish baker Maksymilian Smółka, who has many fond childhood memories of eating *jagodzianki* in summer by a lake, competing for the pastry with curious bees.

***Jagodzianki* are best enjoyed slightly warm. Serve on their own, with sour cream on top, or split and spread with a little thick cream or *crème pâtissière* if you're feeling extra luxurious.**

To make the dough: In the bowl of a stand mixer fitted with the dough hook attachment, mix the flour, milk, eggs, salt, sugar, and yeast and knead on low–medium speed. When the dough comes together and starts to become soft, increase the speed to medium–high. Add the butter in 3 parts, waiting for the dough to absorb the butter in between each addition. The dough should be cohesive, soft, and strong. Aim for a temperature of 82–86°F (28–30°C) after the mixing has stopped. Cover the bowl with a clean, damp dish (tea) towel and proof for 1–1½ hours, until it has risen slightly.

Transfer the dough onto a counter and punch it down, folding the outside parts of the dough to the inside. Place the dough back in the bowl, cover with a clean dish towel, and proof for 1½–2 hours, until it has puffed up.

Divide the dough into 9 × 3½-oz (100-g) pieces. Roll each portion into a ball, then cover and proof for 15 minutes on the counter.

Line a baking sheet with parchment paper and set aside.

Take 1 dough ball and roll it out to around 4–5 inches (10–12 cm) in diameter, being careful not to make it too thin—try to make the middle thicker than the edge. Place the dough in a bowl and fill it with around ⅔ cup (3½ oz/100 g) of the wild blueberries. Connect and pinch the sides as you would make a dumpling, ensuring the seam is well sealed. Turn the bun upside down and place it on the prepared sheet, then repeat with the rest of the buns. Place the sheet in a warm spot, cover, and proof for 1½–2 hours until the buns are nicely puffed up.

Meanwhile, to make the crumble: In a medium bowl, mix together the flour, butter, sugar, and salt until a cohesive sandy texture forms. Set aside.

Preheat the oven to 410°F (210°C/Gas Mark 6). Brush the jagodzianki with the egg wash, then sprinkle on the crumble. Bake for 14–16 minutes. The key to great jagodzianka is not to bake it for too long, as it will cause the inside to cook too much; they should have some texture.

Remove from the oven. They are best enjoyed slightly warm.

HEMNESVÆRINGER

Norway

Submitted by Åshild Blyseth

Makes 18
Prep time: 1 hour, plus proofing time
Cook time: 25 minutes

For the dough:
generous 2 cups (17 fl oz/500 ml) milk
2 eggs
$1\frac{3}{4}$ oz (50 g) fresh yeast
$7\frac{1}{2}$ cups (2 lb 2 oz/950 g) all-purpose (plain) flour
$1\frac{1}{4}$ cups ($4\frac{1}{4}$ oz/125 g) granulated sugar
1 teaspoon ground cardamom
$\frac{1}{2}$ teaspoon salt
9 tablespoons ($4\frac{1}{4}$ oz/125 g) butter, at room temperature

For the vanilla custard filling:
generous 2 cups (17 fl oz/500 ml) milk
$\frac{1}{2}$ cup ($3\frac{1}{2}$ oz/100 g) superfine (caster) sugar
1 vanilla bean (pod), seeds scraped, or 1 teaspoon vanilla sugar or vanilla extract
1 egg, plus 3 egg yolks
4 tablespoons cornstarch (cornflour)

For the egg wash:
1 egg
1 tablespoon heavy (double) cream

To finish:
$3\frac{1}{2}$ tablespoons ($1\frac{3}{4}$ oz/50 g) butter, melted
$\frac{1}{4}$ cup ($1\frac{3}{4}$ oz/50 g) granulated sugar

***Hemnesværinger* is a variation of a pastry that became popular at a bakery in Hemnesberget in the north of Norway. In nearby Bardal, at the cafe and folk museum Wangbrygga, chef and cultural researcher Åshild Blyseth makes her own version, the name of which literally translates to "people from Hemnes"—a tongue-in-cheek joke, but also a tribute. It is said that the buns, which are soft, a bit rich, and quite sweet, are "like a good Hemnesværing."**

Locals in this part of Nordland often buy a tray of *Hemnesværinger* as a part of any celebratory event.

To make the dough: In a small pan, heat the milk to 77°F (25°C). Mix the milk with the eggs and the yeast.

In the bowl of a stand mixer, combine the flour, sugar, cardamom, and salt. Add the milk and egg mixture and knead for 15 minutes. Add the butter in cubes and knead for another 15 minutes. Cover with plastic wrap (clingfilm) and proof in a warm place for 40 minutes.

Meanwhile, to make the vanilla custard filling: Put the milk in a saucepan over medium heat, and bring to boiling point, then remove from the heat.

Whisk the sugar (and vanilla sugar, if using), whole egg and egg yolks, and cornstarch (cornflour) together in a large bowl, then add the warm milk in a thin stream, whisking constantly.

Transfer the egg and milk mixture to a clean pan and cook over low heat, whisking constantly, until the mixture becomes a thick custard. Strain the custard into a clean bowl and stir in the seeds from the vanilla bean (pod) or the vanilla extract, if using. Press some plastic wrap (clingfilm) or parchment paper onto the surface (to prevent a skin from forming) and let cool. You can make this ahead and leave in the refrigerator until needed, and if making more than 2 hours ahead then it should be refrigerated.

Line a baking sheet with parchment paper and set aside.

Once the dough has risen, divide into 18 equal portions. Roll each portion into a rope about 8 inches (20 cm) long and shape them into figure eights. Place on the prepared baking sheet. Fill the holes in the figure eights with vanilla custard. Proof at room temperature for about 40 minutes, or until doubled in size.

Preheat the oven to 410°F (210°C/Gas Mark 6).

To make the egg wash: In a small bowl, mix together the egg and cream. Brush this over the buns, then bake for 12–15 minutes.

Remove from the oven and let cool slightly, then brush with the melted butter and dip in the sugar before serving.

LECHE FLAN

Philippines

***Leche* flan is the Filipino version of crème caramel, introduced originally during the period of Spanish colonization. This version is made richer with egg yolks and sweetened condensed milk. It's a staple at celebrations, particularly during Christmas, birthdays, and fiestas, and is often served in *llanera* (oval pans).**

Submitted by Florence Mae Maglanoc

Serves 6
Prep time: 15 minutes, plus chilling time
Cook time: 45–55 minutes

½ cup (3½ oz/100 g) granulated sugar
10 egg yolks
14-oz (397-g) can sweetened condensed milk
13-oz (370-g) can evaporated milk
1 teaspoon vanilla extract

Preheat the oven to 325°F (160°C/Gas Mark 3).

In a small pan, add the sugar and melt over medium heat, swirling the pan every minute or so to evenly heat—but do not stir—until it turns into golden caramel, 5–10 minutes. Immediately, and carefully, pour into 6 small molds, such as ramekin dishes or llanera, to coat the bottom.

In a bowl, gently whisk the egg yolks. Add the condensed milk, evaporated milk, and vanilla extract. Stir until combined.

Strain the custard mixture into the caramel-lined molds. Cover the molds with aluminum foil. Place in a baking pan, fill with water to come halfway up the sides of the molds, and bake in the oven for 40–45 minutes until set. The flans can also be steamed, if preferred.

Remove from the water bath and let cool completely. Chill in the refrigerator for 3–4 hours, or overnight, before inverting onto a plate to serve.

M'HANNCHA

Morocco

Submitted by Salma Hage

Serves 6
Prep time: 45 minutes, plus chilling time
Cook time: 25 minutes

For the filling:
- 1½ cups (8 oz/225 g) almond meal (ground almonds)
- ⅓ cup (2 oz/75 g) superfine (caster) sugar
- 2 teaspoons ground cinnamon
- ½ teaspoon ground cardamom
- 5 teaspoons orange blossom water
- grated zest of 1 orange
- 1 tablespoon orange juice
- 1 egg, beaten
- pinch of fine sea salt
- 10½ tablespoons (5½ oz/150 g) butter, melted

For the phyllo:
- 4 teaspoons confectioners' (icing) sugar, plus extra for dusting
- 10 sheets of phyllo (filo) pastry
- ¼ cup (1½ oz/40 g) raw pistachios, roughly chopped

For the egg wash:
- 1 egg yolk
- 3 tablespoons (1½ oz/40 g) butter, melted

For the syrup:
- 3 tablespoons runny honey
- ¼ teaspoon ground cinnamon
- 1 tablespoon rosewater

***M'hanncha* (from the Arabic word for snake) gets its name from the dessert's iconic serpentine-like coil of almond-filled pastry. While phyllo (filo) dough is commonly used today, it is traditionally made with *warqa*, a similar Moroccan style of pastry that is a little thicker and also more glutinous, which makes it tougher and less flaky. It's common to find this "snake cake" at feasts and celebrations across the Maghreb region, but especially in Morocco, where the sweet scent of cinnamon and cardamom waft over many a dessert table.**

To make the filling: Mix the almond meal (ground almonds), sugar, and spices together in a mixing bowl or food processor. Add the rest of the filling ingredients, keeping back a quarter of the melted butter, and mix again until the mixture is completely combined.

Brush a baking sheet with a little of the reserved melted butter and dust with confectioners' (icing) sugar.

To make the phyllo (filo): Line a board with parchment paper and lay a sheet of phyllo on it. Brush the sheet all over with some of the melted butter, then lay another sheet of pastry over the top and brush with more melted butter. Add teaspoons of the almond filling down the length of the pastry and shape the filling into a sausage, leaving ½ inch (1 cm) at one side and 1¼ inches (3 cm) at each end (this should leave lots of pastry on the side to roll).

Carefully roll the pastry up and over into a thin log and tuck the edges of the pastry into each end so that no filling is visible. Repeat until the sheets and filling are used up. Transfer the filled dough rolls to the prepared baking sheet and shape into a tight coil. Place in the refrigerator to chill for 20 minutes.

Preheat the oven to 325°F (160°C/Gas Mark 3).

To make the egg wash: Mix the egg yolk and butter together in a bowl. Remove the cake from the refrigerator and brush all over with the egg wash. Bake for 25 minutes, until golden.

Meanwhile, to make the syrup: Mix all the ingredients together in a bowl.

Remove the cake from the oven, then immediately brush it all over with the syrup and top with the chopped pistachios. Let cool completely before slicing.

YEONGYANG CHAL-TTEOK

South Korea

Submitted by Bitna Kang

Serves 4
Prep time: 20 minutes, plus soaking time
Cook time: 1 hour

For the black beans:
- scant ½ cup (2¾ oz/80 g) black beans with green kernels, soaked for 12 hours, or overnight, then drained
- 2 tablespoons granulated sugar

For the rice cake:
- ¼ cup (¾ oz/20 g) sliced almonds
- ¾ oz (20 g) walnuts, chopped
- 3 tablespoons pine nuts
- ⅓ cup (1 oz/30 g) dried jujubes
- 1⅓ cups (7 oz/200 g) glutinous rice powder
- scant 1 teaspoon salt
- 2 tablespoons granulated sugar
- ¾ teaspoon baking powder
- scant 1 cup (7½ fl oz/220 ml) unsweetened almond milk

One of the most iconic Korean desserts, *tteok* (rice cake) is a centerpiece in many celebrations, ceremonies, and rituals. It is typically made for sharing within a community, rather than for enjoying oneself, and this long-standing tradition is so ingrained that there is an expression for it: "*Tteok dolida*," which literally means "to circulate rice cake"—to mark a special occasion by sharing rice cakes with others.

In every town in Korea there are mills called *bangatgan,* where locals can press sesame oil or perilla oil, or order a customized *tteok*. While you can purchase premade *tteok* there, Korean people often bring their own grains from their hometowns or special regional ingredients to a *bangatgan* just to make bespoke *tteok* for a truly special day.

***Yeongyang chal-tteok* (영양 찰떡 / nutritional rice cake) is made primarily from sweet rice powder, enriched with different grains and nuts available throughout the year. This *tteok* is also prepared for celebrations, as giving out *yeongyang chal-tteok* is a customary way to share good news with one's neighbors. Because of its high nutritional value, many Koreans have this *tteok* as a quick breakfast. *Tteok* becomes stale quickly when exposed to air, but you can simply freeze individual portions and defrost overnight for tomorrow morning.**

Preheat the oven to 350°F (180°C/Gas Mark 4). Line a rectangular heatproof glass dish (11 × 7.8 × 3.8-inches/28 × 20 × 9.5 cm) with parchment paper and set aside.

To make the black beans: Combine the beans, sugar, and 3½ tablespoons of water in a pan. Bring to a boil, then reduce the heat to low, and simmer for 15 minutes.

To make the rice cake: Spread the sliced almonds, walnuts, and pine nuts on a baking sheet, and toast in the oven for 3 minutes. Let cool.

Meanwhile, soak the dried jujubes in cold water for 10 minutes. Drain, wipe dry, remove the pits, and shred thinly.

In a large bowl, sift together the rice powder, salt, sugar, and baking powder. Pour in the almond milk and stir until fully incorporated. Add the bean mixture, toasted nuts, and jujubes, then gently combine. Spread the mixture evenly in the prepared dish, aiming for a thickness of about ¾ inch (2 cm). Bake for 40 minutes, until the top is lightly golden.

Remove from the oven and let cool. Slice into bite-size pieces and serve. They will keep in an airtight container at room temperature for 24 hours. Alternatively, cut into small pieces (1¼ × 1½ inches/3 × 4 cm) and freeze. Before eating, allow frozen pieces to come to room temperature for 3–4 hours. You can also microwave them for 2–3 minutes or pan-fry in perilla oil over low heat until both sides are golden brown.

BIKO

Philippines

Submitted by Florence Mae Maglanoc

Serves 8
Prep time: 10 minutes
Cook time: 40–55 minutes

2⅓ cups (14 oz/400 g) glutinous rice
3⅓ cups (27 fl oz/800 ml) coconut milk
½ teaspoon salt
scant 1 cup (7 oz/200 g) dark muscovado sugar or soft brown sugar
banana leaves, for lining, or oil, for greasing
latik (caramelized coconut curds), for sprinkling (optional)

***Biko* is a traditional Filipino rice cake made with glutinous rice, coconut milk, and brown sugar. It's often served at celebrations and family gatherings as a symbol of togetherness and prosperity. Some versions are topped with *latik* (golden caramelized coconut curds) for extra richness. For many Filipinos, *biko* is reminiscent of family parties when growing up—there was always a platter of it on the table, golden and sticky, with *latik* glistening on top. It's one of those desserts that feels generous, filling, and festive, and always disappears quickly.**

Rinse the glutinous rice until the water runs clear. Place in a pot with half of the coconut milk and the salt, bring to a boil, then reduce the heat and simmer for 15–20 minutes. Alternatively, use a rice cooker according to the manufacturer's directions. Set aside once fully cooked.

In a separate pan, combine the remaining coconut milk and the sugar. Bring to a simmer and cook over medium heat for 15–20 minutes until thickened and caramel-like. Reserve a little of the syrup, if desired, then fold the cooked rice into the caramel mixture. Stir continuously over low heat for 10–15 minutes until the rice absorbs the syrup and becomes sticky and glossy.

Preheat the oven to 350°F (180°C/Gas Mark 4). Line a rimmed baking sheet with banana leaves or lightly grease it.

Spread the biko evenly over the sheet, flattening the surface with an offset spatula. Top with latik, or drizzle with the extra reserved syrup if preferred, and bake for 15 minutes, then remove from the oven and let cool. Alternatively, the biko can simply be left to cool and served without baking.

Slice into squares and serve at room temperature.

BIBINGKANG NANNA

Philippines

Submitted by Jasmine Ting

Serves 10–12
Prep time: 30 minutes, plus overnight soaking and cooling times
Cook time: 40–50 minutes

- 1¼ cups (9 oz/250 g) Chinese foxtail millet (xiǎo mǐ, see note)
- 14-oz (400-ml) can coconut milk, plus extra for brushing
- 1 cup (8 oz/225 g) dark brown sugar
- 4 tablespoons butter, plus extra for greasing
- ½ teaspoon salt
- 8 tablespoons macapuno strings or coconut sport strings
- 1 tablespoon condensed milk

Nanna is a type of millet grown in the town of Peñablanca, which is located in the Cagayan Valley in the northeastern part of the island of Luzon. The heritage grain is a labor-intensive, low-yield crop, which can be harvested only once a year. This is why few farmers grow it, thus making it rare and expensive—costing more than twice the price of white rice. It's a luxury reserved for special occasion celebrations like birthdays, fiestas, Christmas, or New Year.

The conventional way to prepare nanna is by simply cooking it in coconut milk and water. This special millet bibingka is based on a recipe by Monica Natividad, who hails from the same town as the recipe's contributor Jasmine Ting, Tuguegarao City (which neighbors Peñablanca), and to whom many locals go specifically for the dish. While nanna is unavailable outside of Cagayan, the closest widely available grain is the Chinese foxtail millet referred to as *xiǎo mǐ*. Cut a slice of this sticky millet cake, and enjoy.

In a bowl, wash and rinse the millet 3–5 times until the water becomes mostly clear. Transfer to a bowl and cover with cold water. Let soak at cold room temperature or in the refrigerator overnight.

The next day, drain and rinse the millet. In a pot, mix the coconut milk with 4¼ cups (34 fl oz/1 liter) of water, and bring to a boil. Once the mixture reaches a rolling boil, add the sugar and stir to dissolve. Add the drained millet, reduce the heat to low, and bring the mixture to a simmer. Cook for 15–20 minutes, stirring frequently to make sure the millet doesn't burn or stick to the bottom of the pot. By the end, the millet should have a thick, porridge-like consistency.

Remove from the heat and let cool for 20–30 minutes, stirring occasionally to allow steam to escape. The mixture should go from piping hot to warm to the touch.

Meanwhile, preheat the oven to 350°F (180°C/Gas Mark 4). Line an 8 × 8-inch (20 × 20-cm) square cake pan with aluminum foil, making sure to get it as flat to the pan as possible. Grease the foil with butter and brush with coconut milk.

Fold the butter and salt into the millet, allowing the butter to melt and fully combine. Add 5–6 tablespoons of the macapuno or coconut sport strings and mix well to evenly distribute.

Pour the millet mixture into the prepared pan, and spread evenly using a rubber spatula. Brush the top with a bit of coconut milk, then spread a dollop of condensed milk on top, and finish it off with a couple of tablespoons (or more) of macapuno strings.

Bake for 25–30 minutes. Remove from the oven and let cool for 10–15 minutes before cutting and serving.

Note: Chinese foxtail millet is called *xiǎo mǐ* or "mini rice millet," or sometimes "glutinous millet", and is available at Chinese grocery stores. Avoid using Indian foxtail millet, which has a grainy, earthy, subtly soil-like taste, even after an overnight soak. The millet used should be nutty and smooth.

DIFO DABO

Ethiopia

Submitted by Ayda Biru

Serves 16
Prep time: 40 minutes, plus proofing time
Cook time: 50–60 minutes

- 1 cup (8½ oz/240 g) active sourdough starter (100 percent hydration)
- 16 cups (4 lb 8 oz/2 kg) unbleached baking flour
- 1 cup (8fl oz/250 ml) warm water
- 1 teaspoon lemon zest
- 1 teaspoon salt
- 1 teaspoon ground fenugreek
- 1 tablespoon nigella seeds (tikur azmud)
- 1 tablespoon baking powder
- 2 tablespoons honey or granulated sugar
- 4 tablespoons vegetable oil, plus extra for greasing
- banana leaves (enset or substitute), washed and lightly oiled

***Difo dabo* is a traditional Ethiopian round sourdough bread known for its soft, slightly tangy flavor and ceremonial presence. Unlike *hambasha* (page 319), which is subtly sweet and patterned like a wheel, *difo dabo* is baked as one large, round loaf, often wrapped in banana leaves (*enset*) that infuse a delicate, earthy aroma into the bread. This bread is a staple at holidays and celebrations, and is also commonly prepared for family gatherings.**

The banana leaves not only give *difo dabo* its characteristic fragrance but also protect the bread during baking, keeping it moist and tender. Its round, generous form makes it ideal for sharing at large gatherings, where each slice symbolizes community and togetherness.

To activate the starter: In a medium bowl, combine the sourdough starter with 1 cup (4¼ oz/125 g) of the flour and the warm water. Mix well, cover with a clean dish (tea) towel, and let sit for 2–3 hours until bubbly and active.

In the bowl of a stand mixer fitted with the dough hook, mix the remaining flour, lemon zest, salt, fenugreek, nigella seeds, baking powder, honey or sugar, and vegetable oil. Stir well to combine. Add the sourdough mixture and 3 cups (24 fl oz/ 700 ml) of water to the flour mixture. Mix on low–medium speed, kneading for about 10 minutes, until the dough becomes soft, smooth, and elastic.

Leave the dough in the bowl, cover with a clean dish towel, and proof for 4–6 hours in a warm, draft-free spot, until doubled in size.

Preheat the oven to 350°F (180°C/Gas Mark 4). Trim the banana leaves to fit a 9-inch (23-cm) cake pan with excess to hang over the edges. Line the cake pan with the oiled leaves. Place the risen dough into the lined pan, shaping it gently into a round loaf. Cover the top with another layer of oiled banana leaves, folding the side leaves over the loaf so it is fully wrapped. Bake for 50–60 minutes, or until the bread is fully cooked through. The banana leaves will darken as the bread bakes, sealing in moisture.

Remove from the oven, unwrap carefully, and allow the bread to cool slightly before slicing. Serve warm.

FOCACCIA BARESE

Italy

Submitted by Roberto Nitti

Serves 10–16
Prep time: 15 minutes, plus resting and proofing times
Cook time: 30 minutes

For the dough:
3½ oz (100 g) potatoes
⅛ oz (5 g) active dry yeast
1 teaspoon granulated sugar
3½ tablespoons warm water
4 teaspoons extra virgin olive oil, plus extra for greasing
2 cups (9 oz/250 g) strong white bread flour, plus extra for dusting
¾ cup plus 2 tablespoons (5½ oz/150 g) coarse semolina
1½ teaspoons salt

For the toppings:
1 lb 2 oz (500 g) cherry tomatoes
1 lb 2 oz (500 g) olives
dried oregano
sea salt
extra virgin olive oil, for drizzling

Characterized by its golden, crisp crust and soft, airy interior, the *focaccia Barese* is typically topped with halved cherry tomatoes, briny black olives, and a generous drizzle of olive oil. The dough is made with a mix of flour and mashed potatoes, which gives it its signature tenderness and slightly chewy texture, and baked in round pans until the edges turn crisp and golden. Locals may eat it on a daily basis, but it is also a festive food and never missing from the tables of Apulians—from Christmas to Easter to a family lunch on Sunday.

To make the dough: Place the potatoes in a pan and cover with cold water. Bring to a boil, then simmer until the potatoes are soft and fully cooked. Rinse under cold running water, then peel and mash with a potato masher. Set aside to cool.

Meanwhile, in a small bowl, combine the yeast, sugar, and warm water. Set aside for 5–10 minutes, until frothy.

Generously grease 2 × 12-inch (30-cm) cast-iron pans with oil, then set aside.

In a large bowl, combine the bread flour and semolina. Add the mashed potato and the yeast mixture. Gradually add ⅞–1 cup (7–8 fl oz/200–250 ml) of water while mixing with your fingers or a wooden spoon. Add the salt and continue to mix. Add the olive oil.

Turn out the dough onto a lightly floured counter and knead for 5–8 minutes until smooth. The dough should be slightly sticky, but you should still be able to knead it with the help of some flour. Divide the dough in half and place in the prepared pans. Oil the top of the dough, cover with plastic wrap (clingfilm) or a clean dish (tea) towel, and proof in a warm place for 1½–2 hours, or until doubled in size.

Preheat the oven to 450°F (230°C/Gas Mark 8). Spread the dough with your hands to cover the whole surface of each pan.

For the toppings: Crush the tomatoes lightly with your hands and sprinkle evenly over the surface of the focaccia. Press firmly into the dough so that they release their juices. Add a handful of olives, and sprinkle with dried oregano and salt. Drizzle with olive oil.

Bake for 30 minutes, until golden. Remove from the oven and serve warm.

FESTIVE "CORNET" POGAČA

Southeast Europe and the Balkans

Submitted by Irina Janakievska

Serves 12–16
Prep time: 30 minutes, plus proofing time
Cook time: 25–30 minutes

¾ oz (20 g) fresh yeast or ¼ oz (7 g) quick-rise dry yeast
1 tablespoon superfine (caster) sugar
1 cup (8 fl oz/250 ml) milk, lukewarm
generous ⅓ cup (3½ fl oz/100 ml) sunflower oil
2 eggs, 1 beaten for egg wash
scant 4 cups (1 lb 2 oz/500 g) strong white bread flour, plus extra for dusting
½ teaspoon fine sea salt
3½ tablespoons (2 oz/50 g) butter, softened, plus extra for greasing
1 tablespoon black or white sesame seeds, or nigella seeds, or a mix

***Pogača*, etymologically an adaptation of Italian *focaccia*—is an umbrella term for a wide variety of breads prepared from various types of flour using different techniques all over the Balkans, and can be anything from a simple unleavened loaf to a very elaborately decorated one.**

It is especially prepared and enjoyed for Slava (the celebration of a family's patron saint) across southeast Europe and the Balkans.

This recipe's shaping technique is sometimes referred to as "cornet (ice-cream cone) *pogača*" and it falls somewhere in the middle of the spectrum in terms of *pogača* difficulty levels. It certainly makes for a rather special centerpiece on the table as part of a celebratory feast, to serve alongside salads, mezzes, olives, spreads, cured or smoked meats, and cheeses.

In a small bowl, combine the yeast, sugar, and lukewarm milk, and set aside for 5–10 minutes, until frothy. Add the oil and 1 egg, and mix well to combine.

In a large bowl, sift together the flour and salt. Add the wet ingredients and mix until combined into a shaggy dough. Turn out onto a lightly floured counter and knead for 5–7 minutes until the dough becomes smooth and soft. Divide it into 8 equal parts, then roll each piece into a ball and put on a lightly floured counter. Cover the dough balls with a clean, damp dish (tea) towel and proof for 20 minutes.

Line the bottom of a 10-inch (25 cm) round baking dish or springform pan (3 inches/7.5 cm deep) with parchment paper and grease the sides with butter.

Dust your counter and a rolling pin with flour, then roll out each ball into 8-inch (20-cm) diameter disks. Brush one of the disks with a little butter (leaving a small unbuttered border around the edge), then stack another disk on top, and brush with butter. Repeat until you have one disk left; place this, unbuttered, on top.

Dust your counter and your rolling pin with flour again. First using your fingertips, gently stretch out the dough stack into a larger circle, about 12 inches (30 cm) in diameter. Then, with your rolling pin, roll out the dough into a 20-inch (50-cm) circle. With a pizza cutter (or sharp knife), cut a 1¼-inch (3-cm) border all the way around the outer edge of the dough circle. Separate the border and cut it into 3 strips of dough. Brush with butter, then roll them up so they look like roses, tucking the ends underneath. Set aside on a lightly floured counter.

Brush the remaining dough circle with butter, then cut into 8 wedges. Starting with the long edge of a wedge, roll it up like a croissant, tucking the tip of the wedge in at the bottom. Repeat with all the wedges, then cut each crescent roll down the middle, crosswise, so you have little pastry cones. Arrange the cones (wide ends at the edge of the dish, thin ends facing the center) evenly around your baking dish, so they look like petals. Place the 3 pastry roses in the middle—it's fine if they overlap the thin ends of the cones. Brush the egg wash over the pastry, then sprinkle with the seeds. Set aside to proof a second time for around 1 hour, or until the pastry has risen enough so there are no gaps between the pastry cones and roses.

Preheat the oven to 425°F (220°C/Gas Mark 7). Bake for 10 minutes, then reduce the temperature to 400°F (200°C/Gas Mark 6) and continue to bake, rotating the dish to ensure an even bake, for another 15–20 minutes, or until the top and bottom are both golden brown and cooked through.

Remove from the oven, transfer to a wire rack, and let cool in the baking dish for at least 15 minutes. Serve warm on a large plate or serving board.

BURMALı AMASYA ÇÖREĞI

Turkey

Submitted by Cemre Torun

Makes 12–14
Prep time: 1 hour, plus proofing, cooling, and resting times
Cook time: 30 minutes

For the dough:
- ⅞ cup (7 fl oz/200 ml) milk, warmed
- ⅓ oz (10 g) quick-rise dry yeast
- 2 tablespoons granulated sugar
- generous ⅓ cup (3½ fl oz/100 ml) sunflower oil
- 1 teaspoon salt
- 1 egg white
- generous ⅓ cup (3½ fl oz/100 ml) warm water
- 4½ cups (1 lb 4 oz/550 g) all-purpose (plain) flour
- 1 egg yolk, beaten, for egg wash

For the filling:
- ¾ cup (3½ oz/100 g) poppy seeds
- 1 cup (8 fl oz/250 ml) boiling water
- 6 tablespoons granulated sugar
- ⅞ cup (7 fl oz/200 ml) olive oil
- 3 tablespoons crushed walnuts

***Burmalı Amasya çöreği*, or twisted Amasya pastries, are a specialty from the northern Turkish city of Amasya in the Black Sea region that likely originated in the early twentieth century. These flaky and delectable twists are prepared with a filling of poppy seed paste and ground walnuts—and interestingly, the warm liquid used to dissolve the yeast is sometimes specified to be that from soaked or fermented chickpeas. Bakeries in Amasya commonly make these pastries in brick ovens, and they are especially popular on religious holidays and special occasions.**

To make the dough: In a large bowl, mix together the milk, yeast, sugar, sunflower oil, salt, egg white, and warm water until the yeast is fully dissolved. Gradually sift in the flour and mix until a soft and sticky dough forms. Cover the bowl with a clean, damp dish (tea) towel and place in a warm spot to proof for 40 minutes, or until doubled in size. Once risen, the dough should be light, airy, and still slightly sticky.

Meanwhile, to make the filling: Place the poppy seeds and boiling water in a heatproof bowl, then let soak until cool.

Drain, then transfer to the bowl of a food processor. Add 3 tablespoons of sugar and process until a paste forms. Transfer to a bowl, add the olive oil, and mix together until fully incorporated and spreadable. It should have a tahini-like consistency. Set aside.

Line a baking pan with parchment paper and set aside.

With lightly greased hands to prevent sticking, turn the dough out onto a work counter and divide into 4 pieces. Stretch each piece into a rough rectangle about ¼ inch (5 mm) thick and as wide as your baking pan. Spread 3–4 spoonfuls of the poppy seed mixture across the surface of 1 piece of the dough, then sprinkle 1 tablespoon of the walnuts and 1 tablespoon of sugar over the top.

Stretch another piece of dough and place it on top of the first one. Spread with the poppy seed paste, then sprinkle with another layer of walnuts and sugar. Repeat for the third piece of dough. Stretch the last piece of dough and place on top. Make sure the dough is still as wide as your baking pan, stretching again if necessary. Using a knife, cut the rectangle crosswise into 12 or so strips 1¼–1½ inches (3–4 cm) wide. Twist the strips into ropes and place on the prepared baking pan, leaving space between each as they will expand in the oven. Let rest at room temperature for 15–20 minutes.

Preheat the oven to 350°F (180°C/Gas Mark 4). Brush the egg wash over the surface of the dough, then bake for 30 minutes, or until the dough is deeply golden brown on top and browned on the bottom.

Remove from the oven and let cool slightly before slicing and serving.

IMERULI KHACHAPURI

Georgia

No special occasion, big or small, in Georgia is complete without a glistening round of *imeruli khachapuri* on the table. Hailing from the western region of Imereti, the cheese bread—with its soft, tender dough and gooey, slightly tangy cheese filling—makes an instant fan of anyone who tries it, and is served as part of a larger *supra* (feast) with plenty of amber wine. Georgians typically make this bread with *imeruli* cheese, or blend it with *suluguni* cheese. Here, a mix of mozzarella, feta, and *queso fresco* gets you a close approximation.

Submitted by Polina Chesnakova

Serves 6–8
Prep time: 45 minutes, plus resting and proofing times
Cook time: 10 minutes

For the dough:
- ¾ cup (6 oz/170 g) plain whole kefir, at room temperature or slightly warmed
- ¾ cup (6 oz/170 g) sour cream, at room temperature or slightly warmed
- 4 teaspoons sunflower oil or other neutral oil, plus extra for greasing
- 2 teaspoons granulated sugar
- 1½ teaspoons instant yeast
- 3½ cups (15 oz/430 g) all-purpose (plain) flour, plus extra for dusting
- 1 teaspoon fine sea salt

For the filling:
- 9½ oz (265 g) low-moisture whole milk mozzarella, coarsely grated, at room temperature
- 9½ oz (265 g) feta cheese, coarsely grated, at room temperature
- 9½ oz (265 g) queso fresco, coarsely grated, or dry, crumbly farmer cheese, at room temperature
- cold butter, for finishing

To make the dough: In a large bowl, whisk together the kefir, sour cream, oil, sugar, and yeast until combined. Switch to a wooden spoon and gradually begin to add the flour, along with the salt, a little at a time, mixing to incorporate after each addition. Once the spoon becomes cumbersome to work with, switch to using your hands and knead until all the flour has been incorporated and you have a cohesive dough.

Transfer the dough to a work counter. Knead until the dough is smooth, elastic, and no longer sticky, 8–10 minutes. With lightly greased hands, form the dough into a ball and transfer to an oiled bowl. Cover the bowl with a slightly damp dish (tea) towel and set aside to proof in a warm place for 1–1½ hours until doubled in size.

To make the filling: In a large bowl, mix the cheeses until evenly combined.

To assemble: A half-hour before the dough has finished proofing, put an overturned rimmed baking sheet or pizza stone inside the oven on the center rack. Preheat the oven to 500°F (265°C/Gas Mark 10). Have a baking-sheet-sized piece of parchment paper ready.

When the dough has finished proofing, turn it out onto a lightly floured counter. Divide the dough in half and form into even balls. Cover with the dish towel and let rest for 10–15 minutes.

Generously dust your work counter with flour. Take 1 piece of dough, keeping the other covered, and round it out gently with your fingers into a 10-inch (25-cm) circle, with the center a little thicker than the edges. Place half of the filling in the middle. Carefully take 1 edge of the dough and pull it up toward and over the center. Hold it securely with one hand while you bring the remaining edges over the filling, pleating as you go, and pinching the ends together tightly at the top to secure like a drawstring purse. Dust the top with flour and gently start flattening out the filled dough using your hand. Continue to flatten out the dough with your fingers and palms (you can also use a rolling pin), working from the center out to the edges to spread the filling out evenly, until you have a 13-inch (33-cm) round. Dust the work counter as you go so that the dough doesn't stick. If there are any tears, try to lightly pinch the dough together to patch up the hole. Carefully transfer the round onto your piece of parchment paper. Use your fingers to make a little hole in the center to allow steam to escape while it bakes. Holding on to the edges of the parchment paper, transfer the round to the baking sheet (or pizza stone).

Bake until the top firms up and takes on a golden color, 6–8 minutes. If one side begins to brown faster than the other, turn it so that it bakes evenly.

Remove the khachapuri from the oven and transfer to a serving plate. Use a fork to coat it evenly with a little butter (the heat of the khachapuri will instantly melt it). Repeat with the other half of the dough. Allow to cool for 10 minutes before cutting and serving immediately. Any leftovers can be wrapped in plastic wrap (clingfilm) and kept at room temperature for 1 day, then moved to the refrigerator for another 2 to 3 days.

SAMSA

Uzbekistan

Submitted by Malika Sharipova

Serves 3–4
Prep time: 20 minutes, plus chilling time
Cook time: 30–35 minutes

For the dough:
1¼ cups (10 fl oz/300 ml) milk
5 tablespoons (2½ oz/70 g) butter
1 teaspoon salt
4–4½ cups (1 lb 2 oz–1 lb 4 oz/500–550 g) all-purpose (plain) flour, plus extra for dusting

For the filling:
10½ oz (300 g) lamb or beef, finely chopped
2 onions, chopped
1 teaspoon cumin seeds, ground
½ teaspoon ground coriander
3½ oz (100 g) lamb's tail fat, diced, or 3 tablespoons olive oil
8½ tablespoons (4¼ oz/120 g) butter, melted
1 egg, beaten, for egg wash
sesame seeds, for topping
salt and freshly ground black pepper, to taste

***Samsa* (also spelled *somsa*) is a savory pastry popular in Uzbekistan and across all Central Asia. Scholars and historians believe the dish traveled along the Silk Road, around the eleventh century or earlier, as it was a portable, delicious, and very nourishing meal. Originally it was prepared with meat (lamb or beef) and whole wheat flour, but later on new ingredients such as premium flour, potatoes, and cabbage became more common, broadening the range of *samsa* you could find.**

Uzbek *samsa* dough varies from region to region but is often made from flour, warm water or milk, salt, butter, and sometimes egg and yeast. Within Uzbekistan, each region cherishes its own *samsa* style. The classic filling is made of ground (minced) lamb or beef, finely chopped onions, rich lamb tail fat, and spices—cumin, black or red pepper, and coriander.

Traditionally it would be baked in a coal-fired *tandyr* (clay oven), but today it is very often made in home ovens as well. Wherever in Uzbekistan you are, however, *samsa*'s beloved status keeps it ever-present on holiday and festive tables for all occasions.

To make the dough: Warm the milk gently in a pan—do not boil. Add the butter and salt. Stir until the butter has fully melted and the salt dissolved. Gradually sift in the flour while mixing continuously, until a soft but elastic dough begins to form. Knead it gently for a few minutes until smooth. Cover the dough with a clean dish (tea) towel and let rest in the refrigerator for 15 minutes.

Meanwhile, make the filling: In a large bowl, combine the finely chopped meat with the chopped onions. Add the ground cumin seeds, ground coriander, season to taste, and mix everything thoroughly. If using olive oil, drizzle it over the mixture and stir well to incorporate.

Remove the rested dough from the refrigerator and turn it out onto a counter. Roll it out into a large, thin rectangle about ⅛ inch (3 mm) thick. Brush the butter generously over the entire surface of the dough. Starting from 1 long edge, tightly roll the dough into a log or spiral, just like a jelly (Swiss) roll, to create multiple buttery layers. Wrap the log in plastic wrap (clingfilm) or a clean dish towel and refrigerate for 30 minutes—this helps the butter set and enhances flakiness.

Meanwhile, preheat the oven to 400°F (200°C/Gas Mark 6). Line a baking sheet with parchment paper and set aside.

After chilling, cut the dough log into even 2-inch- (5 cm)-thick pieces. Place each piece upright (cut-side facing up) on a lightly floured counter, and gently roll it out into a thin circle—around 4 inches (10 cm) in diameter. The beautiful spirals in the dough will become crisp layers when baked. Place about 1 tablespoon of the meat filling in the center of each circle. If using lamb fat, place 2–3 cubes on top of the filling. Pinch the edges tightly to seal—shape them into the desired shape, such as traditional half-moon, triangular, or even round pillow forms. Arrange the shaped samsas on the prepared baking sheet, leaving sufficient space between each as they will expand in the oven. Brush the top of each samsa with the egg wash for a glossy golden finish. Sprinkle with the sesame seeds for extra aroma and crunch, then bake for 30–35 minutes, or until they puff up and turn golden brown on top, with a beautifully crispy edge and moist, flavorful center.

Remove from the oven and serve warm.

BOSNIAN-STYLE BUREK & KROMPIRUŠA

Bosnia and Herzegovina

Many people in Bosnia and Herzegovina will say that the only pastry that may be called *burek* is one filled with meat, onion, and seasoning, and made using the technique in this recipe. This same technique combined with any other filling warrants the name of *pita sa...* (pita with...), with the next word being the relevant filling; alternatively, it is named after the filling. A pita filled with *krumpir* or *krompir* (potato) is known as *krompiruša* (see second filling option below). It is famously heavy on the black pepper, but use white pepper if you prefer a gentler, earthier heat.

Submitted by Irina Janakievska

Serves 6–8
Prep time: 1 hour, plus resting time
Cook time: 35 minutes

For the dough:
- 3¼ cups (15 oz/425 g) strong white bread flour, plus extra for dusting
- ½ teaspoon fine sea salt
- 2 tablespoons sunflower oil, plus extra for greasing and brushing
- 1 cup (8 fl oz/250 ml) lukewarm water
- 2 teaspoons (⅓ oz/10 g) butter
- 3½ tablespoons boiling water

For the meat (burek) filling:
- 4½ cups (1 lb 2 oz/500 g) ground (minced) beef or veal
- 1 onion, grated or very finely chopped
- 2 garlic cloves, minced
- 1 teaspoon sunflower oil
- 1 teaspoon vegetable bouillon powder
- ½ teaspoon sea salt flakes
- ¼ teaspoon freshly ground black pepper

For the potato (krompiruša) filling:
- 1 lb 5 oz (600 g) waxy potatoes, peeled, coarsely grated, and water squeezed out
- 1 onion, finely chopped
- 1 teaspoon sunflower oil
- 1 teaspoon vegetable bouillon powder
- ½ teaspoon sea salt flakes
- ½ teaspoon freshly ground black pepper, or more to taste

cold drinking yogurt or kefir, to serve

To make the dough: In a large bowl, sift together the flour and salt. Add the oil and lukewarm water, then use a fork (or your hands) to bring the mixture together into a shaggy dough. Turn out the dough onto a lightly floured counter and knead for 5–6 minutes until smooth. Shape into a ball, return to the bowl, brush the top with oil, cover, and let rest in a warm place for at least 30 minutes.

Meanwhile, prepare your filling of choice.

To make the meat (burek) filling: Combine all the ingredients in a bowl and knead with your hands until well combined, then set aside.

To make the potato krompiruša filling: Combine all the ingredients in a bowl and mix together. Drain any excess moisture, then set aside.

Preheat the oven to 425°F (220°C/Gas Mark 7). Line a large baking sheet with parchment paper and set aside.

Working in a warm room (at least 70°F/21°C), cover a large table with a cotton tablecloth. Lightly dust a section of the tablecloth with flour and turn out the dough (it should feel elastic). Give the dough a gentle knead and shape it back into a ball. Dust the top with flour, then dust flour over an oklagija (long, thin rolling pin), if you have one, or a regular rolling pin. Start to gently roll out the dough, always pushing from the middle out to the edges, into as large a circle as you can (at least 20 inches/50 cm in diameter). Brush with oil all over, then let rest for 10–15 minutes.

Gently lift one side of the dough and, using the palm of your hand, start to stretch the dough from the middle outward. Work slowly and use the pads of your fingers, not your nails. Work all the way around the dough until it is paper thin. Don't worry if there are a few little rips, but if you are getting too many, pause, brush the dough with a little more oil, and let it rest for 5–10 minutes before you continue. The dough should overhang the edge of your table, roughly 3¼ × 2½ feet (100 × 80 cm). Use your fingertips to stretch the edges, or trim any doughier overhanging pastry.

Place a line of filling along one of the longer edges of the dough and, using the edge of the tablecloth, gently roll it over itself 2–3 times. Cut off the roll from the rest of the sheet with a knife, then swirl it, seam-side down, into a spiral, and place on your prepared baking sheet. Repeat with the remaining dough and filling. Brush the top of each spiral with oil and use your hand to flick a little water (no more than 1 tablespoon) over the tops. Bake for 20 minutes.

Meanwhile, melt the butter in the boiling water. Remove the burek from the oven and reduce the temperature to 400°F (200°C/Gas Mark 6). Drizzle half the water and butter mixture over the burek, then return to the oven and bake for another 15 minutes, until golden brown. Turn the oven off, drizzle over the rest of the water and butter mixture, and return to the warm oven for 5 minutes.

Remove from the oven and serve with a glass of cold drinking yogurt.

SU BÖREĞI

Turkey

Submitted by Cemre Torun

Serves 8
Prep time: 30 minutes, plus resting time
Cook time: 1 hour 10 minutes

For the dough:
- 1¾ sticks (7 oz/200 g) butter, melted
- 4¾ cups (1 lb 5 oz/600 g) all-purpose (plain) flour, plus extra for dusting
- 6 extra-large eggs
- 1 teaspoon salt

For the filling:
- 9 oz (250 g) Turkish white cheese, crumbled
- 1⅓ cups (2¾ oz/80 g) finely chopped flat-leaf parsley
- 1 teaspoon freshly ground black pepper

For the cooking water:
- 2 teaspoons salt
- 2 teaspoons olive oil
- ice, for the ice bath

This delicate *börek*, made of layers of thin *yufka* dough, takes its name from the way it's prepared. *Su* means water in Turkish, and the freshly rolled sheets are first cooked in boiling water before baking. The cake dates back to the Ottoman times, when it was a favorite of sultans. The most common recipe is filled with just cheese (usually Turkish *beyaz peynir* white cheese—a saltier, fattier feta) and parsley, but variations include ground (minced) meat and sometimes vegetables.

This dish is not simple to make—it requires time and skill—but the result is well worth it, with the layers of delicate, melt-in-your-mouth, hand-rolled dough and salty, tangy filling.

Today, you can buy *su böreği* at specialty stores anytime of the year, but homemade *su böreği* is reserved for all kinds of special occasions, from religious holidays to engagement parties.

Lightly grease a 12-inch (30-cm) cake pan with 1 tablespoon of the melted butter and set aside.

To make the dough: Place the flour in a large mixing bowl and make a well in the center. Add the eggs and mix with a fork or your hands until a dough forms. Add the salt and drizzle in 3–4 tablespoons of water, kneading until smooth.

Divide the dough into 10 equal pieces. Roll into balls, lightly flour them, and cover with a clean, damp dish (tea) towel. Let rest at room temperature for 30 minutes.

Meanwhile, to make the filling: Mash the cheese with a fork in a medium bowl. Add the chopped parsley and black pepper, and mix well. Taste and season if needed.

For the cooking water: Bring 1.5 quarts (1.5 liters) of water to a rolling boil in a large pan. Add the salt and the olive oil. In a separate large bowl, prepare an ice bath.

Working with 1 piece at a time on a lightly floured counter, roll each ball into a circle slightly larger than the cake pan. Dust the rolled sheets lightly with flour and keep covered with a damp cloth to prevent them from drying out.

Place the first sheet of rolled dough into the prepared cake pan, letting the edges hang over the sides. Drizzle 2–3 tablespoons of melted butter over the top.

Working with 1 at a time, boil each remaining dough sheet for 1 minute. Transfer immediately to the ice water to stop the cooking. Once cooled, gently remove, pat dry with a clean towel, and allow the excess moisture to drain.

Preheat the oven to 325°F (160°C/Gas Mark 3).

Layer 5 boiled and dried sheets in the cake pan, brushing each one generously with melted butter. Evenly distribute the cheese and parsley mixture over the fifth layer. Continue layering the remaining sheets, brushing each with butter as you go. Fold the hanging edges of the bottom sheet over the top sheet to enclose the börek. Brush the top with the remaining butter. Transfer to the oven and bake for about 1 hour, until golden brown and crisp.

Remove from the oven and let the börek rest before serving.

PASTEL DE CHOCLO

Peru

Submitted by Gastón Acurio

Serves 4
Prep time: 15 minutes
Cook time: 1¼ hours

For the yellow chili paste:
- 2 lb 4 oz (1 kg) yellow chiles, seeded, membrane removed, and cut into pieces
- 1 tablespoon vegetable oil

For the meat mixture:
- ½ cup (4 fl oz/125 ml) vegetable oil
- 1 tablespoon garlic paste
- ⅔ onion, diced
- 14 oz (400 g) beef tenderloin, cut into ½-inch (1-cm) cubes
- 3 tablespoons chopped pitted black olives
- scant ½ cup (2¼ oz/65 g) raisins, soaked in hot water
- 2 hard-boiled eggs, chopped
- salt and freshly ground black pepper

For the corn mixture:
- 6 corncobs
- ½ cup (4 fl oz/125 ml) vegetable oil
- ⅓ onion, diced
- 1 cup (8 fl oz/250 ml) milk
- 1 cup (7 oz/200 g) granulated sugar
- 1 tablespoon salt
- 1 egg
- 1¾ cups (5 oz/150 g) grated Parmesan cheese
- freshly ground black pepper
- 4 parsley sprigs, to garnish (optional)

The recipe for this *pastel de choclo*, or "corn pie," comes from Peruvian chef Gastón Acurio, whose grandmother Genoveva, hailed from Trujillo in the northwest of the country. Childhood memories of this particular *pastel de choclo* resurfaced when he opened his restaurant Tanta, and Gastón worked with his team to make a version reminiscent of the nostalgic flavors.

It is very important for the corn to be really creamy so that the pie can be eaten with a spoon.

Make the yellow chili paste: Place the chiles in a pan with enough cold water to cover, and bring to a boil, then remove from the heat and drain. Repeat the process 3 times, changing the water each time.

Transfer the blanched chiles to a blender, add the vegetable oil and 1 tablespoon of water and blend for about 5 minutes, to form a thick paste. Once the mixture is well blended, push it through a fine-mesh sieve. The chili paste is best used immediately, though it will keep refrigerated in an airtight container for 2 days.

Preheat the oven to 350°F (180°C/Gas Mark 4).

To make the meat mixture: Heat half the oil in a pan over medium heat. Add the garlic paste and onion, sauté for 3 minutes until the onion has softened, then add the chopped meat, olives, raisins, and chopped hard-boiled eggs. Cook for another 4–5 minutes, stirring until the meat has browned all over. Season with salt and pepper to taste. Set aside.

To make the corn mixture: Remove the corn kernels from the cobs, transfer to a blender, and blend to a smooth puree. Set aside.

Heat the oil in a pan. Add the onion and ½ cup (4 oz/125 g) chili paste and sauté until the onion is golden, then add the pureed corn and milk. Cook, stirring, for a few minutes until the corn is just cooked. Add the sugar and salt, remove from the heat, and pour into a bowl. Add the egg and 4 tablespoons of the Parmesan cheese, season with black pepper, and mix together thoroughly with a wooden spoon. Set aside.

Spoon half the corn mixture into a baking dish, top with the meat filling, and cover with the rest of the corn mixture. Sprinkle over the remaining Parmesan cheese. Bake for 40–45 minutes, until cooked and golden.

Remove from the oven and let cool, then remove from the dish and cut into 4 pieces. Serve garnished with sprigs of parsley.

INDEX

RECIPE NOTES

Butter should always be unsalted, unless otherwise specified.

All herbs are fresh, unless otherwise specified.

Eggs are US large (UK medium), unless otherwise specified.

Individual vegetables and fruits, such as onions and apples, are assumed to be medium, unless otherwise specified.

All milk is whole (3% fat), homogenized, and lightly pasteurized, unless otherwise specified.

All salt is fine sea salt, unless otherwise specified.

If you are unable to find fresh yeast, use half the quantity of dried active yeast or one-third the quantity of instant yeast. Dried active yeast will require activating in lukewarm water for 15 minutes before use; instant yeast can be used without the need for preactivation. Follow packet directions for use.

Exercise a high level of caution when following recipes involving any potentially hazardous activity, including the use of high temperatures, open flames and when deep-frying. In particular, when deep-frying add food carefully to avoid splashing, wear long sleeves, and never leave the pan unattended.

Cooking times are for guidance only. If using a fan (convection) oven, follow the manufacturer's instructions concerning the oven temperatures.

All herbs, shoots, flowers, and leaves should be picked fresh from a clean source. Do exercise caution when foraging for ingredients, which should only be eaten if an expert has deemed them safe to eat.

Exercise caution when making fermented products, ensuring all equipment is spotlessly clean, and seek expert advice if in any doubt.

When no quantity is specified, for example of oils, salts, and herbs used for finishing dishes, quantities are discretionary and flexible.

All spoon and cup measurements are level, unless otherwise stated. 1 teaspoon = 5 ml; 1 tablespoon = 15 ml. Australian standard tablespoons are 20 ml, so Australian readers are advised to use 3 teaspoons in place of 1 tablespoon when measuring small quantities.

Cup, metric, and imperial measurements are used in this book. Follow one set of measurements throughout, not a mixture, as they are not interchangeable.

ABOUT THE AUTHOR

Ben Mervis is a respected food historian, researcher, and writer. Born in America and now based in Scotland, he is the founder of the food-focused travel magazine *Fare*, which explores city culture, community, and history through food. Mervis is also the author of *The British Cookbook*, an exploration of the diversity, depth, and history of British food culture. He has been a contributor and researcher on Netflix's *Chef's Table* since 2017 and consults internationally with Michelin-starred chefs and award-winning food festivals across Europe.

CREDITS

Pages 32, 78, 279, 284: Recipes from *The Indonesian Table* by Petty Pandean-Elliott (Phaidon, 2023)

Page 36: Recipe from *Recipes from the American South* by Michael W. Twitty (Phaidon, 2025)

Pages 58 and 350: Recipes from *Middle Eastern Sweets* by Salma Hage (Phaidon, 2021)

Pages 64 and 102: Recipes from *Tava* by Irina Georgescu (Hardie Grant, 2022)

Pages 70 and 100: Recipes from *The Palestinian Table* by Reem Kassis (Phaidon, 2017)

Pages 96 and 366: Recipes from *The Balkan Kitchen* by Irina Janakievska (Hardie Grant, 2024)

Page 101: Recipe from *Sour Cherries and Toast* by Diana Iovescu Tatucu (2025)

Page 106: Recipe from *Carpathia* by Irina Georgescu (Frances Lincoln, 2020)

Page 206: Recipe from *Recipes for Broken Hearts* (Rizzoli, 2026)

Page 224: Recipe from *Bakken met Barbara* by Barbara Serulus (Uitgeverij P, 2025)

Page 236: Recipe from *The British Cookbook* by Ben Mervis (Phaidon, 2022)

Pages 243 and 252: Recipes from *Classic German Baking* by Luisa Weiss (Ten Speed Press, 2016)

Page 255: Recipe from *Spain: The Cookbook* by Simone and Inés Ortega (Phaidon, 2016)

Page 277: Recipe from *The Caribbean Cookbook* by Rawlston Williams (Phaidon, 2026)

Page 368: Recipe from *İçindekiler II* by Cemre Torun and Begüm Yaramanci (2020)

Page 370: Recipe from *Peru: The Cookbook* by Gastón Acurio (Phaidon, 2015)

Phaidon Press Limited
2 Cooperage Yard
London E15 2QR

Phaidon Press Inc.
111 Broadway
New York, NY 10006

Phaidon SARL
55, rue Traversière
75012 Paris

phaidon.com

First published 2026

ISBN 978 1 83729 261 5

A CIP catalogue record for this book is available from the British Library and the Library of Congress.

Commissioning Editor: Sophie Hodgkin
Project Editor: Rachel Malig
Production Controller: Andie Trainer
Design: Associate
Photography: Liz Seabrook
Food Stylist: Katie Smith
Food Stylist Assistant: Aine Pretty-McGrath

Printed in China

The publisher would like to thank all the recipe contributors for their time, knowledge, and generosity, along with Vanessa Bird, Julia Hasting, Hamza Jahanzeb, João Mota, Faye Robinson, Claire Rogers, Ellie Smith, Tracey Smith, Caroline Stearns, Kathy Steer, and Christina Tosi.